This book is to be returned on or before

New Casebooks

ANTONY AND CLEOPATRA

D0301125

29115

028477

New Casebooks

PUBLISHED

Hamlet
Middlemarch
Tristram Shandy
Macbeth
Villette
Emma
Waiting for Godot and
    Endgame
Shakespeare's History Plays:
    Richard II to Henry V
King Lear
Wordsworth
Tess of the d'Urbervilles
Wuthering Heights
Mrs Dalloway and
    To the Lighthouse
Antony and Cleopatra

FORTHCOMING
Sense and Sensibility and
    Pride and Prejudice
Jane Eyre
Great Expectations

Jude the Obscure
Sons and Lovers
Ulysses
Chaucer
Blake
Othello
Hard Times and
    David Copperfield
Frankenstein
E. M. Forster
Heart of Darkness and
    The Secret Agent
A Midsummer Night's
    Dream
Philip Larkin
Twelfth Night
Post-Colonial Literature
Victorian Women Poets
Coleridge, Keats and Shelley
Seamus Heaney
Julius Caesar and
    Coriolanus
Feminism and Shakespeare
Feminist Theatre

New Casebooks

ANTONY AND CLEOPATRA

WILLIAM SHAKESPEARE

EDITED BY JOHN DRAKAKIS

MACMILLAN

First published 1994 by
THE MACMILLAN PRESS LTD
Houndmills, Basingstoke, Hampshire RG21 2XS
and London
Companies and representatives
throughout the world

ISBN 0–333–55531–7 hardcover
ISBN 0–333–55532–5 paperback

A catalogue record for this book is available
from the British Library

Printed in Hong Kong

Shakespeare: Antony and Cleopatra: ed. John Russell Brown

This title is available in the original *Casebook Series*, offering a wide range
of earlier critical views on the text.

For a full listing of the original *Casebook Series*, please write to the
Customer Services Department, Macmillan Distribution Ltd, Houndmills,
Basingstoke, Hampshire RG21 2XS

For Christine, Alexia, and Helena,
and in memory of my father
Emmanuel Drakakis (1910–1992)

Contents

Acknowledgements   ix

General Editors' Preface   xi

Introduction: JOHN DRAKAKIS   1

1. *Antony and Cleopatra*: A Shakespearean Adjustment   33
   JOHN F. DANBY

2. Nature's Piece 'gainst Fancy: Poetry and the Structure
   of Belief in *Antony and Cleopatra*   56
   JANET ADELMAN

3. Shakespeare's Boy Cleopatra, the Decorum of Nature
   and the Golden World of Poetry   78
   PHYLLIS RACKIN

4. *King Lear* and *Antony and Cleopatra*: The Language
   of Love   101
   TERENCE HAWKES

5. Jacobean *Antony and Cleopatra*   126
   H. NEVILLE DAVIES

6. 'Let Rome in Tiber melt': Order and Disorder in
   Antony and Cleopatra   166
   MARGOT HEINEMANN

7. Egyptian Queens and Male Reviewers: Sexist Attitudes
   in *Antony and Cleopatra* Criticism   182
   LINDA T. FITZ

8. Shakespeare's *Antony and Cleopatra* and the Rise
   of Comedy   212
   BARBARA C. VINCENT

vii

9. *Antony and Cleopatra: Virtus* under Erasure   248
JONATHAN DOLLIMORE

10. *Antony and Cleopatra*   262
MARILYN FRENCH

11. 'Travelling thoughts': Theatre and the Space of
the Other   279
ANIA LOOMBA

12. Renaissance Anti-theatricality, Anti-feminism, and
Shakespeare's *Antony and Cleopatra*   308
JYOTSYNA SINGH

Further Reading   330

Notes on Contributors   334

Index   336

Acknowledgements

The editor and publishers wish to thank the following for permission to use copyright material:

Janet Adelman, 'Nature's Piece 'gainst Fancy: Poetry and the Structure of Belief in *Antony and Cleopatra*' in *The Common Liar* (1973), pp. 102–21, by permission of Yale University Press; John F. Danby, '*Antony and Cleopatra*: A Shakespearean Adjustment' in *Elizabethan and Jacobean Poets* (1952), pp. 128–51, by permission of Faber and Faber Ltd; Jonathan Dollimore, '*Antony and Cleopatra*: *Virtus* under Erasure' in *Radical Tragedy: Religion, Ideology and Power in the Drama of Shakespeare and his Contemporaries* (1984) pp. 204–17, by permission of Harvester/Wheatsheaf; Linda T. Fitz, 'Egyptian Queens and Male Reviewers: Sexist Attitudes in *Antony and Cleopatra* Criticism', *Shakespeare Quarterly*, 28, 3, Summer (1977), 297–316, by permission of Shakespeare Quarterly; Marilyn French, '*Antony and Cleopatra*' in *Shakespeare's Division of Experience* (1982) pp. 251–65, by permission of Jonathan Cape and Charlotte Sheedy, Inc. on behalf of the author; Margot Heinemann, '"Let Rome in Tiber melt": Order and Disorder in *Antony and Cleopatra*' (1991), by permission of Vera Gottlieb, executor of Margot Heinemann's Estate; Terence Hawkes, '*King Lear* and *Antony and Cleopatra*: The Language of Love', in *Shakespeare's Talking Animals: Language and Drama in Society* (1975) pp. 166–93, Edward Arnold, by permission of the author; Ania Loomba, '"Travelling thoughts": Theatre and the Space of the Other', in *Gender, Race, Renaissance Drama* (1989) pp. 119–41, by permission of Oxford University Press, India; H. Neville Davies, 'Jacobean *Antony and Cleopatra*', *Shakespeare Studies*, 17 (1985) 123–58, by permission of the author; Phyllis Rackin, 'Shakespeare's Boy Cleopatra, the Decorum of Nature and the Golden World of Poetry', *PMLA*, 87 (1972) 201–12, by permission of the Modern Language Association of America; Jyotsyna Singh, 'Renaissance Anti-theatricality, Anti-feminism, and Shakespeare's *Antony and Cleopatra*' in *Renaissance Drama*, 20 (1989) 99–119, by permission of the Northwestern University Press; Barbara C. Vincent, 'Shakespeare's *Antony and Cleopatra* and the Rise of Comedy', *English Literary Renaissance*, 12, 1, Winter (1982) 53–86, by permission of English Literary Renaissance.

Every effort has been made to trace all the copyright holders but if any have been inadvertently overlooked the publishers will be pleased to make the necessary arrangement at the first opportunity.

General Editors' Preface

The purpose of this series of New Casebooks is to reveal some of the ways in which contemporary criticism has changed our understanding of commonly studied texts and writers and, indeed, of the nature of criticism itself. Central to the series is a concern with modern critical theory and its effect on current approaches to the study of literature. Each New Casebook editor has been asked to select a sequence of essays which will introduce the reader to the new critical approaches to the text or texts being discussed in the volume and also illuminate the rich interchange between critical theory and critical practice that characterises so much current writing about literature.

In this focus on modern critical thinking New Casebooks aim not only to inform but also to stimulate, with volumes seeking to reflect both the controversy and the excitement of current criticism. Because much of this criticism is difficult and often employs an unfamiliar critical language, editors have been asked to give the reader as much help as they feel is appropriate, but without simplifying the essays or the issues they raise. Again, editors have been asked to supply a list of further reading which will enable readers to follow up issues raised by the essays in the volume.

The project of New Casebooks, then, is to bring together in an illuminating way those critics who best illustrate the ways in which contemporary criticism has established new methods of analysing texts and who have reinvigorated the important debate about how we 'read' literature. The hope is, of course, that New Casebooks will not only open up this debate to a wider audience, but will also encourage students to extend their own ideas, and think afresh about their responses to the texts they are studying.

John Peck and Martin Coyle
University of Wales, Cardiff

Introduction

JOHN DRAKAKIS

I

> To read the great wealth of criticism this play has provoked and then
> return to the text itself is to become involved in a splendid, substantial
> hieroglyph, a presentation of human life in political, moral, intellec-
> tual, sexual, sensual, spiritual and instinctive terms that has raised
> conflicting judgements and emotions. Perhaps most agreement could
> be found if we say that it is difficult, finely balanced, energetic,
> fascinating; but even then some critics would insist that, in effect, the
> play is grandly, even simply, triumphant, difficult only for those who
> seek difficulty.
>
> (John Russell Brown)[1]

This conclusion, by the editor of an original Casebook selection of
essays on *Antony and Cleopatra*, represents the summation of a
critical tradition which viewed the play as a Roman 'history', a
heroic drama, and a monument to romantic passion. While for
Russell Brown, what he calls 'the great wealth of criticism' that the
play has generated, involves us as readers 'in a splendid, substantial
hieroglyph, a presentation of human life in political, moral, intellectual, sexual, sensual, spiritual and instinctive terms that has raised
conflicting judgements and emotions',[2] the main emphasis during
this century has been on the play's poetic texture, its unifying imagery, its transcendent themes, and a prurient fascination with the
allegedly feminine wiles of Cleopatra. Even in a volume such as *Some
Shakespearean Themes* (1959), L. C. Knights, sensitive to the ambivalences of the play, and to the opposition between Rome and
Egypt, can assert that the energy radiated by Antony and Cleopatra

1

represents 'an absolute value', and 'communicates itself to all that comes within the field of force that radiates from the lovers, and within which their relationship is defined'.[3] In recent years, John Bayley, in a sophisticated revival of Bradleyan Shakespeare criticism, has observed that the anchoring style of the play's rhetoric contains a sexual charge: 'a to-and-fro, negative and positive indefinitely repeated, like the image of the fans that both cool and inflame Cleopatra's cheeks. The whole effect is one of sexual rise and fall, endorsing and yet ironically contradicting the admiration of Cleopatra as making hungry where most she satisfies.'[4]

In many ways this fascination with Cleopatra, which can be collapsed into a question of the occasional promiscuity of Shakespeare's own literary style, can be traced back to Samuel Johnson. Here, the alleged equivocality of Shakespeare's poetic language was given an ethical gloss through its inscription as a fascination with the verbal excesses comparable in their affective power to 'the fatal *Cleopatra* for which he lost the world, and was content to lose it'.[5] For the Romantics the strength of the play's poetry was often aligned with the seductive impression made by the figure of Cleopatra herself. In a manner which anticipates much of the subsequent masculine criticism of the play, both August Wilhelm von Schlegel and Coleridge highlighted in their different ways the seductive power of Cleopatra; Schlegel regarded Antony as 'Hercules in the chains of Omphale', and went on to remark: 'The seductive arts of Cleopatra are in no respect veiled over; she is an ambiguous being made up of royal pride, female vanity, luxury, inconstancy, and true attachment.'[6] Coleridge, in much the same vein, identified the profound nature of 'the art displayed in the character of Cleopatra' but found that 'the sense of criminality in her passion is lessened by our insight into its depth and energy, at the very moment that we cannot but perceive that the passion itself springs out of the habitual craving of a licentious nature';[7] Hazlitt too commented on Cleopatra's being 'voluptuous, ostentatious, conscious, boastful of her charms, haughty, tyrannical, fickle'.[8] It was this tradition that provided the foundation for the criticism of A. C. Bradley, who did not admit *Antony and Cleopatra* to the pantheon of 'Shakespearean Tragedy' because of what he claimed was its fundamentally undramatic nature.

Bradley contrasted the play's relative lack of dramatic action with the memorable nature of those, for the most part, non-tragic scenes involving Cleopatra: 'Cleopatra coquetting, tormenting, beguiling her lover to stay; Cleopatra left with her women and longing for him;

Cleopatra receiving news of his marriage; Cleopatra questioning the messenger about Octavia's personal appearance.'[9] Moreover, on the larger question of the relationship between dramatic structure and content, Bradley felt that the emphasis upon dramatic form distinguished the play from the other major tragedies, which, he argues, were more concerned with content; Bradley puts the point in the following manner in his *Oxford Lectures on Poetry:*

> One may notice that, in calling *Antony and Cleopatra* wonderful or astonishing, we appear to be thinking first of the artist and his activity, while in the case of the four famous tragedies it is the product of his activity, the thing presented, that first engrosses us . . . It implies that, although *Antony and Cleopatra* may be for us as wonderful an achievement as the greatest of Shakespeare's plays, it has not an equal value. Besides, in the attempt to rank it with them there is involved something more, and more important, than an error in valuation. There is a failure to discriminate the peculiar marks of *Antony and Cleopatra* itself, marks which, whether or not it be the equal of the earlier tragedies, make it decidedly different.[10]

For Bradley, dramatic self-consciousness is a fault in that it diverts attention from the content, or the representation itself, an issue which we shall return to later. But his main objection is that the play may not be tragic at all. At the fall of Antony and Cleopatra he suggests that 'we are saddened by the very fact that the catastrophe saddens us so little; it pains us that we should feel so much triumph and pleasure . . . With all our admiration for the sympathy of the lovers we do not wish them to gain the world. It is better for the world's sake, and not less for their own, that they should fail and die.' He concludes that the play 'gives us what no other tragedy can give, and it leaves us, no less than any other, lost in astonishment at the powers which created it'.[11]

Implicit in Bradley's evaluation of the play is a sense of transcendental optimism which later, anti-Bradleyan critics, such as G. Wilson Knight, were to find attractive. What Bradley does is to respond to the play's *poetry* as an emanation of Shakespearean genius, whereas, even from within the same critical tradition, John Bayley can draw attention to the tragic irony consequent upon the removal of the lovers from the physical world which they have inhabited as a condition of their union: 'What moves as its tragedy is that only in dying will the pair be close to one another, but then they will be close indeed.'[12] However, where Bradley evinced an impatience with the play's self-consciousness, Bayley comments that in the tragedies generally 'Dramatic poetry seems . . . to study its subject, and sometimes itself as well"[13] and that even in the 'consciousness' of a character such as Antony, there exists a form of modernist fragmentation of the sort to be found in the novels of Virginia Woolf or James Joyce: 'sensations and events fall on him: his death sequence itself is a rich and confused accumulation of them'.[14] Interestingly enough, the world of vacillating sensation to which Bayley refers does no more than reaffirm the influence of Cleopatra herself upon Antony, the initiation of a 'stream of consciousness' that attacks the ordering rationality of Rome. It is perhaps for this reason, with a firm sense of the danger that Cleopatra poses, that critics have been fascinated by what they take to be her linguistic and sexual power. What they fail to realise is that implicit in such an approach is, in the circumstances, a racist, as well as a sexist, component which traditional criticism has done much to ignore.

The image of Cleopatra which criticism has bequeathed to us represents an unconscious but gradual eroticisation of Egypt, which has only recently come to be understood at the level of theory. This is part of a much larger process that has recently been identified by the American/Palestinian critic Edward W. Said under the term 'orientalism', which is a way the West has of constructing, and looking at the East, the unfamiliar, and the exotic. Said has observed that the western constructions of the Orient constitute 'a field' which is 'an enclosed space'. He continues:

> The idea of representation is a theatrical one: The Orient is the stage on which the whole East is confined. On this stage will appear figures whose role it is to represent the larger whole from which they emanate. The Orient then seems to be, not an unlimited extension beyond the familiar European world, but rather a closed field, a theatrical stage affixed to Europe . . . In the depths of this Oriental stage stands a prodigious cultural repertoire whose individual items evoke a fabulously rich world: the sphinx, Cleopatra, Eden, Troy, Sodom and Gomorrah, Astarte, Isis and Osiris, Sheba, Babylon, the Genii, the Magi, Nineveh, Prester John, Mahomet, and dozens more; settings, in some cases names only, half-imagined, half-known; monsters, devils, heroes; terrors, pleasures, desires.[15]

Traditional criticism has simply indulged its own fascination with the East that Cleopatra represents, but if we apply Said's thinking to *Antony and Cleopatra*, this changes our critical perspective considerably, and offers us new ways of looking at the play. That eroticisation, formerly a male critical indulgence, takes the form of what can be called a carnivalesque challenge to the values of Rome in the play, but it also underscores the Roman propensity to colonisation: that fascination with Egypt which focuses its attention upon the infatuation with Cleopatra, but which is in fact concerned with conquest and subjugation. In this case Cleopatra's much vaunted sexuality – which the play renders problematical through the Jacobean theatrical convention of having the role played by a male actor – is what attracts successive Roman leaders to Egypt, but it is also her defence against the militaristic rigours of colonisation. When, in the opening dialogue of the play, Philo observes the extent to which Antony's infatuation with Cleopatra 'O'erflows the measure', relinquishing his erstwhile personification as the figure of 'plated Mars' to 'become the bellows and the fan\To cool a gipsy's lust' (I. i. 2–10), Demetrius responds with a statement about transformation:

> Take but good note, and you shall see in him
> The triple pillar of the world transform'd
> Into a strumpet's fool: behold and see.
>   (I. i. 10–13)

Even before we have had the opportunity to savour Egyptian fecundity, which the play goes on to articulate as a oneness with the earth: 'The higher Nilus swells,\ The more it promises: as it ebbs, the seedsman\ Upon the slime and ooze scatters his grain,\ And shortly comes to harvest' (II. vii. 20–3),[16] – it is subjected to the moralistic judgement of a Roman censoriousness. Of course, as John Danby observed,[17] that judgement is itself shown in the play to be less than stable in that it discloses the limitations of Roman values as well as seeking to provide a means of positioning the threat posed by Cleopatra and Egypt. Here what the Coleridgean tradition was content to identify as Cleopatra's seductive powers, themselves allegedly a response to masculine sexual/literary attention, become in this radically revised context, an element in a much larger *politics* which posits the cultural production of Cleopatra's own identity as an adversary of Roman military power; Egypt itself becomes 'feminised', a place of political danger and sexual fascination against whose subversive strategies Rome defines and tests its own values. Here the 'character' of Cleopatra is relatively unimportant compared to the *process* of which the dramatic representation is a part. Cleopatra represents one half of that *difference* in and through which Rome defines itself, the means whereby value is established along the axis of gender, and nationality. The dialectical opposition which the play sets up between Rome and Egypt embraces a struggle for power which is articulated through the *difference* between Rome and Egypt, male and female. Here politics are not incidental to the drama, an addition which many traditional critics have been happy to acknowledge, but are in fact *constitutive* of it.

In the play sexuality and fecundity are represented in carnivalesque terms as the threatening 'other' of Roman restraint, a binary opposition which the play uses, perhaps inadvertently, to sustain the violent hierarchy of colonisation. But we should understand this *not* as a simple disclosure of the operations of Roman 'power'; rather, *Antony and Cleopatra* focuses for us the interaction between Rome's imperial colonising impulse and the response of the colonised Egypt, to the extent that it is appropriate to talk of the play in terms of a politics of colonisation. Antony, we should do well to remember, is not the first Roman to have faced the crisis which confronts the imperial coloniser; before him Caesar had succumbed to Cleopatra's festive charms, exchanging his sword, the phallic symbol of his imperial power, for a more literal manifestation of his manhood which paradoxically *undoes* Roman succession even as it colonises the body of Cleopatra herself; in conversation with Enobarbus, Agrippa observes:

> She made great Caesar lay his sword to bed;
> He ploughed her, and she cropp'd . . .
> (II. ii. 227–8)

In Agrippa's account it is difficult to know exactly which of the two, Caesar or Cleopatra, exerts the greater power. A military encounter is transformed into a sexual encounter, Egypt becomes the body of Cleopatra herself who willingly diverts the energies of her aggressor.

It is, perhaps, not unreasonable to suggest that the traditional male critic of the play has persistently emphasised the fascination of Cleopatra and for his 'ordinary, pays his heart,\For what his eyes eat only' (II. ii. 225–6), whereas in Jacobean theatrical performance the eye itself may be deceived since beneath the role of the seductress is a male actor. One way of examining this is through the way in which the metaphor of food is deployed in the text. The image which Agrippa makes use of here is, translated into the metaphor of colonisation, similar to that which Donne deploys in his Elegie XIX when he describes his mistress in the following terms: 'O my America! my new found land,/My kingdome, safeliest when with one man man'd/ My Myne of precious stones, My Emperie.'[18] It is also one which

Elizabethan colonisers deployed, as Sir Walter Raleigh does in his description of *The Discovery of the Large, Rich and Beautiful Empire of Guiana etc.* as he moves between descriptions of the carnivalesque figures of the Amazonian women who for one month in the year 'feast, dance, and drink of their wines in abundance', through comparisons between Guianese women and their English counterparts, to a view of the land itself as a feminised entity untouched by civilisation:

> To conclude, *Guiana* is a Country that hath yet her Maidenhead, never sacked, turned, nor wrought, the face of the earth hath not been torn, nor the virtue and salt of the soil spent by manurance, the graves have not been opened for gold, the mines not broken with sledges, nor their Images pulled down out of their temples. It hath never been entered by any army of strength, and never conquered or possessed by any Christian Prince.[19]

Although the details are different from what we find in the Egypt of *Antony and Cleopatra*, the process is, in principle, the same. Ingestion of food and colonisation are often in these texts aligned with issues of masculine possession. What Shakespeare's text exposes is a much more complex *politics* than the naïve and self-contradictory description which Raleigh offers. It is none the less a motif that has remained consistent in the literature of colonisation, and which surfaces again in passing in texts such as Joseph Conrad's *Heart of Darkness*, where the continent of Africa is feminised and subjected to a moralising critique which locates an evil, and a savagery at its core through the figure of Kurtz. Where Shakespeare's text resists ascribing moral categories to geographical regions, Conrad's Marlow projects outwards onto the landscape an ironically formulated psychology that recuperates Africa as part of the internal dialogue between civilisation and savagery endemic in western culture. *Antony and Cleopatra* stands at the beginning of this process.

Thus we can see how, beginning from a series of critical positions whose own naïveté betrays a system of values which literary theory has done much in recent years to discredit, the details of the text of *Antony and Cleopatra* can be shown to produce new configurations, which force us to ask serious questions about the play's poetry, its characterisations, its heroic themes, and its restless shifts of focus. Some of these issues have recently been problematised in other Shakespearean texts, but the fact that the action of this play moves constantly between two radically opposed locations has often puzzled a number of critics, and led them to conclude that either the play self-consciously violates the Aristotelian unity of time, or alternatively, represents the dramatist's response, along modernist lines, to the shifting consciousness of the dramatic characters themselves.

The play's restless shifts of focus were first located by John Danby in his collection of essays, *Elizabethan and Jacobean Poets* (1952), from which the first essay in the present collection is taken. For him the play is truly 'cinematic' offering 'more panning, tracking, and playing with the camera, more mixing of shots than in any other of Shakespeare's tragedies'. The play may swim 'with glamour' but the judgements which the audience is asked to make are always partial and can never be mutually exclusive. Indeed, Danby argues that although Caesarism in the play may represent 'the World', and Cleopatra 'the flesh', 'There is no suggestion that the dichotomy is resolvable: unless we are willing to take the delusions of either party as a resolution, the "universal peace" of Caesar, the Egypt-beyond-the-grave of Antony and Cleopatra in their autotoxic exaltations before they kill themselves'. Against the transcendental humanism of earlier criticism, which celebrated the spiritual love of Antony and Cleopatra, Danby locates the 'meaning' of the play in a more sceptical and dialectical ethos; for him the tragedy resides in *disjunction*, not ultimate unity, and the figure who represents this process above all is Antony, caught between the conflicting but irresolvable demands of Rome and Egypt. For Danby Rome is the world of 'politics', which he defines as 'the manipulation of the common body they despise by the great men whom the commons can never love until they are safely rid of them'; by contrast, Egypt is 'the world of the flesh', and Antony's tragedy is that he is caught between these two opposing forces which play through him 'and finally destroy him'. Danby views Shakespeare's dramatic technique in the play as one of making an adjustment to 'the new Jacobean tastes', but he also sees the play as being built around a central paradox which culminates in the tragedy of Antony: 'the tragedy of the destruction of man, the creative spirit, in perverse war and insensate love – the two complementary and opposed halves of a discreating society'.[20] It is the instability of the world that Danby identifies as the play's guiding ethos, although the same may be said about the much earlier play *Troilus and Cressida* (1602), whose own discreating society persistently relativises all human values. Where other critics have been content to gloss over the play's discontinuities, Danby, remarkably, makes them the very centre of his own critical argument, an argument that engages the audience in the dramatic process of problematising the act of judgement itself.

The fact that the play presents us with a dilemma of judgement is something that the American critic Janet Adelman takes up and develops further in the first major book-length study of the play, *The Common Liar* (1973), part of which is reprinted below as essay 2. For her the play persistently questions emotion, to the point that 'The desire to judge and be judged correctly is one of the dominant passions of the play'.[21] But it is a process which draws the audience into its aegis as onlookers of the drama – something which Danby suggests but does not fully develop – and it is problematical because, as she suggests, 'the experience of *Antony and Cleopatra* is curiously indirect; the play consists of a few actions and almost endless discussion of them'.[22] It is interesting to see how a critic such as Adelman incorporates detail such as this, which can be traced back to Bradley, although she makes something much more positive of it.

This uncertainty of judgement is linked by Adelman to the play's rhetorical deployment of poetic language which leads to a perception of the 'partiality of truth', and to the view that 'we can neither believe nor wholly disbelieve the claims made by the poetry'.[23] This scepticism contrasts both with Bradley, and with the unrestrained optimism of critics such as G. Wilson Knight. To this extent the play may be said to be about, among other things, the power of poetic language to structure the world, and the difficulties which follow from acting upon the structures thus created. We may well be invited to 'kneel down and wonder' at Cleopatra, who as a figure constructed out of poetic rhetoric is replete with an inordinate affective power, but the question which Adelman's analysis raises, but does not quite answer, because it cannot wholly break from the conceptual framework of earlier criticism, concerns the forces which are at play in this process. In both her analysis and that of Danby's which precedes it, there is a clear perception of a process of deconstruction *avant la lettre* which is going on in the play. In the same way that Roman values are subjected to a critical scrutiny from an Egyptian perspective, so the seductive power of Egyptian poetic rhetoric – or to put it more precisely, of Roman rhetoric under the power of a carnivalesque Egyptian otherness – is systematically dismantled, and shown to be fictional. And yet these fictions continue to exert an affective power over us, offered as they are by Cleopatra as a truth of nature. Or at least, that 'other nature', which, for Sir Philip Sidney, was the exclusive preserve of poetry in its disdaining of subjection in order to create 'things either better than Nature bringeth forth, or, quite anew, forms such as never were in Nature, as the Heroes, Demigods, Cyclops, Chimeras, and the like'.[24] This is nowhere more clearly indicated than in the exchange at the end of the play between Cleopatra and Dolabella in which Cleopatra's image of a superhuman Antony as an amalgamation of magnanimous Roman power and Egyptian fecundity is placed before a sceptical Dolabella:

> His legs bestrid the ocean, his rear'd arm
> Crested the world: his voice was propertied
> As all the tuned spheres, and that to friends:
> But when he meant to quail, and shake the orb,
> He was as rattling thunder. For his bounty,
> There was no winter in't: an autumn 'twas
> That grew the more by reaping: his delights
> Were dolphin-like, they show'd his back above
> The element they lived in: in his livery
> Walk'd crowns and crownets: realms and islands were
> As plates dropp'd from his pocket.
>   (V. ii. 82–92)

In response to her question 'Think you there was, or might be such a man/As this I dreamt of?', he replies: 'Gentle madam, no' (V. ii. 93–4). But Cleopatra's rejoinder is to relegate poetic imagery to the status of a dream, and to privilege the creative power of the imagination as a feature of nature itself: 'nature wants stuff/To vie strange forms with fancy, yet to imagine/An Antony were nature's piece 'gainst fancy,/Condemning shadows quite' (V. ii. 97–100). Here poetry *and* nature are brought together as part of a strategy designed to oppose Roman scepticism, amalgamating Roman and Egyptian values in a new imaginative synthesis which ascribes to Cleopatra a positive and resistant identity rather than that prescribed by Rome for her.

Adelman's response to the poetry of the play represents an important step forward, even though its preoccupation is with the formal characteristics of the Shakespearean text. As with much criticism of the play up to the early 1970s, the emphasis is upon explication and the recovery of a meaning, rather than upon the theoretical investigation of the conditions under which meanings are produced. What Danby and Adelman began to realise, however, was that *Antony and Cleopatra* was too unstable a text to yield to such monolithic reading, and that more complex critical and theoretical strategies would be needed.

Another American critic, Phyllis Rackin (essay 3), writing some ten years later than Adelman, reinforces the critical vision of a subversive Cleopatra, and pinpoints the ways in which both theatrically and linguistically Egypt violates the rules of decorum, challenging the essentially rationalist outlook of Rome. Her focus is a little more narrow, however, in that it draws attention to the conditions of theatrical performance, and the meanings that it can generate historically. Against Rome's capacity to measure and to analyse, Egypt is a place of theatrical shows, and Cleopatra sustains this capacity for 'showmanship' right up to the end. When Rome encounters Egypt, especially through the figure of Enorbarbus, then it responds imaginatively to 'Cleopatra's creative arts'.[25] For Rackin Cleopatra is to be identified as a neo-Shakespearean artist who authorises theatrical performance at the same time as she challenges 'reality' as conceived by Rome. There is, Rackin argues, a fundamental contradiction in Sidney's theory of poetry, insisting, as it does, on its capacity for mimesis as well as on its ability to construct a 'golden' world. For her, Sidney proposes two mutually contradictory theories of poetry, but, she goes on, 'while Sidney seems to be unaware of the contradiction, Shakespeare insists upon it'.[26]

One half of the contradiction which the play keeps before us is the sheer unrepresentability of part of the reality to which it lays claim. For Rackin it is the figure of the boy-actor who underlines this, in so far as the theatrical device gives Cleopatra 'access to a level of reality beyond what has been presented'.[27] In a move which to some extent anticipates certain rhetorical strategies of New Historicist criticism, Rackin remarks on the capacity of Cleopatra's acts of staging to affect even her most ardent and rational Roman adversaries; it is as if the theatre itself, through the figure of Cleopatra, is displaying its artistic virtuosity in the matter of transforming reality at the same time as it undertakes to represent its contours. It is through a desire to recover a 'golden' world from the quotidian reality of a sordid imperialist politics that the play forsakes parody (the boy actor imitating Cleopatra, who is made to fear in captivity her imitation by a boy actor), and through death elevates itself to the status of tragedy. In some respects we might recast Rackin's argument to say that a search for origins in the play, initiated through a poetic and theatrical representation of a reality which is humanly unattainable, is what lies at the core of the conflict which sustains the drama. Here theories of referentiality and representation collide, move through a series of generic ambivalences, and culminate in the ultimate sacrifice, which makes of the play, not a divine comedy but a mature tragedy of enormous complexity. Moreover, we can begin to detect in Rackin's argument an awareness of New Historicist methods of textual analysis, although they do not of themselves underpin the conceptual framework of her argument which still has one foot in the traditionalist camp.

Clearly language itself in the play is rendered problematical as the drama foregrounds the very materials out of which it is made, and holds them up for critical scrutiny. Self-consciousness, from becoming a deficiency in Bradley, has now become a virtue. Moreover, the oppositions in the play have themselves been subjected historically to that Drydenesque choice of *All for Love* whereby Antony is alleged to have sacrificed his worldly power for the love of Cleopatra. In attempting to locate a similarity between the act of loving and the act of communication, Terence Hawkes, in the fourth essay in this collection, observes that to reject that merging into oneness that characterises love itself, is analogous to a rejection both of communication and community. The model of communication to which Hawkes alludes throughout his book *Shakespeare's Talking Animals* (1975) distinguishes clearly between 'written' and 'spoken' language, each functioning within distinct conceptual frameworks. At one level, Hawkes is right to insist upon the distinction between Rome as a kind of disembodied 'voice', and Egypt as the realm of the body: 'the play assigns voice alone to Rome, body alone to Egypt. Rome is a place of words, Egypt a place of actions. Rome is where love is talked of, Egypt is where love is made'.[28] This opposition of the rational, the logocentric, and the linguistic on the one hand, and the tactile, the irrational, the fecund, and the physical on the other identifies a structural motif in the play which effectively makes way for a carnivalesque reading of Egyptian excess. At one level in the play the body rises to confront the rational constraints of an imperial coloniser, but that sexually inflected arousal is augmented by a poetic rhetoric which is no less tactile in its imagery and imaginative power, but equally effective as a strategy of resistance. In the play languages resist each other, and these resistances take a series of surprising turns. Hawkes's reading of the play is one of the first to align the Rome/Egypt opposition with a gender division: 'If Egypt emphasises the body, one level of language, one sort of "love", and the concomitant womanly powers of Cleopatra, Rome is a place of words, another level of language, another kind of love, and of self-confident "manly" prowess.' Hawkes's analysis breathes a new meaning into the Johnsonian phrase 'fatal Cleopatra' in his suggestion that just as *King Lear* puns on 'love', so *Antony and Cleopatra* puns on 'death'. In this reading a residual commitment to Egypt as a place of undoing remains, although Hawkes firmly resists the reductive binary opposition of Rome and Egypt as 'all' versus 'love'; this, he insists, 'ignores the complementary function of both places'.[29]

What distinguishes the first four essays in this collection from much of the criticism that precedes them is their readiness to admit that there are problems with *Antony and Cleopatra* that cannot be readily resolved. Danby, holding on to the notion of authorial intention, locates a shift in Shakespeare's poetic technique; Adelman and Rackin develop that perception in different directions, while remaining within the same conceptual framework recognised by traditional criticism. Hawkes, influenced by early studies of the media by Marshall McLuhan and Walter J. Ong, seeks to rethink the relationship between language, drama and society, and begins the process of historicising the Shakespearean text through an argument which aligns the pre-literate Jacobean public theatre with the post-literate world of technological media. In the case of Danby, Adelman and Hawkes, the evidence can be shown accumulating which begins to threaten to transform our perceptions of the text of *Antony and Cleopatra*. Hovering around all three readings, and foregrounded much more in the case of Rackin, is an embryonic awareness of subversive questioning within the text itself, later to become an issue in relation to New Historicism, as well as a perception of the critic her/himself as an interrogator of cultural values and assumptions. Of the three, Hawkes, in 1975, is clearly the most adventurous, working as he was then from a theory of language radically different from the other two. It is only with the advent of Critical Theory, and particularly with the interest in language generated by the advent of Structuralism, that the context in which these individual forays into the play, and by implication, into the entire field of Renaissance drama, undergoes radical change.

II

One of the consequences of the development of theoretical ways of approaching *Antony and Cleopatra* is that we are required to be much more sensitive than in the past to questions concerning the relationship between the text and its immediate historical context.

What has already been identified as an impression of restlessness which the text evinces, its theatrical self-consciousness and its linguistic ambivalences, all find echoes in the larger narrative context out of which the play itself emerged. Historically the story of Antony and Cleopatra was regarded in the early seventeenth century as a dangerous and unstable narrative. Fulke Greville, for example, 'sacrificed in the fire' a play of that name which might have been 'construed or strained to a personating of vices in the present governors and government'. Greville went on to display his own political caution in elaborating on the contemporary significance of his play:

> From which cautious prospect I, bringing into my mind the ancient poet's metamorphosing man's reasonable nature into the sensitive of beasts or vegetative of plants, and knowing these all in their true moral, to be but images of the unequal balance between humours and times, nature and place; and again, in the practice of the world, seeing the like instance not poetically but really, fashioned in the Earl of Essex then falling (and ever till then worthily beloved both of Queen and people) – this sudden descent of such a greatness, together with the quality of the actors in every scene, stirred up the author's second thoughts to be careful, in his own case, of leaving fair weather behind him, he having, in the Earl's precipitate fortune, curiously observed how long that nobleman's birth, worth and favour had been flattered, tempted and stung by a swarm of sect-animals whose property was to wound and fly away, and so, by a continual affliction, probably enforce great postures, perchance to tumble sometimes upon their sovereign's circles.[30]

Greville in no sense forsakes an awareness, which he had already demonstrated in his earlier *A Treatise on Monarchy* (c. 1600), of the representational nature of narrative. In this earlier text the desire for power is inscribed within an economy of sexual pleasure with human subjects cast as 'blankes where pow'r doth write her lust'.[31] What is frustrating is that Greville should have destroyed so dangerous a text as *Antony and Cleopatra* in which questions of power, lust, identity, theatrical representation and imperial aspiration were inextricably intertwined.

Greville destroyed a potentially controversial play that may have been written at any time between 1604 and 1610. Shakespeare appears to have shown similar caution in waiting some eight years before returning to develop further material he had already begun to work through in *Julius Caesar* in 1599. Clearly, at the beginning of the seventeenth century the resonances of the narrative of Antony and Cleopatra were such that the story, far from assuming a stable iconic value, could offer no guarantees of stability of meaning. It is hardly surprising, therefore, that in Shakespeare's *Antony and Cleopatra* fiction and history, the personal and the political, along with representations of power, as well as the powers and dangers of theatrical representation, might be shown to converge.

There are, of course, a number of ways of looking at the relationship between a text such as *Antony and Cleopatra* and the historical context in which it is embedded. Clearly, it would be misleading to assume that any literary or theatrical text should be a direct and unproblematical reflection of non-literary and non-theatrical historical events. We know, however, from Sir John Hayward's *The First Part of the Life and Raigne of King Henrie the IIII* (1599), that historical texts could be read as direct reflections of contemporary events and personages,[32] and Fulke Greville's destruction of his own text of *Antony and Cleopatra* confirms the power of theatrical representation to mirror in a controversial and partisan way social and political reality. But any mirroring is likely to have been inflected in such a way that, given the liminal status of the public theatre itself, it would be more accurate to describe the process as one of mediation.

The moment that we move from the concept of 'reflection' to 'mediation', we actually raise questions which result in an unsettling of the relationship between theatrical performance and accepted historical categories, and what we might make of the connections between them as modern readers. One way of overcoming the difficulties that this conceptual shift produces, is to think of a text such as *Antony and Cleopatra* as a 'representation' and a point of convergence of a series of contemporary historical concerns. The relationship between text and history then, becomes one of complex interaction where questions of aesthetic form and genre are shown to be interwoven with social and cultural concerns which give the theatrical representation itself point and contemporary relevance. In what is, arguably, the most detailed excavation of that relationship between text and historical context, H. Neville Davies, in the fifth essay in the collection, seeks to situate the play firmly in the field of discourse of Jacobean court politics, arguing that in its representation of 'the transition from triumvirate to Augustan empire'[33] the play should not only be placed alongside *King Lear*, but that it offers a commentary upon James's own propagandist claims to be a new Augustus. A play which adopts a very ambivalent attitude towards

Augustan Rome in the making, and which foregrounds the subversive strategies of a feminised Egypt, is one that would be less than unequivocal in support of James. As Davies points out, though in a critical vocabulary that retains a traditional allegiance to a neo-Coleridgean view of the author: 'The myriad-minded creator of the serpent of old Nile might reasonably be expected to have adopted a highly ambiguous attitude toward the policies and person of his unattractive sovereign.'[34] Davies goes on to propose Christian, King of Denmark, as a likely model for the figure of Antony and to suggest that it is 'possible to form surprisingly detailed impressions of what happened' when Christian was feasted by James, 'and by so doing to recover a real-life contributory source for one particular scene in Shakespeare's *Antony and Cleopatra*',[35] the scene on Pompey's galley (II. vii).

Davies's treatment of the historical context of *Antony and Cleopatra* represents a very significant advance on Tillyard's assumptions concerning the secondary and supportive value of 'background ideas'. For Tillyard, the work of art was of paramount importance, although it was assumed to rest upon a body of ideas which it was the function of the literary historian to excavate. Those ideas, which for Tillyard make up what he calls 'the Elizabethan World Picture' are shown to inform the art of the period, but they are regarded as something neutral, not active necessarily in the specific tensions which structure social process. What Tillyard takes for granted as *ideas*, which he finds stated in literary and theatrical texts, have a strong ideological charge in that they represent *not* so much a historical reality but the way in which a particular heterogeneous culture was encouraged to view that reality. Once we begin to excavate historically specific events, and particular literary texts, then that body of ideas which according to Tillyard functioned as a kind of *zeitgeist*, lose their coherence, with the result that investigation opens up the much more fragmentary and discontinuous nature of a culture which from the historical distance of our own perspective was once considered unified and harmonious. Davies's article goes a long way to revise Tillyard's position, but it remains nonetheless cast in a discourse of bardolatry. What is useful about this essay, however, is the way in which it proposes a dynamic relationship between theatre and court which is much more than a neo-New Historicist account of the dependent relationship of the former upon the latter. For Davies the theatre is an institution capable of producing a critique of power. Also, although he is concerned primarily with what Tom

Healy, in a larger context, has called 'moments of production',[36] there is a sense in which Davies extends his discussion to speculate upon the possible context for the reception of the play. What this essay does not engage with is that modern encounter with a text of the past, which draws together 'past text, critical representation, and reader's response'.[37]

Working from some of the same historical material, but much more explicitly aware of the materiality of history, Margot Heinemann (essay 6) identifies *Antony and Cleopatra* as a transitional text, produced during the interval between one epoch and another, when 'history' itself had become a narrative open to radically opposed interpretations. She identifies the Tacitean mode of the play, and to this extent augments Davies's observation that it is critical of Augustan imperialism. Moreover, Heinemann reinforces the view that *Antony and Cleopatra* refuses 'a single historical or ethical centre', and she traces this through Dr Johnson, Keats's idea of 'negative capability', to the more politically orientated work of Bertold Brecht. What is especially significant about this essay is the way in which textual ambivalence is shown to open the way to 'widely differing theatrical productions'.[38] Heinemann regards *Antony and Cleopatra* as a text which is characterised by a chaotic openness that certain kinds of performance and, by implication, criticism, seek to smooth out. Thus, what begins as a historical contextualising of the play moves swiftly on to a consideration of its reception in the modern theatre where 'choices' made by director and actor alike carry with them an implicitly ideological charge. Heinemann's justification for reading the play is to locate a 'chaos' with which a modern commentator might identify, and to suggest that we resurrect dramatic literature of the past primarily in so far as it speaks to our current pressing moral, ethical and political concerns.

III

The first six essays in the present collection, ranging from John Danby's attempt to problematise the act of judgement in *Antony and Cleopatra*, through Janet Adelman's and Phyllis Rackin's focus on the rhetorical function of poetry, to Terence Hawkes's account of its social context, and then beyond to Neville Davies's and Margot Heinemann's varying accounts of the play's negotiations of 'history', all in their different ways mark a distinct departure from those traditional approaches which privilege transcendental themes, and which express an uncritical fascination with the seductive allure of Cleopatra. They depart significantly from the kind of criticism that is exemplified in G. Wilson Knight's essays on the play in *The Imperial Theme* (1931) in which he argued that the play contains a 'prevailing optimism' and a 'visionary imagination' which transcends all 'evil': 'Such visionary imaginations far outweigh the minor stressing of Antony's shame or disgrace', and he sees the two central characters as 'both strongly idealised, ablaze with impossible beauty or infinite majesty and power'.[39] Wilson Knight was not alone in seeking to impose *unity* on the play, what he calls 'the single vision', and although he is prepared to concede that *Antony and Cleopatra* contains what he regards as 'realistic' elements, his conclusion is that what we are left with at the end is:

> a dramatic microcosm of human and other, life viewed from within the altitudes of conscious Divinity; that we have here the most perfect statement of the real; that whereas the sombre plays are aspects of 'appearance' in *Antony and Cleopatra* we touch the Absolute.[40]

Many of the issues, such as the veracity of poetic utterance, the dialectical opposing of Rome and Egypt, the generic ambivalence of the play, and the involvement of the audience in the dynamics of performance, are all raised in various ways in the first six essays of the following collection. With the exception of Neville Davies's essay (1985) and Margot Heinemann's (1990), these essays span the years 1952–75. The remaining six essays in the collection date from 1977 onwards, and exhibit a radical shift in the ways in which much of the material uncovered in earlier work is deployed.

Much of this new work has emerged from the encounter between literary criticism and what is generally labelled 'theory', whose influence began to be felt from the late 1960s onwards, but the results of which began to filter through into the area of Renaissance studies generally, and Shakespeare studies in particular, during the late 1970s and early 1980s. At stake in this debate is the issue of how a reading of a particular text is produced. For Bradley, and Wilson Knight, and to a lesser extent Danby and Adelman, reading involves a projection onto the text of *Antony and Cleopatra* of a set of selective hermeneutic practices in an effort to locate the eternal 'truths' which are said to reside at its centre. That is to say, they are concerned with the question of locating a single meaning in the text, which will lead to some 'truth' at its centre which is in some sense beyond language. But even here, in the essays that form part of this collection, the text is shown to be resistant to this process, although the nature of that resistance is neither clearly perceived nor fully articulated. The sort of critical readings evident in the first six essays, however, are a very different affair in principle and in practice from readings generated from within an argument that proposes, as Rosalind Coward and John Ellis put it, that 'text and context are seen as mutually determining, caught in the same process of production'.[41] The shift is one from the naïve, referentially based assumption that it is the *text* that 'means' – a feature which Bradley's criticism of *Antony and Cleopatra* takes as axiomatic – and that meaning can be traced to authorial *intention*, either implicitly or explicitly, to a critical practice which involves a much fuller, more problematical articulation of the conditions, sometimes unconscious, which govern a text's construction, as well as those which govern its reconstitution and reception. In this radically revised context no single truth prevails as the key to the text's meaning, but neither is it accurate to speak of an unrestrained pluralism; readings of the text are capable of producing multiple meanings, but those readings always emerge from particular positions, and it is one of the functions of critical practice to identify those positions as determinants of particular readings.

The concept of meanings produced in and through language – essentially the project initiated by structuralism, and pursued at a more complex level by poststructuralism – is precisely what the late Paul de Man argued was the challenge which 'theory' posed to more established modes of Critical Practice, when he observed that:

> Literary theory can be said to come into being when the approach to literary texts is no longer based on non-linguistic, that is to say historical and aesthetic considerations or, to put it somewhat less crudely, when the object of the discussion is no longer the meaning or the value but the modalities of production and of reception of meaning and of value prior to their establishment – the implication being that this establishment is problematic enough to require an autonomous discipline of critical investigation to consider its possibility and status.

He goes on to argue that 'The resistance to theory is a resistance to the use of language about language',[42] precisely the kind of resistance A. C. Bradley evinced in relation to his judgement of the self-consciousness of the text of *Antony and Cleopatra*.

This shift of methodological emphasis is part of that larger transformation which has been taking place in English studies over the
past decade or so, whose focus is, as Peter Widdowson has observed,
'what English *is*, where it has got to, whether it has a future, whether
it *should* have a future as a discrete discipline, and if it does, in what
ways it might be reconstituted'.[43] The concept of 'crisis' has been pre-
eminent in the sphere of Shakespeare studies; Bradleyan 'Shakespeare' with its commitment to 'character' was replaced in the 1930s
by an emphasis upon poetic structure and theme in the work of
G. Wilson Knight, L. C. Knights and others, while cognate develop-
ments in Practical Criticism and American New Criticism ensured
that a literary (and dramatic) text was self-contained, sometimes the
expression of an authorial intention, sometimes an 'experience' itself,
'detached from the author at birth'.[44] In either case 'history' was
admitted as 'continuity', 'unity' or 'totality': 'History as the teleological unfolding of a promised end' as Frank Lentricchia puts it,[45] or
dispensed with altogether in the preoccupation with formal characteristics of the text. Even when modes of enquiry that we might label
'theoretical' appeared (as in the case of Northrop Frye's *Anatomy of
Criticism* [1957]), they did not deviate substantially from the idealist
notion that literary texts were ultimately the repositories of universal
truths about the human condition.

However, the greater concentration on literary theory from the
1960s onwards did much to change the situation, in that it served to
provide a new kind of focus for what had hitherto existed either on
the margins of Shakespeare criticism, or for questions that had
simply not been asked before of these texts. It would, of course, be
a mistake to think of 'Theory' in monolithic terms, since what was
released during the 1960s – and what emerged substantively in the
area of Shakespeare studies some two decades later – was a range of
committed radical positions, 'alternatives', each with their own particular emphasis, but overlapping in questions of methodology and
conceptual orientation. Common to each was a challenge to teleological and metaphysical notions of 'history', introducing in a variety of ways, concepts already familiar to Marxist and materialist
analysis: 'discontinuity', 'rupture', 'contradiction', 'difference', 'fragmentation' and 'heterogeneity'. Or to put the matter even more
polemically, narrative and historical explanation ceased to be regarded 'objectively'; in the words of the historian Hayden White,
'there is no value neutral mode of emplotment, explanation, or even
description of any field of events, whether imaginary or real', with

the result that, 'the very use of language itself implies or entails a specific posture before the world which is ethical, ideological, or more generally political; not only all interpretation, but also all language is politically contaminated'.[46] The development of structuralist and poststructuralist theories of language – particularly in relation to the concept of the generation of meaning through 'difference' as opposed to an unproblematic referentiality – served to draw together a range of disciplines and philosophies in new and provocative alignments. Questions could now be asked about the precise rhetorics of 'representation'; feminism, Marxism, and psychoanalysis, while not entirely compatible, provided the interdisciplinary bases for raising radical questions about the status of literary texts in society, their representations of gender difference as a constitutive principle, the precise manner in which individual human subjects are constructed within the social formation. In short, literature in general, and Shakespearean texts in particular, could be shown to be deeply implicated, and in a variety of ways, in the ethical, ideological and political currents both of the first moment of their production, and in the subsequent histories of their critical reception.

IV

Antony and Cleopatra is a text that submits itself to a variety of theoretically-informed approaches, partly because of its obviously dialectical structure, but also because it traverses a range of issues which have direct relevance to current questions of history, theatre, genre, race, gender and politics. The two essays by Neville Davies and Margot Heinemann, concerned as they are with different approaches to 'history' and theatrical representation, mark a transition from earlier criticism of the play already beginning to free itself from the straitjacket of traditional response. However, in a very real sense, criticism itself may be said to mediate the text of *Antony and Cleopatra*, and indeed, any Shakespearean text for that matter. The break came in 1977 with Linda Fitz's scathing review of the 'sexism' endemic in much criticism of the play.

Fitz's argument, in essay 7 of this collection, begins from the suggestion that 'male critics feel personally threatened by Cleopatra and what she represents to them'.[47] That fear stems, she argues, from the impression that Cleopatra gives of being 'aggressive' and 'manipulative', but Fitz goes on to suggest that Shakespeare justifies her behaviour in the play on the grounds that it is a response to her awareness of encroaching age. In addition to observing the critical location of love and lust in the allegedly inferior 'feminine' world of Egypt, and politics in the masculine world of Rome, Fitz ascribes a psychological motive to Cleopatra, at the same time as she observes the critical insistence that it is Antony who is the protagonist of the play. This alignment of male protagonist with tragic hero, something which is evident even in those more 'responsible' critics, such as Janet Adelman, that Fitz cites, effectively draws together questions of genre and gender. What Fitz does not do is to attempt to align what she adduces is Shakespeare's psychological motivation of Cleopatra's character with her political situation as a victim of Roman colonisation. What she does do, however, is to make a case for treating Cleopatra as a tragic hero whose own inner struggle is at least equal to that of Antony. This 'demythologising' of Cleopatra is part of a larger feminist project which is designed to force a rethinking both of the structure of the play itself, and of the critical responses that it has elicited.

Fitz's attempt to reclaim the figure of Cleopatra for the genre of tragedy depends, to some extent, upon disengaging her from that of comedy and from comparison with the larger range of Shakespeare's comic heroines. But, as Barbara C. Vincent shows, in essay 8 of the collection, the contestation of genres is effectively one of the play's structuring motifs. Terence Hawkes's analysis of the play centred around a radical opposition between the rational world of Rome, and the world of festive excess that is Egypt. For Vincent comedy and tragedy are intertwined in the play almost in a kind of *differential* relationship with each other, and the two genres interact in such a way that the Egyptian 'irrational world of monstrous fertility'[48] presents a real challenge to the objectively realistic, restraining mode of tragedy. Although Vincent situates in Rome the ironic and realistic vision most commonly associated with tragedy, the play's comic counter-movement subsumes tragedy into itself, with the result that a resolution of the genre difference is effected through the ultimate theatricalising of the figure of Cleopatra.

Whereas Linda Fitz asserted the feminine ethos of comedy, Barbara Vincent offers a more deconstructive reading of the genre in which Cleopatra as 'the prime desirer in the play' creates a heroic identity for Antony, and also a world 'which encompasses tragedy and is only made the loftier for it, which grows the more by reaping'.[49] Vincent carries forward Enobarbus's account of the endless fecundity of

Cleopatra into the imaginative structure of the play itself, to show that even in her suicide there is an ambivalence: the realistic view is that the tactile world of Egypt can no longer function in the face of death, whereas the 'comic' view is that Cleopatra's theatrically realised transcendence hollows out an aetherial sphere for her and Antony which undoes tragic realism. In short, in her death, Cleopatra enacts that excess which has characterised her life in relation to Rome. Vincent affirms the play's own literary self-consciousness, in its negotiation of genres, but she concludes with the view that the 'comic vision' is not exclusive but inclusive, and *includes* tragedy. The play, in short, accommodates both genres, and part of the metadrama is preoccupied with their critical interaction.

It is often assumed that the distinction between comedy and tragedy is that the one is primarily social while the other is concerned with the plight of the individual. With the advent of New Historicism and British Cultural Materialism, along with the interest in the human 'subject' evinced by feminism and psychoanalysis, the social orientation of tragic form, and its implication in the structures of ideology and power have received a new emphasis. Barbara Vincent is concerned with the implications of the shift from the classical to the world of Renaissance humanism as it emerges in the thematic and dramatic structure of *Antony and Cleopatra*, and she associates the 'desire' located in Egypt with Cleopatra as a feature of comedy. In Jonathan Dollimore's analysis of the play, which comprises the ninth essay in this collection, and in the larger argument which informs *Radical Tragedy: Religion, Ideology and Power in the Drama of Shakespeare and his Contemporaries* (1985), desire, 'far from transcending the power relations which structure this society, is wholly in-formed by them'.[50] For Dollimore the tragic subject is constituted in and through the contradictions which reside at the heart of Jacobean culture, and which ideology functions to mediate. In Antony's case the tragic character is decentred by a commitment to a form of 'transcendent autonomy' or self-sufficiency which Dollimore labels *'virtus'*, and the material fact that 'those with power make history yet only in accord with the contingencies of the existing historical moment'.[51] Dollimore conflates Foucault's theory of the operations of power with Raymond Williams's analysis of the internal dynamics of culture as an amalgamation of what he calls 'the dominant' (i.e. 'the definitive lineaments and features' which determine the hierarchical structure of any society at a given moment in history), the 'residual' (or that which still remains from a previous stage), and the 'emergent' or 'new meanings and values, new practices, new relationships and kinds of relationship'.[52] According to Dollimore, Antony's identity in the play is structured according to two contradictions: firstly, it is constituted by a wider conflict 'between the residual/dominant and the emergent power relations' in the play, and secondly, not only is the love relationship with Cleopatra inscribed in relations of power, but Antony's own sexuality 'is informed by the very power relations which he ambivalently is prepared to sacrifice for sexual freedom; correspondingly, the heroic *virtus* which he wants to re-affirm in and through Cleopatra is, in fact, almost entirely a function of the power structure which he, again ambivalently, is prepared to sacrifice for her'.[53]

The interaction between 'State power and cultural forms'[54] is how Dollimore describes the concerns of New Historicism. This is to be distinguished from Cultural Materialism in that the latter is less concerned with 'those genres and practices where State and culture most visibly merge' than with a distinct socio-political perspective whereby the relationship between 'signification and legitimation: the way that beliefs, practices and institutions legitimate the dominant social order or *status quo* – the existing relations of domination and subordination'. Whereas New Historicism shows a distinct tendency to emphasise what Dollimore calls 'the process of consolidation',[55] that is, the ideological means whereby the dominant power secures and legitimates its own political interests, the emphasis in Cultural Materialism is upon resistance to that power at a variety of levels. At a theoretical level Cultural Materialism amalgamates the materialist criticism of writers such as Raymond Williams, with the work of Michel Foucault, especially, in the case of the latter, the assertion that the connection between 'power relations' and 'resistance' is 'strictly relational':

> Their existence depends on a multiplicity of points of resistance: these play the role of adversary, target, support, or handle in power relations. These points of resistance are present everywhere in the power network. Hence there is no single locus of great Refusal, no soul of revolt, source of all rebellions, or pure law of the revolutionary.[56]

What this sacrifices is a notion of the *telos* of history, but its advantage is that it enables the full complexity of any historical context to be investigated, not as part of a general tendency, but as a series of relatively autonomous points of convergence. Thus, a text such as *Antony and Cleopatra*, performed in a theatre which occupied a very ambivalent position within early Jacobean society, discloses a discontinuous range of power relationships which are imperfectly resolved through being displaced into the arena of the aesthetic and the generic. Once these relationships have been identified – and a distinction should be made here between what the text *consciously* and intentionally articulates, and the manner of its articulation, and what exists beneath the level of its ideologically inflected utterance – then the complexity of the connection between text, cultural practice, and social process can be more carefully and more fully analysed, and, in the case of *Antony and Cleopatra*, can be shown to be operating, as Dollimore demonstrates, at a number of levels.

Earlier it was suggested that in *Antony and Cleopatra* the feminisation of Egypt, the according of a gender identity to a geographical space, was itself part of a strategy of colonisation. What this does is to point up the issue of gender and hence make the play amenable to feminist readings. Of those which concern themselves with the ways in which the text structures and shapes gender identities, the excerpt from Marilyn French's *Shakespeare's Division of Experience* (1982) which comprises the tenth essay in this collection, presents the most stark, and hence most problematical statement of what a certain kind of feminist reading might look like. Whereas British materialist feminists tend to emphasise the social construction of identity (and hence posit the possibility of *change*), French insists that there is some essential and irreducible *difference* between male and female. For her, the 'masculine principle' is associated with the acquisition of power, and what she calls 'suprapersonal goals', whereas the 'feminine principle' is concerned with sexual pleasure and personal satisfaction.[57] French sees what she calls 'the outlaw feminine principle' as a challenge to the masculine world of hierarchy, order and authority, whereas 'the in-law feminine principle' functions to support 'the male establishment'.[58] We can begin to see how this categorisation might fit a play such as *Antony and Cleopatra*, which in challenging the principle of female chastity challenges the kind of 'female subordination to the male' which 'guarantees male legitimacy'.[59] For French the tragic drama emerges from the opposition between masculine and feminine, where what is at issue are those social institutions in and through which human constancy is defined. In presenting a radical challenge to those institutions, particularly that of marriage, Cleopatra becomes a force for liberation in the play, and as such challenges the civilising principles of Rome.

Although French is aware of the ways in which sexual identity is mediated through social and cultural institutions, she falls back on a positive restatement of female sexuality as a force which, though it 'may be doomed; it may always be defeated', yet offers a liberating 'richness of emotional and erotic dimensions of life – pleasure, play, and sex'.[60] In some ways this approach, which revives in a different context the notion of carnivalesque which we observed earlier as a feature ascribed to Egypt, reduces the dialectical structure of the play *not* to the axis of gender, but to one of an essential sexuality. In an attempt to restate positively what a number of traditional critics have stated negatively through their treatment of Cleopatra as a *femme fatale*, French neglects to consider the historical conditions of performance which would have had Cleopatra played by a male actor. Her view of the play, as a celebration of female sexuality outwith the constraints of debilitating social institutions, is part of an agenda designed to free women from their inferior roles within masculine power structures. But her locating of female power in an essential sexuality threatens to undermine the cultural force of her argument, and to marginalise issues of politics and race, which feminists of a more materialist persuasion have recently attempted to excavate. Indeed, we can detect in French an enthusiastic restatement of the opposition between 'the world and the flesh' as a structuring principle in the play, although it is here recontextualised in order to produce a much more positive characterisation of Cleopatra as the epitome of 'life' itself.

One way of pointing up this crucial difference is by a return to the position which Jonathan Dollimore has taken up, and from there to the essays by Ania Loomba and Jyotsyna Singh which address all of these questions although from a different perspective from Marilyn French. Dollimore's identification of the radical discontinuity of dramatic form and its relationship to material reality has its origins in part in the writings of Bertold Brecht. It is this approach, what Ania Loomba, in the eleventh essay in this collection, calls 'such proto-Brechtian multiplicity and montage', that enables her to rethink the relationships between race, gender and patriarchy in *Antony and Cleopatra* and other Renaissance plays, particularly from a pedagogic perspective which is itself implicated in a series of assumptions directly attributable to the process of colonialism. Methodologically speaking, Loomba's quarry is that 'non-linear, non-climatic, episodic structure, and montage' which discloses 'the *construction* of identity and social relations'.[61] What she rejects is the view that it is the ultimate, teleological objective of a dramatic form such as tragedy to reveal a universal truth, about an undifferentiated 'human condition'. For her *Antony and Cleopatra* is a play whose heterogeneity and montage effects militate firmly against the achievement of tragic harmony, but what is at issue is much more than the dialectical movement of the text first remarked by John F. Danby.

The 'epic' scope of the play, often alluded to in criticism, is given a fully materialist emphasis in Loomba's account, while the constant shifting of geographical location between Rome and Egypt functions to contradict 'the classical elevation of character or teleological progression towards catharsis' and produces 'a radical interrogation of the imperial and sexual drama'. The public masculine world of Rome is shown to demonstrate a patriarchal control over the apparently private female world of Egypt, and in the process produces a particular form of demonised subjectivity for Cleopatra. Except, of course, that Cleopatra exemplifies a subversive threat to Roman authority, so that Egypt can never be regarded as 'merely a lovers' retreat'. In this respect, Antony alternates between different *political* positions in his oscillation between Rome and Egypt, while Cleopatra's blackness, of which her sexual power is but a manifestation, locates her as a marginal figure caught in contradiction as 'a sexually active non-European female ruler'.[62] Loomba suggests that the fluctuations which so many male critics have come to regard as an endearing feature of Cleopatra's femininity represent a much larger difficulty, eliding as they do emotional and political space in the play:

> As 'foul Egyptian' she will always stand outside Roman society: Antony can never fully trust her and will marry safe and obedient women like Octavia to ensure his stability within that society. Her gender renders her politically unacceptable, her political status problematises her femininity, and her racial otherness troubles, doubly, both power and sexuality.[63]

After the death of Antony Cleopatra appears to capitulate to Roman values, in what seems to be a 'resolution' of the dramatic conflict. But, Loomba suggests, once the prospect of sharing power with Antony is lost, then Cleopatra shifts her attention to the expression of 'absolute emotion'.[64] What is recognised here is the sublimity of the poetry, but there is something more fundamental at issue: 'Cleopatra's words display an effort to cloak personal and political loss in the language of a transcendental, eternal romance', and the process may thus be described as 'a politics of sublimation, rather than a transcendence of politics'.[65] Here the aesthetic is shown to be inextri-

cably intertwined with the political, and in such a way that a purely
empirical response to the affective power of the poetry would itself
be less than adequate. Moreover, the play ends, not in a final closure,
but in Cleopatra's subverting its possibility through her 'final performance'. Loomba concludes her analysis of the play with the
suggestion that the conflict between Rome and Egypt is articulated in
self-consciously theatrical terms, to the point that the contrast between Caesar and Cleopatra may be seen 'as partially deriving from
the contrasting *styles* of James and Elizabeth'.[66] Here theatrical practice becomes a rich source of metaphor in which the opposition
between Rome and Egypt, as well as the historical differences between Elizabeth I and her successor, are inscribed. In some ways, the
play's *theatricality* is aligned with the demonised figure of Cleopatra,
and opposed to the ordered Augustan power which James himself
was known to have favoured, and in such a way that that classically
validated authority becomes, as Neville Davies earlier suggested, the
object of criticism.

Ania Loomba's full contextualising of the issues focused in *Antony
and Cleopatra* and a number of other plays of the period, is part of
a larger project which forms the subject of her book *Gender, Race,
Renaissance Drama* (1989). Her alignment of gender and theatricality is an issue which is taken up in the final essay in this collection by
Jyotsyna Singh in a way which reinforces and extends the debate. For
Singh the cross-dressing in the play, earlier observed by Phyllis
Rackin, is rearticulated in terms of a theatricality which is, for
Cleopatra, a strategy of resistance and 'a source of empowerment as
a positive value in the play'. The radical decentring of the human
subject, observed earlier by Dollimore, is here further developed as a
means of challenging, at a thematic level in the play, a Roman
masculinity which is predicated upon 'a universalised and coherent
male subject'. Cleopatra's challenging theatricalism is not, therefore,
contained by Roman restraint, rather Singh's feminism leads her
away from a New Historicist account of power, towards an alignment of femininity and theatricality which, 'as embodied in Cleopatra function specifically both to reveal and to subvert the existing
ideology of order by which traditional sexual and social hierarchies
were held in place'. While from a Roman perspective the play medi-
ates the preservation of a patriarchal order – Caesar's victory is
legitimised by history itself – Cleopatra's breaking free of such restraint in an excess of theatricalisation employs the strategy of 'improvising Roman fictions and revealing them as constructed and

arbitrary'.[67] By analogy Singh's own critical strategy is to puncture the *illusion* of subjective coherence in order to disclose the ideological shaping of gendered identity, and to suggest, even if only by implication, that things could be different.the fluidity of Cleopatra's identity, as exemplified in her cross-dressing, serves to underline the cultural practice of gender construction and leads to the conclusion that:

> no identity is fixed and immutable, and that agents of representation on the Renaissance public stage could freely take on identities that transgressed boundaries of gender and hierarchy.[68]

The unfixing of gender identity is, of course, part of a larger feminist project which seeks to expose and eradicate the oppression associated with patriarchal authority. In this respect Cleopatra's dramatisation of human identity as 'multiple, varied, and protean',[69] presents not simply a challenge to Rome in the play, but a larger challenge to 'history' itself.

Antony and Cleopatra stretches to the limit the full resources of the Jacobean stage. Octavius's sustained contempt for Antony's entrapment by Cleopatra disguises an anxiety generated by the 'feminine' which presents itself as a challenge to the masculine imperialism of patriarchal Rome: a Rome which only thinly disguises its distinctly English points of reference. But even more than that, and as the collection of essays in this volume demonstrate, *Antony and Cleopatra* invests its excavation of episodes from a classical past with a self-conscious foregrounding of the processes whereby history and politics are bound up with larger questions of representation, both social and theatrical, and the conflict for control of those regimes in and through which meanings themselves are produced.

NOTES

1. John Russell Brown, *Shakespeare: Antony and Cleopatra* (London, 1968), p. 21.
2. Ibid.
3. L. C. Knights, *Some Shakespearean Themes and an Approach to Hamlet* (Harmondsworth, 1966), p. 124.
4. John Bayley, *Shakespeare and Tragedy* (London, 1981), p. 135.

5. W. K. Wimsatt (ed.), *Johnson on Shakespeare* (Harmondsworth, 1969), p. 68.

6. Jonathan Bate (ed.), *The Romantics on Shakespeare* (Harmondsworth, 1992), pp. 262–3.

7. Ibid., pp. 263–4.

8. Ibid., p. 265.

9. A. C. Bradley, 'Shakespeare's *Antony and Cleopatra*', *Oxford Lectures on Poetry* (1905, reprinted London, 1965), p. 284.

10. Ibid., p. 282.

11. Ibid., pp. 304, 305.

12. Bayley, *Shakespeare and Tragedy*, p. 146.

13. Ibid., p. 121.

14. Ibid., p. 136.

15. Edward W. Said, *Orientalism* (Harmondsworth, 1978), p. 63.

16. Cf. Frantz Fanon, *Black Skin, White Masks*, trans. Charles Lam Markmann (2nd impression, London, 1991), p. 45: 'I am black: I am the incarnation of a complete fusion with the world, an intuitive understanding of the earth, an abandonment of my ego in the heart of the cosmos, and no white man, no matter how intelligent he may be, can ever understand Louis Armstrong and the music of the Congo. If I am black, it is not the result of a curse, but it is because, having offered my skin, I have been able to absorb all the cosmic *effluvia*.'

17. See p. 40 below.

18. Sir Herbert Grierson (ed.), *The Poems of John Donne* (1933, reprinted London, 1960), p. 107.

19. Sir Walter Raleigh, *Selected Writings*, ed. Gerald Hammond (Harmondsworth, 1986), pp. 89, 103, 120.

20. See pp. 45, 50, 54 below.

21. Janet Adelman, *The Common Liar* (New Haven and London, 1973), p. 24.

22. Ibid., p. 30.

23. See p. 57 below.

24. Sir Philip Sidney, 'An Apology for Poetry', in *English Critical Essays of XVI–XVIII Centuries*, ed. Edmund D. Jones (1922, reprinted London, 1961), p. 7.

25. See p. 87 below.

26. See p. 89 below.

27. See p. 93 below.

28. See p. 112 below.

29. See p. 123 below.

30. Fulke Greville, *A Dedication to Sir Philip Sidney*, ed. John Guows, *The Prose Works of Fulke Greville, Lord Brooke* (Oxford, 1986), p. 93.

31. Fulke Greville, *The Remains Being Poems of Monarchy and Religion*, ed. G. A. Wilkes (Oxford, 1965), p. 49.

32. See Lily B. Campbell, *Shakespeare's Histories: Mirrors of Elizabethan Policy* (1947, reprinted London, 1970), p. 187.

33. See p. 135 below.

34. See p. 135 below.

35. See p. 145 below.

36. Tom Healy, *New Latitudes: Theory and English Renaissance Literature* (London, 1992), p. 11.

37. Ibid.

38. See p. 178 below.

39. G. Wilson Knight, *The Imperial Theme* (1931, reprinted London, 1965), pp. 199, 255, 261.

40. Ibid., pp. 322, 326.

41. Rosalind Coward and John Ellis, *Language and Materialism* (London, 1977), p. 62.

42. Paul de Man, *The Resistance to Theory* (Manchester, 1986), pp. 7, 12.

43. Peter Widdowson (ed.), *Re-reading English* (London, 1982), p. 7.

44. W. K. Wimsatt, *The Verbal Icon: Studies in the Meaning of Poetry* (London, 1954), p. 5.

45. Frank Lentricchia, *After the New Criticism* (London, 1980), p. xiii.

46. Hayden White, *Tropics of Discourse: Essays in Cultural Criticism* (Baltimore and London, 1985), p. 129.

47. See p. 183 below.

48. See p. 220 below.

49. See p. 242 below.

50. See p. 250 below.

51. See p. 251 below.

52. Raymond Williams, *Marxism and Literature* (Oxford, 1977), pp. 121, 123.

53. See p. 260 below.

54. Jonathan Dollimore and Alan Sinfield (eds), *Political Shakespeare: New Essays in Cultural Materialism* (Manchester, 1985), p. 3.

55. Ibid., pp. 3, 6, 11.

56. Michel Foucault, *The History of Sexuality*, vol. 1, trans. Robert Hurley (Harmondsworth, 1978), pp. 95–6.

57. See Marilyn French, *Shakespeare's Division of Experience* (London, 1982), p. 24.

58. Ibid., p. 28.

59. See p. 262 below.

60. See p. 276 below.

61. See p. 284 below.

62. See p. 288 below.

63. See p. 289 below.

64. See p. 290 below.

65. See p. 290 below.

66. See p. 294 below.

67. See pp. 316, 322 below.

68. See p. 324 below.

69. See p. 325 below.

1

'Antony and Cleopatra': A Shakespearean Adjustment

JOHN F. DANBY

At each stage in his development Shakespeare displays a surprising capacity for renewal. Let us assume that *Antony and Cleopatra* comes after *King Lear*, that it goes with *Coriolanus*, and that both it and *Coriolanus* immediately precede the so-called 'last period'. Between *Antony and Cleopatra* and the plays that have gone before there is no obvious connection in theme or technique. At the same time, only Plutarch links it with *Coriolanus*. Nothing in it would normally prepare us for *Cymbeline* or *The Winter's Tale* to follow. This apparent isolation is one of the main obstacles to a correct focus on the play. There seems to be a break in the internal continuity of the Shakespearean series – a continuity of series which stretches, I think, from *Henry VI* to *King Lear* at least, and which could possibly be extended to include *Timon*: though here again there is something of a lesion, and special factors, external to the 'inner biography' of Shakespeare as a playwright, might have to be invoked to explain all that is happening. *Timon*, however, it might be granted, is the aftermath of *King Lear*. Can the same be said about *Antony and Cleopatra*?

I

To describe the swiftness of *Antony and Cleopatra* we need to draw on the imagery of the cinema. There is more cinematic movement, more panning, tracking, and playing with the camera, more mixing

33

of shots than in any other of Shakespeare's tragedies. At the same
time the technique is always underdeliberate, almost cool, control.
Antony and Cleopatra has none of the haphazardies of *Pericles* nor
any of the plot-imposed vagaries of the last period. The technique is
inwardly related to the meaning Shakespeare has to express. What is
indicated is not enervation or indifference, but rather what Coleridge
recognised as 'giant power', an 'angelic strength'.

The swift traverse of time and space has often been commented
upon. There is also the mixing. Egypt is called up vividly in Rome by
Enobarbus's descriptions. Rome is always felt as a real presence in
Egypt. On the frontiers of Empire Ventidius discusses what repercus-
sions his victories will have on the people at staff-headquarters.
Equally the present is interpenetrated by the past. Antony's past,
particularly, is always powerfully put before us:

> Antony,
> Leave thy lascivious wassails. When thou once
> Wast beaten from Modena, where thou slew'st
> Hirtius and Pansa, consuls, at thy heels
> Did famine follow, whom thou fought'st against
> Though daintily brought up, with patience more
> Than savages could suffer; thou didst drink
> The stale of horses, and the gilded puddle
> Which beasts would cough at; thy palate then did deign
> The roughest berry on the rudest hedge;
> Yea, like the stag, when snow the pasture sheets,
> It is reported thou didst eat strange flesh,
> Which some did die to look on.
>   (I. iv. 55–68)

So, too, is Cleopatra's:

> I found you as a morsel cold upon
> Dead Caesar's trencher; nay, you were a fragment
> Of Cneius Pompey's; besides what hotter hours,
> Unregister'd in vulgar fame, you have
> Luxuriously pick'd out.
>   (III. ix. 116–20)

The hinterland of the quarrels that alternately divide and bring
together again the triumvirate is constantly being suggested,
troubles, truces, and manoeuvres that go back (like Cleopatra's love-
affairs) to Julius Caesar's days. In no other of his plays is Shakespeare at such pains to suggest the stream of time past and its steady

course through the present. In the public world of Roman affairs this is especially so. In the other world of Cleopatra the same suggestion of perspective always frames what is said and done. Is Antony merely the last of a long succession of such lovers? Or is this affair singular and unique as all love-affairs claim to be? Not enough weight has been given in recent assessments of the play to the ambiguity which invests everything in Egypt equally with all things in Rome. Yet this ambiguity is central to Shakespeare's experience in the play. If it is wrong to see the 'mutual pair' as a strumpet and her fool, it is also wrong to see them as a Phoenix and a Turtle.

In addition to the swiftness and the variety of the impacts, and the interpenetration of the parts of time and space as they mix in the speech of the people immediately before us, there is also the added burden which Shakespeare's 'giant power' of compelling presentation imposes. The effects are at once those of a rapid impressionism and a careful lapidary enrichment. Each figure, however minor, has its moment when it comes up into the brilliant foreground light – the Soothsayer with his 'infinite book of secrecy', the Old Man wishing 'much joy o' the worm', Enobarbus describing the barge on the Nile, Lepidus asking 'What manner o' thing is your crocodile?' Ventidius giving once for all the field-officer's view of the higher-ups, the Eunuch and the game of billiards, Dolabella, Octavia, even Fulvia whom we never see: the canvas seems covered with Constable's snow.

Another feature of Shakespeare's technique which makes for the impression of uniqueness might be pointed to here. Shakespeare seems to be innovating also in methods of character-portrayal. Some of the stage conventions, as described by Miss Bradbrook, do not seem to apply. Which, for example, are we to believe – what Caesar says about Antony after he is dead, or what he says about him, and his conduct towards him, while he is alive? What was Fulvia's 'character', about whom we have such conflicting reports? Throughout the play we are forced by Shakespeare himself not to take comment at its face value. Judgements are more personal here than elsewhere. Goneril and Regan discussing their father's condition are reliable judges. Caesar, Antony, Enobarbus, the soldiers Demetrius and Philo, are not – or not to the same extent. Judgement knits itself back into character as it might do in Ibsen, and character issues from a mutable and ambiguous flux of things. Antony's momentary *agnorisis* can be generalised to cover the whole play:

Sometimes we see a cloud that's dragonish;
A vapour sometimes like a bear or lion,
A tower'd citadel, a pendant rock,
A forked mountain, or blue promontory,
With trees upon't, that nod unto the world
And mock our eyes with air: thou hast seen these signs;
They are black vespers pageants . . .
That which is now a horse, even with a thought
The rack dislimns, and makes it indistinct
As water is in water . . .
My good knave, Eros, now thy captain is
Even such a body: here I am Antony,
Yet cannot hold this visible shape, my knave.
                                    (IV. xii. 2–14)

There is something deliquescent in the reality behind the play. It is deliquescence to the full display of which each judgement, each aspect pointed to, and each character, is necessary, always provided that no single one of these is taken as final. The proportion of comment and judgement on the central characters is higher in *Antony and Cleopatra* than anywhere else in Shakespeare. This further underlines its uniqueness and the difficulties of coming by an adequate final assessment. Antony and Cleopatra are presented in three ways. There is what is said about them; there is what they say themselves; there is what they do. Each of these might correspond to a different 'level' of response. Each is in tension against the others. Each makes its continuous and insistent claim on the spectator for judgement in his own right. The pigments vividly opposed to each other on the canvas have to mix in the spectator's eye.

Underlying, however, the bewildering oscillations of scene, the overlapping and pleating of different times and places, the co-presence of opposed judgements, the innumerable opportunities for radical choice to intervene, there is, I think, a deliberate logic. It is this which gives the play its compact unity of effect and makes its movement a sign of angelic strength rather than a symptom of febrility. It is the logic of a peculiarly Shakespearean dialectic. Opposites are juxtaposed, mingled, married; then from the very union which seems to promise strength dissolution flows. It is the process of this dialectic – the central process of the play – which we must trace if we wish to arrive anywhere near Shakespeare's meaning.

II

The first scene opens with Philo's comment on the 'dotage' of his general:

> those his goodly eyes
> That o'er the files and musters of the war
> Have glow'd like plated Mars: now bend, now turn
> The office and devotion of their view
> Upon a tawny front; his captain's heart,
> Which in the scuffles of great fights hath burst
> The buckles on his breast, reneges all temper,
> And is become the bellows and the fan
> To cool a gipsy's lust.
>
> (I. i. 2–10)

Nothing more has time to be said. Antony and Cleopatra themselves appear. Their first words express the essence of romantic love, a tacit contradiction of all that Philo seems to have just suggested:

> Cleo. If it be love indeed, tell me how much.
> Ant. There's beggary in the love that can be reckon'd.
> Cleo. I'll set a bourn how far to be belov'd.
> Ant. Then must thou needs find out new heaven, new earth.
>
> (I. i. 14–17)

Again immediately, an attendant announces the arrival of news from Rome. The atmosphere of the Egyptian court changes. We see the opposite effects of the intrusion on the two it most concerns. Antony will not hear the messengers. Cleopatra insists that he shall. Antony is taunted with a wicked caricature of what the news might be, and of the relation in which he stands to Rome. Yet the version is sufficiently like to make Antony blush – from anger, or shame, or both:

> Your dismission
> Is come from Caesar; therefore hear it, Antony,
> Where's Fulvia's process? Caesar's would I say? both?
> Call in the messengers. As I am Egypt's queen,
> Thou blushest, Antony, and that blood of thine
> Is Caesar's homager; else so thy cheek pays shame
> When shrill-tongued Fulvia scolds.
>
> (I. i. 26–32)

Antony's reaction is to pitch his romantic vows higher still, asserting his independence of Rome in terms that should leave no doubt as to where he stands:

> Let Rome in Tiber melt, and the wide arch
> Of the rang'd empire fall! Here is my space.
> Kingdoms are clay; our dungy earth alike
> Feeds beast as man: the nobleness of life
> Is to do thus; when such a mutual pair
> And such a twain can do't, in which I bind
> On pain of punishment, the world to weet
> We stand up peerless.
>
> (I. i. 33–40)

This again has all the ring of absolute and heroic self-committal. Cleopatra's reply, however, is typical both of herself and of the ambivalence that runs through everything in the play:

> Excellent falsehood!
> Why did he marry Fulvia and not love her?
> I'll seem the fool I am not; Antony
> Will be himself.
>
> (I. i. 40–3)

Her first words might be oxymoron or plain disbelief. The next call up the vista of Antony's past, with its broken pledges and unconscious insincerities – if they were no more. Her last words are highly ambiguous and turn the whole situation upside-down: she is the helpless creature wilfully blinding and deceiving herself, Antony is the self-contained and calculating manipulator of her weaknesses. In replying, Antony is like the man innocent of ju-jitsu who thinks he is pushing when really he is being pulled:

> But stirr'd by Cleopatra.
> Now, for the love of Love and her soft hours,
> Let's not confound the time with conference harsh . . .
> . . . What sport tonight?
>
> (I. i. 43–7)

Shakespeare gives the operative lines a subtle falsity of note that could equally indicate hearty play-acting, slightly awkward self-consciousness, or wilful evasion. Cleopatra's answer is realist and comes with a new urgency:

Hear the ambassadors.
             (I. i. 48)

It drives Antony also to something we can recognise as more fully himself – something that is perceptive and tinged with the masterful as well as the reckless:

> Fie, wrangling queen!
> Whom everything becomes, to chide, to laugh,
> To weep; whose every passion fully strives
> To make itself in thee fair and admir'd.
> No messenger, but thine; and all alone,
> Tonight we'll wander through the streets and note
> The qualities of people. Come, my queen;
> Last night you did desire it: speak not to us.
>   (I. i. 48–55)

This is not only Antony's view of Cleopatra's character, and a reliable account of what she is really like. It is also an expression of the deliquescent reality at the heart of the play which incarnates itself most completely in the persons of the hero and heroine. After Antony's speech, with this two-fold authority it bears, the comment of the soldiers seems peculiarly limited and out of place:

> **Dem.** Is Caesar with Antonius priz'd so slight?
> **Phil.** Sir, sometimes when he is not Antony,
>   He comes too short of that great property
>   Which still should go with Antony.
> **Dem.** I am full sorry
>   That he approves the common liar, who
>   Thus speaks of him at Rome; but I will hope
>   Of better deeds tomorrow.
>   (I. i. 56–62)

It serves to remind us, however, of the world that stands around the lovers, the world of the faithful soldier who can only understand the soldierly, the world of 'the common liar' that enjoys the unpleasant 'truth', the world, too, of Rome and Caesar that is radically opposed to the world of Egypt and Cleopatra.

The first scene is only slightly more than sixty lines long. Yet it is sufficient to illustrate all the main features of the play we have pointed to, and extensive enough to set up the swinging ambivalence – the alternatives and ambiguities constantly proposed to choice – which will govern and control our whole reaction to the play. There is the speed and oscillation, the interpenetration of Rome and Egypt and of present and past. Above all there is the dialectic marriage of the contraries and their dissolution through union. The jealousy of Cleopatra towards Fulvia, the outrage of Caesar to Antony's *amour propre* – these negative repulsions can serve to hold the mutual pair together as firmly as positive attractions. Antony and Cleopatra are opposed to the world that surrounds and isolates them. In this isolation their union seems absolute, infinite, and self-sufficient. Yet the war of the contraries pervades the love, too. In coming together they lapse, slide, and fall apart unceasingly.

The outstanding achievement of the first scene is the way in which it begins with the soldiers' condemnation and returns us at the end to the same thing – allowing for this side eighteen lines out of the sixty-two. Yet at the end we are no longer satisfied as to the adequacy of what Demetrius and Philo say. Not that what they say has been disproved by what we have seen of Antony and Cleopatra. They are and they remain a strumpet and her fool. To have any judgement at all is to choose, apparently, either the judgement of the soldiers at the beginning of the scene or the lovers' own self-assessment that immediately follows it. (Coleridge chose the former; Dr Sitwell and Mr Wilson Knight take the latter.) To entertain either judgement, however, is not enough. The deliquescent truth is neither in them nor between them, but contains both. *Antony and Cleopatra* is Shakespeare's critique of judgement.

Scene i played out romantic love and lovers' quarrels on a lofty stage. It also gave the sharp local comment of the soldiery. Scene ii takes the theme of love below-stairs and changes key. It also gives the universal comment of the Soothsayer, with its suggestion that everything is already decided, the tragedy is in the nature of things, now is already over, the future past, the present always:

> In nature's infinite book of secrecy
> A little can I read . . .
> I make not but foresee. . . .
> You have seen and prov'd a fairer former fortune
> Than that which is to approach.
>   (I. ii. 11–36)

In place of the 'romance' of love, Charmian, Iras, and Alexas give the 'reality'. The reality in this case is strong succession of rich, powerful, and adequate males:

> Let me be married to three kings in a forenoon, and widow them all;
> let me have a child at fifty, to whom Herod of Jewry may do homage;
> find me to marry me with Octavius Caesar, and companion me with
> my mistress.
>
> (I. ii. 25–30)

It reads like a parody of Cleopatra's aspirations, just as the women's
bickering and teasing of Alexas mimics Cleopatra's handling of
Antony:

> Alexas – come, his fortune, his fortune. O! let him marry a woman
> that cannot go, sweet Isis, I beseech thee; and let her die too, and give
> him a worse; and let worse follow worse, till the worst of all follow
> him laughing to his grave, fifty-fold a cuckold!
>
> (I. ii. 60–5)

This seems a nightmare version of Antony's fate – the reflection in a
distorting mirror of the thoughts and feelings that course through
Antony after Cleopatra's desertion in the disastrous sea-fight.

The group is interrupted in its fortune-telling by the entry of
Cleopatra. She is looking for Antony. Her remarks prepare us for the
different mood about to establish itself:

> Saw you my lord? . . .
> He was disposed to mirth; but on the sudden
> A Roman thought hath struck him.
>
> (I. ii. 86–91)

Antony is heard approaching. Cleopatra immediately goes off. Now
that he is coming she will refuse to see him.

When Antony appears he is surrounded by the messengers from
Rome and immersed in Roman affairs. He veers savagely to the point
of view both of the soldiers in the first scene and 'the common liar'
in Rome. Throughout the play this is what marks him off from
Cleopatra and makes him a more complex meeting-ground for the
opposites than even she is herself. He can understand and respond to
the appeal of Rome as much as he can understand and respond to
Egypt:

> Speak to me home, mince not the general tongue;
> Name Cleopatra as she's called in Rome;
> Rail thou in Fulvia's phrase; and taunt my faults
> With such full licence as both truth and malice
> Have power to utter. O! then we bring forth weeds

When our quick winds lie still; and our ills told us
Is as our earing. Fare thee well awhile . . .
These strong Egyptian fetters I must break,
Or lose myself in dotage.

(I. ii. 113–26)

The second messenger brings news of Fulvia's death. It is characteristic of the play that what is hated during life should find favour once
it is dead. Later in this scene that is reported to be the case with
Pompey in the popular reaction to him:

> our slippery people –
> Whose love is never link'd to the deserter
> Till his deserts are past – begin to throw
> Pompey the great and all his dignities
> Upon his son.

(I. ii. 198–202)

This is what happens, too, in Antony's case when, once he is dead,
Octavius sings his praises. It also happens when Cleopatra is thought
to have committed suicide and Antony flings from vituperation to
acclamation almost without pausing. It happens now with Fulvia.
Antony says:

> There's a great spirit gone! Thus did I desire it:
> What our contempts do often hurl from us
> We wish it ours again; the present pleasure,
> By revolution lowering, does become
> The opposite of itself: she's good being gone.
> The hand could pluck her back that shov'd her on.
> I must from this enchanting queen break off.

(I. ii. 131–7)

Typically, when he joins the general, Enobarbus summons all the
counter-arguments. To leave Egypt would be to kill Cleopatra. 'She
is cunning,' Antony says, 'past man's thought.' 'Alack, sir, no,'
Enobarbus rejoins,

> her passions are made of nothing but the finest part of pure love. We
> cannot call her winds and waters sighs and tears; they are greater
> storms and tempests than almanacs can report: this cannot be cunning
> in her; if it be, she makes a shower of rain as well as Jove.

(I. ii. 156–62)

Even if we read Enobarbus's words as irony, the double-irony that works by virtue of the constant ambivalence in the play still turns them back to something approaching the truth: and Cleopatra's real distress and anxiety over Antony's departure have already cut through the scene like a knife. The ding-dong continues:

> **Antony** Would I had never seen her!
> **Eno.** O, sir! you had then left unseen a wonderful piece of work.
> **Antony** Fulvia is dead.
> **Eno.** Sir?
> **Antony** Fulvia is dead.
> **Eno.** Fulvia?
> **Antony** Dead.
> **Eno.** Why, sir, give the gods a thankful sacrifice . . . this grief is
>   crown'd with consolation; your old smock brings forth a new
>   petticoat.
>
> (I. ii. 163–81)

Antony, however, has made up his mind to go back to Rome.

Antony does go back to Rome – but not in the mood and not with the motives of thorough-going reformation in which he remains at the end of Scene ii. In Scene iii the alchemy of the Shakespearean process is further at work. It works to make Antony do the thing resolved upon but for reasons the very opposite of those which led him to the resolve. The scene of his departure is chosen for Cleopatra's most sincere avowal. Having tormented Antony beyond all bearing she suddenly breaks off with:

> Courteous lord, one word.
> Sir, you and I must part, but that's not it;
> Sir, you and I have loved, but there's not it;
> That you know well: something it is I would –
> O my oblivion is a very Antony,
> And I am all forgotten.
>
> (I. iii. 86–91)

Antony's final words in the scene almost catch the very idiom of *The Phoenix and the Turtle*:

> Let us go. Come.
> Our separation so abides and flies,
> That thou, residing here, go'st yet with me,
> And I, hence fleeting, here remain with thee.
> Away!
>
> (I. iii. 101–5)

It is, so to speak, the honeymoon of the contraries – only possible while the lovers are apart.

III

The first three scenes show how pervasive is that quality in technique and vision which we have called the Shakespearean 'dialectic'. It comes out in single images, it can permeate whole speeches, it governs the build-up inside each scene, it explains the way one scene is related to another. The word 'dialectic', of course, is unfortunately post-Hegelian. The thing we wish to point to, however, in using the word, is Shakespearean. In *Antony and Cleopatra* Shakespeare needs the opposites that merge, unite, and fall apart. They enable him to handle the reality he is writing about – the vast containing opposites of Rome and Egypt, the World and the Flesh.

Rome is the sphere of the political. Shakespeare uses the contraries (long before Blake) to give some sort of rational account of the irrationals there involved. The common people, for example, is 'the common liar'. Antony has already noted that its love is 'never link'd to the deserver till his deserts are past'. Caesar, too, has his own cold knowledge of the same fact:

> It hath been taught us from the primal state
> That he which is was wished until he were;
> And the ebb'd man, ne'er loved till ne'er worth love,
> Comes dear'd by being lack'd. This common body,
> Like to the vagabond flag upon the stream,
> Goes to and back, lackeying the varying tide,
> To rot itself with motion.
>
> (I. iv. 41–7)

The great men, however, behave exactly as they say the commons do, too. With Antony, Fulvia becomes dear'd by being lack'd. In Caesar's case it is the same. The threat of Pompey makes him suddenly appreciate the grandeur of Antony's leadership, courage, and endurance. The magnanimous praise of Antony in Act V is only possible because Antony by then is dead. The law is general: judgement is a kind of accommodation to the irrational on reason's part:

> men's judgments are
> A parcel of their fortunes, and things outward
> Do draw the inward quality after them,
> To suffer all alike.
>
> (III. ix. 31–4)

Even soldierly 'honour' is rooted in the ambiguous. When Pompey's
man mentions his treacherous scheme for disposing of all Pompey's
rivals at one blow (the rivals are also Pompey's guests on board ship),
Pompey exclaims:

> Ah, this thou should'st have done
> And not have spoken on't. In me 'tis villainy;
> In thee 't had been good service. Thou must know
> 'Tis not my profit that does lead mine honour;
> Mine honour it. Repent that e'er thy tongue
> Hath so betray'd thine act; being done unknown,
> I should have found it afterwards well done,
> But must condemn it now.
>
> (II. vii. 80–7)

The law is general because it reflects the nature of the terrene world
– the tidal swing of the opposites on which all things balance in a
motion that rots them away.

The self-destruction of things that rot with the motion which their
own nature and situation dictate is almost obsessive with Shakespeare throughout the play. The political world is the manipulation
of the common body they despise by the great men whom the
commons can never love until they are safely rid of them. The pattern
which remains constant in all the possible groupings is that of open
conflict alternating with diseased truce, neither of them satisfactory:

> Equality of two domestic powers
> Breeds scrupulous faction. The hated, grown to strength,
> Are newly grown to love. . . .
> And quietness, grown sick of rest, would purge
> By any desperate change.
>
> (I. iii. 47–54)

Compacts between the great men merely represent the temporary
sinking of lesser enmities in front of greater:

> lesser enmities give way to greater.
> Were't not that we stand up against them all
> 'Twere pregnant they should square amongst themselves.
>
> (II. i. 43–5)

Pompey's is a correct appreciation. It is because of him that Octavius and Antony are reconciled. They will rivet the alliance by means of Antony's marriage to Caesar's sister. Enobarbus knows automatically that this union is a certain way of making conflict ultimately inevitable.

> you shall find the bond that seems to tie their friendship together will be the very strangler of their amity.
>
> (II. vi. 7–9)

Octavia is one of Shakespeare's minor triumphs in the play, beautifully placed in relation to the main figures and the tenor of their meaning. Her importance is apt to be overlooked unless her careful positioning is noted. Her presence gives a symmetrical form to the main relations of the play. Octavia is the opposite of Cleopatra as Antony is the opposite of Caesar. She is woman made the submissive tool of Roman policy where Cleopatra always strives to make the political subservient to her. (It is the thought of being led in triumph by Caesar as much as the thought of Antony's death which finally decides Cleopatra for suicide.) Where Caesar and Cleopatra are simple and opposite, Octavia – like Antony – is a focal point for the contraries. There is nothing in her as a 'character-study' to account for the effect her presence has. It is rather that she is transparent to the reality behind the play and one of its least mistakable mediators. On the occasions when she appears herself, or when mention is made of her, it is the interfluent life of this reality rather than the personality of its vehicle which fills the scene.

Her first entry is significant. It comes immediately after the triumvirate and Pompey have made their pact. We have just heard the following satiric account of Lepidus's behaviour – and Lepidus, like Octavia, has to stand between the two demi-Atlases:

> Agrippa   'Tis a noble Lepidus.
> Eno.   A very fine one. O! how he loves Caesar.
> Agrippa   Nay, but how dearly he adores Mark Antony.
> Eno.   Caesar? Why, he's the Jupiter of men!
> Agrippa   What's Antony? the god of Jupiter.
> Eno.   Spake you of Caesar? How, the nonpareil!
> Agrippa   O Antony! O thou Arabian bird!
>
> (III. ii. 6–12)

Then the triumvirate and Octavia come on. Octavia stirs Antony deeply. But the imagery in which his vision of her is clothed carries

us past the person described to the 'varying tide' by which everything
in the play is moved:

> Her tongue will not obey her heart, nor can
> Her heart obey her tongue; the swan's down-feather
> That stands upon the swell at full of tide,
> And neither way inclines.
>   (III. ii. 47–50)

Octavia never escapes from her position midway between the contraries that maintain and split the world. With Antony away in Athens,
her brother first falls on Pompey then finds a pretext to destroy
Lepidus. He is now ready to mount his attack on the last remaining
rival, his 'competitor in top of all design'. Hearing of it, Octavia
cries:

> A more unhappy lady,
> If this division chance, ne'er stood between,
> Praying for both parts. . . .
>   . . . Husband win, win brother,
> Prays and destroys the prayer; no midway
> 'Twixt these extremes at all.
>   (III. iv. 12–20)

Octavia's is the alternative plight to Cleopatra's for womanhood in
the play. The choice is merely between alternative methods of destruction – either at one's own hands, or through the agency of the
process. The 'swan's down-feather', like the 'vagabond flag', can
only swing on the tide until it rots with motion.

Rome is the world of politics and policy. Its supreme term is
Octavius Caesar himself. He, like Octavia, must be brought into
relation with the pattern which he helps in part to define. Half his
significance is lost if he is seen only as a 'character'. In Octavius's
case we have aids external to the play which help towards a clear
focus on what Shakespeare intends by him. He falls recognisably into
Shakespeare's studies of the 'politician' – the series that begins with
Richard III and continues down through Edmund.

Octavius is a notable development in the figure which started as a
machiavel pure and simple. Shakespeare now betrays no sign of
alarm, no hint of revulsion or rejection, almost no trace of emotion
in putting him into a story. He is taken completely for granted. He
has arrived and he will stay. He is part of the structure of things. He
is 'Rome'. In matters of politics and policy it is obvious that only the

politicians count: and politics is one half of life. The politician is a perfectly normal person. Given all his own way he would doubtless bring – as Octavius is certain his triumphs eventually will bring – a 'universal peace'. To be normal like him, of course, and to enjoy the peace he offers, two conditions are necessary. First, one must sacrifice the other half of life; then, one must be prepared to make complete submission. By the time Shakespeare comes to depict Octavius he has refined away all the accidentals from the portrait – the diabolism, the rhetoric, the elaborate hypocrisy, the perverse glamour: everything but the essential deadlines and inescapability. Octavius marks an advance on Goneril and Regan. He shares their impatience with tavern and brothel. He has no share in the lust which entraps even them. We might almost doubt whether Octavius has any personal appetite at all, even the lust for power. His plan to lead Cleopatra in triumph has the appearance of a desire for personal satisfaction, but it is more likely that it fits into an impersonal wish on Caesar's part to subdue all things to Rome. Caesar, of course, is Rome – but a kind of impersonal embodiment. He is more like a cold and universal force than a warm-blooded man. He is the perfect commissar, invulnerable as no human being should be. Egypt has no part in his composition.

Caesar has the deceitfulness of the machiavel, but he plays his cards without any flourish. He can rely on his opponents to undo themselves: they are more complicated than he. He puts the deserters from Antony in the van of his own battle:

> Plant those that are revolted in the van,
> That Antony may seem to spend his fury
> Upon himself.
>
> (IV. vi. 9–11)

The strength and weakness of those ranged against him constitute Caesar's fifth column. The opposition will rot away or eat the sword it fights with.

It is in the last act that Egypt and Rome confront each other singly, the duplicity of Caesar pitted against the duplicity of Cleopatra. There is no doubt as to who shall survive the contest. The tension is maintained throughout the fifth act only by the doubt left in the spectator's mind right up to the end as to which way Cleopatra will jump: will she accept submission or will she take her own life? The whole play has prepared us for just this doubt. In a sense, whichever way the decision goes it is immaterial. The point of the play is not the decisions taken but the dubieties and ambivalences from which choice springs – the barren choice that only hastens its own negation. Rome, from the nature of things, can admit no compromise. Egypt, equally, can never submit to its contrary. So Cleopatra kills herself.

Cleopatra has been loved by recent commentators not wisely but too well. As Caesar impersonates the World, she, of course, incarnates the Flesh. Part of Shakespeare's sleight of hand in the play – his trickery with our normal standards and powers of judgement – is to construct an account of the human universe consisting of only these two terms. There is no suggestion that the dichotomy is resolvable: unless we are willing to take the delusions of either party as a resolution, the 'universal peace' of Caesar, the Egypt-beyond-the-grave of Antony and Cleopatra in their autotoxic exaltations before they kill themselves.

Cleopatra is the Flesh, deciduous, opulent, and endlessly renewable:

> she did make defect perfection . . .
> Age cannot wither her, nor custom stale
> Her infinite variety; other women cloy
> The appetites they feed, but she makes hungry
> Where most she satisfies; for vilest things
> Become themselves in her, that the holy priests
> Bless her when she is riggish.
> (II. ii. 239–48)

The Flesh is also the female principle. Cleopatra is Eve, and Woman:

> No more but e'en a woman, and commanded
> By such poor passion as the maid that milks
> And does the meanest chares.
> (IV. xiii. 73–5)

She is also Circe:

> Let witchcraft join with beauty, lust with both!
> (II. i. 22)

Shakespeare gives Cleopatra everything of which he is capable except his final and absolute approval. Cleopatra is not an Octavia, much less a Cordelia. The profusion of rich and hectic colour that surrounds her is the colour of the endless cycle of growth and decay, new greenery on old rottenness, the colour of the passions, the wild flaring of life as it burns itself richly away to death so that love of life and greed for death become indistinguishable:

> there is mettle in death which commits some loving act upon her, she hath such a celerity in dying.
>
> (I. ii. 152–4)

The strength of the case Shakespeare puts against her is undeniable. The soldiers, and Caesar, and Antony when the consciousness of Rome speaks through him, are right, as far as they go. The strength of the case for her is that it is only Rome that condemns her. And Egypt is a force as universal as Rome – as hot as the other is cold, as inevitably self-renewing as the other is inescapably deadly. And the only appeal that can be made in the play is from Egypt to Rome, from Rome to Egypt. And neither of these is final, because between them they have brought down Antony, the 'man of men'.

For the tragedy of *Antony and Cleopatra* is, above all, the tragedy of Antony. His human stature is greater than either Cleopatra's or Caesar's. Yet there is no sphere in which he can express himself except either Rome or Egypt, and to bestride both like a Colossus and keep his balance is impossible. The opposites play through Antony and play with him, and finally destroy him. To Caesar (while Antony is in Egypt, and alive) he is:

> A man who is the abstract of all faults
> That all men follow.
>
> (I. iv. 9–10)

To Cleopatra he appears instead a 'heavenly mingle':

> Be'st thou sad or merry,
> The violence of either thee becomes,
> So it does no man else.
>
> (I. v. 59–61)

When she sees him returning safe from the battlefield she cries:

> O infinite virtue! Com'st thou smiling from
> The world's great snare uncaught?
>
> (IV. viii. 17–18)

After he is dead she remembers him as a kind of Mars:

> His face was as the heavens, and therein stuck
> A sun and moon, which kept their course, and lighted
> This little O, the earth . . .
> His legs bestrid the ocean; his rear'd arm
> Crested the world; his voice was propertied
> As all the tuned spheres, and that to friends;
> But when he meant to quail and shake the orb,
> He was as rattling thunder. For his bounty,
> There was no winter in't, an autumn 'twas
> That grew the more by reaping; his delights
> Were dolphin-like, they show'd his back above
> The element they lived in; in his livery
> Walk'd crowns and crownets, realms and islands were
> As plates dropped from his pocket . . .
> . . . Nature wants stuff
> To vie strange forms with fancy, yet t'imagine
> An Antony were nature's piece 'gainst fancy,
> Condemning shadows quite.
>   (V. ii. 79–99)

This, of course, is again the past catching fire from the urgent needs of the present, flaring in memory and imagination as it never did in actuality. Antony is nothing so unambiguous as this. The most judicious account of him is that of Lepidus when he is replying to Caesar's strictures:

> I must not think there are
> Evils enow to darken all his goodness:
> His faults in him seem as the spots of heaven,
> More fiery by night's blackness; hereditary
> Rather than purchased, what he cannot change
> Than what he chooses.
>   (I. iv. 10–15)

Here the ambiguities of the play's moral universe get their completest expression: faults shine like stars, the heaven is black, the stars are spots. Ambivalence need go no further.

IV

The earlier criticism of *Antony and Cleopatra* tended to stress the downfall of the soldier in the middle-age infatuate. More recent criticism has seen the play as the epiphany of the soldier in the lover, and the reassurance of all concerned that death is not the end. In the view that has been put forward here neither of these is right. The meaning of *Antony and Cleopatra* is in the Shakespearean 'dialectic' – in the deliquescent reality that expresses itself through the contraries.

Antony and Cleopatra swims with glamour. Once we lose sight of the controlling structure of the opposites which holds the play together we are at the mercy of any random selection from its occasions. And occasions abound – moments, opinions, moods, speeches, characters, fragments of situation, forked mountains and blue promontories, imposed upon us with all the force of a 'giant power'. It is, then, eminently understandable that critics should succumb like Antony or hold aloof like Demetrius and Philo.

The Roman condemnation of the lovers is obviously inadequate. The sentimental reaction in their favour is equally mistaken. There is no so-called 'love-romanticism' in the play. The flesh has its glory and passion, its witchery. Love in *Antony and Cleopatra* is both these. The love of Antony and Cleopatra, however, is not asserted as a 'final value'. The whole tenor of the play, in fact, moves in an opposite direction. Egypt is the Egypt of the biblical glosses: exile from the spirit, thraldom to the flesh-pots, diminution of human kindness. To go further still in sentimentality and claim that there is a 'redemption' motif in Antony and Cleopatra's love is an even more violent error. To the Shakespeare who wrote *King Lear* it would surely smack of blasphemy. The fourth and fifth acts of *Antony and Cleopatra* are not epiphanies. They are the ends moved to by that process whereby things rot themselves with motion – unhappy and bedizened and sordid, streaked with the mean, the ignoble, the contemptible. Shakespeare may have his plays in which 'redemption' is a theme (and I think he has), but *Antony and Cleopatra* is not one of them.

Antony and Cleopatra is an account of things in terms of the World and the Flesh, Rome and Egypt, the two great contraries that maintain and destroy each other, considered apart from any third sphere which might stand over against them. How is it related to the plays of the 'great period', the period which comes to an end with *King Lear*?

The clue is given, I think, in the missing third term. *Antony and Cleopatra* is the deliberate construction of a world without a Cordelia, Shakespeare's symbol for a reality that transcends the political and the personal and

> redeems nature from the general curse
> Which twain have brought her to.
>
> (*King Lear*, IV. vi. 211–12)

One must call the construction deliberate, because after *King Lear* there can be no doubt that Shakespeare knew exactly where he was in these matters. Both *Antony and Cleopatra* and *Coriolanus* follow North's Plutarch without benefit of clergy. Both Antony and Coriolanus were cited by the sixteenth-century moralists as notable examples of heathen men who lacked patience – the one committing suicide, the other rebelling against his country. In *Antony and Cleopatra* suicide is the general fate of those who wish to die. Cleopatra gives the audience a conscious reminder of the un-Christian ethos involved:

> All's but naught;
> Patience is sottish, and impatience does
> Become a dog that's mad: then is it sin
> To rush into the secret house of death
> Ere death dare come to us?
>
> (IV. xiii. 78–82)

The Christian world-view in Shakespeare's time turned round a number of conceptions which were covered by the Elizabethans in their examination of the meanings of 'Nature'. The theme of 'Nature' runs through the whole of *Macbeth*, *King Lear*, and *Timon*. Its absence from *Antony and Cleopatra* suggests Shakespeare's satisfaction that for him the theme is exhausted. He is inwardly free now to look at a classical story, deliberately excise the Christian core of his thought, and make up his account of what then remains over.

This explains the effect, I think, of *Antony and Cleopatra*. Freedom from the compulsive theme of the Natures, the conscious security gained from having given it final expression, enabled Shakespeare to handle something new and something which was bound to be intrinsically simpler. Part of the energy absorbed in grappling with theme now bestows itself on technique. *Antony and Cleopatra* gives the impression of being a technical *tour de force* which Shakespeare enjoyed for its own sake.

The excision also explains, I think, the tone of the play – the sense of ripe-rottenness and hopelessness, the vision of self-destruction, the feeling of strenuous frustration and fevered futility, that which finds its greatest expression in Antony's speech before he gives himself his death-blow:

> Now
> All length is torture; since the torch is out,
> Lie down and stray no further. Now all labour
> Mars what it does; yea, very force entangles
> Itself with strength; seal then, and all is done.
> (IV. xii. 45–9)

The excision, finally, explains what might be regarded as a diminution of scope in *Antony and Cleopatra*. (We are, of course, only comparing Shakespeare with himself.) The theme of Rome and Egypt, however, is simpler than the theme of 'Nature', the trick of using the contraries (again, for Shakespeare) relatively an easy way of organising the universe. It is unusual, at any rate, for Shakespeare to rely on one trick so completely as he seems to do in *Antony and Cleopatra*. At times we are almost tempted to believe he has fallen a victim of habitual mannerism.

One last comment might be made. We referred at the beginning of this chapter to Shakespeare's surprising capacity for self-renewal. *Antony and Cleopatra* is not the aftermath of Lear in any pejorative sense. There is something in it that is new and exciting and profound. Shakespeare remained still the youngest as the greatest of his contemporaries. In *Antony and Cleopatra* he is making his own adjustments to the new Jacobean tastes. The play is Shakespeare's study of Mars and Venus – the presiding deities of Baroque society, painted for us again and again on the canvases of his time. It shows us Virtue, the root of the heroic in man, turned merely into *virtu*, the warrior's art, and both of them ensnared in the world, very force entangling itself with strength. It depicts the 'man of men' soldiering for a cynical Rome or whoring on furlough in a reckless Egypt. It is the tragedy of the destruction of man, the creative spirit, in perverse war and insensate love – the two complementary and opposed halves of a discreating society.

For more obvious, if less great manifestations of the same discreating society, interested almost exclusively in love and war (and these both more narrowly conceived and more over-valued emotionally than they ever are by Shakespeare) we must turn to Beaumont.

From John F. Danby, *Elizabethan and Jacobean Poets* (London, 1952), pp. 128–51.

NOTES

[This essay comes from a larger collection of essays on Elizabethan and Jacobean writers by the late Professor John Danby. It was the first to address seriously the complex question of perspective in *Antony and Cleopatra*, although it is clear from the essay itself that what Danby lacked was the kind of theoretical vocabulary now available to critics of Shakespeare to deal with some of the insights that his own perceptive reading of the play uncovered. Ed.]

2

Nature's Piece 'gainst Fancy: Poetry and the Structure of Belief in 'Antony and Cleopatra'

JANET ADELMAN

Throughout *Antony and Cleopatra*, we have seen Cleopatra indulge in visions of Antony whenever he was absent; and after his death, she creates the most monumental vision of all. Her emperor Antony is a gigantic and godlike figure, virtually a human form divine. To what extent can we share her vision, or the other hyperbolical visions of the play? The study of the traditional interpretations of myth can set her emperor in an appropriate context, but it cannot in itself verify her vision. Mythic and iconographic meaning can participate in the significance of a play only if the play first invites their participation; if the work itself does not provide a fertile seedbed, then no amount of mythic analogy will flourish. We must consequently turn back to the play itself.

SCEPTICISM AND BELIEF

You lie up to the hearing of the gods.
(V. ii. 95)

From the first words of the play ('Nay, but'), our reactions have been at issue. We are given judgements that we must simultaneously accept and reject; we are shown the partiality of truth. But finally we are not permitted to stand aside and comment with impunity any more than Enobarbus is: we must choose either to accept or to reject the lovers' versions of themselves and of their death; and our choice will determine the meaning of the play for us. But the choice becomes increasingly impossible to make on the evidence of our reason or our senses. How can we believe in Enobarbus's description of Cleopatra as Venus when we see the boy actor before us? The Antony whom Cleopatra describes in her dream is not the Antony whom we have seen sitting on stage in dejection after Actium or bungling his suicide. Although the lovers die asserting their postmortem reunion, all we see is the dead queen and her women, surrounded by Caesar and his soldiers. The stage action necessarily presents us with one version of the facts, the poetry with another.[1] This is the dilemma inherent in much dramatic poetry; and the more hyperbolical the poetry, the more acute the dilemma.[2] Critics are occasionally tempted to read *Antony and Cleopatra* as a very long poem; but it is essential that we be aware of it as drama at all times. For how can one stage hyperbole? Reading the play, we might imagine Antony a colossus; but what shall we do with the very human-sized Antony who has been before us for several hours? In a sonnet, for instance, an assertion contrary to fact will be true within the poem; standards must be imported from outside the work by which to find the assertions improbable. As Shakespeare points out, not every girl be-sonneted has breasts whiter than snow, despite the assertions of her sonneteer. But a play carries its own refutation within itself: even with the most advanced stage technology, the action and the human actors will undercut these assertions even as they are made. Precisely this tension is at the heart of *Antony and Cleopatra*: we can neither believe nor wholly disbelieve in the claims made by the poetry.

The poetry of the last two acts is generally acknowledged as the sleight-of-hand by which Shakespeare transforms our sympathies toward the lovers, in despite of the evidence of our reason and our senses. Although even Caesar speaks in blank verse, the language of most richness and power is in the service of the lovers: it is the language in which Enobarbus creates Cleopatra as Venus and the lovers assert the value of their love and their death. In this play, the nay-sayers may have reason and justice on their side; but as Plato suspected when he banished poetry from his republic, reason and justice are no match for poetry. The appeal to mere reason will not always affect fallen man; according to Renaissance theorists, it was

precisely the power of poetry to *move*, occasionally against the
dictates of all reason, that made it at once most dangerous and most
fruitful. And modern critics are as wary of the power of poetry as
their predecessors: the poetry in *Antony and Cleopatra* is almost
always praised, but the praise frequently coincides with the suspicion
that it has somehow taken unfair advantage of us by befuddling our
clear moral judgement. It is that doubtless delightful but nonetheless
dubious means by which the lovers are rescued from our condemnation at the last moment, rather as Lancelot rescues Guinevere from
her trial by fire. We are pleased but suspect that strictest justice has
not been done. If it is true that Shakespeare uses the poetry to dazzle
our moral sense and undo the structure of criticism in the play, then
we may find *Antony and Cleopatra* satisfying as a rhetorical show-
case, but we cannot admire the play as a whole.[8] It is refreshing to
find this charge made explicit by G. B. Shaw, who clearly enjoys
expressing his contempt for a poet who finds it necessary to rescue
his lovers from our moral judgement by means of a rhetorical trick.

> Shakespear's Antony and Cleopatra must needs be as intolerable to
> the true Puritan as it is vaguely distressing to the ordinary healthy
> citizen, because after giving a faithful picture of the soldier broken
> down by debauchery, & the typical wanton in whose arms such men
> perish, Shakespear finally strains all his huge command of rhetoric &
> stage pathos to give a theatrical sublimity to the wretched end of the
> business, & to persuade foolish spectators that the world was well lost
> by the twain. Such falsehood is not to be borne except by the real
> Cleopatras & Antonys (they are to be found in every public house)
> who would no doubt be glad enough to be transfigured by some poet
> as immortal lovers. Woe to the poet who stoops to such folly! . . .
> When your Shakespears & Thackerays huddle up the matter at the
> end by killing somebody & covering your eyes with the undertaker's
> handkerchief, duly onioned with some pathetic phrase . . . I have no
> respect for them at all: such maudlin tricks may impose on tea-house
> drunkards, not on me.[4]

The final poetry, detached from character and situation, does
indeed give us the glorified vision of love that Shaw mistrusted, a
vision not wholly consistent with the merely human Antony and
Cleopatra, though Antony is far more than a debauchee and Cleopatra anything but typical, no matter how wanton. But the poetry is
not a rhetorical Lancelot. Its assertions and the problems they present
to our scepticism have been inherent throughout: and if the poetry
strains our credulity toward the end, the strain itself is a necessary

part of our experience. Are the visions asserted by the poetry mere fancies, or are they 'nature's piece 'gainst fancy'? Precisely this tension between belief and disbelief has been essential from the start. When the lovers first come on stage, very much in the context of an unfriendly Roman judgement, they announce the validity of their love in a hyperbolical poetry which contrasts sharply with Philo's equally hyperbolical condemnation. Here, at the very beginning, two attitudes are set in juxtaposition by the use of two equally impossible images which appeal to two very different modes of belief. Philo uses hyperbole as *metaphor*: 'his captain's heart / . . . is become the bellows and the fan / To cool a gipsy's lust' (I. i. 6–10). This is the deliberate exaggeration which moral indignation excites; it does not in any sense call for our literal belief. The hyperbolical metaphor is morally apt, and that is all. The Roman metaphor is carefully delineated as metaphor: it never pretends to a validity beyond the metaphoric. But what of the lovers? 'Then must thou needs find out new heaven, new earth' (I. i. 17); 'Let Rome in Tiber melt' (I. i. 33). Strictly speaking, these hyperboles are not metaphor at all. Antony's words assert his access to a hyperbolical world where such things actually happen, a world beyond the reach of metaphor. They claim, like Cleopatra's dream, to be in the realm of nature, not of fancy. His words do not give us the protection of regarding them merely as apt metaphors: they make their claim as literal action. We may choose to disbelieve their claim; but in doing so, we are rejecting a version of reality, not the validity of a metaphor. And precisely this kind of assertion will become more insistent – and more improbable – as the play progresses.

The poetry of the final acts should not take us unawares: if at the last moment it surfaces, like the dolphin who shows his back above the element he lives in, the whole of the play and a good deal of Shakespeare's career should have prepared us for its appearance. The validity of the imaginative vision as it is asserted in the poetry is a part of Shakespeare's subject in *Antony and Cleopatra*. But the play is not therefore 'about' the vision of the poet: we are presented with lovers creating the image of their love, not with poets poetising. For the association of love with imagination or fancy is one of Shakespeare's most persistent themes. Love in Shakespeare almost always creates its own imaginative versions of reality; and it is almost always forced to test its version against the realities acknowledged by the rest of the world. Theseus in *A Midsummer Night's Dream* tells us that the lover, like the lunatic and the poet, is of imagination all compact (V. i. 7–8): in that play, 'fancy' is generally used as synonymous with 'love'. We remember Juliet, valiantly making day into night in despite of the lark that sings so out of tune. Imagination is essential to love; but if it is totally unmoored to reality, it becomes love's greatest threat. Othello's love will turn to hate as Iago poisons his imagination. Spenser circumscribes his book of chaste love (*The Faerie Queene*, book 3) with just this kind of warning about the uses and misuses of imagination in love. Britomart falls in love with Artegall when she sees him in Merlin's magic mirror; she immediately assumes that the vision has no basis in reality and that she is doomed to 'feed on shadowes' (*FQ* 3.2.44). But her vision is directed by Merlin's art: her Artegall exists, though she does not recognise him when she first meets him in the real world. The vision here is no shadow but an idealised version of reality; and in time Britomart will recognise the real Artegall whose ideal form she has seen. Her love depends initially on the idealising vision, but it passes the test of reality. But at the end of book 3, we see the consequences of an abandonment to self-willed imagination. Amoret is subject to Busirane's tormented perversion of love: and the masque of Cupid which holds her captive is led by Fancy (*FQ* 3.12.7).

Love is an act of imagination, but it cannot be an act of *mere* imagination. In the plays that deal with lovers, Shakespeare continually emphasises the need to circumscribe the tyranny of imagination in love. The arbitrary loves of *A Midsummer Night's Dream* must be subjected to the chaos of unbridled fancy (stage-managed by Puck) before they can be sorted out. At the end of *As You Like It*, Orlando proclaims that he can live no longer by thinking (V. ii. 55). But in the Forest of Arden, thinking makes it so: Orlando's imagined Rosalind can reveal herself as the real Rosalind because her game has permitted her to test the realities of love. The matter is more complex in *Twelfth Night*, where mere imagination prevails in the self-willed loves of Olivia and Orsino. Here the emblem for the dangerous prevalence of the imagination in love is Malvolio, reading the supposed letter from Olivia and finding himself in every word. Malvolio here is exactly like any lover, searching reality for clues to confirm his own delusions; that the letter is constructed precisely so that he will find such confirmation simply emphasises the process. Given all this imagination run rampant, it is no wonder that Viola insists on testing her imagination, even to the point of stubbornness: 'Prove true, imagination, O, prove true' (*Twelfth Night* III. iv. 409), she says, and then quizzes Sebastian extensively about his parentage and his early history before she will allow herself to believe that he is her brother.

If the theme of imagination in love is a concern in these plays, it is an obsession in *Troilus and Cressida*, where the consequences of mere imagination are delineated with chilling accuracy. Before Troilus meets with Cressida, 'expectation' whirls him round; 'th' imaginary relish is so sweet' (III. ii. 19–20) that it enchants his sense. But even Troilus knows that the imaginary relish will exceed the act; and his description of the physiology of sex is true of all enterprise in this world of frustration:

> This is the monstruosity in love, lady, that the will is infinite and the execution confin'd, that the desire is boundless and the act a slave to limit.
>
> (*Troilus and Cressida* III. ii. 87–90)

Troilus watching Cressida give herself to Diomed will learn exactly how much desire or imaginary relish is bound by the limits of reality. He has throughout the play assumed that thinking makes it so: during the council scene he asks, 'What is aught, but as 'tis valu'd?' (II. ii. 52). At the end, he will learn the hard facts of value, the facts implicit in Hector's answer to his question:

> But value dwells not in particular will;
> It holds his estimate and dignity
> As well wherein 'tis precious of itself
> As in the prizer.
> (*Troilus and Cressida* II. ii. 53–56)

Troilus and Cressida is Shakespeare's most horrifying vision of untested imagination in love. In that sense, it is a necessary counterpoise both to the earlier comedies and to *Antony and Cleopatra*. For *Antony and Cleopatra* is *Troilus and Cressida* revisited: if *Troilus and Cressida* portrays desire as a slave to limit, *Antony and Cleopatra* asserts the power of desire to transcend limits; if Troilus's subjection to mere imagination nearly destroys him, Cleopatra's imagination of her Antony virtually redeems them both. Later, in the romances, the desires of the lovers will usually become their realities: the art itself is nature, and imagination purely redemptive. *Troilus* and the romances are in this sense at opposite ends of the scale: in *Troilus and Cressida*, our credulity is at the mercy of our scepticism, as Troilus himself will discover; in the romances, our scepticism is banished by an act of total poetic faith. But *Antony and Cleopatra* is poised in a paradoxical middle region in which scepticism and credulity must be balanced. In this sense, the perspectives of both *Troilus and Cressida* and the romances are included within *Antony and Cleopatra*; and it is precisely because of this inclusiveness that imagination can emerge triumphant.

The process of testing the imagination is essential to the assertion of its validity: for only through an exacting balance of scepticism and assent can it prove true. And more than any other play, *Antony and Cleopatra* insists on both our scepticism and our assent. For it is simultaneously the most tough-minded and the most triumphant of the tragedies, and it is necessarily both at once. Throughout, Shakespeare disarms criticism by allowing the sceptics their full say: the whole play is in effect a test of the lovers' visions of themselves. Cleopatra herself presents the most grotesquely sceptical view of her own play:

> . . . The quick comedians
> Extemporally will stage us, and present
> Our Alexandrian revels: Antony
> Shall be brought drunken forth, and I shall see
> Some squeaking Cleopatra boy my greatness
> I' the posture of a whore.
> (V. ii. 215–20)

Once she has spoken, this Roman version of her greatness becomes untenable; we know that Shakespeare's *Antony and Cleopatra* is not an item in Caesar's triumph. It is only in the context of 'Nay, but' that we can answer 'yes': if the imaginative affirmations were not so persistently questioned, they could not emerge triumphant. The extreme of scepticism itself argues for affirmation: and here the affirmations are no less extreme than the scepticism. Throughout the play, we are not permitted to see Cleopatra merely as a fallen woman: we are asked to see her in the posture of a whore. And when the time has come for affirmation, we are asked to believe not in the probable but in the palpably impossible: not that the lovers are worthy though misguided, but that they are semi-divine creatures whose love has somehow managed to escape the bonds of time and space, and even of death. Whore or goddess, strumpet's fool or colossus: the play allows us no midpoint. After all the doubt which has been central to our experience, we are asked to participate in a secular act of faith. This is the final contrariety that the play demands of us: that the extreme of scepticism itself must be balanced by an extreme of assent.

If we come to believe in the assertions of the poetry, it is, I think, precisely because they are so unbelievable. One of the tricks of the human imagination is that an appeal to the rationally possible is not always the effective means of ensuring belief: occasionally an appeal to the impossible, an appeal to doubt, works wonders. *Antony and Cleopatra* embodies in its structure the paradox of faith: the exercise of faith is necessary only when our reason dictates doubt; we believe only in the things that we know are not true. The central strategy of *Antony and Cleopatra* depends upon this process: we achieve faith by deliberately invoking doubt. And in fact this process dictates not only the broad structure of the play but also its poetic texture. The imaginative vision of the play is based firmly on the two rhetorical figures that are themselves dependent on this strategy: paradox and hyperbole.[5]

The incidence of paradox and hyperbole in *Antony and Cleopatra* is not merely an accident or Shakespeare's sleight-of-hand: these figures inform the shape and the substance of the play. For they posit in their very structure the tension between imaginative assertion and literal fact that is part of the state of love. Even Bacon is willing to concede that love is appropriately expressed in hyperbole, precisely because its assertions are palpably untrue.

> It is a strange thing to note the excess of this passion, and how it braves the nature and value of things, by this: that the speaking in a perpetual hyperbole is comely in nothing but love. Neither is it merely in the phrase; for whereas it hath been well said that the arch-flatterer, with whom all the petty flatterers have intelligence, is a man's self; certainly the lover is more. For there was never proud man thought so absurdly well of himself as the lover doth of the person loved.[6]

As Bacon points out, love infects the thought as well as the language of lovers with hyperbole. Biron and other lovers fall hopelessly into paradox as they fall in love in *Love's Labour's Lost*; even Hamlet is subject to paradox and hyperbole in love, as his poem to Ophelia demonstrates. Only the contradictions of paradox are capable of expressing the contradictions of love: for paradox is a stylistic *discordia concors*, a knot intrinsicate like love itself. In his discussion of the Neoplatonic doctrine of Blind Love, Wind says,

> In reducing the confusions of the senses to reason, the intellect clarifies but it also contracts: for it clarifies by setting limits; and to transcend these limits we require a new and more lasting confusion, which is supplied by the blindness of love. Intellect excludes contradictions; love embraces them.[7]

In embracing contradictions, love transcends the limits of the intellect and of reality as the intellect normally perceives it: and no figure more vehemently asserts this transcendence than hyperbole, Puttenham's overreacher. Shakespeare expresses his sense that love transcends the limits of reason and fact in the overreaching paradoxes of 'The Phoenix and the Turtle': here the lovers can transcend number ('Two distincts, division none', l. 27), space ('Distance, and no space was seen / 'Twixt this turtle and his queen', ll. 30–1), and identity ('Property was thus appalled, / That the self was not the same', ll. 37–8). Reason itself is confounded by these paradoxes and cries: 'Love hath Reason, Reason none, / If what parts can so remain' (ll. 47–8).

Antony and Cleopatra is the exploration of this *if*: it is the working out of these paradoxes in human terms, with all their human contradictions. The paradoxes so easily stated in 'The Phoenix and the Turtle' are the hard-won conclusions of the lovers: that one must lose oneself to gain oneself; that the only life is in death, the only union in separation. To regard either paradox or hyperbole as merely rhetorical ornament is to overlook their enormous potency in the play: in a very literal way, they shape not only the language but also the presentation of character, the structure, and the themes. And if the tension between scepticism and belief is resolved for a moment at the end, it is resolved only in so far as we for a moment accept paradox and hyperbole as literally true, despite their logical impossibilities. These are large claims; in order to substantiate them, I shall have to discuss the figures and some related concepts at length.

The structure of *Antony and Cleopatra* is the structure of paradox and hyperbole themselves: according to Renaissance figurists, both gain our credence by appealing to our doubt.

> *Paradoxon*, is a forme of speech by which the Orator affirmeth some thing to be true, by saying he would not have beleeved it, or that it is so straunge, so great, or so wonderfull, that it may appeare to be incredible.[8]

Thus Henry Peacham defines paradox.[9] The figure *paradoxon*, or as Puttenham calls it, 'the wondrer',[10] affirms faith by appealing to doubt.[11] Paradox was for the Renaissance a figure pliable to any use: if John Donne as a young man could use it as an occasion for the display of witty and cynical extravagance, he could also use it in his sermons to express the central tenets of Christianity. A seventeenth-century theologian cast these tenets into the form of paradox precisely because they impose such a strain on our logical categories and nonetheless are not to be questioned – that is to say, because they demand the operation of our faith, not our reason.[12] All paradox demands an act of faith; but hyperbole is that species of paradox which poses the crisis in its most acute form.[13] Hyperbole must, by definition, assert that which is literally untrue. George Puttenham in *The Arte of English Poesie* discusses hyperbole along with other figures which work by altering the meaning of words or phrases:

> As figures be the instruments of ornament in every language, so be they also in a sorte abuses or rather trespasses in speech, because they passe the ordinary limits of common utterance, and be occupied of purpose to deceive the eare and also the minde, drawing it from plainnesse and simplicitie to a certaine doublenesse, whereby our talke is the more guilefull & abusing, for what els is your *Metaphor* but an inversion of sense by transport; your *allegorie* by a duplicitie of meaning or dissimulation under covert and darke intendments: one while speaking obscurely and in riddle called *Aenigma*: another while by common proverbe or Adage called *Paremia*: then by merry skoffe called *Ironia*: . . . then by incredible comparison giving credit, as by your *Hyperbole*.[14]

'By incredible comparison giving credit': this is the paradox of hyperbole. And if all these figures are in some sense deceivers, then the worst in this kind are the hyperboles. Puttenham later says,

> Ye have yet two or three other figures that smatch a spice of the same *false semblant* but in another sort and maner of phrase, whereof one is when we speake in the superlative and beyond the limites of credit, that is by the figure which the Greeks called *Hiperbole*, the Latines *Dementiens* or the lying figure. I for his immoderate excesse cal him the over reacher right with his originall or (lowd lyar) & me thinks not amisse: now when I speake that which neither I my selfe thinke to be true, nor would have any other body beleeve, it must needs be a great dissimulation, because I mean nothing lesse than that I speake.[15]

Precisely this great dissimulation gives credit, as Puttenham has told us earlier; and although the speaker does not believe himself and expects no one else to believe him, he means no less than what he says. This very illogical state of affairs reduces Puttenham to a similar illogic; but with this illogic he suggests the central force of hyperbole and its fascination for poets at the end of the sixteenth century. If we are to take it seriously, hyperbole must elicit some sort of belief or assent: that is to say that it demands of us the simultaneous perception of its literal falsehood and its imaginative relevance. It presents the spectacle of man making his own imaginative universe in despite of all reality, in despite of all human limitation: the struggle of Tamburlaine, or Richard II, or the lover in Donne's love poetry.

But can we take paradox and hyperbole seriously? If the two figures challenge our reason by their very structure, the play takes up that challenge: for paradox and hyperbole are to some extent embodied in the lovers; and the degree to which we can believe in these figures will determine our response to the play. Cleopatra herself seems to embrace contradictions; she is usually described in terms which confound all our logical categories. One need only look at Shakespeare's additions to Plutarch's description of Cleopatra at Cydnus for confirmation: by the use of paradox, Shakespeare transforms Plutarch's beautiful but entirely probable description into something rich and strange.[16] The wind from the fans of her Cupids 'did seem / To glow the delicate cheeks which they did cool' (II. ii. 203–4). Her barge burns on the water. She animates nature with love for her: the waters follow her barge, 'As amorous of their strokes' (II. ii. 197), as Antony will follow her at Actium. 'She did make defect perfection, / And, breathless, power breathe forth' (II. ii. 231–2). She embodies all the paradoxes of sexual appetite, which grows the more by reaping: she 'makes hungry, / Where most she satisfies' (II. ii. 237–8). Like the woman in the sonnets, she is black with Phoebus's amorous pinches (I. v. 28) and yet the day of the world (IV. viii. 13): black and wholly fair.[17] She is wrinkled deep in time (I. v. 29), and yet age cannot wither her. And if Cleopatra is paradoxical in her nature, Antony is hyperbolical in all that he does: in his rage, his valour, his love, and his folly.[18] From Philo's description of him as Mars to Cleopatra's description of him as her colossus, he is seen in hyperbolic terms; and his own passionate use of hyperbole confirms its association with him.

The paradoxes surrounding Cleopatra are in a sense verified early in the play by Enobarbus's portrait of her at Cydnus. Enobarbus's speech is placed between Antony's resolution to marry Octavia and his decision to leave her; placed here, it serves to tell us why Antony will return to Cleopatra. In this sense, it functions as a substitute for a soliloquy in which Antony could announce his intentions to us. But a soliloquy would tell us about Cleopatra only as Antony perceives her: this description comes from Enobarbus, the most consistently sceptical voice in the play. That Enobarbus is the spokesman for Cleopatra's paradoxes establishes the portrait of her as one of the facts of the play.[19] We are presented with her paradoxical nature as a *fait accompli*, as one of the premises from which the action of the play springs. In this sense, paradox itself is embodied in the person of Cleopatra, and we are forced to acknowledge its presence on stage.[20] Her nature is fixed from that moment: and although she changes constantly, paradox can accommodate all the change; it is, after all, central to the paradox that everything becomes her and that she becomes everything. Cleopatra's definition by paradox comes early in the play and remains relatively static; Antony's definition by hyperbole is a continuing process, a continuing attempt to redefine him. And our education is at stake in his definition: for we are continually re-educated in the possibilities of hyperbole and in the kind of belief we can accord it. If Antony's hyperboles are verified, it is only at the end of the play, after a continual process of testing. The entire play leads us to Cleopatra's hyperbolical portrait of him; but it leads us there by subjecting hyperbole to scepticism as well as to assent.

Like the play itself, Antony's hyperboles can be verified only by surviving the test of the comic structure. Hyperbole can indicate either the similarity or the discrepancy between assertion and reality; or it can indicate both together. Whether the effect of the hyperbole is comic or tragic depends largely on the extent to which we are permitted to believe in the untruth it asserts.[21] In purely comic hyperbole, the effect lies precisely in the discrepancy between the fact and the assertion. The hyperbolical claims about Antony are frequently subject to just such mockery. For Ventidius, who has just won a battle by his own harsh labour, Antony's name is 'that magical word of war' (III. i. 31). Agrippa and Enobarbus mock Lepidus's sycophantic love for his two masters by citing his hyperbolical praise of them:

> Eno.   Caesar? Why he's the Jupiter of men.
> Agr.   What's Antony? The god of Jupiter.
> Eno.   Spake you of Caesar? How, the nonpareil?
> Agr.   O Antony, O thou Arabian bird!
>   (III. ii. 9–12)

But not all the hyperboles in the play are comic: and as hyperbole becomes imaginatively relevant, it begins to invoke our belief, in despite of all reason. For *Antony and Cleopatra* is virtually an experiment in establishing the imaginative relevance of hyperbole and consequently the kind of belief we can accord it: and our final sense of Antony depends on this process.

Throughout the play, we are given a medley of hyperboles ranging from the purely comic to the purely tragic. Antony, as one of the three triumvirs, is 'the triple pillar of the world', according to Philo (I. i. 12); and even Antony seems to imagine that when he takes his support from the world, a significant portion of it will collapse ('Let Rome in Tiber melt, and the wide arch / Of the rang'd empire fall!' [I. i. 33–4]). Cleopatra later imagines Antony bearing up the heavens rather than the earth: her Antony is 'the demi-Atlas of this earth' (I. v. 23).[22] But these very hyperboles are mocked when the drunken Lepidus is carried offstage:

> Eno. There's a strong fellow, Menas.
> Men. Why?
> Eno. 'A bears the third part of the world, man; see'st not?
> Men. The third part, then, is drunk.
> (II. vii. 88–91)

When Octavius hears of Antony's death, he comments, 'The breaking of so great a thing should make / A greater crack' (V. i. 14–15). In his words, the concept of universal order crumbles; but so does our hyperbolical vision of Antony upholding earth and heaven. At his death, there is no crack. But the effect of this sequence of hyperboles is balanced by another sequence. When the serving men on Pompey's barge compare the drunken Lepidus to a star, the poetical clothing is clearly too large for him, and the effect is comic:

> To be called into a huge sphere, and not to be seen to move in't, are the holes where eyes should be, which pitifully disaster the cheeks.
> (II. vii. 14–16)

The servant's shift from the cosmic and outsized to the human and minute in mid-metaphor is wholly appropriate: for poor Lepidus is in a sense a mere mortal caught in a world filled with hyperbolical figures. But when we find Antony dressed in the same poetical clothing, he wears it with grace. Lepidus compares his faults to the spots of heaven (I. iv. 12–13); and the comparison is not ludicrous.

By the time the second guardsman responds to Antony's suicide by reiterating the hyperbolical association ('The star is fall'n' [IV. xiv. 106]), we are, I think, quite prepared to believe him. And he in turn prepares us for Cleopatra's assertion that the crown of the earth doth melt and the soldier's pole is fallen.

If the hyperboles that describe Antony are subject to a continual process of testing, so are the hyperboles that Antony himself uses. In his education in the hyperbolical, Antony appeals to his ancestor Hercules as teacher:

> The shirt of Nessus is upon me, teach me,
> Alcides, thou mine ancestor, thy rage.
> Let me lodge Lichas on the horns o' the moon,
> And with those hands that grasp'd the heaviest club,
> Subdue my worthiest self.
>
> (IV. xii. 43–7)

But Antony does not even manage to subdue his worthiest self. What is possible for the god inevitably remains impossible for the mortal – impossible and consequently slightly foolish. Cleopatra suggests by her mockery at the beginning of the play that this emulation is folly in a mere mortal: she notes to Charmian 'how this Herculean Roman does become / The carriage of his chafe' (I. iii. 84–5). In imitating his ancestor' gigantic rage in Act 1, Antony is merely playacting and is as foolish as Pistol or any other Herculean stage braggart whose language is clearly too big for his worth – he is a slightly larger version of Moth.[23] The frequent reference to Herod, the conventional stage blusterer, would remind the audience of the dangers inherent in the use of hyperbole: it was the language of tyrants.[24] For much of the play, Antony's hyperbolical passion is subject to this kind of comic testing. The long scene in which Antony rages in Hercules' vein and Enobarbus consistently undercuts him (Act III, scene xiii) is fundamentally comic in structure; as I have noted elsewhere, it follows the classical pattern of *miles gloriosus* and servant. His rage here does not fully engage our sympathy; when he says, 'O that I were / Upon the hill of Basan, to outroar / The horned herd, for I have savage cause' (III. xiii. 126–8), we are disinclined to believe in the extent of his grievances or in his hyperbolical expression of an action appropriate to them. The hyperbole here dissuades us from belief and becomes mere rant. But the situation is more complex after the Egyptian fleet has joined with Caesar's. Antony in calling on his ancestor for instruction seems to recognise that his own hyperbolical language is not altogether equal to the occasion. His language here is proportionate to the cause of his rage: it is not merely rant, and it is surely no longer comic. Moreover, Cleopatra immediately verifies the heroic extent of his rage: 'O, he's more mad / Than Telamon for his shield, the boar of Thessaly / Was never so emboss'd' (IV. xiii. 1–3). Though we still cannot believe in Antony's hyperbolical actions as literal, at least we believe in his rage. The hyperbole becomes an appropriate expression for the gigantic rage and, in that sense, imaginatively relevant. And after Antony hears of Cleopatra's death, he echoes her reference to Ajax in an image which sounds hyperbolical but is in fact absolutely literal: 'The seven-fold shield of Ajax cannot keep / The battery from my heart' (IV. xiv. 38–9).

If Cleopatra is the first to mock Antony's hyperboles, she is also the final advocate of their truth. Cleopatra asserts to Dolabella that her dream of Antony belongs to the realm of nature, not of fancy: 'to imagine / An Antony were nature's piece, 'gainst fancy, / Condemning shadows quite' (V. ii. 98–100). But this assertion comes only after five acts of continual testing. Even while Antony is dying, Cleopatra can acknowledge the folly of hyperbole. As she struggles to lift him into her monument, she says,

> . . . Had I great Juno's power,
> The strong-wing'd Mercury should fetch thee up,
> And set thee by Jove's side. Yet come a little,
> Wishers were ever fools.
>
> (IV. xv. 34–7)

Yet side by side with this quiet resignation to the literal is her hyperbolical appeal to the sun ('Burn the great sphere thou mov'st in' [IV. xv. 10]): precisely the crack the absence of which Caesar notes. 'Wishers were ever fools': 'O, see, my women: / The crown o' the earth doth melt' (IV. xv. 62–3). If we are finally able to believe Cleopatra's hyperbolical portrait of her Antony, it is only because she herself tells us that wishers are fools.

From Janet Adelman, *The Common Liar* (New Haven and London, 1973), pp.102–21.

NOTES

[In her reading of *Antony and Cleopatra* Janet Adelman pursues rigorously the view which Danby formulates, concerning the perplexing range of perspectives on the action that the play offers. Throughout she pays particular attention to the affective power of the play's poetry as something which points the spectator and the reader to some degree of stability in what is otherwise a very unstable dramatic world. Adelman traces Shakespeare's own fashioning of source material, and develops a series of classical analogies: Dido and Aeneas, and Venus and Mars, as types which provide the basis for the dramatic characterisation of Antony and Cleopatra. Her concern is, nonetheless a formalistic one: she is preoccupied with the play's internal structure, and with the problems of perspective, genre and judgement which this structure produces. Ed.]

1. Harry Levin's discussion in *The Overreacher* (Cambridge, 1952) first made me aware of the problem of staged hyperbole, though his view of it is very different from mine. He says, 'The stage becomes a vehicle for hyperbole, not merely by accrediting the incredible or supporting rhetoric with a platform and sounding board, but by taking metaphors literally and acting concepts out. Operating visually as well as vocally, it converts symbols into properties; triumph must ride across in a chariot, hell must flare up in fireworks; students, no longer satisfied to read about Helen of Troy, must behold her in her habit as she lived. Whereas poetry is said to transport us to an imaginative level, poetic drama transports that level to us: hyperbolically speaking, it brings the mountains to Mohammed' (p. 24). But we can never see Helen; any actual face is a poor substitute for the face that launched a thousand ships. In fact, the literal action will always to some extent contradict the assertions of the poetry: it will be up to the individual playwright to emphasise these contradictions or to ignore them, as he chooses.

2. This concern with the problem of staged hyperbole may have been suggested to Shakespeare by Marlowe's *Dido, Queen of Carthage*; Marlowe insists upon the discrepancy between literal action and verbal assertion throughout *Dido*.

3. In fact, many of the critics who praise the poetry extravagantly seem by implication to condemn the play as a whole, as though it were necessary for us to adjudicate between the claims of the Poetry and those of the Play. G. B. Harrison, for instance, says, '*Antony and Cleopatra* is gorgeous, with the loveliest word-music, but it never reaches down to the depths of emotions' ('*Antony and Cleopatra*', *Shakespeare's Tragedies* [London, 1951], p. 226). A. C. Bradley ('Shakespeare's *Antony and Cleopatra*', *Oxford Lectures on Poetry* [London, 1909]) suggests that in praising the play, we are praising 'the artist and his activity, while in the case of the four famous tragedies it is the product of this activity, the thing presented, that first engrosses us' (p. 282). In fact, very few people attempt to reconcile the final claims of the poetry with the play as a whole. Those who wish for certainty inevitably wish that Shakespeare had condemned the lovers a little more, or exalted them a little more; and according to their preference, they either minimise or

emphasise the poetry. In either case, the poetry becomes in effect detachable from the play. Thus Bethell (*Shakespeare and the Popular Tradition* [London, 1944]), Griffiths (G. S. Griffiths, '*Antony and Cleopatra*', *Essays and Studies*, vol. 31, ed. V. De Sola Pinto [Oxford, 1946], pp. 34–67), and Knight (*The Imperial Theme* [London, 1951]), rely too exclusively on the poetry; Danby, Rosen (*Shakespeare and the Craft of Tragedy* [Cambridge, 1960]) et al. are too eager to ignore it altogether. Proser (*The Heroic Image in Five Shakespearean Tragedies* [Princeton, 1965]) suggests that the lovers create their own poetic universe which can compete with the everyday universe, but he does not show how this poetic universe is related to the rest of the play. Though his discussion is suggestive, he still seems to regard the poetry as finally detachable. Traversi is almost alone among major critics in insisting that the 'lyrical' and 'realistic' visions of the play are part of the same organic whole: 'It is the play's achievement to leave room for *both* estimates of the personal tragedy, the realistic as well as the lyrical; and if each has to be continually balanced against its opposite, so that the total impression can never, even at the last, depend upon one to the exclusion of the other, full understanding of what is intended rests upon an appreciation of the poetic quality so marvellously, richly present throughout the play. The gap between what is clearly, from one point of view, a sordid infatuation, and the triumphant felling which undoubtedly, though never exclusively, prevails in the final scenes is bridged by a wonderful modification of connected imagery. Rottenness becomes the ground for fertility, opulence becomes royalty, infatuation turns into transcendent passions, all by means of an *organic* process which ignores none of its own earlier stages, which, while never denying the validity of the realistic estimates of the situation which accompany it to the last, integrates these in the more ample unity of its creative purpose' (*An Approach to Shakespeare* [Garden City, 1969], 2: 224–5). In his view, the lyricism grows from the realism as all the vitality in the play grows from its corruption. The central metaphor for this process is Nilus's slime, quickened by the fire of the sun (p. 230). Though the terms of our arguments are very different, Traversi's demonstration that the poetry is not detachable from the play and his emphasis on the corrupt vitality of the Nile are similar to my own.

4. Bernard Shaw, *Three Plays for Puritans* (London, 1930), pp. xxx–xxxi.

5. Both figures have been recognised as essential to the poetic texture of the play; see, for example, Benjamin T. Spencer, '*Antony and Cleopatra* and the Paradoxical Metaphor', *Shakespeare Quarterly*, 9 (1958), 373–8; and Madeleine Doran, '"High Events as These": The Language of Hyperbole in *Antony and Cleopatra*', *Queen's Quarterly*, 72 (1965), 25–51. Spencer notes most of the paradoxes in the play and finds paradox 'the matrix from which much of the characterisation and the action sprang' (p. 376). He finds it characteristic of a discourse 'obliged to take account of the contradictions and unpredictability and irration-

ality of human affection and passion' (p. 373). His suggestion that at the end 'the paradoxical hints at the transcendental' (p. 375) is tantalising; unfortunately he does not tell us how, nor does he discuss the tension between belief and disbelief which is, I think, essential to paradox in the play. Doran's essay is particularly useful in so far as it discusses hyperbole as part of the Elizabethan tendency toward 'the ideal, the excellent, the distinguished, the quintessential' in all areas (p. 28).

6. 'On Love', *The Works of Francis Bacon*, ed. James Spedding, Robert Leslie Ellis and Douglas Denon Heath (London, 1859), vol. 6, pp. 397–8.

7. Edgar Wind, *Pagan Mysteries in the Renaissance* (New York, 1968), pp. 55–6.

8. Henry Peacham, *The Garden of Eloquence* (1593), ed. William G. Crane (Gainesville, Fla., 1954), p. 112.

9. It is suggestive that Peacham's only example of the figure is Paul's words to King Agrippa, a sceptic about the miracles of Christianity: '"Why should it be thought a thing incredible unto you: that God should raise againe the dead. I also thought in my selfe that I ought to do many contrary things against the name of Jesus of *Nazareth* . . ." Here Paul sheweth, that not long before he was of the same opinion that his adversaries and the judge were now of, and was in the like maner an open enemy to the professor of that name' (pp. 112–23).

10. George Puttenham, *The Arte of English Poesie*, ed. Gladys Doidge Willcock and Alice Walker (Cambridge, 1936), p. 226.

11. Peacham, Puttenham, and the other English figurists seem to regard paradox as a strictly verbal phenomenon, in which the doubt is expressed explicitly in so many words. Thus Day's example of paradox is, 'Could it possibly bee thought that learning and place of good education might ever have produced such monstrous effects?' (Angel Day, *The English Secretary* [1599], ed. Robert O. Evans [Gainesville, Fla., 1967], pt. 2, p. 90). James Blair Leishman (*Themes and Variations in Shakespeare's Sonnets* [London, 1963]) eloquently warns against the danger of putting the cart before the horse in this matter: the use of 'hyperbole' as 'a rhetorical or literary-critical term represents an attempt by rhetoricians and "grammarians" to describe something which had struck them in the practice of great poets, not an attempt by great poets to realise something which had first been suggested as a possibility by rhetoricians and grammarians. This may perhaps seem too obvious to require insistence, but I think it is not so at a time when so many scholars, especially in America, seem to have persuaded themselves, not only that we can learn something really valuable from a study of medieval or semi-medieval textbooks on rhetoric which great renaissance poets may or may not have read at school, but also that it was

from such textbooks that great poets learnt to use rhetorical devices which, long before any textbooks existed, had been used by Homer and Aeschylus and Pindar' (p. 152). The rhetoricians may suggest traditional attitudes toward a figure, but they can never suggest the function a figure actually serves in an author as complex as Shakespeare.

12. The 'Christian Paradoxes', originally printed under Bacon's name, are almost certainly not by him. According to the editors of the collected *Works*, 'It is the work of an orthodox Churchman of the early part of the seventeenth century, who fully and unreservedly accepting on the authority of revelation the entire scheme of Christian theology, and believing that the province of faith is altogether distinct from that of reason, found a pleasure in bringing his spiritual loyalty into stronger relief by confronting and numbering up the intellectual paradoxes which it involved' (*Works*, 7: 290). Paradox in the Renaissance has recently received much attention. See, for instance, A. E. Malloch, 'The Technique and Function of the Renaissance Paradox', *Studies in Philology*, 53 (1956), 191–203. Malloch gives the philosophical background in Aquinas and More and emphasises the importance of the reader's response to the illogic of the paradox. His conclusion is suggestive for *Antony and Cleopatra*: 'Logic operates upon concepts, which are by definition abstracts from the world of existent things. Paradox controls and makes intelligible this multiple world much as two negative units in algebra, when multiplied, bring forth a positive answer' (p. 203). Rosalie Colie defines the traditional *topoi* of paradox in *Paradoxia Epidemica: The Renaissance Tradition of Paradox* (Princeton, 1966). Her discussion is illuminating for *Antony and Cleopatra*, particularly in her emphasis on the self-reflexive quality of paradox (p. 7); on its involvement in dialectic (paradox exploits 'the fact of relative, or competing, value systems' [p. 10]); and on the necessity for brief in the impossible expressed through paradox (p. 23).

13. The figurists generally give paradox and hyperbole approximately equal billing as figures; but nonetheless hyperbole is defined in a way which permits us to see it as a species of paradox in the broadest sense. In fact, the terms of the figurists constitute a quicksand quite as dangerous as the one in which Lepidus almost sinks. One of the few flaws in Sister Miriam Joseph's useful study (*Shakespeare's Use of the Arts of Language* [New York, 1947]) is that she makes the rhetoricians appear far more consistent than they actually are. According to Sister Miriam Joseph, it is very probable that Shakespeare knew Puttenham (p. 44); and there is some evidence to suggest his knowledge of Peacham (pp. 113–14). For most figurists, *paradoxon* does not imply logical contradiction, though this implication is present in Donne's use of the word. The term *oxymoron* had not yet come into use. The closest approximation to it was *sinaciosis* or *synaeceosis* defined by Peacham as 'a figure which teacheth to conjoine diverse things or contraries, and to repugne common opinion with reason, thus: The covetous & the

prodigall are both alike in fault, for neither of them knoweth to use their wealth aright, for they both abuse it, and both get shame by it' (p. 170). Puttenham defines it as 'the *Crossecouple*, because it takes me two contrary words, and tieth them as it were in a paire of couples, and so makes them agree like good fellowes' (p. 206). He uses the same example as Peacham. (Day also uses the same example, incidentally on p. 95: apparently synaeceosis was scarce.) Despite the apparent similarity to paradox in function, these figurists did not connect the two in any way. But I suspect that they would have considered Shakespeare's additions to Plutarch's description of Cleopatra synaeceosis rather than paradox. In general, these figurists tended to divide the figures into three categories: *tropes*, in which the signification of a word or sentence was changed, such as metaphor or allegory (Puttenham calls these 'sensable figures'); *grammatical schemes* such as zeugma, in which the order of spelling of words was changed without affecting the signification (Puttenham calls these 'auricular figures'); and *rhetorical schemes*, in which both the arrangement of words and the signification is changed (Puttenham calls these 'sententious figures'). Unfortunately, hyperbole is by this system a trope and paradox is a rhetorical scheme, and never the twain shall meet, despite their similarity of function. In any event, since hyperbole can be used to create precisely the effect prescribed for paradox, I have chosen perhaps arbitrarily to consider hyperbole as a species of paradox. Colie also concludes that paradox is 'primarily a figure of thought, in which the various suitable figures of speech are inextricably impacted' (p. 22).

14. Puttenham, p. 154.

15. Puttenham, pp. 191–2.

16. Our sense of Cleopatra as a creature who embodies paradox within herself comes largely from Enobarbus's speech; Shakespeare's addition of paradox to Plutarch's description is the more striking because he otherwise follows Plutarch's wording exactly The barge in Plutarch has a gold poop and purple sails, but it does not burn on the water. The winds are not lovesick with the sails. Plutarch's oars are silver and move in time to flutes; the water does not follow, amorous of their strokes. Plutarch's Cleopatra does not beggar description. She is 'apparelled and attired like the goddesse Venus, commonly drawen in picture' and surrounded by boys, 'apparelled as painters doe set forth god Cupide', who are fanning her; but Plutarch's Cleopatra does not overpicture Venus, the picture of Venus does not outwork nature, and the winds fanned by the Cupids do not glow the cheeks which they did cool. The inhabitants of Plutarch's city run to gaze at Cleopatra; but his air seems untempted to follow suit and make a gap in nature.

17. Theseus tells us that it is part of love's madness to see 'Helen's beauty in a brow of Egypt' (*A Midsummer Night's Dream* [V. ii. 11]).

18. In one sense, of course, this distinction is specious: Antony's hyperboles are paradoxical and Cleopatra's paradoxes hyperbolical. The two figures of thought are thoroughly intertwined in the play. Nonetheless, as purely verbal phenomena, the paradoxes tend to be associated with Cleopatra and the hyperboles with Antony.

19. To rectify this obvious implausibility, Dryden transferred the speech to Antony; by the same process, he transferred the mystery out of the speech. There have been other, equally ingenious, solutions to the problems which Enobarbus's speech creates. In Michael Langham's Stratford, Ontario, production of the play (1967), Enobarbus assumed the guise of a city sharpy gulling Roman rednecks, thus obliterating the audience's dangerous tendency to believe the speech.

20. Mack says of Enobarbus's description of Cleopatra at Cydnus, 'This is clearly not a portrait of a mere intriguing woman, but a kind of absolute oxymoron' (introduction to the Pelican *Antony and Cleopatra* [Baltimore, 1960], p. 19).

21. Puttenham cautions against the abuse of this figure on just these grounds: 'this maner of speach is used, when either we would greatly advaunce or greatly abase the reputation of any thing or person, and must be used very discreetly, or els it will seeme odious, for although a prayse or other report may be allowed beyōd all measure' (p. 192). He tells the story of a speaker who compared the task of reciting the virtues of Henry VIII to numbering the stars of the sky and consequently made of himself 'a grosse flattering foole': and though he does not say so, by his own law the speaker probably did nothing to enhance Henry's reputation. The effect of the hyperbole was comic, independent of the speaker's intentions, because the discrepancy between fact and assertion was too great. Puttenham then suggests his own 'more moderate lye' as a substitute for this gross flattery (p. 192).

22. It is not clear whether Cleopatra imagines Antony upholding the heavens (as the Atlas myth would suggest) or the earth: 'of the earth' may imply either that this Atlas belongs to the earth or that he upholds the earth instead of the heavens. The second alternative would be more consistent with the imagery of the play, especially with the collapse of the wide arch of the rang'd empire; but perhaps we should not expect consistency from Cleopatra. According to the myth, Hercules once relieved Atlas of his task; since Caesar and Antony now share the task between them, Antony is only a demi-Atlas, by implication only half as strong as his great ancestor.

23. The hyperbolical braggart is in fact associated with Antony in *Henry V*: Fluellen tells us that he thinks Pistol 'is as valiant a man as Mark Antony' (*Henry V*, III. 613–15).

24. For a discussion of the stage representations of Herod, see Douglas Cole, *Suffering and Evil in the Plays of Christopher Marlowe* (Princeton,

1962), pp. 11–22. Geoffrey Bullough accounts for the references to Herod by suggesting that Shakespeare probably knew the tradition that Cleopatra had attempted to seduce Herod and failed (*Narrative and Dramatic Sources of Shakespeare* [London, 1964]; vol. 5, p. 219). We probably need not refer to any tradition to explain his presence: it is part of the spaciousness of *Antony and Cleopatra* that the grand tyrant himself is in effect one of the superfluous kings who have served as Antony's messengers. When Charmian imagines herself mother of a son to whom Herod will do homage, her fantasy is a comic version of the other grandiose ambitions in the play. But at the same time, her mock ambition makes us strangely conscious of Herod's real power as a tyrant in the Christian context. Stephen Booth has pointed out to me that this curious half allusion to Christ produces a good deal of gratuitous hyperbolical energy at this moment in the play.

3

Shakespeare's Boy Cleopatra, the Decorum of Nature, and the Golden World of Poetry

PHYLLIS RACKIN

> The quick comedians
> Extemporally will stage us, and present
> Our Alexandrian revels: Antony
> Shall be brought drunken forth, and I shall see
> Some squeaking Cleopatra boy my greatness
> I' the posture of a whore.[1]

In these lines, Shakespeare's Cleopatra describes for her women the treatment they will receive in the theatre if they allow themselves to be taken to Rome. The speech was troublesome to Shakespeare's nineteenth-century editors, who were reluctant to read *boy* as a verb. Schmidt suggested that 'Cleopatra-Boy' be read as a compound. Sprenger advised that *boy* be emended to *bow*. Most modern editors accept the passage without comment, and those critics who do discuss it vary widely in their assessments of its impact.

Shakespeare's strategy in this speech is worth exploring, for it is daring to the point of recklessness, and it provides a major clue to his strategy in the play as a whole. The treatment Cleopatra anticipates at the hands of the Roman comedians is perilously close to the treatment she in fact received in Shakespeare's theatre, where the word *boy* had an immediate and obvious application to the actor

who spoke it. Insisting upon the disparity between dramatic spectacle and reality, implying the inadequacy of the very performance in
which it appears, the speech threatens for the moment the audience's
acceptance of the dramatic illusion. And the moment when the threat
occurs is the beginning of Cleopatra's suicide scene – her and her
creator's last chance to establish the tragic worth of the protagonists
and their action.

Recklessness, perhaps most apparent here, is in fact the keynote of
Shakespeare's *Antony and Cleopatra*: it is the characteristic not only
of the love and the lovers the play depicts but also of its dramatic
technique. The play seems perfectly calculated to offend the rising
tide of neoclassical taste and to disappoint rational expectation. The
episodic structure, with its multiplicity of tiny scenes ranging in
setting from one end of the known world to the other, directly
opposed the growing neoclassical demand for the Unities; and even
in the twentieth century it has often seemed unsatisfactory. Most
recent critics, of course, argue that the structure is necessary to do
'justice to the dimensions of the heroic portrayal', to present the
thematic conflict between Roman and Egyptian values, and to evoke
a world where 'time and place do not matter', since 'the dimensions
of the play are not temporal but eternal; not local but spatial'.[2] And
these demonstrations are generally convincing. In the long run, the
structural peculiarities reveal themselves as functional embodiments
of the peculiar vision that informs the play. But in the short run they
remain disturbing. The bewildering parade of tiny, scattered scenes
requires explanation, as does the diffusion of the catastrophe through
the last two acts. If the issue of the action is to unite the lovers in
death, surely the wide separation between Antony's suicide and
Cleopatra's is troublesome.

Recklessness is apparent also in the language of the play, with its
curious mixture of the most elevated Latinisms and the coarsest
contemporary slang, its mixed metaphors, its elliptical constructions,
and its exuberant disregard for grammatical convention. That *boy* is
a verb is no anomaly in a play where hearts can 'spaniel' at Antony's
heels and the moon can 'disponge' the damp of night upon Enobarbus.
Anthimeria, or 'the substitution of one part of speech for another',
was an accepted figure of Elizabethan rhetoric, but like all figures, it
was held to be a vice if used excessively.[3] Moreover, by the time
Shakespeare wrote *Antony and Cleopatra*, the neoclassical demand
for a style 'pure and neat', 'plaine and customary' was beginning to
discredit the older fashion for rhetorical exuberance.[4] The incon-

stancy of style may seem less problematical than the structural eccen-
tricity, for it can be explained as characteristic of Shakespeare's
practice in his later plays or justified as the natural embodiment of
the inconstancy in the behaviour of the protagonists. Recent critics
have also seen in the style an embodiment of the 'metaphysical'
quality of the play, showing 'the same strain and discord within
harmony, the same sense of diversity embraced and fused that is so
characteristic of metaphysical poetry'. In this view, the style becomes
the necessarily paradoxical and hyperbolic expression of a vision
that defies the limitations of logical categories.[5] Yet here, as in the
case of the structure, if the style is finally necessary, it is also initially
reckless; and our initial impression of indecorum and irrationality
contributes as much to the total effect as does our final recognition
of its propriety as the necessary embodiment of a meaning that
transcends rationality.

What is perhaps most reckless of all, and most offensive to neoclassical taste, is Shakespeare's presentation of his heroine, for his
Egyptian queen repeatedly violates the rules of decorum. If Sir Philip
Sidney found the mingling of kings and clowns distasteful, one can
imagine his reaction to a queen who not only consorted with clowns
but behaved suspiciously like one herself.[6] 'A boggler ever', Cleopatra repeatedly betrays Antony's trust. Moreover, in many scenes,
her behaviour is not simply ignoble but comical as well. In the first
act, she repeatedly interrupts Antony's farewell with a ludicrous
harangue. In the second, she hales the messenger from Rome up and
down the stage, threatening, 'I'll spurn thine eyes like balls before
me: I'll unhair thy head.' In the third, she extracts from that same
messenger a patently falsified description of Octavia and drinks it in
with absurd gullibility. What makes all this reckless, of course, is that
Cleopatra is not finally a comic character or an object of scorn. This
same Cleopatra is also, we are told – and told in the longest and most
memorable speech in the play – the apotheosis of magnificence that
greeted Mark Antony on the Cydnus. In the face of the conflicting
evidence, some critics have ignored the comedy, and others have
denied the nobility, but most today would agree with T. J. B. Spencer
that 'the behaviour of Cleopatra in the play, at least in the first four
acts, does not quite correspond with the way in which some of the
others talk about her', although they differ widely in their explana-
tions of the incongruity.[7]

The question of Cleopatra's worth can hardly be answered by
reference to Antony's enslavement, for if Cleopatra is an ambiguous

character, so is Antony, and his ambiguity is inextricably bound up with hers. In Antony's case, just as in Cleopatra's, the hard facts tend to suggest – and a number of the critics tend to agree – that the unsympathetic view is justified. The mismanagement of his military and political affairs, the repeated vacillations of his allegiance, and the bungling of his suicide provide ample evidence that Antony has diminished from the triple pillar of the world into a strumpet's fool. To the rationally minded this evidence is conclusive. George Bernard Shaw, for instance, was thoroughly convinced: 'I always think of what Dr Johnson said: "Sir, the long and short of it is, the woman's a whore!" You can't feel any sympathy with Antony after . . . Actium. . . . All Shakespear's rhetoric and pathos cannot reinstate Antony after that, or leave us with a single good word for his woman.'[8]

It is significant that Shaw quotes the reasonable doctor, for, as Shaw recognised, Shakespeare's play calls the very basis of reason into question. In the tenth book of *The Republic*, Plato argues the inferiority of the imitative arts to those activities that spring from the 'rational principle of the soul' by pointing out the unrealiability of appearance and the consequent necessity of 'the arts of measuring and numbering' to rescue the human understanding from the delusions imposed by the senses:

> The same object appears straight when looked at out of the water, and crooked when in the water; and the concave becomes convex, owing to the illusion about colours to which the sight is liable. Thus every sort of confusion is revealed within us; and this is that weakness of the human mind on which the art of conjuring and of deceiving by light and shadow and other ingenious devices imposes, having an effect upon us like magic. . . . And the arts of measuring and numbering and weighing come to the rescue of the human understanding – there is the beauty of them – and the apparent greater or less, or more or heavier, no longer have the mastery over us, but give way before calculation and measure and weight. . . . And this, surely, must be the work of the calculating and rational principle in the soul.[9]

Plato's view here is very much like Shaw's and Johnson's and very much like that of the Romans in the play. The play opens with Philo's contemptuous judgement that Cleopatra is a worthless strumpet and Antony her degraded fool. The Romans, like Shaw and Johnson, are contemptuous of Antony's devotion to Cleopatra: to them it represents the enslavement of his reason to his baser passions. They are almost puritanical in their scorn for the sensuous delights of

Egypt, and in this too they resemble the great rationalists. But what is perhaps most important is their epistemology. Philo's opening statement – 'this dotage of our general's o'erflows the measure' – demonstrates his rationalistic reliance upon measurement as an index of truth. In direct opposition, Antony's opening statement – 'There's beggary in the love that can be reckon'd' – asserts the inadequacy of a merely quantitative, reckoning standard and denies that the real is always measurable.

This opposition between the rationalistic view and its antithesis is thus represented within the play as well as among its critics. Philo's opening speech ends with the words 'behold and see' – an invitation to the audience, but more obviously to Demetrius. Within the play as without, the rationalistic view insists upon the faults of the lovers, relies upon ocular proof, weighs what Antony sacrifices – a third of the Roman world – against what he gains – the illicit love of the notorious Egyptian – and finds his action foolish. The rationalists within the play, like those among its critics, are unmoved by Cleopatra's arts. They pity and scorn Antony's enthralment because they discount the rhetoric by which the lovers claim for themselves a greatness surpassing the limitations of the Roman world. Antony's and Cleopatra's dialogue in the opening scene implies the inadequacy of a merely reckoning standard because it invokes a transcendent world in which the claims of time and space and measurement are irrelevant. To Demetrius, however, there is only one salient fact to be derived from their performance – Antony's failure to hear Caesar's messengers. When the lovers leave the stage, he speaks one line only – 'Is Caesar with Antonius priz'd so slight?' The language here is significant: according to Demetrius Antony has made an error in measurement. Antony has prized Caesar too 'slight' to satisfy Demetrius' rational standard of reckoning. Thus, Antony's performance has corroborated Philo's opening statement – his dotage does 'o'erflow the measure'. Ignoring the rhetoric, Demetrius has assessed the actions, and although he is sympathetic to Antony and 'will hope of better deeds to-morrow', what he has seen today is just what Philo said he would see.

This refusal of the rationalists, inside and outside the play, to be impressed by delusory shows and seductive rhetoric accounts for their low estimate of Cleopatra. For the critics, it also means that the play itself is deficient. When Shaw says, 'after giving a faithful picture of the soldier broken down by debauchery, and the typical wanton in whose arms such men perish, Shakespear finally strains all his huge command of rhetoric and stage pathos to give a theatrical sublimity to the wretched end of the business, and to persuade foolish spectators that the world was well lost by the twain',[10] he is demonstrating his rationalistic and neoclassical predilection for 'true' imitations of the 'typical' and his Platonic distrust for the delusory powers of the imitative arts. Shaw's objection to the play rests on the same premises as the Roman objection to its heroine: in each case what is finally at stake is the nature and value of art.

Cleopatra's incredible parade of shifting moods and stratagems, together with Shakespeare's notorious reticence about her motives, has led even her admirers to conclude that her one salient quality is, paradoxically, her lack of one – the magnificent inconstancy that Enobarbus calls 'infinite variety'. To the unsympathetic, of course, it is inconstancy pure and simple – the moral weakness of her sex, the vice that directly opposes the Roman virtue of steadfastness. Behind all her turnings, however, one motive does remain constant: from beginning to end, Shakespeare's Cleopatra is a dedicated showman. In the opening scene of the play, she tells the audience, 'I'll seem the fool I am not; Antony will be himself', a remark that serves as a pithy keynote to her character. Cleopatra's action throughout, like that of the playwright or actor, is seeming: she is a contriver of shows, mostly for Antony's benefit, but he is by no means her only audience. Cleopatra's strategy in love is to present a series of shows, to keep Antony unsure of her feelings and motivations, but in most of the play, the audience is also unsure. As Granville-Barker points out, she is 'never . . . left to a soliloquy. Parade fits her character'.[11] Some of Cleopatra's shows are obviously trivial – 'play' in both senses of the word – as when she changes clothes with Antony or has a salt fish hung on his fishing line or acts as his armourer. Others are more calculated stratagems, contrived to ensure her hold over Antony:

> See where he is, who's with him, what he does:
> I did not send you. If you find him sad,
> Say I am dancing; if in mirth, report
> That I am sudden sick. Quick, and return.
> (I. iii. 2–5)

But at the end of the play they prove the last best weapon in the lovers' arsenal, for it is by means of Cleopatra's trickery that Caesar suffers the only defeat inflicted upon him in the course of the play. For once, the luck of Caesar fails him, the great emperor is 'beguiled', and the lovers have their triumph. The death of Cleopatra is in fact a double triumph of showmanship – hers and her creator's. But the two are so entirely related that neither can be seen unless the other is appreciated.

Thus, in a very important sense, the entire play turns on the question of the proper response to a show. To the Romans, and to the critics who follow them in discounting the seductions of rhetoric and the delusions of the senses, the shows are false and their sublimity merely 'theatrical'. To the sympathetic among her audience, Cleopatra's wiles identify her with her creator as a fellow artist – an identification that is especially easy today, when we have read Joyce and Mann and Gide. In contemporary literature this association between the artist and the confidence-man has become almost a cliché. But in *Antony and Cleopatra*, the ancient version of the same association – Plato's charge that the poet is a liar – is also relevant. The Romans in Shakespeare's play, like Socrates in Plato's *Republic*, are able to make a good case against the creator of illusions when they appeal to our rational faculty to discount the evidence of the senses in favour of calculation and measurement. And the too-easy dismissals of these charges by Romantic lovers of art and of Cleopatra have never really succeeded in answering them. Shakespeare's play dramatises the oppositions and relationships between the two versions: only by appreciating both can we approach its dramatic and thematic centre.[12]

Enobarbus clearly illustrates this interplay. Ordinarily, his medium is prose and his perspective rational and ironic. He tends to reduce romantic love to physical appetite and to describe the business in bawdy jokes. Cleopatra is Antony's 'Egyptian dish'. To him Antony's devotion is inordinate and therefore irrational. But Enobarbus can also see Cleopatra very differently. Joking with Caesar's followers about Antony's Egyptian life, he suddenly abandons his characteristic ironic prose for the soaring poetry that creates for his listeners a Cleopatra who transcends anything they could see with the sensual eye or measure with the calculating and rational principle of the soul. In his famous set speech, Enobarbus evokes Cleopatra's arrival on the Cydnus to meet Mark Antony in terms that invite his audience – off the stage as well as on – to rise above these inferior modes of perception and to participate instead in the imaginative vision of the poet. 'I will tell you', he says, introducing the speech that creates one of Cleopatra's greatest scenes. Only the telling will do it: the physical spectacle we have beheld is ambiguous at best. This scene, in contrast, is not physically present: it is evoked by and for the imagination, and it pays tribute not only to Cleopatra's beauty and her incredible powers to enchant but also to the beauty and powers of the medium in which she is created. It is a commonplace of the older criticism that Shakespeare had to rely upon his poetry and his audience's imagination to evoke Cleopatra's greatness because he knew the boy actor could not depict it convincingly.[18] But he transformed this limitation into an asset, used the technique his stage demanded to demonstrate the unique powers of the very medium that seemed to limit him. Like Cleopatra's own art, the economy of the poet's art works paradoxically, to make defect perfection.

It is well known that Shakespeare took most of Enobarbus' speech from the narrative in North's *Plutarch*. The details he added, moreover, instead of making the speech more concrete or dramatic, emphasise that narrative is its necessary medium. They say, in effect, that the scene by its very nature is impossible to stage, and they also suggest that that impossibility is part of its meaning. The speech is full of hyperbole and paradox, rhetorical manifestations of the impossibility of its subject to be contained within the categories of logic and measurement. The subject cannot be represented but only created, embodied in the uncategorical and alogical shifts the poet works with words. Cleopatra's barge, for instance, can perform the miracle of burning on the water because it is 'like a burnish'd throne', and 'burn'd' is contained in 'burnish'd, not logically, and not visually, but verbally. The effect of these words, like that of Sidney's 'golden' world of the poet's making, is that Nature herself is outdone. To Sidney,

> There is no Arte delivered to mankinde that hath not the workers of Nature for his principall object, without which they could not consist, and on which they so depend, as they become Actors and Players, as it were, of what Nature will have set foorth. So doth the Astronomer looke upon the starres, and, by that he seeth, setteth downe what order Nature hath taken therein. So doe the Geometrician and Arithmetician in their diverse sorts of quantities. So doth the Musitian. . . . The naturall Philosopher . . . the Morall Philosopher . . . The Lawyer . . . The Historian. . . . The Grammarian . . . the Rethorician and Logitian. . . . The Phisition. . . . the Metaphisick. . . . Onely the Poet, disdayning to be tied to any such subjection, lifted up with the vigor of his owne invention, dooth growe in effect another nature, in making things either better then Nature bringeth forth, or, quite a newe, formes such as never were in Nature . . . so as hee goeth hand in hand with Nature, not inclosed within the narrow warrant of her guifts, but freely ranging onely within the Zodiack of his owne wit.

Nature never set forth the earth in so rich tapistry as divers Poets have done, neither with plesant rivers, fruitful trees, sweet smelling flowers, nor whatsoever els may make the too much loved earth more lovely. Her world is brasen, the Poets only deliver a golden.[14]

Clearly Enobarbus is speaking of this golden world when he says the winds which filled Cleopatra's sails 'were love-sick with them' and the waters beat by her oars did 'follow faster, as amorous of their strokes'. Moreover, in the description of Cleopatra herself –

> she did lie
> In her pavilion – cloth of gold, of tissue –
> O'er-picturing that Venus where we see
> The fancy outwork nature
> (II. ii. 198–201)

Enobarbus refers directly to the transcendent power of the artistic imagination in terms that closely echo Sidney's, as well as North's.

But my words here are ill-chosen, for Enobarbus does not really describe the queen – he evokes her. 'Her own person', he tells us, 'beggar'd all description.' It transcended description or measurement, for these methods are not applicable to the golden world. To create the golden world, 'the fancy outworks nature'. The world of Nature is the world we can behold, the world the Romans can measure. The world Enobarbus sees here is created by art in the fancy of those who can respond to it. This opposition between the two worlds is implicit from the beginning of the play. Antony and Cleopatra's opening lines, immediately following Philo's 'behold and see', declare it:

> **Cleopatra**   If it be love indeed, tell me how much.
> **Antony**   There's beggary in the love that can be reckon'd.
> **Cleopatra**   I'll set a bourn how far to be belov'd.
> **Antony**   Then must thou needs find out new heaven, new earth.

Antony's new heaven and earth, like Sidney's golden world and Enobarbus' vision, defies logical scrutiny, but its surpassing magnificence makes beggarly the reckonings of the Romans.

In this perfected world, where the ordinary forms of logic are inapplicable, paradox takes over:

> Age cannot wither her, nor custom stale
> Her infinite variety: other women cloy
> The appetites they feed, but she makes hungry,

> Where most she satisfies. For vilest things
> Become themselves in her, that the holy priests
> Bless her, when she is riggish.
>
> (II. ii. 235–40)

Enobarbus here leaps beyond measurement, ordinary morality, and logic itself, for these are the categories our minds design to enable us to cope with the world of time and change and limitation, and in the world produced by the fancy, outworking nature, they are no longer necessary or even relevant.

Enobarbus' vision of Cleopatra is not, of course, a creation ex nihilo. It represents his imaginative response to Cleopatra's creative arts. The entire scene here as in North's *Plutarch* is also her tour de force of artifice. The ageing queen who describes herself earlier (I. v. 28–9) as 'black' 'with Phoebus' amorous pinches . . . and wrinkled deep in time', has staged an elaborate spectacle complete with stage props, perfume, background music, supporting actors, and a carefully constructed setting. And, as Enobarbus five times reminds us, the entire creation belongs to the world of seeming: Cleopatra's barge is '*like* a burnish'd throne', the 'pretty dimpled boys' who wield her fans are '*like* smiling Cupids', the wind they make 'did *seem* to glow the delicate cheeks which they did cool', the gentlewomen tending her are '*like* the Nereides', and the helmsman is 'a *seeming* mermaid'. In creating the spectacle, Cleopatra deals in likenesses and seemings, not in the stuff that Plato would call reality. If she shares the power of the poet, she also shares his limitations.

Thus Cleopatra's ambivalence – the strange combination of degradation and sublimity that seems to lie at the centre of her characterisation – is best understood in connection with the ambivalence of the artist himself. The priests who bless her when she is riggish are not, of course, Christian priests; but the fact of their blessing attests to the lawless and mysterious powers that she, like the artist, possesses. Shakespeare insists upon this ambivalence, for it is not simply the characteristic of his heroine but also the informing principle of the entire dramatic structure. It represents the clash between two radically opposed views of poetry, both of them nicely illustrated in Sidney's *Apologie*, although Sidney seems unaware of the opposition.

Answering Plato's charge that the poet is a liar, Sidney points out that the golden world of poetry is not amenable to ordinary truth-criteria: the poet 'nothing affirmes, and therefore never lyeth':

What childe is there that, comming to a Play, and seeing *Thebes* written in great Letters upon an olde doore, doth beleeve that it is *Thebes*? If then a man can arive, at that childs age, to know that the Poets persons and dooings are but pictures what should be, and not stories what have beene, they will never give the lye to things not affirmatively but allegorically and figurativelie written. And therefore, as in Historie, looking for trueth, they goe away full fraught with falshood, so in Poesie, looking for fiction, they shal use the narration but as an imaginative groundplot of a profitable invention.[15]

However, Sidney contradicts himself in a later portion of the essay and undercuts this defence when he attacks *Gorboduc* for being 'faulty both in place and time, the two necessary companions of all corporall actions':

For where the stage should alwaies represent but one place, and the uttermost time presupposed in it should be, both by *Aristotles* precept and common reason, but one day, there is both many dayes, and many places, inartificially imagined. But if it be so in *Gorboduck*, how much more in al the rest? where you shal have *Asia* of the one side, and *Affrick* of the other, and so many other under-kingdoms, that the Player, when he commeth in, must ever begin with telling where he is, or els the tale wil not be conceived. Now ye shal have three Ladies walke to gather flowers, and then we must beleeve the stage to be a Garden. By and by, we heare newes of shipwracke in the same place, and then wee are to blame if we accept it not for a Rock.[16]

Sidney here offers a standard argument for the Unities – the need to bring the stage as close as possible to the reality of this world. As acting time approaches the time represented in the action, the gap between the poet's imagined world and the world of the spectator's ordinary experience is narrowed – not by appealing to the spectator's imagination to carry him beyond the bounds of his ordinary experience, but by subjecting the poet to the rules of rational expectation in the world of Nature. The Unity of Place is also a means of fixing and limiting the action of the play: in the neoclassical theatre it would collaborate with representational stage sets to localise the production in a finite world recognisably like the one outside the theatre. Thus, when Sidney argued for the Unities as necessary for verisimilitude, he implicitly repudiated his own notion of the golden world of poetry. The golden world, he had said, is separate from the brazen world of Nature experienced by 'our degenerate soules, made worse by theyr clayey lodgings' in 'the dungeon of the body' since the Fall.[17] The poet, in this view, redeems his audience for the moment, enabling them to recapture that prelapsarian vision of perfection. In contrast, the universals imitated by the neoclassicists are firmly rooted in Reason and Nature. What is to be imitated is the highest truth of this world, and the playwright is therefore answerable to all the rationalistic criteria designed to cope with this world.

Although Sidney's essay seems to imply that the golden world conforms to neoclassical rules of decorum, his claim that the poet of the golden world, 'disdayning to be tied to any . . . subjection' to Nature, creates a world which is not amenable to ordinary truth-criteria actually denies the great sanction underlying those rules – the assumption that it is the poet's business to provide just imitations of general Nature. The contradiction in Sidney's essay, like the conflict in Shakespeare's play, is finally a conflict between two theories of poetry and two orders of reality; but while Sidney seems unaware of the contradiction, Shakespeare insists upon it.

Antony and Cleopatra depends for its workings upon a defiance of the rules of decorum, but the defiance is meaningless unless we know the rules and appreciate the arguments by which they were justified. When Shakespeare refuses to be bound by the Unities of Time and Place, he is able to evoke a vision of a transcendent world of the imagination only because we first see that his settings are in fact unreal by the standards of 'common reason' that we bring to 'all corporall actions'. Similarly, his squeaking boy can evoke a greatness that defies the expectations of reason and the possibilities of realistic representation only because we share those expectations and understand the limits of those possibilities. Before the boy can evoke Cleopatra's greatness, he must remind us that he cannot truly represent it. In Egypt – and to the Egyptian imagination – he could become the queen he enacted on Shakespeare's stage, but only after he has reminded us that he would appear in Rome – and that he was in fact in Shakespeare's London – a squeaking boy.[18]

By admitting the reality of Rome, Shakespeare is able to celebrate the power of Egypt: by acknowledging the validity of the threat, he can demonstrate the special power that shows have to overcome the limitations of a reality that threatens to refute them. The Roman comedians Cleopatra describes, like the neoclassical writers in England, derived their authority from their submission to an authority they acknowledged to be higher than their own. They dedicated their art to imitations of the natural world and confined it within the bounds of rational expectation in that world. But since their authority was borrowed, it was also tenuous. Their very scrupulousness in imitating the world of Nature subjected them to its logic and rendered them vulnerable to the charges that banished poets from Plato's Republic. In claiming to satisfy that world's criteria for truth, they became guilty of deception. In contrast, Shakespeare violates those criteria, and admits that he violates them, in order to present a show that cannot lie because it does not affirm.

In this view, Shakespeare's reckless dramatic strategy is not simply justified but necessary. The structure, for instance, must employ frequent and abrupt shifts from Egypt to Rome, not only to convey the scope of the action, and not only to make us finally contemptuous of that scope, but also because the audience, like Antony, must vacillate between the two worlds. When Antony is in Egypt, as in the opening scene, he repudiates Time and Space and Roman thoughts in favour of sensual pleasure, of immersion in the timeless moment of immediate experience. But every time Antony steps outside that moment, into the world of Time and Roman thoughts, its charm evaporates. Like Antony, the audience is swept back and forth between the two worlds until the final scene when they are brought to rest in Egypt to behold Cleopatra's suicide, to see in it the nobility Antony saw in her, and thus, several scenes after Antony's death, to see the full significance of his action.

Similarly, the other structural peculiarity, the wide separation between the deaths of the lovers, can also be seen as a necessary part of Shakespeare's strategy. If the play ended with Antony's suicide, the Roman view would seem fairly well justified. He has given up virtue, honour, and one third of the Roman world and got in return the possession of an ageing, treacherous courtesan, the weak and unreliable support of the Egyptian forces, and, in the end, an ambiguous death. These are the observable facts of his behaviour and its measurable results. Moreover, his suicide, far from being an efficient Roman triumph over mortality, is a rather messy affair. Cleopatra shows her very worst when, her navy having betrayed Antony to his final defeat, she orders Mardian to take him a false report of her death. Her very language – 'Say, that the last I spoke was "Antony", and word it, prithee, piteously. Hence, Mardian, and bring me how he takes my death to the monument' – condemns her. For although her concerns here resemble those of the poet, they are those of Plato's poet, who is indistinguishable from a simple liar. She even uses the same term – 'word it' – with which she later discounts Caesar's attempt to deceive her about his intentions ('He words me, girls, he words me, that I should not be noble to myself' [V. ii. 190–91]). That

Antony is taken in by her lie surely diminishes him in the eyes of the audience, and the awkwardness of his suicide does little to redeem him.

The monument scene, however, complicates the matter. At the beginning, Cleopatra's fearful refusal to descend to Antony reminds us again how little he has got in return for all his sacrifices; and the stage business that follows, in which she and her women laboriously draw him up, has a ludicrous effect which is only partly relieved by the characteristically Shakespearean puns with which she accompanies it:

> Here's sport indeed! How heavy weighs my lord!
> Our strength is all gone into heaviness,
> That makes the weight.
>
> (IV. xv. 32–4)

But of course the spectacle is not simply ludicrous. North describes it as 'lamentable', a 'pitiefull . . . sight'.[19] Modern criticism has taught us to expect and appreciate mixed effects in Shakespeare's tragedies and to recognise that some of his most serious scenes are marked by this kind of bitter, grating humour. In this particular case, the effect is qualified by the fact that Antony's raising provides a visual 'metaphor of elevation' for his death.[20] Being physically presented, the metaphor is especially impressive, and the impression created should remain throughout much of the next act until it is finally overlaid by the next great visual spectacle in the play – Cleopatra's own suicide.

The action of Antony's death thus ends on a much higher note than it began; for once he has ascended into the monument, the language undergoes 'a corresponding heightening of style'.[21] Similarly, the play itself ends on its grandest note. Just as Cleopatra raises Antony into her monument in Act IV, in Act V she raises the entire action beyond the reach of Roman power. At the beginning of Act V, her character is still ambiguous. She sends a submissive messenger to Caesar:

> A poor Egyptian yet; the queen my mistress,
> Confin'd in all she has, her monument,
> Of thy intents desires instruction,
> That she preparedly may frame herself
> To the way she's forc'd to.
>
> (V. i. 52–6)[22]

In the scene that follows, she seems to be taken in by Proculeius' deceit, and in this both lovers are diminished; for just before he died, Antony had warned her to trust none of Caesar's men but Proculeius. In the much-debated interview with Caesar, there is at least some warrant for believing she is still 'boggling', looking for opportunities to preserve herself and her treasure by coming to ignominious terms with her conqueror. As is attested by the critical debates, the scene with Seleucus is sufficiently ambiguous that the audience, like Caesar, is very likely to take at face value the act she performs with her treasurer.[23] It is not until Caesar leaves the stage that Cleopatra turns to her women and says, 'He words me, girls, . . . that I should not be noble to myself', thus revealing that she has only pretended to trust him.

At this point, Cleopatra takes charge of the action. She says, 'I have spoke already, and it is provided', 'it' being the basket of figs which is the necessary prop for the show by which she will dramatise her nobility and Antony's. Up to this point, her manipulations have been covert and her motives ambiguous, but in her suicide she will stage directly before us the spectacular vision of herself that Antony had seen and Enobarbus recalled. But first she must describe the Roman comedies. Just as her knowledge of their sordidness and vulgarity helps to motivate her suicide, her allusion to them helps the audience to appreciate it. When Cleopatra contracts for a moment to the squeaking boy who acted her part, she reminds us that what we have been watching is a deceitful show. The reminder should make us doubt the validity of the conclusions we have reached on the basis of what we have beheld. In effect, she turns Plato's argument against poetry inside out and uses its major premise to refute its conclusion. For if the objects of our perception are delusive and inadequate misrepresentations, then how seriously can we take the calculations we have made on the basis of what we have seen? The audience is thus forced into a kind of 'double take' which prepares them to reorganise their disparate and jarring impressions of Cleopatra into a new synthesis.

The squeaking boy speech brings to a head the two major issues of the play – the issue of Cleopatra's character and the issue of the nature of plays. Throughout, Cleopatra has been depicted as a showman: showing has been her great defect and also her consummate virtue. In this speech, and in the scene that follows, the question of her worth is directly associated with the question of the worth of shows. Here she seems to set the two at odds: only if we reject the shows we have seen can we accept the unseen greatness of Cleopatra. But in her suicide she will present a new show that validates both, and even in this speech the validation begins. The very fact that Cleopatra can talk about the show and claim that it is a poor parody implies that she has access to a level of reality beyond what has been presented. By implying the inadequacy of the representation, she implies also that she can transcend it.

That Cleopatra's suicide is a show would be apparent in the theatre: she even changes costume for it onstage. 'Show me, my women, like a queen', she says, 'go fetch my best attires.' Much is made of dressing, and Charmian's dying gesture is to straighten her dead queen's crown. Her words, 'Your crown's awry, I'll mend it and then play', echo Cleopatra's order for the costume, 'when thou hast done this chare, I'll give thee leave to play till doomsday.' The word *play* emphasises both the hedonistic and the theatrical aspects of the very Egyptian death these women are contriving, but the fact that the crown is their central concern unites these aspects with another – the wholly serious matter of royalty. For the crown is the emblem of Cleopatra's royalty, and when she puts it on here, it establishes in a fully theatrical manner the nature of this queen who is so thoroughly involved with the world of art and illusion that she is incomprehensible except within its terms.

Cleopatra commands her women to 'show' her 'like a queen', but for the characters onstage, as well as the audience, the likeness becomes reality. After Cleopatra dies, Charmian says, 'golden Phoebus, never be beheld of eyes again so *royal*!' When Caesar's guard asks, 'Is this well done?' she replies, 'It is well done, and fitting for a princess descended of so many *royal* kings'. Discovering Cleopatra's death, Caesar says, 'Bravest at the last, she levell'd at our purposes, and being *royal* took her own way'. Of these lines, only the interchange with the guard is taken from North, and North's adjective is 'noble'. All these tributes to Cleopatra's royalty act as refutations to the earlier charge that she violated the decorum of her station. Those charges remained valid only so long as she was content to 'seem the fool' in a performance susceptible to neoclassical standards of propriety and realism. Once she repudiates that performance, she can invoke a fully theatrical world where she can put on her royalty with its emblems. In this world, the costume we see, the poetry we hear, and the act we see performed are sufficient, for they satisfy the only kind of truth-criteria available within the context of the theatre. The strategy is very much like that of Enobarbus' great speech, as we are reminded when Cleopatra says, 'I am again for Cydnus, to meet Mark Antony'. But Enobarbus' vision is only now fully validated, for he evoked it by words alone and only to the inner eye. In this scene it will be evoked by all the resources of Shakespeare's theatre, by spectacle as well as poetry, and the show will be theatrical reality. The stage itself, no less than the audience, is here freed from the demands of rationally plausible neoclassic verisimilitude, and for once in the play we can see before us the greatness that was only boyed in what we beheld earlier.

The interview with Dolabella, which has no real basis in North,[24] indicates the difference. It contrasts not only with the interview with Proculeius, which immediately precedes it, but also with the scene where Enobarbus describes his vision at the Cydnus. When Cleopatra tells Dolabella her dream of Antony, he betrays Caesar's confidence to tell her the truth that Antony's experience of Rome made him expect Proculeius would tell. In effect, her conquest of Dolabella is a microcosm of her conquest of the whole texture of values and aspirations with which he, as a member of Caesar's party, is associated. Her dream of Antony, like Enobarbus' vision of her, evokes a greatness that is not physically present, and it uses the language of paradox and hyperbole: 'For his bounty, there was no winter in 't: an autumn 'twas that grew the more by reaping. . . . In his livery walk'd crowns and crownets: realms and islands were as plates dropp'd from his pocket.' There are some important differences, however. The cosmic imagery – 'His face was as the heavens, and therein stuck a sun and moon, which kept their course, and lighted the little O, the earth. . . . his voice was propertied as all the tuned spheres' – directly establishes the translunary context of the vision.[25] In Enobarbus' vision, Cleopatra was associated with 'that Venus where we see the fancy outwork nature'. In Cleopatra's, Antony is 'past the size of dreaming: nature wants stuff to vie strange forms with fancy, yet to imagine an Antony were nature's piece, 'gainst fancy, condemning shadows quite'. At this point the truth of the imagination has become reality for Cleopatra: her dream is a vision of the golden world from a vantage point within that world rather than outside of it.

Cleopatra's ascent to the golden world is also an ascent from comedy, which shows men worse than they are, to tragedy, which shows them better. When the clown arrives to bring her the means by which she will ascend, she says, 'Let him come in. What poor an instrument may do a noble deed!'; and in the scene that follows he serves as her scapegoat, for he attracts the laughter which has become a fairly well-conditioned response to the figure of the queen while she preserves the decorum of her superior station. Similarly, the clown's speeches serve, as Donald C. Baker has remarked, to purge 'the baser elements of the language of the plays as Cleopatra purges herself and leaves her other elements "to baser life"'.[26] The clown's basket helps to define the transition. Early in the play (I. ii. 32), Charmian says, 'I love long life better than figs'. Now she and her mistress will choose the deadly figs and by their choice transform themselves from comic characters devoted to the life and sensual pleasures of this world to tragic characters who have the nobility to choose a good higher than mere survival. The asps as well as the figs are the products of the Nile, and the deaths of the Egyptian women demonstrate that their 'o'erflowing' river breeds material for high tragedy as well as low comedy.[27] Like Cleopatra's description of the asp as a babe that sucks its nurse asleep, the clown's basket unites appetite and death to sublimate both. His jokes make the same point: if 'a woman is a dish for the gods', appetite is godly.

Cleopatra's death sublimates appetite, but first she rejects it, in both its Roman and its Egyptian manifestations. She rejects the coarse diet available in Rome, where 'mechanic slaves with greasy aprons . . . shall uplift us to the view. In their thick breaths, rank of gross diet, shall we be enclouded, and forc'd to drink their vapour';[28] and she also resolves, 'Now no more the juice of Egypt's grape shall moist this lip'. Similarly, she denies the woman's nature that made her a boggler in the sublunary world – 'I have nothing of woman in me: now from head to foot I am marble-constant; now the fleeting moon no planet is of mine' – before she assumes the name of Antony's wife in the world of immortal longings. In each case, and in the case of all the other qualities that have led us to doubt her nobility, the renunciation is only a prelude to redefinition and fulfilment.

During the suicide scene, Cleopatra systematically and explicitly renounces the weaknesses charged against her by the Romans and made credible to the audience by her earlier performance. If she drank Antony under the table, she will now renounce the grape. If she was his strumpet, she will now become his wife. If her vacillation lost him battles, she will now be marble-constant. If his devotion to her made him effeminate, she will now renounce her sex. But she does not renounce her sex in order to collapse into a squeaking boy, any more than her rejection of his shows meant that she was done with showing. Her character, like her showmanship, is not destroyed in the final scene but sublimated. Even her sensuality remains: 'the stroke of death is as a lover's pinch, which hurts, and is desir'd'; and the new heaven and new earth she anticipates with Antony, where he is 'curled' just as he was 'barber'd ten times o'er' at the Cydnus,[29] will abound in sensuous delights. One way to describe this process of sublimation is to say that we are now made to share the romantic lovers' own vision of their passion; another way is to say that the passion in the world of Nature is destroyed in order to be reborn in a new incarnation in the golden world, which is also the afterlife that Cleopatra envisions with Antony.

In the opening scene, Antony's rhetoric rejected the world for a kiss:

> Let Rome in Tiber melt, and the wide arch
> Of the rang'd empire fall! Here is my space.
> Kingdoms are clay: our dungy earth alike
> Feeds beast as man; the nobleness of life
> Is to do thus: when such a mutual pair,
> And such a twain can do't . . .
>   (I. i. 33–8)

In the final scene, Cleopatra's act validates his choice. In the first scene, Antony suggested that to know the limits of their love, Cleopatra 'find out new heaven, new earth'. Here she prepares to find them out. In this final vision of Cleopatra's, Antony at last triumphs over Caesar. 'Methinks', she says 'I hear Antony call. . . . I hear him mock the luck of Caesar, which the gods give men to excuse their after wrath.' In the natural world, the soothsayer's warning to Antony holds true: Caesar will win at any game, for 'of that natural luck, he beats thee 'gainst the odds. Thy lustre thickens, when he shines by . . . thy spirit is all afraid to govern thee near him; but he away, 'tis noble'. Cleopatra can see Antony triumphing over Caesar because she looks beyond the world of time and change and luck where Caesar is always triumphant to a world where Antony's magnanimity can find its proper milieu. In the brazen world of Nature, where most of the play is set, Caesar is the master politician, but when Cleopatra chooses to leave that world, she can call him 'ass, unpolicied' and his intents 'most absurd'.

After Cleopatra's death, when she has in act as well as in vision repudiated Caesar's world, her vision becomes reality in Caesar's world as well as her own. Caesar, says the guard who finds her dead, has been 'beguil'd'. And Caesar is beguiled in two, equally significant, senses. In the first place, he is tricked out of his triumph: Cleopatra outwits the master manipulator at the end. But just as important, he is beguiled in the sense that he responds to Cleopatra's charm. Seeing the dead queen, Caesar says, 'she looks like sleep, as she would catch another Antony in her strong toil of grace'. For the first and only time in the play, Caesar sees what Antony saw in Egypt. He now knows Cleopatra's charm, not as an abstract consideration to be reckoned in Rome, troublesome or useful to him in his political manoeuvrings, but as a response within himself. Caesar has come to Egypt for his final vision of Cleopatra, and his response, like Enobarbus' memory of the Cydnus, attests the validity of the vision that drew Antony from Rome. Caesar is moved by Cleopatra's act and her staging of it. The audience, having seen the entire spectacle, is even better prepared to appreciate her worth. And once they have done so, Antony is necessarily elevated. When he died in Act IV, there was still considerable reason to believe him a strumpet's fool. But when the strumpet turns out to be a queen, Antony's sacrifice is shown to be worthwhile.

The last speech in the play, like the first one, is spoken by one Roman to another. And, like the first, it ends with an injunction to 'see':

> Our army shall
> In solemn show attend this funeral,
> And then to Rome. Come, Dolabella, see
> High order, in this great solemnity.

If we make the kind of association I have been suggesting and identify the Roman view of the lovers with the perceptions available to fallen man in the brazen world of mundane life, we might say that the audience, about to leave the theatre, is about to return to the 'Rome' from which they entered it. Like Caesar, however, they have been in the interval to Egypt where they have, at first, beheld Cleopatra's deceptive show and, at the end, seen her in another show, of 'high order' and 'great solemnity'.

Before the final scene can be enacted and the sight of Cleopatra's greatness made available to the audience, Shakespeare must establish and then undermine the comic conception of her character that was based on the boy actor's imitation of her appearance in the natural world to which the Roman comedians are limited. Like the Romans, we must accept its verisimilitude before we can appreciate the force of Cleopatra's charge that it is a poor parody of the greatness she possesses in the golden world which is the high product of the tragic poet's making. Thus the ambivalence of our reactions to the first four acts is as important an element of our total experience of the play as is our response to the final scene, which resolves the ambivalence. The golden world of poetry became necessary only after the Fall of man, and the worth of the poet can only be seen when his handiwork is compared to the products of the arts that are bound by the limitations of Nature.

From *PMLA* (March 1972), 201–12.

NOTES

[In this relatively early essay Phyllis Rackin deals with some of the same material as Janet Adelman, except that she focuses her attention on the Jacobean stage convention of having the role of Cleopatra played by a male actor. This is an issue which has recently been reconsidered in the work of a number of feminist critics, such as Lisa Jardine, *Still Harping on Daughters: Women and Drama in the Age of Shakespeare* (Brighton, 1983), and the issue of 'cross-dressing' is closely associated with larger questions of gender identity in Shakespeare's plays generally. See also Marjorie Garber, *Vested Interests* (London, 1992). Ed.]

1. *Antony and Cleopatra*, V. ii. 215–20. All textual references are to the Arden edition, ed. M. R. Ridley (Cambridge, Mass., 1954).

2. Eugene M. Waith, *The Herculean Hero in Marlowe, Chapman, Shakespeare and Dryden* (New York, 1962), p. 121; and Robert Speaight, *Nature in Shakespearian Tragedy* (London, 1955), p. 123.

3. Sr Miriam Joseph, *Rhetoric in Shakespeare's Time* (New York, 1947), p. 299.

4. 'Timber: or Discoveries', in *Ben Jonson*, ed. C. H. Herford, Percy and Evelyn Simpson (Oxford, 1947), vol. 8, p. 620.

5. Anthony Caputi, 'Shakespeare's *Antony and Cleopatra*: Tragedy without Terror', *SQ*, 16 (1965), 188. See also Maurice Charney, *Shakespeare's Roman Plays: The Function of Imagery in the Drama* (Cambridge, Mass., 1961), pp. 79 ff.

6. Sir Philip Sidney, *An Apologie for Poetrie*, in *Elizabethan Critical Essays*, ed. G. Gregory Smith (London, 1904), I, 199. For a more extreme statement, see George Whetstone's 'Dedication to *Promos and Cassandra*', Smith, I, 58–60.

7. 'The Roman Plays', in *Shakespeare: The Writer and His Work*, ed. Bonamy Dobrée (London, 1964), p. 314.

8. From an interview entitled 'Mr. Shaw on Heroes', signed A. D, *Liverpool Post*, 19 Oct. 1927, quoted by Gordon W. Couchman in '*Antony and Cleopatra* and the Subjective Convention', *PMLA*, 76 (1961), 421.

9. *The Dialogues of Plato*, trans. Benjamin Jowett (New York, 1937), I, 860.

10. 'Better than Shakespear?' Preface to *Three Plays for Puritans*, in *Prefaces by Bernard Shaw* (London, 1934), p. 716; also quoted by Couchman, p. 420.

11. *Prefaces to Shakespeare* (Princeton, 1946), I, 440.

12. The critics illustrate the ambivalence. Virgil K. Whitaker argues in *The Mirror up to Nature: The Technique of Shakespeare's Tragedies* (San Marino, Calif., 1965), p. 295, that since Cleopatra 'has been established as a consummate and habitual actress from the first scene', the audience remains sceptical 'of her heroics' at the end. Like Shaw, Whitaker combines a distaste for Cleopatra with a dislike for the play as a whole. In direct contrast, Robert Ornstein argues in 'The Ethnic of the Imagination: Love and Art in *Antony and Cleopatra*', in *Later Shakespeare*, ed. John Russell Brown and Bernard Harris, Stratford-upon-Avon Studies, No. 8 (London, 1966), pp. 44–5, that 'the artist in Cleopatra . . . stirs Shakespeare's deepest imaginative sympathies and . . . receives the immeasurable bounty of his artistic love'.

13. See, e.g., Granville-Barker, 1, 435–40 and Guy Boas, 'The Influence of the Boy-Actor on Shakespeare's Plays', *Contemporary Review*, 152 (1937), 74–7.

14. *Apologie*, pp. 155–6.

15. *Apologie*, pp. 184–5.

16. *Apologie*, pp 197.

17. *Apologie*, pp. 160, 161, 157.

18. Cf. the similar relationship in *MV* between Portia's Venetian 'disguise' as a boy and her Belmont 'reality' as a girl. Here, too, the rationalistic brazen world within the play demands a disguise which conforms to the reality of Shakespeare's London, while the imaginative golden world in the play presents an actuality which is identical with the illusion presented on Shakespeare's stage.

19. Arden edition, p. 281.

20. Charney, p. 135.

21. Charney, p. 135.

22. If we follow Schmidt in preferring the Folio punctuation of the first line ('yet, the'), the message is positively obsequious.

23. See Arden edition, pp. xlv–xlvii; Elmer Edgar Stoll, *Shakespeare Studies* (New York, 1927), p. 143; and Brents Stirling, 'Cleopatra's Scene with Seleucus: Plutarch, Daniel, and Shakespeare', *SQ*, 15 (1964), 299–311.

24. See Arden edition, pp. 283–4: 'There was a young gentleman Cornelius Dolabella, that was one of Caesars very great familiars, and besides did beare no evil will unto Cleopatra. He sent her word secretly as she had requested him, that Caesar determined to take his jorney through Suria, and that within three dayes he would sende her away before with her children.'

25. Matthew N. Proser, *The Heroic Image in Five Shakespearean Tragedies* (Princeton, NJ, 1965), pp. 181–2, argues that Cleopatra's language here dislodges Antony from the world of mundane forms and raises him to "Platonic" proportions: "Platonic" in the sense of the *Symposium*, where art brings to birth new forms which mirror and immortalise the artist-lover and the beloved'. J. A. Bryant, Jr., *Hippolyta's View: Some Christian Aspects of Shakespeare's Plays* (Lexington, 1961), p. 183, sees the process as a miraculous redemption 'such as only a Christian poet can understand'. Other critics, like John Middleton Murry, *Shakespeare* (London, 1936), pp. 359–61, emphasise the imaginative and dreamlike qualities of the speech.

26. 'The Purging of Cleopatra', *ShN*, 9–10 (Dec. 1959– Feb. 1960), 9.

27. On the significance of the basket, cf. Charney, pp. 99–100.

28. Cf. Caesar's description of a noble Roman diet (I. iv. 55–71).

29. Noted by R. H. Case, Arden edition, p. 230, n.

4

'King Lear' and 'Antony and Cleopatra': The Language of Love

TERENCE HAWKES

Language may be man's distinctive means of communication, yet traditionally it is surpassed by love. Love's goal is utter communion: the merging of two human beings into one. Such unity makes language redundant. To the outside world, lovers are blind, deaf and dumb.

No doubt this presents an indealised and unrealistic picture, and the extent to which actuality fails to match it provides a constant theme for art. Lovers who betray each other, love itself which falls short of total physical and spiritual merging, the alienating demands of lust, all offer large subjects of concern.

If man can be regarded as a creature 'designed' to communicate with others, one for whom 'reality' resides only in that activity, then a deficiency in the capacity to love must prove seriously diminishing. To resist the ultimate 'merging' with others, to retain singularity, to remain inviolable, is finally to reject communication itself, and so community.

For an oral society, with its vested interest in reciprocation at all levels, this represents a serious subversion. And a special odium remains traditionally reserved for those who abrogate mutuality in this sphere; who offer trust in order to betray, 'love' that they may satisfy lust. Traditionally the acts of villains, these also rank as less than human.

In respect of the reciprocities of love itself, the nature of the debasement takes classic form in the imposition on them of the standards of another 'lower' kind of human interaction.

The exchange of money, buying, selling, and negotiating, is a human activity of a communicative sort. Indeed, it acts as a kind of 'language' in which counters, coins, notes, goods, are interchanged on the basis of set conventions, to enable a society to apportion and divide the work requisite for its existence. The language of money is as necessary to society (and thus to human life) as the language of love. Both can claim involvement at their different levels in the procreation of life which ensures the society's continued existence. Yet our scale of values is such that we place these activities at opposite extremes, in the sense that we require them to inhabit areas whose moral assumptions we judge to be mutually exclusive. And although financial interaction is as 'natural' to human beings as the sort of interaction we term 'love', any activity which connects them incurs a deep distaste. Money and love are traditionally 'opposed' in our culture. One can marry for love, or for money, never for both.

If love represents the highest point of interaction, prostitution – in its largest sense, with reference to a range of human behaviour far beyond that of the girl on the streets – represents the lowest. And the odium it incurs is the greater because its *modus operandi* is spuriously to invoke its opposite. 'Love' of one kind poses as love of another; the least good pretends to be the best. When the values of money obtrude on those of love, the process seems deeply inappropriate, mocking, and reductive. The Faustus legend gains much of its permanent applicability from the fact that its protagonist puts a price on that which is priceless.

If we now turn to those two mature plays of Shakespeare's most concerned with human interaction in the form of love, it will be seen that they naturally tend to explore the situation in terms of the gigantic 'interactive' instrument of language; in particular in terms of the language of 'love' itself.

I

The first scene of *King Lear* has been described as improbable. Lear's disturbing question 'How much do you love me?' has been called imponderable and improper. And his proffered 'equation' – so much love 'equals' so much land – probably ranks as immoral. Yet somehow these negative epithets, 'improbable', 'imponderable', 'improper', 'immoral' fail to capture the scene's immense positivity, the sense that its concern is with matters fundamental to human existence. Lear's 'darker purpose' evokes a complex response in performance. It is as if his question probed us to the core.

In fact the first scene of the play probes nothing less than the nature of love. And it does so by means of a simple, stark confrontation between the language of love and the language of money.

Of course a similar confrontation also occupies the play at the level of character and theme, with the spiritual quality of Cordelia's love pitted against the material gains for which Goneril and Regan vie, as well as at a symbolic level where the divisive forces of ambition tear asunder the unity of family and kingdom. But the subtlest probing of the issue seems initially to take place in terms of the actual words used by the participants in this first scene; particularly the word *love* itself. The two distinct, almost opposite meanings which this word could carry at the time the play was written suggest, in miniature, the movement of the whole piece.

The *Oxford English Dictionary* gives as a developed meaning of *Love*, v.² (OE. *lofian* 'praise') 'to appraise, estimate or state the price or value of'. This is an entirely different word in origin and phonetic history from *Love*, v.¹ (OE. *lufian*), and was not originally a homophone of it. Its normal development to [lɔː v] is shown by the sixteenth-century spelling *loave*; but there are fourteenth- and fifteenth-century spellings, *louve*, and *lowf*, which indicate a raising of the vowel as may be found before v in several words.¹ The apparent development of *Love*, v.² into a homophone of *Love*, v.¹ by this process – whether or not followed by shortening – would make possible the punning use quoted by the *Dictionary* from the *Towneley Mysteries*, in which the meaning of 'to estimate the value of' is made to intrude on the more usual 'to feel affection for'. The pun as used in this particular situation might be said to acquire something of an archetypal nature, for it is Judas who is asked how much he *loves* Jesus Christ. In the punning sense his answer is inevitable:

> **Pilatus** Now, Iudas, sen he shalbe sold,
>   how *lowfes* thou hym? belyfe let se.
> **Iudas** ffor thretty pennys truly told
>   or els may not that bargan be
>   (xx, 238 ff.)

As late as 1530 this use of *love* is recognised in John Palsgrave's

Lesclaircissement de la Langue Francoyse, in the English-to-French section of a 'Table of Verbes':

> I love, as a chapman loveth his ware that he wyll sell. *Je fais.* Come of, howe moche love you it at: *sus, combien le faictiez vous?* I love you it nat so dere as it coste me: . . . I wolde be gladde to bye some ware of you, but you love all thynges to dere . . .[2]

This sense does not appear in any dictionary after 1530, but seems to have been singled out for close attention here. It seems fair to say, then, that this other verb *to love*, with its clearly defined meaning, was well known at this time, and probably for some time afterwards.

In his book *Words and Sounds in English and French* (Oxford, 1953), Professor John Orr writes of a homonymic 'collision' which took place between the Old French verbs *esmer* and *aimer*. In the evolution of the French language, says Orr, *esmer* 'to reckon, calculate', although later replaced by the modern *priser*, nevertheless tended, in the final states before *priser* supplanted it, to invade the 'psychological field' of *aimer* 'to love'. To illustrate his point he quotes from the *Roman de Brut* by Wace (one of the sources of the *Lear* story and significantly very like Holinshed's version).[3] Cordelia, disgusted at her sister's flattery, answers, when asked by her father how much she loves him:

> Mes peres iés, jo aim tant tei
> Com jo mun pere amer dei.
> E pur faire tei plus certein,
> Tant as, tant vals e jo tant t'aim.
> (1739 ff.)

The apparent translation of this last line is 'so much you have, so much you are worth, and so much I love you'. But Orr goes on to show that the line has the status of a recognisable proverbial saying, in the manner of a pun, where the equivocation is between *aimer* 'to love' and the similarly pronounced *esmer* 'to estimate the value of'. So the punning translation of this line becomes 'So much you have, so much you are worth, *of such a price (or value) you are to me*'.

Thus the fact that there was a homonymic intrusion of *esmer* into the psychological field of *aimer* is established. It persists in the use of *aimer cher* in the Old and Middle French period, cognate with English 'to love dearly'. Palsgrave and the other evidence of *O.E.D.* shows that a similar intrusion, of the sense of *lofian* into the field of *lufian*, was possible in English at this time.[4]

It is generally accepted that Holinshed's *Chronicles* were among Shakespeare's sources for *King Lear*. Holinshed's version of Cordelia's reply to Lear in the 'division' scene is almost exactly taken from Wace:

> ... I protest vnto you that I haue loued you euer, and will continuallie (while I liue) loue you as my naturall father. And if you would more vnderstand of the loue that I beare you, assertaine your selfe, that *so much as you haue, so much you are worth, and so much I loue you and no more.*[5]

Whether the pun is intended in this version of the line mentioned above is not apparent. But linguistically it is implicit in the two senses of *love* whether Holinshed meant it to be there or not.

Shakespeare's grasping of the potentialities of the pun upon *love*, whether or not from Holinshed, can be detected without doubt in *King Lear*. Not surprisingly, Goneril's *love* presents a fairly precise, tabulated catalogue in the manner of an 'estimate':

> Sir, I love you more than word can wield the matter,
> Dearer than eyesight, space, and liberty;
> Beyond what can be valued rich or rare;
> No less than life, with grace, health, beauty, honour;
> As much as child e'er loved or father found;
> A love that makes breath poor and speech unable;
> Beyond all manner of so much I love you.
> (I. i. 56–62)

It is left to Regan to colour this estimate in terms of money, which she does with an image of coinage:

> I am made of that self metal as my sister,
> And prize me at her worth. . . .
> (I. i. 68–9)

Cordelia's remark at a very early stage in the proceedings has indicated her absolute rejection of the concept of *love* as an expressible 'value'. She seizes on the notion that the largest and truest sense of *love* implies something impossible to conceive of and 'estimate or state the value of' in any terms. Discarding the punning use of the other verb *to love* which her sisters have offered to Lear, she says 'What shall Cordelia speak? Love, and be silent' (I. i. 63). Her reply to the king comes with all the force of Wace's play:

> . . . I love your majesty
> According to my bond; no more nor less.
>
> (I. i. 93)

If we now turn to the beginning of the play we notice that love of one sort or another permeates the language from the start, and that the significance of these two opposed punning meanings thus takes on a kind of centrality in the action.[6] In fact a bewilderment about Lear's 'loving' and its vagaries prompts Kent's observation to Gloucester, which is the play's first line:

> I thought the King had more affected the Duke of Albany than Cornwall.
>
> (I. i. 1)

Lear's 'affection' and its nature remain of crucial importance throughout, and Gloucester's reply hints at its most alarming quality:

> It did always seem so to us; but now in the division of the kingdom, it appears not which of the dukes he values most, for equalities are so weighed that curiosity in neither can make choice of either's moiety.
>
> (I. i. 3 ff.)

Lear's 'valuing' of the dukes is an instance of his 'affection' at its most divisive, his 'love' at its most 'estimating'. He has 'loved' them, Gloucester is saying, at equal weight. Each has been assigned a 'moiety' of land and money in accordance with Lear's assessment. His subsequent attempt to gauge the 'love' of his daughters is here prefigured as an attempt to impose the values of one sort of love on those of another: to set a price on that which should be priceless.

At this point, Kent suddenly appears to change the subject. He notices Edmund:

> Is not this your son, my Lord?
>
> (I. i. 8)

Of course the subject has not been changed so much as ironically reinforced in another key. For Edmund is a child of love; at least, of the act which bears that name. And Gloucester's attitude towards him, and towards the circumstances of his birth, reveals a good deal:

> His breeding, sir, hath been at my charge. I have so often blushed to acknowledge him that now I am brazed to it.
>
> (I. i. 9 ff.)

It reveals an attitude towards love at once no less reprehensible than
that of Lear, and cognate with it. If Lear imposes an improper
linguistic 'shrinking' upon love, making it a matter of money and
land, Gloucester imposes on it the equally improper reductions of
mere lust and levity. As he says, 'though this knave came something
saucily to the world before he was sent for, yet was his mother fair,
there was good sport at his making, and the whoreson must be
acknowledged' (I. i. 21 ff.).

Both Gloucester and Lear thus deny love its full range of demands
and they rank as unmoved, unresponsive, single individuals in a
society which requires them above others to be the opposite. Both
apply to their respective situations a reduced notion of human
relationships which proves literally, as well as metaphorically, illegitimate. Edmund, the 'natural' in the sense of 'illegitimate' child,
dedicates himself thereafter to an unredeemed Nature whose com-
pulsions prove as positively destructive in respect of human community as the actions of Lear's 'unnatural' daughters. Both Lear and
Gloucester are shown from the beginning to be merely 'users' and
'assessors' of people for their own pleasure. Such 'use' or 'assessment' stands condemned in this play as 'love' of one very limited
kind.

And it is not until both Gloucester and Lear are purged of this
'estimating' kind of love that they can admit the existence of another
sort. For Gloucester, this involves a rejection of worldly, material
values, symbolised first by the loss of the sight which formerly made
him 'blind', and later by a complete renunciation of the 'assessable'
visual world:

> This world I do renounce, and in your sight
> Shake patiently my great affliction off.
> (IV. vi. 35–6)

His 'fall' from the cliff results in a new life, as well as a new concept
of love ushered in by his meeting with Lear in the fourth Act.

Lear's irrationality in this scene (IV. vi), itself a liberation from a
hitherto excessively rational, 'measuring' state of mind, gives his
language a width of reference far beyond the events he actually
encounters on the stage. Significantly, his words centre on love,
offering to Gloucester, as to all men, a broad and all-embracing
acceptance:

> What was thy cause?
> Adultery?
> Thou shalt not die: die for adultery! No!
>   (IV. vi. 111–13)

The 'pardon' comes, notably, not because the sin is now condoned, but because Lear's new 'loving' refuses to assess or measure it, recognising in it a common compulsion, and so a matter for larger compassion:

> The wren goes to 't and the small gilded fly
> Does lecher in my sight.
> Let copulation thrive; for Gloucester's bastard son
> Was kinder to his father than my daughters
> Got 'tween the lawful sheets.
>   (IV. vi. 114–18)

The observation is wry, not bitter, in its refusal to distinguish between 'legitimate' and 'illegitimate' loving, and it suggests a much more expanded response to life than that of the play's first scene. Noting Gloucester's blindness, Lear sees in it both the image of the sin whose punishment it represents, and the complementary image of its possible redemption:

> I remember thine eyes well enough. Dost thou squiny at me? No, do thy worst, blind Cupid. . . .
>
>   (IV. vi. 138 ff.)

The figure of 'blind Cupid' juxtaposes instantaneously the sin, its consequence, and the means of redemption appropriate to it. For Gloucester has sinned against love of one sort in the name of 'love' of another sort, and the reference is not only to the painted sign of 'blind cupid' traditionally said to be hung outside brothels – and so to Gloucester's own fornication – but also to the punishment of his own 'blindness' and ultimately to the God of Love which his redeemed person now suggests. As Edgar says to Edmund at the end of the play:

> The Gods are just, and of our pleasant vices
> Make instruments to plague us:
> The dark and vicious place where thee he got
> Cost him his eyes.
>   (V. iii. 172–5)

By means of that purgation, Gloucester has moved from the realm of one sort of Cupid to that of another; from a false, merely visual, and so 'painted' love, to its real 'seeing' counterpart which in his blindness he paradoxically embodies. He stumbled when he saw.

Lear, too, has changed. His hand now 'smells of mortality', and he assures Gloucester that 'I'll not love' (IV. vi. 140). He refers to his former way of 'loving' – associated here as before with Gloucester's physical lust – which involved simple measurement in physical terms so reductive that they could diminish the complexities of an oral culture to the merely visual dimension of a map crudely divided into three parts.

Of course, by this time Lear has undergone a purgative, literally maddening experience in which such 'loving' has been applied to himself. His 'needs' in respect of the body of knights necessary for him to retain his 'kingly' way of life have been assessed by his daughters much as he formerly assessed theirs, in terms of calculable number. And as their 'loving' has progressively diminished that number, he has experienced the bitterness evidenced in his shattering comment to Goneril about Regan:

> Thy fifty yet doth double five and twenty
> And thou art twice her love.
> (II. iv. 258–9)

Now love of that 'estimating' sort has been replaced in him by love of a larger kind. His super-rational 'madness', cognate with Gloucester's 'seeing' blindness, represents the price Lear has had to pay for that love in a world where sanity and sight and the sort of 'loving' in which they deal are very restricted and restricting affairs indeed.

That world, of course, derives from and relates to the post-Renaissance world experienced by Shakespeare himself. It is one in which, as Karl Manheim describes it, 'quantity and calculation' inexorably became the basis of a 'new ideal of knowledge' wholly dissociated from 'personalities and concrete communities':

> This 'quantitative' rationalist form of thought was possible because it arose as part of a new spiritual attitude and experience of things which may be described as 'abstract' . . . A symptom of this change is the . . . tendency to 'quantify' nature. . . . With the substitution of a system of commodity production for a subsistence economy there takes place a similar change in the attitude towards things as in the change-over from qualitative to quantitative thinking about nature. Here too the quantitative conception of exchange value replaces the qualitative

conception of use value. In both cases therefore the abstract attitude of which we have been speaking prevails. It is an attitude which gradually comes to include all forms of human experience. In the end, even the 'other man' is experienced abstractly. In a patriarchal or feudal world the 'other man' is somehow regarded as a self-contained unit, or at least as a member of an organic community. In a society based on commodity production, he too is a commodity, his labour-power a calculable magnitude with which one reckons as with all other quantities. The result is that as capitalist organisation expands, man is increasingly treated as an abstract calculable magnitude, and tends more and more to experience the outside world in terms of these abstract relations.[7]

It is a world easily recognisable as the forerunner of our own. Nevertheless, in the teeth of it, and as a comment on it, Lear's new-found love proves one in which the 'other man's' concrete reality finds full affirmation. It is a love, at last, which refuses to assess, to measure, to apportion praise or blame in any abstract mode:

> None does offend, none, I say, none.
> (IV. vi. 170)

The argument of the play seems finally to affirm a faith in this kind of 'loving' negation. Both Cordelia's 'Nothing' and Lear's 'None' represent, in the end, the same refusal to take part in that inhuman process of division, that improper degree of 'assessment', that impertinent and preposterous form of 'loving' which formerly characterised Lear's way of life. Such negativity represents perhaps the only proper rejoinder to the abstract quantifying of a world whose most fitting epigraph, then as now, is Lear's own earlier calculation: 'Nothing will come of nothing' (I. i. 92). Rejection of that mechanistic prospect, and deliverance from the aridity of its equations, can only come about, *King Lear* seems to say, through an ultimate compassionate recognition of the unity of human life and of the interdependence of the language, the culture, and the kingdom which then comprised it.

The sort of love which reinforces the faith that something *can* come of nothing, and which refuses to be divided, 'estimated' and assessed in accordance with a merely 'visual' quantification of land and money-values, may itself be said to be divinely blind in the way of those who genuinely 'see'. And its 'blindness' must serve to reinforce its mutuality with the non-visual nature of the words in which it is expressed.

For if mechanistic thinking is rejected, so is mechanistic language, abstracted by a false 'objectivity' and 'clarity' from its speaker's living being. It is replaced by the kind of unity in which speech itself inherently deals, particularly in the form of the homonym. To establish an argument, as poets of this period characteristically do, by pun and by analogy, is endemic in an oral society. The pun on 'love' manifests and resolves, orally and aurally, the division *King Lear* probes. In so doing it sheds its own valuable light on the nature both of the art form itself and of the audience towards which it is directed.

II

The relationship between *King Lear* and *Antony and Cleopatra* is often misconceived because of certain critical presuppositions about the nature of the latter play. Most of these find themselves crystallised in Dryden's version of the same subject, *All for Love or The World Well Lost*. The title itself gives a sense of the degree of sentimentality generated in that play by the trite distinction it proposes between 'all' on the one hand, and 'love' on the other. And it may, not unfairly, exemplify the kind of unthinking preconception that a casual reading of *Antony and Cleopatra* often involves. Happily, Shakespeare's play is of a subtler order.

In fact, it proves a work of high complexity, probing and testing the values and the language of love in a variety of ways to reach a more complex view of the world we live in, and of the intricacies of those communicative means which serve us both to shape and to apprehend it.

Antony's tragedy derives, like Dryden's, from an assumption that a choice has to be made between mutually exclusive opposites. In this, he resembles Lear.

But the action of *Shakespeare's* play provides a clear illustration of the falsity of that imagined choice by virtue of the very mode in which it casts Antony's perception of the proposed central distinction between Egypt and Rome. It is not that 'love' resides in Egypt, 'all' in Rome, or some such sentimental disposition of the demands of existence, but that the distinction itself is a false one, because too readily reductive of the complications of human experience. Life demands no uncompounded choice between Egypt and Rome, 'love' and 'all'. It would be simple if it did.

It has been argued that man is the talking animal. But nobody just talks. Man does not communicate by words alone, and complex combinations of voice and body, sounds and gestures, contrive to form in us a total multi-stranded apparatus finally inclusive of a wide range of activities. Over-simple 'divisions' of this communicative structure serve only to mislead and confuse.

And yet the distinction maintained in *Antony and Cleopatra* between Egypt and Rome seems to be precisely of this order. It ascribes to each location a simplistic notion of the nature of human language, and, cognately, bestows on each a simplistic concept of the nature of love itself. If man's communicative system depends, finally, on two interdependent units, voice and body, the play assigns voice alone to Rome, body alone to Egypt. Rome is a place of words, Egypt a place of actions. Rome is where love is talked of, Egypt is where love is made.

A powerful sense of 'reduction' can thus be felt to haunt even Cleopatra's first words in the play, particularly when we realise that her apparently lighthearted question is the self-same chilling demand that Lear put to his daughters:

> If it be love indeed, tell me how much.
> (I. i. 14)

Antony's response – and his first words in the play too – recalls Cordelia's:

> There's beggary in the love that can be reckoned
> (I. i. 15)

The spectres concerning the nature of loving explored in *King Lear* also stalk this play. And in the succeeding interchange

> **Cleopatra** I'll set a bourn how far to be beloved.
> **Antony** Then must thou needs find out new heaven, new earth
> (I. i. 16–17)

the crude 'assessing' limitations she proposes, the grandiosely im-measurable nature of his rejoinder, both point to the same tragic withering of genuine human proportion in matters of communica-tion that has manifested itself conspicuously in *Hamlet, Othello, Lear* and *Macbeth*.

The 'bourns' Cleopatra imposes on love will prove very confining indeed. They extend, in the event, to only half of what we are, for their limits are those of the body. And Antony finds himself accordingly committed to a way of life in which the body predominates; where, to use his own memorable phrase,

> . . . The nobleness of life
> Is to do thus.
>
>   (I. i. 36–7)

At this, he embraces Cleopatra.

Many critics have commented on the play's sense of universality. Una Ellis-Fermor felt this to be a matter of the pervading feeling of 'space', and Granville-Barker termed it 'the most spacious of the plays'.[8] A kind of encircling amplitude certainly seems to inform the action. In its vivid *montage* of places and people, love and death, the play appears to embrace the whole known world. To go beyond its limits would indeed apparently require a new heaven and a new earth.

But on another level, that same sense of 'embracing', of encircling in close physical contact, may be said to give rise to an opposite, claustrophobic effect. It is as if, despite the play's clamour, we and it remain no less obstinately tied down to this old earth and its older heaven. *Antony and Cleopatra*'s amplitude does not prevent it from looking inward as much as outward.

Philo's opening words have already pointed out that Antony's eyes, formerly famed as overt, outward-directed emblems of hostility, which

> . . . o'er the files and musters of the war
> Have glowed like plated Mars
>
>   (I. i. 3–4)

now 'bend, now turn' embracingly on Cleopatra. His 'captain's heart', inured to violent physical combat, and the 'scuffles of great fights' (l. 8) has also 'turned' to take up a smaller, circular, repetitive function as the bellows and the fan to heat and to cool a gypsy's lust. In Egypt, we quickly discover, close physical, tactile, 'embracing' contact constitutes the mode of everyday existence. Space there may be, but it exists to be constantly encircled and filled by willing flesh.

In effect, Antony's embrace of Cleopatra turns out to be paradigmatic. At that moment when their bodies unite on the stage, the word 'thus' and its concomitant gesture stand for 'embrace', the totality of the Egyptian way life life. For the rest –

> Kingdoms are clay; our dungy earth alike
> Feeds beast as man.
>
> (I. i. 35–6)

The reduction is staggering. Animals can 'do thus' as well as man, and unless man is to be accounted merely a beast, there must be more to him than 'thus' allows. To embrace is also to enclose, to restrict. Even Cleopatra recognises the depth of the implied degradation. But it is an 'excellent falsehood!' (I. i. 40), and if life were really of this order, it would be wonderfully simple.

In fact, every effort is made to *make* life that simple in Egypt; a simple matter of the body alone, of sexual coupling, of doing 'thus' and little else. The beds in the east are soft. There, 'the love of Love and her soft hours' clashes only with the 'conference harsh' of Rome (I. i. 45–6). There, the intensest kind of bodily communion prevails. Antony's blush (I. i. 30) 'speaks' volumes. Hands, not words, are 'read' (I. ii). The tactile potential of figs, 'oily' palms and 'inches' is idly and lengthily discussed (I. ii. 32 ff.), and the senses are drugged with mandragora (I. v. 3). In fact, Cleopatra and her attendants tend to use language itself not so much as a vehicle for rational discourse, but rather as a physically luxurious thing, part of a totality of sensuous indulgence in which all events rank as potential sources of bodily pleasure. Thus even a messenger charged with the office of simple verbal communication is urged alarmingly to

> Ram thou thy fruitful tidings in mine ears,
> That long time have been barren.
>
> (II. v. 23–4)

In short, in Egypt, Cleopatra seems to inhabit a virtually 'non-verbal' sphere more closely connected with unredeemed Nature than with its civilised human analogue:

> We cannot call her winds and waters sighs and tears; they are greater storms and tempests than almanacs can report.
>
> (I. ii. 150 ff.)

It is a world in which spatial, gestural relationships 'speak' potently, however silently:

> **Cleopatra** Pray you, stand farther from me.
> **Antony** What's the matter?
> **Cleopatra** I know by that same eye there's some good news . . .
>
> (I. iii. 18–20)

– a world of tastes, textures and perfumes where the visitor finds

> . . . Epicurean cooks
> Sharpen with cloyless sauce his appetite.
> (II. i. 24–5)

and what Pompey slyly calls 'your fine Egyptian cookery' on which Julius Caesar 'Grew fat with feasting' (II. vi. 62–4). Mere discourse, promises, 'mouth-made vows / Which break themselves in swearing' (I. iii. 30–1) count for little in an atmosphere in which the body deals in its own language-disdaining futurity, where lovers find that

> Eternity was in our lips and eyes,
> Bliss in our brows' bent, none our parts so poor
> But was a race of heaven.
> (I. iii. 35–7)

In short, the language of love in Egypt is the silent language of the body, whose covert meanings softly usurp overt utterance, however exotic. In performance, the spatial relationship between the actors' bodies must be a good deal closer in the Egyptian scenes than in those set in Rome. Significant and suggestive groupings, gestures, winks and nods are obviously called for to communicate their full ambience.[9] How else could Cleopatra's account of Antony,

> His delights
> Were dolphin-like, they showed his back above
> The element they lived in
> (V. ii. 88–90)

aptly deliver its meaning? Words alone are held in little regard: discursive speech seems to be a Roman vice. As Cleopatra curses when Enobarbus alleges that her presence 'puzzles' Antony:

> Sink Rome, and their tongues rot
> That speak against us.
> (III. vii. 15–16)

As the messenger discovers, a normal talking-listening interchange is out of the question in this atmosphere. Cleopatra's 'conversation' proves almost entirely a matter of physical, not verbal, encounter, with blows being struck, knives drawn, hands kissed, and a haling up and down. Her obsession with Octavia's physical appearance, her

size, shape, posture and gait (see also III. iii. 14 ff.) overrides any
other consideration:

> Bring me word how tall she is. – Pity me Charmian,
> But do not speak to me.
>   (II. v. 118–19)

Even at the edge of disaster, Antony grandiloquently 'rates' tears and
kisses beyond all military losses,

> Fall not a tear, I say; one of them rates
> All that is won and lost. Give me a kiss;
> Even this repays me.
>   (III. xi. 69–71)

And later, in pursuit of the final 'gaudy night' which presages defeat,
his gestures must 'speak' as much as the words in lines like these:

> Come on, my queen
> There's sap in't yet! The next time I do fight
> I'll make death love me for I will contend
> Even with his pestilent scythe.
>   (*Exeunt*)
>   (III. xiii. 191–4)

Antony's body, his 'inches', thus carry more weight in Egypt than his
protestations. His words of sorrow at Fulvia's death (in the face of
Cleopatra's cynical sexual pun, 'Can Fulvia die?') only meet demands for physical signals as proof that such sorrow exists:

> O most false love!
> Where be the sacred vials thou shouldst fill
> With sorrowful water?
>   (I. iii. 63–4)

And when he wishes to leave her, Cleopatra catches him in one of
her embraces, and pursues her argument with positive bodily
movements:

> Cleopatra   Good now, play one scene
>   Of excellent dissembling, and let it look
>   Like perfect honour.
> Antony   You'll heat my blood: no more.
> Cleopatra You can do better yet; but this is meetly.
> Antony Now by my sword –
> Cleopatra   And target. Still he mends. . . .
>   (I. iii. 78–82)

The physical gestures which must accompany this interchange suggest themselves. Their importance to the play's theme can be gauged from the risk that this self-consciously takes of embarrassing or distracting the audience in a theatre in which women's parts were played by boys. Like most of the contemporary dramatists, Shakespeare rarely permits much physical contact between men and 'women' on the stage for this reason. Morever, the 'theatrical' references to 'playing' a sexual 'scene' draw covert attention to Cleopatra's actual maleness just when her virtual 'female' wiles are seen at their overt height. The 'reminder' here that 'she' is a boy focuses an 'alienated' and so powerfully reiterated attention on the physical nature of her relationship with Antony.

This scene ends, incidentally, with Antony's breaking away from Cleopatra's attempt to make him 'do thus', and her archly botched effort, as a last resort, to use words to reach him:

> Courteous lord, one word,
> Sir, you and I must part, but that's not it:
> Sir, you and I have loved, but there's not it:
> That you know well. Something it is I would –
> O my oblivion is a very Antony,
> And I am all forgotten.
>   (I. iii. 86–91)

Mere words, she seems to argue with contrived pathos, are not her medium.

Of course, she is right. Enobarbus's famous evocation of her rests on that premiss. She embodies the senses, and 'embracing', nothing discursive:

> . . . the poop was beaten gold;
> Purple the sails, and so perfumed that
> The winds were lovesick with them; the oars were silver
> Which, to the tune of flutes kept stroke and made
> The water which they beat to follow faster,
> As amorous of their strokes. . . .
>   (II.ii. 198–203)

Perhaps the 'beggary' that inheres in 'the love that can be reckoned' finds itself mirrored in her word-defeating person which 'beggared all description'. Even her colour (she is 'with Phoebus' amorous pinches black' [I. v. 28]) suggests 'embracing', and her gustatory qualities receive constant mention:

> . . . other women cloy
> The appetites they feed, but she makes hungry
> Where most she satisfies.
>
> (II. ii. 242–4)

She is a 'morsel for a monarch' (I. v. 31) 'Salt Cleopatra' (II. i. 21) Antony's 'Egyptian dish' (II. vi. 126), her proper tribute a wordless admiration:

> great Pompey
> Would stand and make his eyes grow in my brow;
> There would he anchor his aspect, and die
> With looking on his life.
>
> (I. v. 31–4)

Unfortunately, the play strongly hints, just as 'death' (in its punning meaning of sexual climax) ends embracing, so (in its ordinary meaning) does it end a life based on that limited and limiting activity. The play exploits the pun on death at length, to make this point. Of a way of life whose 'nobleness' resides in 'doing thus' with such frequency Enobarbus can rightly say

> I do think there is mettle in death, which commits some loving act upon her, she hath such a celerity in dying.
>
> (I. ii. 143 ff.)

There his meaning was overtly sexual. At the play's end, after a last drawn-out and ultimately ludicrous 'embrace' from Antony, to achieve which he has been heaved 'aloft' to her side with cries of 'Here's sport' and 'How heavy weighs my lord' and 'O come, come come. . . . Die where thou hast lived' (IV. xv. 33 ff.), she finds 'Immortal longings' in her own body, discovers that

> The stroke of death is as a lover's pinch,
> Which hurts, and is desired.
>
> (V. ii. 295–6)

– and the pun's final irony becomes explicit. A life based on the body alone, on physical love-making, on doing 'thus' as its sole end, finds nothing at its conclusion but a grimmer version of the 'death' it has punningly sought many times. Embracing, as a way of life, proves ultimately sterile, meaningless, only half human. So Cleopatra's physical death mocks her many sexual 'deaths'. She dies fondling the phallic asp, whose vulgar symbolism has been fully exploited by the

Clown. Many women have indeed 'died' of this worm. So her death fittingly takes on an orgasmic dimension:

> As sweet as balm, as soft as air, as gentle –
> O Antony! . . .
>
> (V. ii. 311–12)

It is not insignificant that Antony, enveloped in this atmosphere, should seal his projected alliance with Caesar with an embrace and a phrase that ironically recalls it:

> . . . Tis spoken well.
> Were we before our armies, and to fight,
> I should do thus.
>
> (II. ii. 25–7)

He meets his own death, not surprisingly, in sexual terms, resolving to be

> A bridegroom in my death, and run into't
> As to a lover's bed.
>
> (IV. xiv. 100–1)

And he falls in suggestive mockery of the sexual 'embrace' on his sword, symbol of his potency, claiming, to the aptly named Eros that

> . . . To do thus
> I learned of thee.
> (102–3)

He has been one kind of love's apt pupil, but its life of 'embracing' and of orgasmic 'dying' has brought about a course of disaster which leads inevitably to death of a more final sort. And it leads, conclusively, to Caesar's apt epitaph which draws its irony from the finality, and grisly quality, of the very last 'embrace' the lovers enjoy:

> No grave upon the earth shall clip in it
> A pair so famous.
>
> (V. ii. 358–9)

Rome is Egypt's direct opposite in every way. If Egypt emphasises the body, one level of language, one sort of 'love', and the concomitant womanly powers of Cleopatra, Rome is a place of words, another level of language, another kind of love, and of a self-confident 'manly' prowess. Our first sight of Octavius Caesar (I. iv) shows him very much concerned with discursive verbal matters (he is reading a letter) and complaining of Antony's unmanly behaviour. He finds him

> . . . not more manlike
> Than Cleopatra, nor the queen of Ptolemy
> More womanly than he. . . .
>
> (I. iv. 5–7)

Rome is a place where precise distinctions are preferred, where men are men and women are women, each accorded a distinct role in the community. In fact Caesar evokes Antony's former 'manliness' in terms of his ability to stomach much more starkly unadulterated food than the exotic 'dishes', the 'lascivious wassails' he now encounters:

> ... Thy palate then did deign
> The roughest berry on the rudest hedge. . . .
>
> (I. iv. 63–4)

The scene in which Antony, Octavius, and Lepidus meet together to resolve their differences (II. ii) perhaps has the most distinctive Roman flavour. Formal spatial relationships prevail between them. They sit (and so remain in fixed positions throughout) and talk. They speak of relationships between politicians. The question of relationships between men and women only arises in connection with arrangements for a politically convenient marriage between Antony and Octavia. Interchanges such as this suggest the prevailing atmosphere:

> **Caesar** Speak, Agrippa.
> **Agrippa** Thou hast a sister by the mother's side,
>   Admired Octavia: great Mark Antony
>   Is now a widower.
> **Caesar**   Say not so, Agrippa:
>   If Cleopatra heard you, your reproof
>   Were well deserved of rashness.
> **Antony** I am not married, Caesar: let me hear
>   Agrippa further speak.
> **Agrippa**   . . . Pardon what I have spoke;
>   For 'tis a studied, not a present thought,
>   By duty ruminated.

Antony	Will Caesar speak?
Caesar	Not till he hears how Antony is touched

With what is spoke already.

(II. ii. 123–46)

'Speaking' not only dominates the communicative process of the seated men, but imposes its discursive mode of communication, perhaps, on an area of experience which Antony normally encounters by means of non-discursive action and bodily gesture. To speak of the institution of marriage in Rome, for reasons of policy, is the exact opposite of doing 'thus', illicitly in Egypt, for no 'reason' at all. In Rome, words 'speak' louder than actions, where the reverse is true of Egypt. In Rome, love is a word; in Egypt, love is a deed. And if Antony's 'Egyptian dish' offers love as sustenance for the body, his wife, we learn ominously, has opposite Roman virtues. As Enobarbus perhaps unkindly reminds us, she manifests 'a holy, cold, and still conversation' (II. vi. 122). Indeed, for both Antony and Cleopatra Rome is a place where life as they know it can only be parodied: where Antony would be 'windowed'

> . . . with pleached arms, bending down
> His corrigible neck, his face subdued
> To penetrative shame, whilst the wheeled seat
> Of fortunate Caesar, drawn before him, branded
> His baseness that ensued.
>
> (IV. xiv. 72–6)

and Cleopatra would see

> Some squeaking Cleopatra boy my greatness
> I' th' posture of a whore.
>
> (V. ii. 220–1)

The ironic reference these lines make to the maleness of the painted boy-actor who himself utters them on the stage, again induces a powerful 'alienation effect' at a crucial point in the play, which casts its own sardonic light on the limiting sexuality of the 'greatness' to which she lays claim. If death seems preferable to life in such circumstances, it clearly does so in the way that 'death' of a sexual sort provides release from the Roman world of words. Cleopatra surely speaks of both sorts of 'dying' when she recognises that 'Tis paltry to be Caesar' and therefore 'great'

To do that thing that ends all other deeds,
Which shackles accidents and bolts up change;
(V. ii. 5–6)

Since 'that thing' finally makes cognate the act of love and the act of
death, it can only claim to be as much, and so as little, as 'to do thus'.

III

Love and death perhaps represent opposite extremes of human experience. Where love implies the absolute and virtually complete
union of two formerly separate persons, death implies the reverse. Its
essence is loss of communication, and the experience itself, though
common to all humans, remains incommunicable. The act of love
creates life. Death literally defeats man's nature, and its victory can
be regarded either as fulfilment, or at another extreme, as violation.
In any event, it finally prevents man from being himself, where love,
perhaps, enables him to be most himself.

A good deal of the 'universality' which can be sensed in *King Lear*
and *Antony and Cleopatra* perhaps springs from the fact that both
love and death are fundamental concerns of both plays. Like all great
works of art, they span the range of human experience. And they do
so through the central image of man as the talking animal. In *King
Lear* the notion of man's communicative relationship with other men
proves fundamental to the play. As Maynard Mack remarks,

> Existence is tragic in *King Lear* because existence is inseparable from
> relation; we are born from and to it; it envelops us in our loves and
> lives as parents, children, sisters, brothers, husbands, wives, servants,
> masters, rulers, subjects – the web is seamless and unending. . . . There
> is no human action, Shakespeare shows us, that does not affect it and
> that it does not affect. Old, we begin our play with the need to impose
> relation – to divide our kingdom, set our rest on someone's kind
> nursery, and crawl toward our death. Young, we begin it with the
> need to respond to relation – to define it, resist it even in order to
> protect it, honour it, or destroy it. Man's tragic fate, as *King Lear*
> presents it, comes into being with his entry into relatedness, which is
> his entry into humanity.[10]

A particular concern with the language of love, and especially the
word 'love' itself, focuses attention on an aspect of that issue which
the body of *King Lear* develops fully. What, it asks, is the nature of
the relationship between human beings with regard to love? What

duties does it impose, what responses are required? By means of a careful juxtaposition of overt and covert 'meanings' of the word, dimensions of these questions are revealed, so that the play's larger action can explore them. The fundamental question, lying at the play's heart, can thus be approached: can love be measured? What can one reply to 'how much do you love me?' The simplest, and most honest reply must be Cordelia's 'nothing', and it is *King Lear*'s wonderfully fulfilled task to justify the apparent harshness it contains: to point out that such negation is the only reply worthy of love itself.

Antony and Cleopatra begins, in a sense, where *King Lear* ends. Death, which seemed so inexplicable and even unnecessary in the earlier play, here undergoes the same kind of probing that was formerly given to love and, significantly, in the same oral manner. Where *King Lear* explored a pun on 'love', *Antony and Cleopatra* explores a pun on 'death'. The two extremes, love and death, unite in speech. To 'die' becomes, punningly, to love. Conversely, to love is also to 'die', sexually in terms of the pun, psychologically in the sense that one 'loses' one's individual existence in another, and finally – almost as a 'natural' consequence – physically, in terms of the word's literal meaning: the lover's embrace prefigures that of the grave.

Thus the logic of these plays seems to locate 'loving' – the ultimate communicative activity as it has been argued – as central to man's nature, and requiring death in both senses to complete both that activity and that nature. Death, and its counterpart 'death', become the climax, the purpose, the focal point of a human existence whose mode is – must be – love. Love affirms reciprocation, and guarantees community. It lies at the heart of all societies, and is in the forefront of those which are oral. Antony's tragedy springs from his mistaken response to such a metaphor. In effect, he proves unable to grasp its unity, and improperly separates the elements of which it is composed. He remains unable to see, in the play's oral terms, that the two 'sides' of the pun on death are complementary, not opposed, in utterance. Like Dryden, Antony conceives of Egypt's 'love' as an 'all' that necessarily opposes Roman demands, and he ignores the complementary function of both places. Thus, like Lear, he violates the complex nature of language by means of reductive objectification and a simplistic and divisive insistence on unitary 'meaning'.

In short, if a 'tragic flaw' exists in Antony and Lear, it could be characterised as an inability – or refusal – to respond to the full social and moral complexity of oral language; especially the language of love. Shortcomings in this respect must inevitably rank as tragic. Where Lear insists on a narrow and exclusive meaning of the word 'love' itself, Antony bases a 'way of life', or joins a culture whose way of life is based on an equally narrow and exclusive meaning of the complementary word 'death'. Ultimately, what Lear means by 'love' – assessment – and what Antony means by 'death' – sexual climax – become coterminous as betrayals and diminutions of the larger 'meanings' of those words which circumstances inevitably thrust on them.

Where overt and covert usages of words themselves interact in a version of the oral-aural colloquy of the human beings who use and are shaped by them, Shakespeare's mature dramatic skill is literally heard at its most powerful. Life, these plays seem to say, is language; language life. Drama may often say less than that. It can say no more.

From Terence Hawkes, *Shakespeare's Talking Animals: Language and Drama in Society* (London, 1975), pp. 166–93.

NOTES

[Terence Hawkes's *Shakespeare's Talking Animals* represents one of the first serious attempts to bring together the study of Shakespeare and his contemporaries and a consideration of the influence of popular media theory, especially that of Marshall McLuhan. Throughout it is Hawkes's contention that the Elizabethan audiences who watched Shakespeare's plays were 'non-literate' and that they had developed skills of listening which have disappeared in literate cultures. Hawkes argues that the heir to the Elizabethan popular theatre is television, and that we can learn much from the techniques and structures of television which is of value in an appreciation of Shakespearean drama. Hawkes develops much further a particular strand of criticism, aware of popular culture, that was begun by S. L. Bethell in his book *Shakespeare and the Popular Tradition* (London, 1944), but he also develops a view of language and drama in society which owes much to early structuralist thinking, for example that of Claud Lévi-Strauss, as well as to the work of the late Raymond Williams. Ed.]

1. See E. J. Dobson, *English Pronunciation 1500–1700* (Oxford, 1957), p. 151 and n. 2.

2. Quoted from the Paris edition of 1852, p. 614.

3. See W. Perrett, *The Story of King Lear* (Berlin, 1904).

4. The existence of a punning connection of the two meanings of *love* for a length of time cannot be conclusively demonstrated, but it would be

ridiculous to suppose that immediately after the publication of *Lesclaircissement* the verb *Love*[2] fell out of use. Often examples of the equivocation crop up unexpectedly, such as in Marvell's *To His Coy Mistress:* 'An hundred years should go to praise / Thine eyes, and on thy forehead gaze. . . .' 'For lady you deserve this state, / Nor *would I love at lower rate.*' The connection of *love* and *rate* fairly invites the equivocal interpretation of *love* as 'value'.

5. Everyman edn. (London, 1927), p. 226.

6. Cf. Alfred Harbage's essay on *Lear*, 'The Fierce Dispute', in his *Conceptions of Shakespeare* (Harvard, 1966) pp. 77–98, which places 'love' as the central concern of the play, and concludes that 'no greater symbols have been offered anywhere of man's capacity of love, and need to love and be loved' (pp. 95–6).

7. Paul Kecskemeti (ed.), Karl Mannheim, *Essays on Sociology and Social Psychology* (London, 1953), pp. 86–7.

8. Una Ellis-Fermor, 'The Nature of Plot in Drama', *Essays and Studies*, 13 (1960), pp. 65–81. H. Granville-Barker, *Prefaces to Shakespeare, Second Series* (London, 1930), p. 111.

9. John Russell Brown's remarks on the use of gestures and 'business' in this play support this point of view, and contribute an excellent commentary. *Shakespeare's Plays in Performance* (London, 1966), pp. 40 ff.

10. Maynard Mack, *King Lear in Our Time* (Berkeley, Calif., 1965), pp. 110–11.

5

Jacobean 'Antony and Cleopatra'

H. NEVILLE DAVIES

When the New Penguin editor of *Antony and Cleopatra* comments, in the final paragraph of his introduction, on Shakespeare's play as an imperial work, he speculates about the possibility of there having been a performance by the King's Men at the court of James I. 'James was England's, or rather "Britain's", own modern Augustus', he reminds us,

> for whom Caesar's lines in the play –
>
> > The time of universal peace is near.
> > Prove this a prosperous day, the three-nooked world
> > Shall bear the olive freely –
>
> > > (IV. vi. 5–7)
>
> would have had special significance. James was himself an imperial, quasi-Augustan, peacemaker. So the British Augustus may have watched this Augustan tragedy.[1]

This valedictory speculation is my starting point and prompts me to wonder how, should such a court performance ever have taken place, the king (and others) are likely to have reacted. Certainly we ought not to assume that Shakespeare's royal patron must necessarily have been embarrassed, like a guilty Claudius at *The Tragedy of Gonzago*. Adrian Noble's Royal Shakespeare Company (RSC) studio production recently presented a commanding and passionate Octavius, strongly played by Jonathan Hyde, a performance in which James I could readily have taken pleasure. Peter Brook's RSC main house production in 1978 gave us Jonathan Pryce's memorable Octavius – a sensible, peace-loving man who never wears armour and whose warmhearted concern for his sister's well-being was movingly demonstrated in Act II, scene ii, when he acceded to the marriage proposal. The way Pryce paused and then said with marked emotion

> A sister I bequeath you whom no brother
> Did ever love so dearly
>
> (ll. 155–6)

ruled out any question of Octavia's being sacrificed to political expediency. But perhaps Pryce went too far. Such was the evident probity of his Octavius that when Act V came, it was difficult to take seriously Cleopatra's savagely spoken 'He words me, girls, he words me'. Before that production, there was Keith Baxter's genial Octavius at Chichester in 1969, which seems to have set something of a fashion for sympathetic Octaviuses on the English stage. Nevertheless, the age of universal peace that Octavius inaugurates inevitably promises to be less exciting than the mélange of 'high events' and 'garboils' that it replaces. With the deaths of Antony and Cleopatra

> The odds is gone,
> And there is nothing left remarkable
> Beneath the visiting moon.
>
> (IV. xv. 66–8)

And the deprivation is devastating, for without Cleopatra's voice we seem even to lack a speaker able to record the loss.

For James's contemporaries, too, a great age had recently passed with the death of Queen Elizabeth, and similarities have been observed between the behaviour of Shakespeare's lass, supposedly unparalleled, and Elizabeth that may reveal the dramatist's perception of a comparable diminishment.[2] James, however, while honouring his predecessor, as Caesar honours the 'pair so famous' in the final speech of the play, was more attentive to the garboils than to high events. The new order he envisaged was the Augustan one of peace, and the powerful appeal of that lofty vision is not permanently impaired by Shakespeare's backward glance. There is loss at the end of the play, but the irresponsibility of Antony and of Cleopatra is hardly an example for princes. Fortunately, though, irreconcilable states like stability and excitement can co-exist in art. So it is that the lovers become united in death as they never were in life, and an audience may imagine them hand in hand 'where souls do couch on flowers', while at the court of a new Augustus their story, with all its turmoil, could live in performance when government yielded to recreation.

But no matter how James might have reacted, it is inconceivable that a dramatist late in 1606, the time when Shakespeare is usually supposed to have been writing or planning his play, could have failed to associate Caesar Augustus and the ruler whose propaganda was making just that connection.[3] The coronation medal, for instance, minted for distribution to his new subjects, had depicted James wearing a laurel wreath, while a Latin inscription proclaimed him Caesar Augustus of Britain, Caesar the heir of the Caesars.[4] Such versifiers as Henry Petowe and Samuel Rowlands had been quick to respond with titles like *Englands Caesar: His Majesties Most Royall Coronation* (1603) and *Ave Caesar: God Save the King* (1603). With greater art, Samuel Daniel, in April 1603, had spoken of 'this Empire of the *North*' united by 'one Imperiall Prince' who was 'more then Emperor / Over the hearts' of his people.[5] Although an outbreak of plague had cramped the style of the coronation itself, in March 1604 James's postponed entry into London had been celebrated with great magnificence. Both at Temple Bar and in the Strand James had been feted as successor to Augustus, so that when the Commons then declined to accept the proposal of a Welsh MP that James be styled 'emperor of Great Britain', they were rejecting a concept already gaining currency.[6]

At Temple Bar James had passed through a triumphal arch representing the temple of Janus. On the far side and so 'within' the temple, as it were, the principal figure was Peace, a wreath of olive on her head and an olive branch in her hand. As the king approached, the Genius of the City was ready to reveal that 'this translated temple' was now consecrated to James, and over the altar an elaborate Latin inscription hailed him as *Augustus Novus*. In the Strand, Electra, in the figure of a comet suspended between two 70-foot-high pyramids, had been provided with these words by Ben Jonson to conclude the pageantry:

> Long maist thou live, and see me thus appeare
> As omenous a comet, from my spheare,
> Unto thy raigne; as that did auspicate
> So lasting glory to AUGUSTUS state.[7]

When Francis Bacon dedicated *The Advancement of Learning* (1605) to his new sovereign, it was only politic that he too should find some way of relating James and Augustus. They are, he asserts, alike in eloquence.

Divines contributed at yet another level, the Dean of Salisbury, in a sermon of 1604, pursuing the parallel between Augustus and James with particular zeal.[8] James's motto, *beati pacifici*, which recalls not only the Sermon on the Mount but also the fact that Christ's birth was in the days of Caesar Augustus (Luke ii:1), encapsulates and, what is more, envelops in the odour of sanctity a domestic policy of which the chief objective was the unification, or reunification, of a divided 'Britain', and a foreign policy of which the overwhelming purpose was peace. Besides being reluctant to embrace any policy that might lead to hostility abroad, James even strove, by offering his services as mediator, to resolve conflicts in which he was not directly involved. Significantly, his first major action as king of England was to end Elizabeth's long war with Spain, and in May 1604 formal peace talks opened. But enthusiasm among his new subjects for union with Scotland and peace with Spain was, at best, limited; and if Octavius' eager anticipation of the approaching time when 'the three-nooked world / Shall bear the olive freely' is at odds with the responses primarily invoked by Shakespeare's play, we may see this as reflecting the conflict, particularly acute in 1606, between James's peace policy and public feeling. Ten years later, it is true, the bishop of Winchester could refer to James as '*our* Augustus *in whose dayes our blessed* Saviour Christ Jesus *is come to a full and perfect aage*' and claim that 'Never hath there bene so *universal a Peace in* Christendome *since the time of* our Saviour Christ, *as in these his Dayes*'; but such were not the popular sentiments of 1606.[9] A degree of historical myopia is required if the mood of a particular time is to be accurately established.

After the discovery of the Gunpowder Plot, relations with Spain deteriorated, and there was widespread grumbling about the peace. In the House of Commons on 8 March 1606, Sir Edwin Sandys spoke for many when he declared that 'the peace . . . had wormwood in it'.[10] Sir Henry Neville, in a letter of June 4, tells how

> Upon *Sunday* last there were divers Merchants and Merchant's Wives at the Court, and made greivous Complaint unto the King, the one of their Servants, and the other of their Husbands, *imprisoned and put to the Gallies in* Spaine, *and of much Injustice and Oppression done there to our Nation, besides some particular Contumely to the King personally*; the like Complaint was made before to the Lords. I hear it

hath *moved much*, and this I will assure you, *that the Kingdom generally wishes this Peace broken*, but Jacobus Pacificus *I believe will scarce incline to that Side*.[11]

In fact, the merchants kept on complaining. The following February a petition was laid before the Commons and a committee duly appointed to investigate the grievances. Following the report of that committee, the strongly sympathetic Commons sought a conference with the Lords to consider drawing up a joint petition to the king 'for the redress of Spanish wrongs', but in June, when the conference eventually took place, Cecil produced a barrage of arguments to undercut and belittle the claims of the merchants while professing solicitous concern about their sufferings. Furthermore, he made it clear that matters of war and peace were *arcanum imperii*, no business of the Commons.[12] Thus the Spanish grievances remained an emotive issue throughout the time Shakespeare was, as we think, writing *Antony and Cleopatra*, and a particular reason for deploring the royal pacifism.

At the diplomatic level, a rapidly worsening situation is revealed by the letters sent to Cecil in the early summer of 1606 by Sir Charles Cornwallis, ambassador at Madrid. In May, when he protested about the treatment of those unfortunate English merchants apprehended at sea by the Spaniards, Cornwallis was 'answered with a Shrinke of the Shoulder'.[13] In June he reports that when he pressed the matter, the Duke of Lerma retorted derisively that the person responsible '*shall be called to account for that he did not instantly execute them*'.[14] A later letter details many instances of the Spanish authorities dragging their feet and describes, for example, how when Cornwallis sent his representative to accompany an English captain attempting to seek the redress already agreed by Lerma, the dignitary to whom they went instructed '*his Dorekeeper*' to say 'that they should depart *en mala hora, and that he would not speake with any Engleses*'.[15] In addition, Cornwallis reports that the Spaniards were themselves complaining that their ambassador at Westminster was being disgracefully treated, although they would give no particulars. He reports, too, that English fugitives were being harboured in Spain and even warns Cecil of an assassination plot being hatched there.[16]

All this was calculated to provoke Cecil and James into abandoning their foreign policy of 'unadventurous and inoffensive goodfellowship'.[17] The penultimate letter in the series then goes farther by disclosing that murderous thoughts about Cecil were being widely voiced, and Cornwallis openly advocates the termination of the peace: 'Occasion to call all to a new question, will arise out of the Cruelty of *Don Luys Fyrardo* to the Merchants taken in the Indies. . . . And sure I am, that his Majestie will not think it for his Honor, to give so much way to the *Spanish Pride*, as to consent to deprive his Subjects to trade thither.'[18] The occasion should be seized, argues Cornwallis, because the failure of their treasure ships to reach port had deprived the Spaniards of the resources needed 'to maintain their Warrs abroad [and] themselves at home': 'To be short, *their Estate (were they now well set upon) is Irrecoverable; this Peace being an Impediment to the greatest Advantage and Meanes to enrich our King and Realme that in any Age hath ever been offered.'*[19]

The last letter in the sequence refers contemptuously to the stupidity of the Spaniards, unable to recognise impending disaster, and reverts to the recommended rupture:

> I make no doubt but that his Majestie will resolve upon that which shall most agree with his own Honor, Safetie and Profit; and *before any publique* knowledge *be taken of a Disposition to breake*, will make such Bargaine with the United *Provinces, assure the* French, and treate with the *Venetians*, the *Florentine*, and all such others, from whom may be expected either Ayde or Ayme.[20]

This was the ideal moment, as Cornwallis explains to another correspondent, for James to revoke the peace with Spain: '*to set his Foot on their Heads and sinck them for ever.*'[21] But *Jacobus Pacificus* was not to be hustled into belligerent action. Late in August, Cecil replied to Cornwallis in a letter that manages to sound sympathetic about Cornwallis's frustrations while firmly rejecting his hawkish advice. Instead, there had been some straight talking with the reluctant Spanish ambassador at a conference called by the Privy Council, and Cornwallis himself is reminded of James's commitment to peace, and the need to wait upon events: 'Here on build your Foundation; whatever you hear or collect thus standeth his Majestie's *inward Affections*, (I may say to you) *to conserve Peace as long as he may with Honor and Safety, or to make a Warre upon good Foundation.*'[22] It is a policy that the French Ambassador in May had characterised as *timide et irresolu* and that showed, as many Englishmen thought, that James lacked that 'heart and Stomach of a King' that Elizabeth had claimed as hers at Tilbury in 1588.[23]

Contrasting James and Elizabeth, the Venetian Ambassador may have exaggerated James's unpopularity in 1607; but the essential difference is accurately observed:

> He loves quiet and repose, but has no inclination to war, nay is opposed to it, a fact that little pleases many of his subjects. . . . He does not caress the people nor make them that good cheer the late Queen did, whereby she won their loves; for the English adore their Sovereigns, and if the King passed through the same street a hundred times a day the people would still run to see him; they like their King to show pleasure at their devotion, as the late Queen knew well how to do; but this King manifests no taste for them but rather contempt and dislike. The result is he is despised and almost hated.[24]

There is evidence, too, some of it in plays and poems, that by 1607 the memory of Queen Elizabeth was being revived with affection.[25] In 1606 Thomas Dekker's *Whore of Babylon* (published 1607), which ends with the defeat of the Armada, was not the first Jacobean play to include a speaking part for the late queen, presented though she is under the name of Titania, the Faerie Queene. The play is anti-papist and significantly anti-Spanish, with Elizabeth prospering as mighty opposite to the empress of Babylon, 'Under whom is figured *Rome*'. Dekker's extravagant notion, though, that James, a 'second Phoenix', would be a successor 'of larger wing / Of stronger talent, of more dreadfull beake', a monarch who would strike terror into every opponent and 'shake all *Babilon*', is absurdly unrealistic wishful thinking that serves only to reveal the width of the gulf between popular aspiration and royal policy.[26] Bishop Goodman was later to remember that although people were 'generally weary of an old woman's government' by the end of Elizabeth's reign, experience of James soon prompted a revival of her reputation: 'Then was her memory much magnified, – such ringing of bells, such public joy and sermons in commemoration of her, the picture of her tomb painted in many churches, and in effect more solemnity and joy in memory of her coronation than was for the coming in of King James.'[27] It has been suggested that the dissolution of the Society of Antiquaries in 1607 was one result of James's resentment of this nostalgia.[28]

During the first parliamentary session of the new reign, a major issue had been James's overhasty attempt to establish Anglo-Scottish unity, a process that was, in the end, to require a hundred years. *Unus Deus, una fides, unum baptismum* was seen at the beginning of the seventeenth century as no warrant for *unus rex, una Britannia, unum imperium*, and opposition proved far stronger than the self-styled British Augustus had anticipated. In response to parliamentary rebuff, therefore, James began a determined campaign. By a royal proclamation in October 1604, this monarch of a constitutionally separate England and Scotland assumed 'The Name and Stile of KING OF GREAT BRITTAINE, including therein according to the truth, the whole Island'; and by referring to 'one Imperial Crowne' and 'our owne Imperial Power', he emphasised his notion of a newly founded empire in which the olive would be freely borne: 'Wee think it unreasonable, that the thing, which is by the worke of God and Nature so much in effect one, should not be one in name; Unitie in name being so fit a meanes to imprint in the hearts of the people, a character and memoriall of that Unitie, which ought to be among them indeed.'[29] The second parliamentary session, because of the disruption caused by the Gunpowder Plot, failed to find time for the union issue, although a select commission that had first met on the very day of James's proclamation was waiting to report. By the end of the summer of 1606, the king's new style had begun to have an impact, while Parliament was waiting to return to the constitutional question as soon as the third session commenced in November.

If James supposed, that autumn, that the lapse of time would have operated in his favour, he was mistaken. The opposition was as intransigent as ever, and the conflict throughout the third session was bitter. But even while the battle raged, and it was undecided whether James or the Commons would prevail, the emblems of empire were on display. The coinage, now uniform for North Britons and South Britons, proclaimed .IACOBVS. D' .G' .BRIT' .FRAN' .ET HIB' .REX., and bore such tendentious legends as *Faciam eos in gentem unam* ('I will make them one nation' – Ezek. xxxvii:22), *Quae Deus conjunxit nemo separet* ('What God hath joined together, let no man put assunder' – Matt. xix:6), *Henricus rosas regna Jacobus* ('Henry [united] the roses, but James the kingdoms'), *Tueatur unita Deus* ('May God protect these united [kingdoms]').[30] Designs on the coins combined the thistle and the rose, the 20-shilling 'sovereign' had been replaced by the 20-shilling 'unite', and the 5-shilling piece had become a 'Britain crown'. From April 1606, ships were required to fly a new union flag combining the red cross of Saint George with the white cross of Saint Andrew.[31]

The lord mayor's pageant presented in London in the autumn of 1605 had been Anthony Munday's *The Triumphes of Re-united Britania*. The printed text is prefaced by a survey of 'British' history that besides providing an introduction to the device itself, also sup-plies perspectives for *King Lear* and *Antony and Cleopatra*. Munday records how Noah, who after the flood 'was sole Monarch of the World', divided the earth in three so that each of his sons would inherit a third. Britain formed part of Japhet's inheritance and was ruled by him and his descendants until Neptune's son Albion and a race of giants wrested it from them. Eventually, Brute and his Trojan followers rescued the island from these savage usurpers and gave it the name of Britain. All would then have been well had not Brute, like Noah, out of misguided love for his three sons, divided the kingdom between them: to Camber, Wales (or Cambria); to Locrine, most of England (or Loegria); to Albanact, an enlarged Scotland (or Albania). This division of the land introduced strife, and only with the accession of James, the second Brute, was the disastrous error of the first Brute repaired and the unity and peace of Britain restored.[32]

The folly of division is the folly of *King Lear*, a play first staged within a few months of Munday's pageant's being presented; but the tripartite division of the world by Noah and the similar division of Britain by Brute also help to account for Octavius' allusion to his future empire as 'three-nooked'. A reference to Asia, Africa, and Europe, possibly envisaged as a tripartite T-in-O map, seems appropriate, as is recognition of the distinct responsibilities distributed in the triumvirate among Antony, Octavius, and Lepidus.[33] More significantly, however, by announcing that if his forces prevail, an age of peace will dawn for the 'three-nooked world', Octavius is made to speak with a recognisably Jacobean voice – and more than a trace of a Scottish accent. Brute's territorial division mirrors Noah's and thereby provides a circumstance that aligns the world at large with the smaller *orbis Britannicus*, whereas Munday's depiction of 'the Island of *Britayne*' as 'triangular' gives geometric form to the Shakespearean concept of a three-cornered world. In his Twelfth Night masque at the beginning of 1605, *The Masque of Blackness*, Jonson similarly used the Virgilian notion of James's unified Britain as a *'world, divided from the world'* (cf. *Eclogue* I,66), as, indeed, he had already done when he celebrated James's entry into London in 1604, and as James himself regularly contrived to do when addressing Parliament. In the masque, the new unity of the little world of Britain receives the approbation of the larger and disunited world, significantly described as 'triple' in a way that anticipates Shakespeare:

> Britannia, which the triple world admires,
> This isle hath now recovered for her name.[34]

This British union of three in one is further hallowed by its trinitarian association, as the dean of Salisbury had noted in his sermon of 1604 when he descanted upon the 'union of three Realmes . . . in one royaltie'.[35] *Antony and Cleopatra* is a play that shows the transition from triumvirate to Augustan empire, and it should not be forgotten that its Jacobean context places it with *King Lear* (performed 26 December 1606, and probably earlier too), where the effects of division are terrifyingly recorded, and Jonson's *Hymenaei* (performed 5 January 1606), where the multifaceted blessings of union are, perhaps, most fully honoured.[36]

With hindsight we can recognise that despite widespread opposition at the time, James's notion of union was, in essence, a noble one. James's most thorough biographer warns us that 'to consider King James as merely a crafty politician grasping at a great prize is quite to misjudge his character. He was a man who could be fascinated by lofty ideals and sublime aspirations; and no ideal attracted him more strongly than that of unity, in the sense of universal agreement and concord.'[37] Choice spirits such as Francis Bacon in England and Thomas Craig in Scotland appreciated the merits of these ideals in 1606, and there is no reason to think that Shakespeare must necessarily have been less perceptive.[38] Unequivocal support of James by Shakespeare, however, is equally unlikely. The myriad-minded creator of the serpent of old Nile might reasonably be expected to have adopted a highly ambiguous attitude toward the policies and person of his unattractive sovereign.

Assessments of the historical Octavius have varied.

> *Augustus Cesar* was not such a saint
> As *Virgill* maketh him by his description[39]

says Ariosto in Harington's translation, and assessments of Shakespeare's Octavius have varied too. British playgoers remember the ice of Corin Redgrave (RSC, 1972), as well as the warmth of Jonathan Pryce; and critics offer similarly diverse views. Robin Lee, for instance, has it that 'Shakespeare's Octavius Caesar is not at all true to what we know of history's (or even Plutarch's) Octavius. Shakespeare emphasises his qualities of self-interest, remorseless ambition for himself and his Empire, and total unconcern for individuals who stand in the way of his aims.'[40] On the other hand, A. P. Riemer insists that commentators are wrong to regard Caesar as

> . . . a ruthless megalomaniac with an almost psychological dislike of his elder partner and a jealousy of his Egyptian revels. . . . Caesar is a noble, well-intentioned and generally just ruler; he does virtually nothing treacherous or underhand, he does not abuse his powers, and he is much more than the Machiavellian opportunist many critics see in him. We misread Shakespeare's subtlety if we regard the presentation of this character as merely unfavourable or unsympathetic: he is, in fact, a model of political wisdom as well as of virtue; that he is unattractive, perhaps sinister, is a result of Shakespeare's mature understanding of the forces of life and history.[41]

What is important is that the complexity of Shakespeare's portrait be acknowledged, for the ambiguity derives not from failure to achieve consistency but from Shakespeare's perceptive response to the question, What sort of a man must Caesar Augustus have been? During the crucial period of his career, when the accomplishment of his ambition was just within sight, and in the events leading up to that time, the future emperor of universal peace, later to be deified, is revealed by Shakespeare as an adept politician, an opportunist on the make, as well as a visionary whose oracular pronouncement offers the imminent realisation of one of mankind's noblest aspirations. Caesar, eagerly espousing empire and the *pax Romana*, is observed in a context that celebrates values that eclipse, if only existentially, the worth of any empire. His pre-eminence is among those who cannot condone the flaunting of a subversive transcendentalism that reduces kingdoms to clay and love that can be reckoned to beggary. And if James really did recall this Augustus, then perhaps Augustus could be glimpsed in James. Inevitably, the clever, scheming, canny, cautious Scotsman, the new Augustus whose theoretically admirable peace policy seemed in actuality less golden than the vigorous turmoil it replaced, provided Shakespeare with a sufficiently parallel life to supplement what he read in North. But to understand King James has never been simple. The ambiguities and contradictions of the 'wisest foole in Christendome' have always attracted comment: pacifist or cowardly, circumspect or devious, indolent or busy, chaste or perverted?[42] The antitheses resist easy resolution, and this is reflected in the open verdict that one astute observer was to record: 'Some Parallel'd him to *Tiberius* for Dissimulation, yet Peace was maintained by him as in the Time of Augustus.'[43] Such a response seems to be anticipated in the portrayal of Shakespeare's Caesar.

This is also the typical response of Shakespeare's contemporaries to the historical Octavius, commonly envisaged by them as a Jekyll-and-Hyde figure. For Montaigne he exemplified man's essential inconsistency, but for writers less drawn to sceptical uncertainties a remarkably clear distinction was frequently made between the vicious tyrant and demagogue before Actium and the ideal prince thereafter.[44] Pedro Mexia wittily brings the two aspects together when he remarks that Octavius 'happened wisely and uprightly to governe that, which by force and cunning he had gotten', and Peter Heylyn enigmatically expresses the same idea when he claims that 'it had beene an ineffable benefit to the Commonwealth of Rome, if eyther he had never dyed, or never beene borne'.[45] Shakespeare takes us to the point where the opposing halves of the career meet to catch the ambiguity at the juncture, for that is the key point of critical interest. The last speech of the play, thought by some to be out of character, reveals the new voice of Augustus, its style distinct from the familiar accents of Octavius. But the cleavage is earlier stressed by Octavius describing the time of universal peace as 'near' not 'here', by the irony of this reference to the coming time, and to the olive branch, following Octavius' instructions to Agrippa to 'begin the fight', and by the realisation that on that occasion the military success was to be Antony's. An avant-garde Tacitean refinement of the Jekyll-and-Hyde division delved deeper and discerned a destructive and sordid reality underlying even the appearance of imperial splendour; and that, too, invites a dramatist's irony.[46]

As it happens, the character of James was brought sharply into focus in the summer of 1606, when his brother-in-law Christian IV of Denmark paid the first state visit to England by a foreign ruler for eighty-four years and thereby provided James's subjects with a unique opportunity to compare, or rather contrast, their monarch with one of a very different mould. Christian was everything James was not, and the distinction was not lost on bystanders. The French Ambassador reports people regretting that their king was not like Christian.[47] The Venetian Ambassador, who observed that popular emotion had been so deeply stirred by the treatment of those English merchants sent to the Spanish galleys that 'war is openly demanded', reports:

> And so far have matters gone that at Hampton Court, where the Queen is, a letter has been picked up in which the King is urged to declare war, to leave the chase [that is, hunting, an obsessive pursuit of James's] and turn to arms, and the example of his brother-in-law,

the King of Denmark, is cited, who for his prowess at the joust has won golden opinions.[48]

One can well believe that the queen, anxious to preserve amity between her husband and her brother, 'would not allow the letter, which came into her hands, to be shown to the King'. According to gossip, Christian himself 'did use all means to persuade the King to give over his extraordinary hunting and to follow martial or more serious affairs'.[49] That gossip may have been based on another incident reported by the Venetian Ambassador:

> A deputation of merchants recently waited on the King, complained loudly of what they had to suffer from the Spanish and begged for some redress. The King is said to have grown angry, and the King of Denmark, who was present, expressed surprise that his Majesty could submit to such injuries inflicted on his subjects.[50]

Christian, whose instincts were so different, was an immensely attractive, impulsive, larger-than-life figure, possessed of great vitality and vigour, some eleven years younger than his forty-year-old host. If Shakespeare looked for a modern Antony to compare with the neo-Augustus, he could have found no better likeness than the king of Denmark; and as with Antony and Octavius, the two rulers were brothers-in-law, even though Anne's relationship to brother and husband was the reverse of Octavia's.

Like Antony in his prime, Christian was a military man, in his case patently spoiling for the fight with Sweden that was to ensue in the Kalmar War. The year before his English visit, Christian had seen action for the first time, albeit in a small way, when he had taken five hundred men to Brunswick to intervene, on behalf of his wife's brother Duke Heinrich Julius, in a dispute that was really none of his business. Having already done much to put Denmark's military forces into fighting shape, he was erecting a network of fortresses and fortifications. But his twin passions were artillery and the Danish fleet, and he had personal experience in all matters relating to both of them. Ships were built to his own designs, and in 1606 the navy must have been practically up to the strength of fifty or sixty large and heavily armed warships that it achieved by 1611, substantially larger than James's fleet.[51] Christian's interest in these matters was much in evidence when he visited England, for he came with an imposing squadron of five or six warships and two pinnaces, 'all large and fine'.[52] His flagship, the recently commissioned *Tre Kroner*, a vessel of 1500 tons sumptuously decorated 'with rich gold, and very excellent workmanship', was one of the largest, most impressive, and most heavily armed ships of the period. She carried seventy-two guns, and we are told that she attracted 'many thousands . . . to Gravesend, where she doth ride, to view her'.[53]

The writer of one celebratory pamphlet virtually resorted to blank verse as he strove vainly to do justice to his subject: 'The Ship wherein the King of *Denmarke* went was a moste goodly and famous Vessell . . . shee boare in her, three tyer of Ordinance, all brasse, both great and large: her poope, her forecastle and Beake-head, were all fayre carued and ritchly guilt.'[54] One way of summarising his long prose description, with its awkward lyricism, would be to say simply that the scene at Gravesend 'beggared all description'. For many people, the first impression of the Danish fleet would have been the sound of the guns. Another account records that when Christian left the ships in order to proceed by barge up the Thames, the *Tre Kroner* 'discharged such a thundering peal of ordnance . . . that the smoke dimmed the skies, and their noise was heard a far way off. After her the vice and rear admiral, and so all the rest; which made a long peal; every ship taking his turn, very orderly, in exceeding good sort.'[55] As for Christian himself, it was obvious that he had the makings of an inspired and courageous leader in war, lacking only the judgement to know when to stop: 'His proportion shewes him to bee a man of greate strength, activitie, and indurance, such as are the markes of the best Conquerours'.[56]

The ability to endure personal hardship and privation resolutely while on active service is a particular characteristic that Christian shares with the young Antony. Octavius pays this tribute to the soldier he remembers:

> When thou once
> Was beaten from Modena, where thou slew'st
> Hirtus and Pansa, consuls, at thy heel
> Did famine follow, whom thou fought'st against,
> Though daintily brought up, with patience more
> Than savages could suffer. Thou didst drink
> The stale of horses and the gilded puddle
> Which beasts would cough at. Thy palate then did deign
> The roughest berry on the rudest hedge.
> Yea, like the stag when snow the pasture sheets,
> The barks of trees thou browsed'st. On the Alps
> It is reported thou didst eat strange flesh,
> Which some did die to look on. And all this –

It wounds thine honour that I speak it now –
Was borne so like a soldier that thy cheek
So much as lanked not.

(I. iv. 56–71)

Christian, like his predecessors, was king of Norway as well as
Denmark; but he was by far the most active of the Danish kings in
this other realm, visiting the country some thirty times in the course
of his reign. He was, in fact, the first Danish king to take his northern
responsibilities seriously; and in 1599 to the consternation of courtiers
'daintily brought up' who had to accompany him, he sailed north
along the entire Norwegian coast, through Arctic waters and the
regions of the midnight sun, as far as Finnmark and the island of
Vardøya in the Barents Sea where Norway borders Russia. From
here he made further expeditions with just two of the eight ships.

Naturally, being the man he was, early in the voyage he supplanted his admiral by becoming General-Kapitain Christian
Fredericksen (his father was Frederick II) and taking personal command of the *Victor*. On pain of death it was forbidden to refer to him
by any other title, but for his commanders there was always Ventidius'
problem of reconciling the roles of captain's captain and chief lieutenant. No doubt, stories were still told in 1606 of the privations
endured and the sights seen: of the shaman who foretold danger for
Christian and his ship; of the Lappish witch, perhaps, whose cat they
stole and how the fearful storms that the witch stirred up in revenge
were only allayed by court-martialling the cat and setting it adrift
with a supply of salt herring, smoked ham, and milk; of the Murmansk
Russians who smeared themselves with blubber and wrestled for
Christian; of what practically amounted to an orgy at Bergen; of
ships dismasted and a keel ripped by a submerged reef 'as a stag
would the belly of a hunting dog'. There were great whales, mid-
winter weather in midsummer, and the maelstrom to spice the
stories, and strange food too. On one occasion a party of Russians
could be feasted on board so well that they came from the table 'like
swine and beasts', on others lack of fuel led to hunger. Local produce, such as cheese and butter made of reindeer milk, was eaten
sometimes; but the expedition also browsed on strange herbs, the
arctic stonecrops and moneyworts, to ward off scurvy.[57]

Some of the ships involved in the expedition (the *Victor*, the
Gideon, and the *Raphael*) were among those actually on display at
Gravesend, a matter of special interest in England because in the
course of his Arctic voyage Christian had seized English vessels that

were, he claimed, illicitly in his Norwegian waters. There were English captains, it was said, who had suffered the same punishment as Thidias, but with Christian himself, 'very unprincely', wielding the lash.[58] Although Queen Elizabeth had been outraged, the victims were luckier than they might have been, since the master of a Dutch vessel encountered on the return voyage had been shot. The issue still rankled in 1606, and in August the mayor and aldermen of the ships' home port marked Christian's visit by writing to Cecil about compensation.[59]

Considerable mercantile, diplomatic, and cultural contact between England and Denmark around this period ensured that Christian's reputation preceded him to London.[60] Accounts of his coronation in 1596, with its remarkable festivities, in which Thomas Sackville and the duke of Brunswick's troupe of English players had participated, must have helped to colour that reputation.[61] Whereas James in 1603 at his English coronation only managed to endure 'the *days* brunt with *patience*, being assured he should never have such another', Christian's enthusiasm in 1596 had been boundless.[62] Impetuously he threw himself into everything that was going on. Christian was the designer of his own crown; he led the fire-fighting team, and had himself paraded through the streets on a litter dressed as Pope Sergius VI; and then, still in papal attire, he tilted at the ring. With 150 cannon mounted on the walls of Copenhagen, and another 600 on board ship, the royal delight in the sound of artillery was made hugely evident, while Christian's personal prowess as a fighter was spectacularly demonstrated by his achievements as a tireless competitor in martial exercises. He charged at the ring or at opponents 345 times and tilted against 113 nobles, Danish and foreign. The festivities were further enlivened by shows of Oriental splendour, with nobles appearing as Turkish, Indian, and Persian women, and a fireworks display that represented the defeat of a Persian army – not quite an Alexandrian feast, perhaps, but ripening towards one.

Like Antony, Christian was extravagant, physically strong, and able to take pleasure in the company of all sorts and conditions of men, whether fellow rulers or 'knaves that smell of sweat'. Like Antony, too, he had an appetite for women that the homosexual James certainly lacked. Christian had married, in 1597, the daughter of the margrave of Brandenburg, and Anna Katrine was to bear him six children in little more than twice as many years; but his pleasure lay elsewhere. Almost immediately after his marriage, Christian openly made Kirsten Mansdatter his mistress and fathered the first of many illegitimate children. James, on the other hand, as Bishop Goodman declared, 'was never taxed with the love of any other lady' than his wife.[63] The 'ne'er lust wearied' Christian, however, was to acquire a considerable reputation as a man of little sexual restraint, a reputation that, for instance, enabled a scurrilous exposé of the 'most secret and chamber-abominations' of the Stuart court, published during the Commonwealth, to present the Danish king as an unbridled and tyrannical womaniser.[64]

But above all, Christian was known as a drinker. In this, he followed the settled example of his court – his father had died of drink, and his comparatively sober mother worked her way through two gallons of Rhine wine a day.[65] In his drinking of healths, Shakespeare's Claudius is a truly royal Dane. For Christian's coronation a stock of 35,000 glasses was requisitioned from merchant vessels passing through the Sound; and as in other matters, when it came to drinking, Christian was a match for any man. He was capable of downing thirty to forty goblets of wine in an evening and, recording his excesses by means of the method Hans Christian Andersen was to adopt for relatively minor indulgences more than two centuries later, would mark his diary with a cross if he had been carried to bed incapable. A second or even a third cross was added if his condition had been paralytic.[66] 'Now will drunkards be in request', remarked one letter-writer ominously when he heard that Christian was to visit James; and John Davies of Hereford in his *Bien Venu: Greate Britaines Welcome to Hir Greate Friendes, and Deere Brethren the Danes* (1606) offered the following advice:

> Then let thy Conduits runne with rarest wines,
> That all may freely drinke all health to thee:
> And to those Kings, their Heires, and their Assignes,
> By whom thou art, or maist the better bee:
> Yet, O beware of Drunkards fowle designes,
> Take healthes, while thou from surfet maist be free;
>   'For 'tis no glorie, but a foule reproach,
>   To take (like Tuns) the wine that Shame doth broach'.[67]

In general, James himself was 'not intemperate in his drinking' it seems. 'It is true he drank very often', says Weldon; but this 'was rather out of custom than any delight. [He] seldom drank at any one time above four spoonfulls, many times not above one or two'.[68] There seems, however, to have been real concern in 1606 that Christian and his hard-drinking entourage would teach their English hosts to drink deep and that the state visit would degenerate into gargantuan scenes of alcoholic overindulgence.

Accounts of Christian's activities in England show that he lived up to his reputation. The three weeks included much feasting and entertainment at the royal palaces; and at Cecil's house, Theobalds, Cecil was determined to keep his guests happy. 'God forbid', he remarked to the Venetian Ambassador, 'that these Danes should hear that we devoted ourselves to anything but the table; they would take us all for enemies.'[69] Sir John Harington reported that Cecil was 'overwhelmed in preparations . . . and doth marvelously please both Kings, with good meat, good drink, and good speeches'; and Harington himself felt 'well nigh overwhelmed with carousal and sports of all kinds'.[70] James, too, was anxious to impress Christian and stinted nothing, although he must have found the visit exhausting. There was a great deal of hunting that was more to James's taste than Christian's, and feats of arms to watch and participate in that were certainly more to Christian's taste than James's. When the two kings competed at running at the ring, it was Christian's 'good hap never almost to miss it, and [James] had the ill luck scarce ever to come near it, which put him into no small impatience'.[71]

A wealth of dispersed information about Christian's four-week visit survives, but the sources have never been assembled in a satisfactory account that covers the full range of social, cultural, and diplomatic interest.[72] In a single day of intensive sightseeing, Christian's curiosity took him from the coronation chair and royal tombs at Westminster Abbey to the roof of old Saint Paul's, the shops at the Royal Exchange, and the Tower of London, with its royal mint, armoury, jewel house, and menagerie.[73] The two monarchs must have stood on the platform above the recently completed two-story lions' dens and looked down into the animals' refurbished exercise yard, with its cistern 'for the Lyons to drinke and wasche themselves in';[74] but perhaps they would also have seen among the 'other wilde beasts there kept and maintained for his Highnesses pleasures and pastimes' the 'two young crocodiles . . . presented alive' to James the previous autumn, even if the poor creatures had succumbed to their first London winter and were by then stuffed.[75]

Shakespeare's professional associates were much involved in Christian's visit. The text of the entertainment that Jonson, and probably Thomas Wilson, devised for welcoming the two kings to Theobalds survives.[76] So does the text that Ford provided for the ceremonial meeting of the monarchs, besides the four arguments that Ford wrote in connection with the jousts, when the honour of 'all faire Ladies' was defended by four earls against all challengers.[77] Typically, Christian himself, 'armed very rich', took a vigorous part in the martial sports.[78] Marston's verses, spoken at Cheapside on the occasion of the 'most pompous passage' through London, also survive; and so do the words of a 'moste excellent song sung dialogue wise' that formed part of a pastoral device at Fleet Conduit.[79] Since, in this state procession, 'all our Kinges Groomes and Messengers of the Chamber' marched immediately behind Christian's fourteen trumpeters, Shakespeare, as one of the King's Men (and therefore ranked as a groom extraordinary of the King's chamber), can be assumed to have been present.[80] Furthermore, the King's Men contributed three performances to the programme of royal entertainment that James provided for Christian. One is now thought to have been a performance of the new play *Macbeth*, and another could well have been *Hamlet*, somehow abbreviated – a Danish play to complement a Scottish one.[81] But this was not the only drama, for Christian, like Antony, was a lover of plays. The Children of Paul's are known to have presented 'a playe called *Abuses*: containing both a Comedie and a Tragedie, at which the Kinges seemed to take delight and be much pleased'.[82] In addition, Henry N. Paul has plausibly suggested that the Admiral's Company may have performed at some time during the visit, probably on the evening of the day Christian spent sightseeing in London.[83]

Neither the plot nor the author of *Abuses* is known, but at least we know that the anonymous masque that lives so memorably in Sir John Harington's famous account was intended to be about the meeting of two biblical monarchs, Solomon and the Queen of Sheba. According to Harington, a befuddled Queen of Sheba stumbled and fell as she approached Christian, who in turn collapsed and had to be carried out. Other performers, too, were unable to stay on their feet, 'wine did so occupy their upper chambers'. Hope, Faith, and Charity formed a sadly intoxicated trio. When Hope attempted to speak her lines, 'wine rendered her endeavours so feeble that she withdrew', and Faith 'left the court in a staggering condition'. Both were soon vomiting in the lower hall. Victory, overcome by alcohol, was dumped incapable on some stairs, while Peace, whom drink had made aggressive, attacked with her olive branch those who attempted to restrain her.[84]

Harington tells a good story, and we may suspect that he exaggerated the drunkenness, subordinating truth to readability. After all,

Henry Robarts, who wrote two pamphlets about the visit, stresses the sobriety of the Danes in England; but Robarts protests far too much and was not present at court entertainments.[85] The second of his pamphlets culminates in an account of the punishment devised by Christian for drunkenness among his retinue, and with a prayer prompted by Christian's supposed reformation, a piece of rhetoric that reveals that there was a problem and that it was matter for comment. Another pamphleteer who also stressed the sobriety of the Danes seems to have been some sort of court apologist.[86] Solemn chroniclers are not necessarily more reliable witnesses than amusing letter-writers, and Harington's private report, coloured though it undoubtedly is, is probably close enough to the truth:

> The sports began each day in such manner and such sorte, as well nigh persuaded me of Mahomets paradise. We had women, and indeed wine too, of such plenty, as would have astonished each sober beholder. Our feasts were magnificent, and the two royal guests did most lovingly embrace each other at table. I think the Dane hath strangely wrought on our good English nobles; for those, whom I never could get to taste good liquor, now follow the fashion, and wallow in beastly delights. The ladies abandon their sobriety, and are seen to roll about in intoxication.[87]

Of course, the 'wild riot, excess, and devastation of time and temperance' at Theobalds could not be reported in print or even retailed to the indiscreet. Harington is writing to a friend who he knows 'will not blab'.[88]

Two extraordinary shipboard feasts, one given by James on Sunday, August 10, and one given by Christian the following day, marked the end of the state visit. By dint of combining information from various sources, English and Danish, and remembering Harington's charges of inebriation, it is possible to form surprisingly detailed impressions of what happened on those reciprocal occasions, and by so doing to recover a real-life contributory source for one particular scene in Shakespeare's *Antony and Cleopatra*. Considered purely as narrative, the scene on Pompey's galley (II. vii) is superfluous and for that reason has frequently been omitted in performance; but Shakespeare, boldly introducing a shipboard setting for the first time in his career, seizes an opportunity to present a series of brilliant illuminations of the issues and personalities encompassed by his play with superbly theatrical daring.[89] The episode has its historical source, but the impetus to dramatise a section of Plutarch not easily accommodated in an Antony-and-Cleopatra play came, it seems, from the festivities of 1606. And it even caused Shakespeare to abandon his practice of avoiding scenes on ships.

After attending divine service at Rochester on the final Sunday morning, the royal party proceeded by barge two miles down the Medway to Upnor Castle near Chatham. Anchored on the river for review were twenty-two ships of the fleet, James being provided with a list of the names, tonnages, armaments, and crew of each. A determined effort had been made to present a good show, although in fact the fleet was in poor condition. The kings were then entertained on the *Elizabeth Jonas*, the pride of the English navy, launched almost half a century before but rebuilt and expensively decorated at Woolwich in 1598 and armed with 56 guns, while some of Christian's entourage were entertained on the slightly larger *White Bear* of 40 guns, an even older vessel rebuilt a year or so after the *Elizabeth Jonas*.[90] Like the other ships in the review, these two had been specially prepared for the occasion by Phineas Pett, the master shipwright at Deptford, who records that he 'strove extraordinarily', working night and day to be ready in time.[91] But no English ship could measure up to the magnificence of Christian's new flagship, and to avoid humiliation a startling construction was improvised. The *Elizabeth Jonas* was linked to the *White Bear* by a pontoon or gangway broad enough for four men to walk abreast with ease, railed on either side, and, according to one observer, 200 feet long (a more convincing sounding measurement than that of more than 240 yards mentioned elsewhere).[92] In the middle of this assemblage of masts, planks, and sailcloth supported by lighters or floats was a large merchant ship that served as kitchen for the two prestige warships and was accordingly equipped with ovens and three ranges for roasting. The whole project drew much comment; and evidently the arrangements worked well, for Christian was pleased and expressed his amazement at an abundance of hot food being available on board ship.[93]

The *Elizabeth Jonas* 'perfumed with sweet and pleasant perfume' and hung inside with cloth of gold was specially set up for feasting:

> The Great-chamber, being part of the upper-deck abaft the main-mast, contained a long table for my Lord Chamberlain and other of our English Lordes; the same deck, before the main-mast, had a table for the Ladies. From whence, up a payer of stayers, ther was a passage unto the orelope, where was a faire tente sett up, lined and hanged in

the inside with silkes and cloth of gold; and at the upper end whereof, under a rich cloth of estate, sate the two Kinges, the Queen, and the Prince at dinner.[94]

A Danish diarist mentions Spanish wine, claret, and sweet wines mixed with lemons and various spices being served; and cannon were discharged when healths were drunk.[95]

After feasting, Christian walked across the improvised bridge to the *White Bear*, 'which was fitted in all pointes for the entertainment of the Danish Lordes and others'.[96] On the way, he inspected the kitchen 'and throwout that shippe, went from place to place, noting every roome'[97] and remarking that 'all things . . . were performed with that order and sumptuousness that [he] confessed he could not have believed such a thing could have been done unless he had seen it'.[98] An hour or so after they had dined, the members of the royal party re-entered their barges and, after reviewing the fleet that was dressed overall, came ashore at Upnor Castle. A coach journey of three-quarters of a mile took them to high ground, whence they could survey all the ships at once 'set out in their best equippage' and riding at anchor on the curving Medway below.[99] This was the moment for the ships and the castle to discharge their guns one after the other in strict order. One account mentions 1008 'great shott', another has 'almost twelve hundredth shot', and a third specifies 2300; but whatever the number, Christian was delighted and told James that 'if he had spent half his Kingdom in a Banquet, he could not have contented him so well'.[100]

In his preparation for the writing of *Antony and Cleopatra*, Shakespeare read in Plutarch how Sextus Pompeius, Antonius, and Octavius Caesar 'met all three together by the mount of Misena, upon a hill that runneth far into the sea, Pompey having his ships riding hard by at anchor, and Antonius and Caesar their armies upon the shore side, directly over against him'.[101] When Pompey invites the two brother-in-law rulers to feast on his ship, a problem arises about how the guests are to reach the vessel: 'So he cast anchors enow into the sea to make his galley fast, and then built a bridge of wood to convey them to his galley from the head of Mount Misena; and there he welcomed them, and made them great cheer' (p. 214). In the late summer or autumn of 1606, this would inevitably have suggested a parallel with the shipboard feast on the Medway, and Phineas Pett's remarkable bridge constructed to cope with a slightly different problem of hospitality,while the identification of James with Augustus,

supported by the congruence of Christian and Antony, would only
have reinforced that parallel. It hardly matters whether Shakespeare
himself was an eyewitness (although the Medway festivities did
include some sort of dramatic entertainment), for observers and
reports must have been numerous.[102] And it is easy to see why in his
play Shakespeare should have disregarded Plutarch's ship-to-shore
bridge and made no reference to the ship-to-ship Medway bridge.
Any explicit link between the feasting of 1606 and that on Pompey's
galley would have been unacceptable to the authorities; and besides,
Shakespeare wished to emphasise the vulnerability of Pompey's guests.
The several 'gables of the anchor' that Plutarch's Menas offers to cut
(p. 214) are significantly reduced by Shakespeare to a single one.

   Plutarch's feast on Pompey's galley is followed by a reciprocal
feast when Antonius and Caesar play host to Pompey in their camp
on shore. Shakespeare combined the two occasions but retained the
shipboard setting. James's feast on the Medway was also followed
the next day by a reciprocal feast, this time on the Thames, with
Christian playing host. Since the people were the same and the days
were consecutive, it is only reasonable to expect aspects of the one
shipboard occasion to be associated or conflated with aspects of the
other shipboard occasion. Plutarch gives no indication that the entertainment on Pompey's galley was drunken, and there is no clear
evidence that the feasting on the Medway was either, but what
happened on the Thames could certainly have prompted Shakespeare
to present the scene that way. And since North's Plutarch refers to
Pompey's 'admiral galley', it is easy to associate Pompey's flagship
with Christian's, known by English observers simply as 'the
Admiral'.[103]

   Alcohol and gunpowder were predictably the active ingredients of
Christian's entertainment. On board the Admiral, as I shall now call
the *Tre Kroner*, there was banqueting and the drinking of healths.
With each toast, drums and trumpets brayed out the triumph of the
pledge, and ordnance on ship and shore, from Tilbury to Gravesend,
resounded in response. According to one account, this happened
between forty and fifty times, with between sixty and eighty great
shot in each volley.[104] Another account more modestly says twenty
healths were drunk, with forty-two shot in each volley;[105] but whether
the number of shot was in the region of 3150 or only 840, Dudley
Carleton related in a letter to a friend that James, who disliked the
smell of gunpowder (especially after Guy Fawkes's plot), was not
happy until he had drunk enough to become 'so hearty that he bid

them at last shoot and spare not'. Carleton noted that drinking was heavier than at court, although it can scarcely have been heavier than at the disastrous Solomon-and-Sheba masque, and remarked that 'they played the seamen for good fellowship'.[106]

Two anecdotes reveal how things went on Christian's ship. The first is told by Carleton, although, since he was out of favour at the time, he was not actually present:

> Sir Francis Vere [who commanded the English forces in the Nether-lands] of all the company had the honor to be the soundest drunk; and your good friend Sir Hugh Beeston, who came in his company, was as well wet both without and within but of another liquor: for, standing on the edge of a small boat with Sir John Lucen to get up into the ship, they toppled it over and went both down together to the bottom of the water, to search belike, whether there was no gunpowder treason practicing against the two kings – Sir John Lucen was first ketched up and being pulled by the breeches, which were but taffeta and old linings, had them clean torn off, and the first things which appeared (as Ned Wymark relates, from whom you have this story with especial recommendation) was his cue and his cullions, which as the Danes confessed could be no discredit to Kent or Christendom. Old Hugh, all this while, had his head under the water and, like a crafty knave (as saith mine author), held his breath and having hold with one of his hands on the edge of a boat was spied by a waterman when he was giving over himself and all else had given him for gone. In this interim Sir Francis Darcy with 2 other Darcies in his company had his boat split with the wind of a piece and down went they to look [for] Sir Hugh, but came up again before him. The Knight by this accident hath changed his name and is called about this town Sir Water Beeston.
>
> (p. 88)

The second anecdote, one that caused quite a stir, also seems to indicate that alcohol had had its effect and reveals that the Lepidus of the occasion was the earl of Nottingham, James's senior privy councillor and lord high admiral, a man who in the emergency of 1599 had been for a period of six weeks lord lieutenant-general of all England. He was a powerful figure throughout Elizabeth's reign, best remembered as Howard of Effingham, victor over the Armada; and even in 1606, at the age of seventy, his appearance was impressive. But Charles Howard was really a superannuated Elizabethan, as his modern biographer explains:

> He had a practical common sense which was of great value as long as it did not have to be exercised with uncommon subtlety. Unfortu-

nately, as he grew older, his common sense was no match for the growing intricacy of life and intrigue at court. His lack of courtly wit combined with a growing looseness of tongue to make him often enough sound like a fool. The Jacobean court had no great respect for his past accomplishments and set a rather low value on his present charms. In all truth, by the time James came to England, Howard, now the earl of Nottingham, must have been a bore: a vain, proud, pompous, and garrulous old man whose wealth and talents no longer matched his pretentions.[107]

Like Lepidus, he was open to charges of having grown cruel and of having abused his authority.[108] During James's reign, Nottingham's grasping manipulation of monopolies and the perquisites of high office appeared increasingly objectionable, while the part he played in the prosecution of Sir Walter Raleigh was particularly odious, since he became a principal beneficiary of Raleigh's downfall. His heartless treatment of the ruined Lady Raleigh shows despicable avarice.[109] And when the Naval Commission of 1608–9 reported its findings, it became clearly evident how rife corruption was in the navy under Nottingham's administration.[110] Most damagingly for his reputation, in 1603, less than six months after the death of his wife, Nottingham had made himself ridiculous by courting and marrying a frivolous and indiscreet heiress: he was sixty-eight; she nineteen. The queen referred to the pair mockingly as Mars and Venus, and stories soon circulated, such as the one of how the bridegroom boasted of his virility, and promptly fell ill. A report that the new countess could be heard singing on the wedding night led to debate about whether she was trying to send her husband to sleep or keep him awake, and there were persistent rumours of her infidelity.[111] At the time of Christian's visit, she was thought to be pregnant; and no doubt that gave fresh impetus to malicious wit.[112]

On the occasion of the shipboard feast given by Christian, Nottingham, who must have been elated at his Medway success, as well as exhausted by nervous and physical strain, once again became a figure of ridicule; and once again his marriage was the butt of the joke. Of several accounts, a note in the Egerton papers is the fullest.

The Lord Admirall was the man made choice of to putt his Ma[jes]ty in mynde how the time passed, and when the opportunity of the tide served, . . . he, often consulting with his watch to see how the time slipt away, put the King of En[gland] in mynde that he should leese the benefitt of the tide unlesse he were then gone at that hower. The King of D[enmark], desirous to enjoye the company of theis his deerest

friends as long as possibly he could, was pleased to take notice of this
my L[ord] Ad[miral's] importunitye, and was as ernest on the contrary
side for their longer staye abourde. The L[ord] admirall, in the ende
shewing what hower it was by his watche (which he (as it is sayd) had
purposely advanced some ii howers only for this turne), the K[ing] of
Denmarke, suspecting it, was pleased to aske him what was the hower
by his watche. His Lo[rdshi]p, eyther not willing or not well understanding, still seemed to be of the same opinion. The K[ing of Den-
mark], to make him the better to understand him, was faine to doe yt
by way of demonstration, and, with his foremost fingers directed
towards him, shewed him by the nomber of them the hower of the
day, which was, according to the generall opinion of those present,
neere the true time of the daye; but his Ma[jes]ty in the performance
heerof was so longe in action that the standers by tooke notice that my
Lo[rd] adm[iral] toke some secrett dislike at the manner thereof;
whereof notice being since given to the Countesse of Nottingham, she
hath sent a letter eyther to the King of D[enmark] himself or one very
neere him, the subject whereof was only the discontent she tooke at
the K[ing] of Den[mark]. The particulars of this letter were such as are
very offensively taken heer. Amongst other, shee in expresse plaine
termes writt unto him that she did not thinke that the K[ing] of the
Danes would have offred that abuse to any lady of England as to make
the signe of the hornes at her husband.[113]

Christian had counted on the festivities' continuing until after
dusk; but James, it seems, was determined to leave long before then,
even though this meant having the fireworks set off in the full glare
of the afternoon. Probably James feared that extended entertainment
would become unacceptably drunken; and like Shakespeare's Octavius
bringing Pompey's feast to a premature conclusion as the revelry
begins to get out of control, the British Augustus was anxious to
withdraw while some sobriety remained. But Christian must have
been disappointed by James's restraint; and it was Nottingham who
had the unenviable task of ensuring an early departure, despite the
inevitable reluctance of an expansive host to lose his guest of honour.
Nottingham's unpopularity – he was associated with the Spanish
peace since he had been ambassador extraordinary to Spain in 1605,
and with Anglo-Scottish union since he was one of the commission-
ers for union with Scotland – combined with his vanity and ponder-
ously old-fashioned style, the absurdity of his marriage, and the
problem of communication between Danish speakers and English
speakers made him an easy target for ridicule. The French Ambassador and Dudley Carleton both believed that Christian fully intended
his ambiguous gesture to be more than just a way of indicating the

correct time.[114] Among those present, the incident certainly caused widespread amusement; and the story was enjoyed even in France.[115] By subsequently drawing renewed attention to the insult in her misjudged letter of complaint, the unfortunate countess acted most unwisely, and then compounded her folly with a crassly defiant response when the queen banished her from court.[116]

In Plutarch's accounts of the feast on Pompey's galley and the feast on shore the following day, there is no warrant for the ragging of Lepidus – or, indeed, any indication that the third world-sharer was even present. Shakespeare's immediate source for the addition could well have been the unseemly merriment at Nottingham's expense; and if so, the dramatist followed his model in casting Antony (the character who resembles Christian) as principal leg-puller. But Shakespeare's crocodile joke is a much more appropriate way of making a fool of Lepidus than Christian's two-fingered gesture, although it may also conceivably have had a basis in the state visit. That the two monarchs inspected the royal menagerie, where crocodiles might have been seen, has already been noted. Nottingham was present and could have fallen victim to some humorous allusion to the 'strange serpents'. Once sheer speculation is admitted, however, the way is open for almost any extravagant flight of fancy. For instance, could there not have been, in that confused exchange between Christian and Nottingham, a seminal collision of two key words, the Danish *Klokke* (a two-syllable equivalent of 'clock') and the English *Dial* (the usual Elizabethan word for a watch), so that *klokke-dial*, the composite sound that emerged, suggested a drunken man whose 'tongue / Spleets what it speaks' failing to cope with an intractable letter *r*?

But the natural habitat of crocodiles that tick is, after all, J. M. Barrie's Never Land, and the essential distinction between identifying sources and inventing them must be preserved. Fanciful conjecture is no substitute for knowledge, and the full range of Shakespeare's sources will always elude discovery. Just how much Shakespeare's shipboard scene owes to the shipboard entertainments that marked the end of Christian's visit cannot be ascertained. But when considering Jacobean presences in Shakespeare's Roman play, it is helpful to remember two other Antony-and-Cleopatra plays of the period, one Danish and one English. Hans Thomissøn Stege's Antony-and-Cleopatra tragedy was published in Copenhagen in 1609 with a long, moralising preface. The pious author looks back to Christian's grandfather as a king of blessed memory and spells out six lessons that the play teaches a now degenerate Denmark. The first of these warns against the vice of drunkenness, and the second inveighs against fornication.[117] Stege does not say straight out that Christian resembles Antony, nor could he possibly say it; but there seems to be a message for a reigning monarch whose vices are obvious enough. By implication, therefore, the likeness that Stege flatteringly draws between the virtuous Octavia and Elizabeth Sophie Lindenov, to whom the play is dedicated, is not the only example that this dramatist offers of a parallel between an antique Roman and a modern Dane.[118] The other Antony-and-Cleopatra play is Fulke Greville's. At the time of the fall of Essex, Greville destroyed his manuscript, fearful lest he be thought to have represented 'vices in the present Governours, and government'.[119] How Elizabeth would have reacted to his untimely play we can only guess, and how Christian responded to Stege's admonitions or James to Shakespeare's opalescent fusion of ancient history and Jacobean observation remains beyond our knowledge. But what we can say, when it comes to Shakespeare's play, is that perplexing the dull brain to separate elements so mixed would have been fit occupation only for an ass unpolicied, and James was certainly not that.

From *Shakespeare Studies*, 17 (1985), 123–58.

NOTES

[Neville Davies's discussion of *Antony and Cleopatra* attempts to connect Shakespeare's imaginative reworking of a range of classical material with the historical occasion that may have stimulated the play itself. Fundamental to Davies's approach is the view that there is a connection (though not necessarily direct) between the play and the historical context itself. The one reflects the other. Davies's own methodology is recognisably 'old historicist', concerned as it is with events which lie behind the text. He is not concerned directly with analysing social institutions, although the material that he uncovers can be utilised for an analysis of that kind. Ed.]

I thank B. S. Benedikz (University of Birmingham) and Einar Bjorvand (University of Oslo), who helped me generously in matters Scandinavian in the preparation of this study.

1. William Shakespeare, *Antony and Cleopatra*, ed. Emrys Jones (Harmondsworth, 1977), pp. 46–7. All quotations from the play are from this edition and are cited in parentheses.

2. Helen Morris, 'Queen Elizabeth I "Shadowed" in Cleopatra', *Huntington Library Quarterly*, 32 (1969), 271–8; Kenneth Muir, 'Elizabeth I, Jodelle and Cleopatra', *Renaissance Drama*, NS 2 (1969), 197–206; and Keith Reinhart, 'Shakespeare's Cleopatra and England's Elizabeth', *Shakespeare Quarterly*, 23 (1972), 81–6. In 1624 Thomas Heywood dubbed Elizabeth a 'Cleopatra for her bountie' but only in the course of a series of comparisons that link her with other famous women (Γυναικειον; *or, Nine Bookes of Various History, Concerninge Women*, p. 123). J. H. Walter's contention in his Players' Shakespeare edition of *Antony and Cleopatra* (London, 1969), pp. 305–6, that Shakespeare's Cleopatra recalls Penelope Rich is strained.

3. See Howard Erskine-Hill, *The Augustan Idea in English Literature* (London, 1983), chaps 5–6; Emrys Jones, 'Stuart *Cymbeline*', *Essays in Criticism*, 11 (1961), 84–99; Graham Parry, *The Golden Age Restor'd: The Culture of the Stuart Court, 1603–42* (Manchester, 1981), pp. 16–26; Glynne Wickham, 'From Tragedy to Tragi-Comedy: *King Lear* as Prologue', *Shakespeare Survey*, 26 (1973), 33–48; and D. Harris Willson, *King James VI and I* (London, 1956), esp. pp. 271–87. For the date of composition, see J. Leeds Barroll, 'The Chronology of Shakespeare's Jacobean Plays and the Dating of *Antony and Cleopatra*', in Gordon Ross Smith (ed.), *Essays on Shakespeare* (Pennsylvania, 1965), pp. 115–62, and J. M. Nosworthy, Shakespeare's *Occasional Plays: Their Origin and Transmission* (London, 1965), pp. 9–13.

4. IAC : I : BRIT: CÆ : AVG : HÆ CÆSARVM CÆ. D. D. The medal is well illustrated in Margaret Amstell, *A Start to Collecting Commemorative Medals* (Slough, 1970), p. 15.

5. *A Panegyrike Congratulatorie*, Sts 2, 4, and 13, in Samuel Daniel, *Complete Works*, ed. Alexander B. Grosart (1885–96; rpt. New York; 1963), I, 143–7.

6. See S. T. Bindoff, 'The Stuarts and Their Style', *English Historical Review*, 60 (1945), 193 and 204.

7. Ben Jonson, *Works*, ed. C. H. Herford and Percy and Evelyn Simpson (Oxford, 1931), 7, 109. See also Erskine-Hill, *The Augustan Idea*, pp. 123–9; and Glynne Wickham, 'Riddle and Emblem: A Study in the Dramatic Structure of *Cymbeline*', in John Carey (ed.), *English Renaissance Studies Presented to Dame Helen Gardner* (Oxford, 1980), pp. 100–1. In the event, not all the words that Dekker and Jonson wrote were spoken.

8. John Gordon, 'ενωτικόυ; or, A Sermon of the Union of Great Brittannie' (London, 1604). See also Andrew Fichter, '*Antony and Cleopatra*: The Time of Universal Peace', *Shakespeare Survey*, 33 (1980), 99–111.

9. James I, *Works*, ed. James Montagu (London, 1616), sigs. c2ᵛ and e1ᵛ.

10. Quoted in Wallace Notestein, *The House of Commons, 1604–1610* (New Haven, 1971), p. 200. Anti-Spanish attitudes of the period are surveyed in William S. Maltby, *The Black Legend in England: The Development of Anti-Spanish Sentiment, 1558–1660* (Durham, NC, 1971).

11. [*Winwood's*] *Memorials of Affairs of State in the Reigns of Q. Elizabeth and K. James I*, ed. Edmund Sawyer (London, 1725), II, 217.

12. *The Parliamentary Diary of Robert Bowyer, 1606–1607*, ed. D. H. Willson (Minneapolis, 1931), pp. 333–9, and Francis Bacon, *Works*, ed. J. Spedding, R. L. Ellis, and D. D. Heath, X (London, 1868), 345–61.

13. *Winwood's Memorials*, II, 213.

14. *Winwood's Memorials*, II, 221.

15. *Winwood's Memorials*, II, 225.

16. *Winwood's Memorials*, II, 221, 225, 227, and 229–30

17. Maurice Lee's phrase in his *James I and Henri IV: An Essay in English Foreign Policy, 1603–1610* (Urbana, 1970), p. 13. chap. 3, 'Aftermath of Peace', deals with 1606. Cornwallis's antagonism toward Spain was evident even in 1605, when he accompanied Nottingham on his embassy to the court of Philip III. See Robert W. Kenny, 'Peace with Spain, 1605', *History Today*, 20 (1970), 198–208.

18. *Winwood's Memorials*, II, 235.

19. *Winwood's Memorials*, II, 235–6.

20. *Winwood's Memorials*, II, 237.

21. *Winwood's Memorials*, II, 245. Early in July, news had reached Devon that 'the Commons all about London do cry out for war with Spain', and in September the same diarist recorded that 'there are divers things daily proved against the Spaniards for their treachery to the state of England; and [it is] thought the peace 'twixt us will not long hold' (Walter Yonge, *Diary*, ed. George Roberts [London, 1848], pp. 9 and 11).

22. *Winwood's Memorials*, II, 249.

23. Antoine Le Fèvre de la Boderie, *Ambassades de M. de la Boderie, en Angleterre sous le regne d'Henri IV et la minorité de Louis XIII*, ed. P. D. Burtin (Paris, 1750), I, 45.

24. Horatio F. Brown (ed.), *Calendar of State Papers and Manuscripts Relating to English Affairs, Existing in the Archives and Collections of Venice, and Other Libraries in Northern Italy* (London, 1900), X, 513.

25. Anne Barton, 'Harking Back to Elizabeth: Ben Jonson and Caroline Nostalgia', *ELH*, 48 (1981), 706–31, and David Lindley, 'Campion's *Lord Hay's Masque* and Anglo-Scottish Union', *Huntington Library Quarterly*, 43 (1979), 1–11.

26. Thomas Dekker, *The Whore of Babylon*, III. i. 232–44, in *Dramatic Works*, ed. Fredson Bowers (Cambridge, 1955), II, 541.

27. Godfrey Goodman, *The Court of King James the First* (London, 1839), I, 98.

28. Barton, 'Harking Back', p. 714.

29. James F. Larkin and Paul L. Hughes (eds), *Stuart Royal Proclamations: Royal Proclamations of King James I, 1603–1625* (Oxford, 1973), pp. 94–7. Hereafter cited as *Proclamations*.

30. *Proclamations*, pp. 99–102. The same biblical texts also recur in speeches given and heard by the king, for instance, in James's first address to Parliament (*The Political Works of James I Reprinted from the Edition of 1616*, ed. Charles Howard McIlwain [Cambridge, Mass., 1918], p. 272) and in the chaplain's oration delivered on the occasion of James's entry into the Tower of London, 12 March 1604 (William Hubbocke, *An Oration Congratulatorie* [Oxford, 1604]).

31. *Proclamations*, pp. 135–6. In March 1607 James had to admit to Parliament that he had moved too fast: 'The error was my mistaking; I knew mine owne ende, but not others feares' (*Political Works*, p. 219).

32. R. T. D. Sayle (ed.), *Lord Mayors' Pageants of the Merchant Taylors' Company in the Fifteenth, Sixteenth and Seventeenth Centuries* (London, 1931), 'The Triumphs of Re-United Britania', sig. A2ʳ. See T. D. Kendrick, *British Antiquity* (London, 1950), chap. 5, for 'British' history. Glynne Wickham stresses the relevance of Munday's piece to Shakespeare in his 'Romance and Emblem: A Study in Dramatic Structure of *The Winter's Tale*', in David Galloway (ed.), *The Elizabethan Theatre III: Papers Given at the Third International Conference on Elizabethan Theatre Held at the University of Waterloo, in July 1970* (London, 1973), pp. 82–99, and in his 'From Tragedy to Tragi-Comedy'. See also Marie Axton, *The Queen's Two Bodies: Drama and the Elizabethan Succession* (London, 1977), chap. 9.

33. Donald K. Anderson, 'A New Gloss for the "Three-nook'd World" of *Antony and Cleopatra*', *English Language Notes*, 17 (1979), 103–6.

34. Lines 211–12 and 218 in Jonson, *Complete Masques*, ed. Stephen Orgel (New Haven, 1969), pp. 55–6. For references by James himself, see his *Political Works*, pp. 272, 281, and 290. See also Erskine-Hill, *Augustan Idea*, pp. 130–1, and Bindoff, 'The Stuarts and Their Style', pp. 210–11.

JACOBEAN 'ANTONY AND CLEOPATRA' *157*

35. John Gordon, *England and Scotlands Happinesse in Being Reduced to Unitie of Religion* (London, 1604), pp. 2–4.

36. D. J. Gordon, '*Hymenaei*: Ben Jonson's Masque of Union', *Journal of the Warburg and Courtauld Institutes*, 8 (1945), 107–45, rpt. in his *The Renaissance Imagination: Essays and Lectures*, ed. Stephen Orgel (Berkeley, 1975), pp. 157–84; and Glynne Wickham, 'Masque and Anti-Masque in *The Tempest*', *Essays and Studies*, NS 28 (1975), 1–14.

37. D. H. Willson, 'King James and Anglo-Scottish Unity', in W. A. Aiken and B. D. Henning (eds), *Conflict in Stuart England: Essays in Honour of Wallace Notestein* (London, 1960), p. 43.

38. Joel J. Epstein, 'Francis Bacon and the Issue of Union, 1603–1608', *Huntington Library Quarterly*, 33 (1970), 121–32, and Sir Thomas Craig, *De Unione Regnorum Britanniae Tractatus*, ed. C. Sanford Terry (Edinburgh, 1909).

39. Ludovico Ariosto, *Orlando Furioso*, trans. Sir John Harington (1591), ed. Robert McNulty (Oxford, 1972), book 35, stanza 25 (p. 403).

40. *Shakespeare: Antony and Cleopatra* (London, 1971), p. 23.

41. *A Reading of Shakespeare's 'Antony and Cleopatra'* (Sydney, 1968), pp. 38–9.

42. The clash of opposing judgements is evident in Robert Ashton (ed.), *James I by His Contemporaries: An Account of His Career and Character as Seen by His Contemporaries* (London, 1969). In modern times the debate has been interestingly taken up, and James defended, in Charles Howard Carter, *The Secret Diplomacy of the Hapsburgs, 1598–1625* (New York, 1964), chap. 9.

43. Arthur Wilson's words, first printed in his *The History of Great Britain Being the Life and Reign of James the First* (1653), are quoted in Ashton, *James I by His Contemporaries*, p. 18. Wilson was eleven years old in 1606.

44. Robert P. Kalmey, 'Shakespeare's Octavius and Elizabethan Roman History', *Studies in English Literature*, 18 (1978), 275–87, describes the distinction but holds that Shakespeare dramatises 'only the demagogue Octavius' (p. 279). Erskine-Hill, *The Augustan Idea*, and Howard D. Weinbrot, *Augustus Caesar in 'Augustan' England: The Decline of a Classical Norm* (Princeton, NJ, 1978), also review divided attitudes in the early seventeenth century, with Erskine-Hill attending particularly to Montaigne. David M. Bergeron argues that Shakespeare had a special interest in the Augustan era in '*Cymbeline*: Shakespeare's Last Roman Play', *Shakespeare Quarterly*, 31 (1980), 31–41.

45. Pedro Mexia, *The Historie of All the Romane Emperors*, trans. W. T[raheron] (London, 1604), p. 51, and [Peter Heylyn,] *Augustus; or, An Essay of the Meanes and Counsels Whereby the Commonwealth of*

Rome was Altered, and Reduced unto a Monarchy, ed. Henry Seile (London, 1632), p. 227.

46. Mary F. Tenney's 'Tacitus in the Politics of Early Stuart England', *Classical Journal*, 37 (1941), 151–63, reveals the growing engagement with Tacitus, and Alan T. Bradford, 'Stuart Absolutism and the "Utility" of Tacitus', *Huntington Library Quarterly*, 46 (1983), 127–51, points out the attractiveness of Taciteanism to Jacobean dramatists despite the king's anti-Tacitean views. For the larger context, see Kenneth C. Schellhase, *Tacitus in Renaissance Political Thought* (Chicago, 1976).

47. *Ambassades de M. de la Boderie*, I, 311, where there is mention of *des voix confuses qui disoient, Ah que n'avons-nous un tel Roi*.

48. *Cal S. P. (Venetian)*, X, 398. The French Ambassador relates the same story.

49. M. S. Giuseppi (ed.), *Calendar of the Manuscripts of the . . . Marquis of Salisbury*, pt. XVIII (London: HMSO, 1940), p. 317.

50. *Cal. S. P. (Venetian)*, X, 390.

51. H. G. Garde, *Den dansk-norske Sømagts Historie, 1535–1700* (Copenhagen, 1861), p. 112, and Charles William Petersen, 'English and Danish Naval Strategy in the Seventeenth Century', diss. University of Maine 1975, pp. 68–9. J. C. Tuxen, *Den danske og norske Sømagt fra de ældste Tider indtil vore Dage* (Copenhagen, 1875), p. 185, describes the small Dano-Norwegian fleet that Christian inherited. The activity of Christian's dockyard is recorded in H. D. Lind, *Kong Kristian den Fjerde og hans Mænd paa Bremerholm* (Copenhagen, 1889). In James's fleet in 1606 there were thirty-two warships, not all of which were operational. See the lists for 1604 and 1607 printed in E. H. H. Archibald, *The Wooden Fighting Ship in the Royal Navy AD 897–1860* (London, 1968), pp. 118–19.

52. *Cal S. P. (Venetian)*, X, 383. Seven ships are listed in L. Laursen (ed.), *Kancelliets Brevbøger vedrørende Danmarks indre Forhold i Uddrag 1603–1608* (Copenhagen, 1915), p. 438, three of them built by David Balfour within the preceding five years. But there may have been eight ships altogether, as Preben Holck acknowledges in 'Danish Ships in England', *Mariner's Mirror*, 17 (1931), 295.

53. Henry Robarts, *The Most Royall and Honourable Entertainment of the Famous and Renowned King Christiern the Fourth* (1606), in John Nichols, *The Progresses, Processions and Festivities of King James I, his Royal Consort and Family*, II (London, 1828), 54–69 (p. 56). Johan Dircksen's engraving of Christian Møller's picture of a ship that is probably the *Tre Kroner* (*Three Crowns*) can be seen in Svend Ellehøj, *Christian 4.s Tidsalder, 1596–1660*, 2nd edn, Danmarks Historie, Vol. 7 (Copenhagen, 1970), pp. 186–7, and accompanying R. Morton Nance's

description, 'A "Great Dane" of 1600', *Mariner's Mirror (MM)*, 4 (1914), 225–32. The Latin verses engraved below the picture suggest that the acceptance of the ship by Christian is being celebrated. Nance's description is supplemented in the same journal by R. C. Anderson, 'The Date of the Great Dane', *MM*, 11 (1925), 439, and, under the same title, L. G. C. Laughton, *MM*, 13 (1927), 179–80, and P. Holck, *MM*, 28 (1942), 164–5.

54. *The King of Denmarkes Welcome: Containing His Arivall, Abode and Entertainement, Both in the Citie and Other Places* (London, 1606), p. 4. Only parts of this pamphlet are reprinted in Nichols, *Progresses*, IV, 1072–5.

55. Robarts, *The Most Royall . . . Entertainement*, p. 59.

56. *The King of Denmarkes Welcome*, p. 10. A portrait of 1610 is reproduced in Ellehøj, *Christian 4.s Tidsalder*, p. 33, and serves as frontispiece to Joakim Skovgaard, *A King's Architecture: Christian IV and His Buildings* (London, 1973).

57. For Christian's three-month Arctic voyage see the standard Danish biography, H. C. Bering-Liisberg, *Christian IV, Danmarks og Norges Konge* (Copenhagen, 1890–91), pp. 131–48, and the only book-length biography in English, John A. Gade, *Christian IV, King of Denmark and Norway: A Picture of the Seventeenth Century* (London, 1928), pp. 82–94. The principal sources on which I have drawn are the journal of Jonas Charisius, *Kong Christian den Fierdes Reise omkring de norske Kyster indtil den russiske Grændse, 17 april–13 jul. 1599*, ed. Johann Heinrich Schlegel, in *Samlung zur dänischen Geschichte Münzkenntniss, Oekonomie und Sprache*, I, No. 4 (Copenhagen, 1773), 43–90, and the *diarium vitae* of Sivert Grubbe ('De Curriculo Vitae Sigvardi Grubbii', Royal Library, Copenhagen, Uldallske Saml. MS. 449 4°), translated into Danish by Holger Frederik Rørdam as 'Sivert Grubbes Dagbog', *Danske Magazin*, 4th series, 2 (1873), of which pp. 389–406 cover the voyage. Charisius, who kept his diary at Christian's instigation, was to accompany Christian on the visit to England, while Grubbe was to leave court in 1602. It may be significant that Shakespeare's source in Plutarch for *Ant*, I. iv. 56–71, makes no mention of the snow to which Shakespeare alludes in line 65.

58. Chamberlain to Dudley Carleton, 1 August 1599, *The Letters of John Chamberlain*, I, ed. N. E. McClure (1939; rpt. Philadelphia, 1962), 79. For the background, see Edward P. Cheyney, 'England and Denmark in the Later Days of Queen Elizabeth', *Journal of Modern History*, 1 (1929), 9–39.

59. 'The Mayor and Aldermen of Hull to the Earl of Salisbury, High Steward of Kingston upon Hull', 26 August 1606, *Cal. Salisbury MSS*, XVIII, 253.

60. See Cay Dollerup, *Denmark, 'Hamlet', and Shakespeare: A Study of Englishmen's Knowledge of Denmark Towards the End of the Sixteenth Century with Special Reference to 'Hamlet'* (Salzburg, 1975) and items cited in his bibliography, particularly Ethel Seaton, *Literary Relations of England and Scandinavia in the Seventeenth Century* (Oxford, 1935).

61. The accounts in the biographies by Bering-Liisberg and Gade are supplemented in Gunnar Sjøgren, 'Hamlet and the Coronation of Christian IV', *Shakespeare Quarterly*, 16 (1965), 155–60, rpt. in his *Hamlet the Dane: Ten Essays* (Lund, 1983), pp. 36–45; Otto Andrup, 'Hoffet og dets Fester', in *Danmark i Fest og Glæde*, I, ed. Julius Clausen and Torben Krogh (Copenhagen, 1935), 336–41; and Torben Krogh, 'Optogsbilleder fra Christian IVs Kroningsfest', *Tilskuaren*, 2 (1938), 187–98, rpt. in his *Musik og Teater* (Copenhagen, 1955), pp. 1–11. The chief sources are cited in Frede P. Jensen, 'Peder Vinstrups Tale ved Christian 4.s Kroning. Et teokratisk Indlæg', *Historisk Tidsskrift*, 12th series, 2 (1967), 375–92. Among these Augustus Erich's German account is most important: *Aussfürliche und Hochgeborenen Fürsten und Herrn Herrn Christians des Vierden . . . Krönung* (Copenhagen, 1597).

62. Wilson, *History of Great Britain*, quoted in *James I by His Contemporaries*, p. 12. James's dislike of public occasions is well documented in Josephine Waters Bennett, *'Measure for Measure' as Royal Entertainment* (New York, 1966), esp. pp. 80 and 175–6.

63. *The Court of King James*, I, 168.

64. Edward Peyton, *The Divine Catastrophe of the Kingly Family of the House of Stuarts* (1652) in W. Scott (ed.), *Secret History of the Court of James the First*, II (Edinburgh, 1811), 391–2.

65. Gade, *Christian IV*, p. 72.

66. Gade, *Christian IV*, p. 73.

67. Letter (no source given) quoted in Marchette Chute, *Ben Jonson of Westminster* (London: Hale, 1954), p. 165; and John Davies and Conrad Khunrath, *Greate Britaines Welcome and Relatio oder Erzehlung wie der grossmechtigste Herr Christianus Quartus*, ed. Henry Thejls and Edward C. J. Wolf (Copenhagen, 1957), p. 33.

68. *James I by His Contemporaries*, p. 13.

69. *Cal. S. P. (Venetian)*, X, 386.

70. Thomas Park (ed.), *Nugæ Antiquæ : Being a Miscellaneous Collection of Original Papers*, I (1804; rpt. New York, 1966), 352–3 and 349.

71. Carleton to Chamberlain, 20 August 1606, in Maurice Lee (ed.), *Dudley Carleton to John Chamberlain, 1603–1624: Jacobean Letters* (New Brunswick, NJ, 1972), p. 87.

72. The best account is in Henny Glarbo, *Danske i England: Tre Afhandlinger* (Copenhagen, 1956), supplemented by Bjørn Kornerup, *Biskop Hans Poulsen Resen: Studier over Kirke- og Skolehistorie i det 16. og 17. Aarhundrede,* I (Copenhagen, 1928), 283–90. Certain aspects of the visit are covered by a chapter in Henry N. Paul, *The Royal Play of Macbeth: When, Why, and How It Was Written by Shakespeare* (1948; rpt. New York, 1978), pp. 317–31, and similarly in Torben Krogh, 'Har Christian IV set Shakespeare i England?' in his *Musik og Teater,* pp. 12–18. There are accounts in the biographies of Christian and also in W. Culling Gaze, *On and Along the Thames: James I, 1603–1625* (London, [1913]), pp. 136–45; Skovgaard, *A King's Architecture,* pp. 125–30; and Ethel Carleton Williams, *Anne of Denmark: Wife of James VI of Scotland, James I of England* (London, 1970), pp. 190–23.

73. The principal printed sources are Edmund Howes, the continuator of Stow's *Chronicle,* quoted in Nichols, *Progresses of James I,* II, 88; and Henry Robarts's second pamphlet about Christian's visit, *Englands Farewell to Christian the Fourth* (1606; rpt. in Nichols, *Progresses of James I,* II, 75–85). A Danish view is expressed in an unpublished anonymous diary, 'En kort och richtig Relation skrifsuelsze om den kongelige engelsche Reigse', Royal Library, Copenhagen, Rostgaard Saml. MS. 68 4°.

74. H. M. Colvin, D. R. Ransome, and John Summerson, *The History of the King's Works* (London, 1975), III, pt 1, 272–3.

75. Robarts, in *Progresses,* II, 79; Howes, in *Progresses,* I, 577.

76. Jonson, *Works,* VII, 145–50. For the attribution to Thomas Wilson, see the letter to Dudley Carleton, 5 October 1606, in *The Letters of John Chamberlain,* I, 232. This contradicts the unconvincing attribution to Lyly in *Complete Works of John Lyly,* ed. R. Warwick Bond (Oxford, 1902), I, 537–8. But Inigo Jones may have been involved. See John Harris, Stephen Orgel, and Roy Strong, *The King's Arcadia: Inigo Jones and the Stuart Court* (London, 1973), pp. 31–2.

77. David Clifford Merchant, 'An Edition of *Honour Triumphant and The Monarchs' Meeting',* diss. University of Birmingham, 1970.

78. Robarts in *Progresses,* II, 80, expanded by Drummond's letter, 6 August 1606, in *Progresses,* II, 88. But see Carleton to Chamberlain, p. 87.

79. John Marston, *The Poems,* ed. Arnold Davenport (Liverpool, 1961), pp. 185–8, and *The King of Denmarkes Welcome* in *Progresses,* IV, 1074–5.

80. Paul, *The Royal Play of Macbeth,* pp. 322–3 and 325.

81. The slender evidence about *Macbeth* is challenged by J. Leeds Barroll in 'The Chronology of Shakespeare's Jacobean Plays'.

82. E. K. Chambers, *The Elizabethan Stage* (Oxford, 1923), IV, 121.

83. *The Royal Play of Macbeth*, p. 328.

84. *Nugæ Antiquæ*, I, 349–51.

85. Louis B. Wright, 'Henry Robarts: Patriotic Propagandist and Novelist', *Studies in Philology*, 29 (1932), 176–99 (pp. 191–2).

86. *The King of Denmarkes Welcome* is supposedly 'Written in a discourse from a Gentleman to a friend of his in the northerne parts' (1606 edition, STC 5194, p. 1).

87. *Nugæ Antiquæ*, I, 349.

88. *Nugæ Antiquæ*, I, 352.

89. For examples of exclusion in performance, see William P. Halstead, *Shakespeare as Spoken: A Collection of 5000 Acting Editions and Promptbooks of Shakespeare* (Ann Arbor, 1977–79), XII, 922c, and Strindberg's comment that the scene 'seems superfluous to us and probably can be cut completely' (*Open Letters to the Intimate Theatre*, trans. Walter Johnson [London, 1967], p. 272). Even Granville-Barker, who recognised the scene's 'solidity, variety and colour', described it in 1930 as a 'rest point in the action' (*Prefaces to Shakespeare*, I [London, 1958], 410). Recent commentators have become increasingly aware of the scene's importance. It is the 'great scene . . . to which all this part of the play has been leading' in Derek Traversi's account (*Shakespeare: The Roman Plays* [London, 1963], p. 123), while Maurice Charney, in *Shakespeare's Roman Plays: The Function of Imagery in Drama* (Cambridge, Mass., 1963), locates in this scene the 'most important and direct use of world imagery' (p. 84). Arguing that 'in *Antony and Cleopatra* the pattern of instability and insecurity is basic, and encompasses all elements of the play', William Leigh Godshalk identifies this scene as the 'symbolic centre' of a 'general pattern of political instability' (*Patterning in Shakespearean Drama: Essays in Criticism* [The Hague, 1973], p. 156). Emrys Jones, in his New Penguin edition (1977), declares simply, 'More than any other scene, it encapsulates the vision of the play' (p. 22). Shipboard scenes in the drama of Shakespeare's time are examined in Louis B. Wright, 'Elizabethan Sea Drama and Its Staging', *Anglia*, 51 (1927), 104–18, and Ralph Berry, 'Metamorphoses of the Stage', *Shakespeare Quarterly*, 33 (1982), 5–16. The naval protocol of Shakespeare's scene is explained in Alexander Frederick Falconer, *Shakespeare and the Sea* (London, 1964), pp. 18–20.

90. R. C. Anderson, *List of English Men-of-War, 1509–1649* (Greenwich, 1974), items 139, 154, 216, and 217. The *White Bear*, from one of the C. J. Visscher engravings, is shown in E. Keble Chatterton, *Old Ship Prints* (1927; rpt. London, 1965), plate 14. At the time of the Armada,

this ship was painted red. A description of the carved decoration that she carried after the rebuilding is given in A. L. Rowse, *The Expansion of Elizabethan England* (1955; rpt. London, 1973), pp. 272–3. A photograph of a model based on the rebuilt *Elizabeth Jonas* appears in G. S. Laird Clowes, *Sailing Ships: Their History and Development as Illustrated by the Collection of Ship-Models in the Science Museum*, revised by E. W. White, 3rd edn (London, 1948), plate V.

91. *The Autobiography of Phineas Pett*, ed. W. G. Perrin (London, 1918), p. 29.

92. Letter of John Pory to Sir Robert Cotton, 12 August 1606, *Progresses*, II, 91; Howes's continuation of Stow's *Chronicle* in *Progresses*, II, 89; Robarts, *Englands Farewell* in *Progresses*, II, 83; Charleton to Chamberlain, p. 87; and 'En kort och richtig Relation', p. 32.

93. *Englands Farewell*, in *Progresses*, II, 83.

94. Pory's letter, in *Progresses*, II, 91.

95. 'En kort och richtig Relation', p. 31.

96. Pory's letter, in *Progresses*, II, 91.

97. *Englands Farewell*, in *Progresses*, II, 83.

98. Carleton to Chamberlain, p. 87.

99. Carleton to Chamberlain, p. 87. For an indication of the layout of the scene, see the map of the Medway anchorage (British Library, Cott. MS. Aug. I. i. 52), showing twenty-one ships, reproduced in M. Oppenheim, *A History of the Administration of the Royal Navy and of Merchant Shipping in Relation to the Navy* (London, 1896), I, facing p. 150.

100. Pory, Howes, and Robarts, in *Progresses*, II, 92, 89, and 83. Pory reports Christian's remark.

101. T. J. B. Spencer (ed.), *Shakespeare's Plutarch* (Harmondsworth, 1964), p. 213.

102. The Danish diarist notes, 'Baade paa skibene ok paa Galleierne, med saadand Mūscik ok spil paa samme spiell, Var der med Adtskellige Maskeratter Formummet Udi Atskelige Klededragt', but the precise meaning is unclear ('En kort och richtig Relation', p. 29).

103. For instance, Pory, and Robarts in both his pamphlets. Howes refers to 'the King of Denmarke's shippe, commonly called the Admirall' (*Progresses*, II, 89).

104. Pory, in *Progresses*, II, 92.

105. Carleton to Chamberlain, p. 87.

106. Carleton to Chamberlain, pp. 87–8.

107. Robert W. Kenny, *Elizabeth's Admiral: The Political Career of Charles Howard, Earl of Nottingham, 1536–1624* (Baltimore, 1970), p. 7.

108. *Shakespeare's Plutarch*, p. 244, and *Ant*, III. vi. 32.

109. Kenny, *Elizabeth's Admiral*, pp. 275–7.

110. Donald Robert Martin, 'Corruption and Reform in the Jacobean Navy: The Report of the Naval Commission of 1608–1609', diss. University of Miami, 1974.

111. Patrick Walker and A. Macdonald (eds), *Letters to King James the Sixth* (Edinburgh, 1935), Facsimile 3, and earl of Worcester's letter to earl of Shrewsbury, 24 September 1603, in *Progresses*, I, 274.

112. Carleton to Chamberlain, p. 90.

113. J. Payne Collier (ed.), *The Egerton Papers: A Collection of Public and Private Documents Chiefly Illustrative of the Times of Elizabeth and James I* (London, 1840), pp. 468–9, corroborated by both Carleton and the French Ambassador. Sir Edward Peyton's more scandalous account of Christian's behaviour toward the countess and her husband (*Secret History of the Court of James I*, II, 387) is not reliable.

114. Ledit Roi lui fit par deux ou trois fois les cornes avec les doigts, voulant dire qu'il étoit deux heures, et accompagna cela d'une telle risée entre la reine et lui, que ledit Amiral [Nottingham] s'en sentit infiniment piqué' (*Ambassades de M. de la Boderie*, I, 307). Similarly, 'Our king, asking what o'clock it was and desirous to be gone, my lord admiral as willing to hasten him answered four; the king of Denmark seeking all meanes to stay them said it was but two and for doubt of not being understood made a sign with his two fingers to my lord admiral, which the good man took no worse than it seemed to be meant' (Carleton to Chamberlain, p. 90). Perhaps there was animosity between Christian and Nottingham anyway. They were to be sharply opposed in their attitudes to Raleigh, whom Christian admired; and the alteration of Thomas Cockson's engraving of Nottingham on horseback to represent Christian would undoubtedly have upset Nottingham if it was in circulation in 1606. But although the altered engraving would have sold well at the time of the state visit, it is dated ca. 1630 in Arthur M. Hind, *Engraving in England in the Sixteenth and Seventeenth Centuries: A Descriptive Catalogue with Introductions*, pt. 1 (Cambridge, 1952), pp. 249–50.

115. De Villeroy to Boderie, 9 September 1606, *Lettres d'Henry IV, roi de France et de messeiurs de Villeroy, et de Puisieux, à Mr. Antoine Le Fèvre de la Boderie, ambassadeur de France en Angleterre, depuis 1606, jusqu'en 1611*, I (Amsterdam, 1733), 73.

116. 'Sir Thomas Lake to the Earl of Salisbury', 7 September 1606, *Cal. MSS . . . Marquis of Salisbury*, XVIII, 276.

117. *Cleopatra: Eller en historisk Tragœdia om den sidste Dronning i Egypten, ved Naffn Cleopatra, oc M. Antonio, en romersk Keyser . . . paa danske Riim udsat,* sigs. b1ᵛ–b4ʳ and repeated in the Epilogus, sig. M7ᵛ.

118. Sig. d2ᵛ.

119. *Sir Fulke Greville's Life of Sir Philip Sidney etc. First Published 1652,* ed. Nowell Smith (Oxford, 1907), p. 156.

6

'Let Rome in Tiber melt': Order and Disorder in 'Antony and Cleopatra'

MARGOT HEINEMANN

Thinking about the representation of chaos and order in our interpretation of Shakespeare today I recall the great French actor-
director and cinéaste Jean-Louis Barrault discussing a similar theme
at a comparable time of crisis and upheaval. Speaking at the Edinburgh Festival in 1948, not long after the Second World War and at
the very outset of the Cold War that followed, he explained why at
this moment he fed more on Shakespeare than on Molière (he was
bringing his production of *Hamlet* in French to the festival that year):

> Shakespeare is topical to our time, he lived as we do now, in an age of
> transition, an age of revolutions and calamities in which the old faith
> had been lost, and the new one had not yet appeared. His world was,
> like ours, in the throes of doubt. Molière on the contrary lived in an
> age of prosperity and brilliance, in an orderly society dominated by
> monarchic authority. Wealth, prosperity, order, authority, all these
> notions are very remote from us; Molière stands for equilibrium and
> at this moment we do not know what equilibrium is . . . At this
> moment, and I mean at this moment, and not in fifty years' time when
> things will be different, Shakespeare is more modern than Molière. He
> is closer to us, and the conditions in which he lived are also closer to
> ours.

More than anyone else, Shakespeare immortalised the turmoil of his
time:

The Middle Ages were fading away, and with them the faith which
united the Western world; the religious reformation begun under
Henry VIII was still in progress, and the political revolution which
reached its climax with Charles I was about to begin; the modern age
was about to be born, and Shakespeare was, as we are now, strug-
gling in a vale where murders and catastrophes were part of life, and
where all human values were again questioned . . . To us, who still
have present in our minds the memory of Buchenwald and Auschwitz,
the retreat of Dunkirk or the horrors endured by Coventry and Hiro-
shima, these cries of despair easily find an echo in our souls. We must
confess that we feel rather remote from the antiquated common sense
of Chrysale and the arguments of *les femmes savantes.*

In this situation, Shakespeare replaces the poet in his true function, as the abstract and brief chronicle of his time.

Had he emerged like us from the Second World War, and had he lived,
as we do, through the anxieties caused by the behaviour of the two
world powers which are holding peace in their hands, I doubt if he
would alter in any way Enobarbus's words when he says about
Antony and Caesar who are now face to face:

Then, world, thou hast a pair of chaps – no more;
And throw between them all the food thou hast,
They'll grind the one the other.
            (*Antony and Cleopatra*, III. v. 13–15)[1]

Shakespeare can be seen, says Barrault, as the patron of the
committed artist, but committed to be involved, to bear witness,
rather than to take sides as a political or religious propagandist.[2] And
significantly the first play he refers to is *Antony and Cleopatra*, the
most open, far-ranging and complex of all Shakespeare's historical
plays.

I

Antony and Cleopatra represents the disintegration and transmutation not only of a passionate relationship, but of a whole world and
its values. The chaos looks more radical and shocking, the supposed
restoration of order at the end less firm and reassuring, if we see it in
the light of history. Win or lose, the struggle between the triumvirs
marks the end of the republic, so admired and idealised in the
European Renaissance for its stern Roman virtues and the anti-

absolutist principles of its aristocracy. Chaos seems more than a brief
interlude: it could well be irreversible.

Within the play, everything external is in rapid change. Fixed
points disappear, military and political alliances form and break up,
eastern and western cultures clash, allegiance and authority melt
away. The word 'melt' runs through the play, from Antony's first
scene of defiance:

> Let Rome in Tiber melt, and the wide arch
> Of the ranged empire fall!
>
> (I. i. 35)

to his final loss:

> The hearts
> That spaniel'd me at heels, to whom I gave
> Their wishes, do discandy, melt their sweets
> On blossoming Caesar.
>
> (IV. xii. 20)

Under the pressure of defeat subjective identities and values like
honour and love dissolve and transform too. Devotion is transmuted
(at Actium) into cowardice; valour into the blind ferocity of a dying
animal; love into policy; loyalty under a distracted commander into
stupidity; reason into treason. And meanwhile tens of thousands die.
All over the empire it is

> As if the world should cleave, and that slain men
> Should solder up the rift.
>
> (III. iv. 31)

Yet chaos is not represented as merely a muddle, or a mystery of
pure chance, with a hero whose good fortune has deserted him. That
is certainly part of the story, and Antony, always a gambler rather
than a planner, naturally sees it so. But for the audience, his desertion
by the god Hercules can be seen as the end of a long process. (Even
the Egyptian soothsayer warning him to keep away from Caesar
whose luck is better may be acting as Cleopatra's agent, says Plutarch.)

Disaster and collapse are shown as the outcome of multiple human, psychological, material and political contradictions in that
world, dissected and exposed in the episodic action, cutting across
one another, intersecting one with another and modifying one another with unforeseeable results. The historical process is retrospec-

tively intelligible, though not predictable. Too many local conflicts and insoluble contradictions are indeed observed and revealed for any to provide an overriding causal explanation of the global disorder and thus imply a single way to understand, resolve or control it. Everything – actions and individuals – is shown in a double or more than double light, the rapid shifts of mood and of reporting characters producing a many-sided, endlessly changing view.

The very large cast-list even by Shakespearean standards (some 35 speaking parts, as against 18 in *Coriolanus*, 20 in *Lear*, 22 in *Henry IV Part 1*, 11 in Robert Garnier's *Antonie*) allows the long and diffuse history to be *staged* in brief contrasting episodes, rather than narrated with choric or authorial comment; and this gives space for even minor characters to change (everyone has their breaking-point), and incidentally allows an unforced sense of the price lower ranks have to pay in smaller personal tragedies for the grand designs and follies of those above them.[3] The episodic construction is, of course, in marked contrast to other near-contemporary plays on the same subject,[4] neo-classical or Senecan in form, which focus rigorously on the last stages of the love-tragedy, limiting the historical-political build-up to narrative speeches or the ethical comments of a unified chorus, and thus making the conflicts relatively few, simple and predictable, though the choruses themselves may be (as in Samuel Daniel's *Cleopatra*) poignant and moving.

II

The final conflict of Caesar against Antony, or of Caesar's Rome against Cleopatra's Egypt, is often treated as not only central but exclusive. But other discords are coolly revealed, too, in Shakespeare's wider rendering of the history as he found it in Plutarch:

(a) The constant warfare in which *all* military and political leaders, whether allies or opponents, compete for power, followers and loot.

(b) The danger of a republican revolt by alienated Romans and popular forces, led by Pompey and his pirate friends, which Antony's 'duty' tears him away from Egypt to help quell.

(c) The clash between the older ideas of honour expected of a republican leader (which Pompey still claims to be) and the new, ruthless political manoeuvring and action now required for success, in face of which the republican challenge collapses.

(d) The glamour of the hand-to-hand armoured swordsman (Antony's image from the first lines of the play), and the personal prestige and comradeship which that confers, set against Caesar's logistic planning and efficiency, his ability to move troops and war materials rapidly to the battle-fronts.

(e) The vast distance and alienation between front-line commanders at the borders of the empire and *all* chairborne generals – Ventidius, victorious in Parthia, notes that 'Caesar and Antony have ever won/More in their officer than person' (III. i. 16), and decides he had better not achieve more glory lest he make his master jealous.

(f) The unstable loyalty of subordinates who, whatever their personal preferences, depend on pillage and spoil to pay their legions, and must therefore gravitate to the stronger side; while tributary kings seek the best bargain from whichever conquering emperor or queen they can.

(g) The contrast, obvious to their followers, between uncontrolled power and the selfish, weak or irresponsible men who wield it. As Leipidus is carried off drunk by his slave from the feast on Pompey's galley, the cynical Enobarbus comments 'There's a strong fellow, Menas. . . . A' bears the third part of the world, man' (II. vii. 83).

These complexities of interest, spread over three continents, are bewildering: the whole world is spinning out of control and a firm centre is lacking. Much of this effect is, of course, removed if the more directly political scenes (such as the 'summit meeting' of the triumvirs or the sequence involving Pompey) are omitted to make room for elaborate changes of scenery, as they almost invariably were in the eighteenth- and nineteenth-century theatre, or drastically cut in performance as they still have often been in the twentieth century, at least until quite recently,[5] on the grounds that the 'central' contradiction between love and honour, sexual pleasure and lust for power, is alone capable of interesting an audience.[6]

Moreover, all this detailed historical movement and flux is not just a backdrop to the great love story, but is seen to exert continuous pressure on *all* the personal relationships represented. The passionate relation between the mighty lovers, given through the language with erotic intensity and dizzying comic variety (the jokes, as in Donne's poems, saving the rhetoric from over-sweetness), is not sentimentalised as a private romantic idyll, an enclave of feminine feeling removed from politics and battles, but shown as inseparable from the power struggle for control of Egypt and the world, within which it originates and with which it always remains entangled. Antony's imperial power and military glory, Cleopatra's fabulous wealth as queen of the fertile Nile, are part of the attraction between them, and their delights – the feasting, the splendour, the careless generosity to kings and servants – depend on the continuance of wealth and conquest. If this is carnival it is a rich people's carnival, a scene from Veronese rather than Breughel.

Cleopatra, we are reminded, has always frankly used her sexuality as an element in the struggle to keep hold of Egypt, with Julius Caesar and Pompey long before Antony. We see her still so using it after Antony's death as she tries to escape being led in Caesar's triumph. The violent quarrels and reconciliations between the lovers, the contest for sexual mastery (emblematised in their cross-dressing), her feigned heartbreak or indifference, Antony's unprincipled marriage, are likewise related to the power struggle, not only to men's inconstancy or women's changeable arts. Theirs is a publicly performed affair, not one stolen privately from history (unlike Troilus and Cressida or Romeo and Juliet, they are never seen alone together). Its apex is not a secret night of love, but their enthronement in Alexandria's market-place, she dressed as the goddess Isis, he as divine consort conferring kingdoms on her and her children – an alternative Eastern power base to Rome itself.

The godlike identities they have constructed for one another exalt self-delighting, chaotic sensuous pleasure and fertility – the great 'carpe diem' affirmation of so much Renaissance art – yet require continued power. In the face of military and political defeat they begin to fall apart, and the language enacts this. The dignity and self-image of greatness collapses into depression and confusion, 'dislimns' and becomes 'indistinct as water is in water'. Only the imminence of death revives the heroic identities and allows grief and courage to soar into legend. Yet however it arises, however manipulated, tipping the balance of an unstable world, this transgressive relation is represented as real, warm and compelling. Indeed, the principals often behave as if they do not themselves know how serious it is and are startled at how unbreakable the 'strong Egyptian fetters' prove to be.

Moreover, the experience of chaos and disorder is not harmonised by a clear historical or ethical judgement on the action. Shake-speare's English histories, even at their most savage and terrifying, still provide some kind of bearings through the element of patriotic nationalism which allows the audience, if they so choose, to identify the restoration of order and justice with the immediate national interests of England. After Shakespeare's decisive turn to Roman history (ironically resulting in part from the censorship on English history imposed after the Essex revolt), this direct equation of reason and order with the military victory of one side no longer operates. In the final confrontation between Rome and Egypt, the audience has no such pre-existing emotional alignment. Its sympathies and judge-ments can move for or against each of the protagonists from scene to scene, producing unusual scepticism and detachment together with unusual involvement in the representation. At the centre is not a unifying conviction about authority and order, but a radical contra-diction of interests and values – a question rather than an answer.

Accordingly, critics and readers have notoriously responded to the play in sharply opposed ways – G. B. Shaw and Croce, for example, condemning the lovers for voluptuousness and neglect of their plain duty; others (from G. Wilson Knight to Terry Eagleton and the Bremer Shakespeare Company) treating their reckless transgressive passion as the one meaningful, self-validating experience in a mean-ingless world; others again (like John Danby) sensing a deliberate dialectical ambiguity in the play itself as to whether one should opt for duty or love. This has indeed been regarded as a 'problem play' rather than a tragedy because it makes us, in Ernest Schanzer's phrase, 'uncertain of our moral bearings'.

Much orthodox criticism has simplified away these ambivalences. Caesar's Rome is assumed to represent public duty as against private self-indulgence; the sacrifice of pleasure and personal affection to build a strong state and impose a lasting peace; the armed guarantee of future civilisation. This would have been *the* Jacobean view, we are assured, even if it is not ours, and it is presented by many editors (especially in school texts) as axiomatic. The New Arden edition of M. R. Ridley (1954) is a representative if extreme case:

> When Antony says 'the nobleness of life is to do thus', we know that for himself, and perhaps also for Cleopatra, he is stating the mere truth; but unless his values were wrong it would not be the truth . . . The world loses little by their passing; and indeed we know that for the world it is better that the Roman State should on, cracking their link asunder.[7]

In line with this, the spectacle of Antony, 'a man of considerable qualities wasting them in an infatuation', is not ennobling; their love is 'not the highest kind of love', though it offers us 'a thrill, a quickening of the pulses', and the play cannot be a great tragedy, since it lacks the sense of devastating waste. Octavius, though admittedly an unattractive figure, represents

> the relentless power of Rome . . . something against whose ineluctable march no individuals, however great, can for one moment stand.

And at the end Caesar is 'more than himself'; he is Rome, looking down with a just and not unsympathetic estimation, on the 'pair so famous' over whom her chariot wheels have rolled'.[8] This meshes readily with the imperial magnificence of nineteenth-century staging and the nostalgic image of the British Raj.

Yet despite all this, few theatre audiences seem to side comfortably or unequivocally with Caesar's Rome as the supposed norm of order and moral authority. If we see the play in its historical context, as a Jacobean play about Roman times, now observed by a twentieth-century audience, it becomes clearer why this should be so.

III

Two Versions of History

In the early 1600s this much-dramatised subject, and indeed the representation of the whole period, was felt as much more problematic and politically risky. We know that Fulke Greville burned the manuscript of his tragedy of Antony and Cleopatra because, as he said, it might be 'construed or strained to a personating of vices in the present government', especially after the fall of Essex, 'till then ever worthily beloved both of the Queen and people'.[9] And Shakespeare, Geoffrey Bullough thinks, probably intended to follow *Julius Caesar* (1599) with another play on the break-up of the triumvirate, but postponed it for political and personal reasons:

> No doubt Shakespeare and his company were careful what they played after the [Essex] revolt, when Southampton was still pent in the Tower (where he remained until 1603), and the morale of the country was shaken by the revelation of division in high places.[10]

Antony and Cleopatra was not staged until around 1607–8 (or printed before the Folio of 1623). In the meantime several playwrights dealing with classical themes were hauled before the Privy Council for dangerous political comment – notably Jonson over *Sejanus*, a play based closely on Suetonius' and Tacitus' accounts of the rule of terror under Tiberius, in which the martyred historian Cordus claims freedom for later writers to represent Brutus and Cassius as worthy men. Jonson was lucky to escape with his ears intact, although he was certainly no republican and there was no obvious parallel to be made with the Essex affair. More was involved than possible personal allusions to Essex (whom King James had in fact regarded as his ally). It was rather a matter of subversive ideas latent in the popularising of classical history, questioning the authority of absolute monarchy and the legitimacy of dictatorial rule.

Two quite different ways of seeing the period were indeed available. There was a radical split both in the original historiography and in the contemporary interpretation of classical history as a mirror for the times – a split, very roughly, between Caesarian and republican traditions. And this division surely contributes to the sense of ambiguity and ambivalence in the play itself.

In the older traditional historiography, the decisive victory of a single ruler and the establishment of the Empire was seen as the beginning of a new Virgilian golden age. James I, like other absolutist monarchs in Europe, liked to identify himself with Augustus, especially in his role as peacemaker. The medieval tradition of Julius Caesar as the greatest of the Nine Worthies, and Brutus and Cassius as scoundrelly regicides burning in Dante's Hell along with Cleopatra, could be readily fused with one Tudor myth of benevolent despotic power, to make the Empire established by Octavius the type of stable and peaceful rule. This is the kind of reading assumed by Emrys Jones in his Penguin edition of *Antony and Cleopatra*:

> The play is an imperial work in a special sense – written by the leading dramatist of the King's Men, whose patron was James I . . . It is hard to resist the notion that this most courtly of Shakespeare's tragedies must have been performed at James' court. James was England's modern Augustus. James was himself an imperial quasi-Augustan peacemaker. So the British Augustus may have watched this Augustan tragedy.[11]

However, for many of Shakespeare's contemporaries and patrons this crucial historical turning-point had quite a different significance, and a tragic one, pointing not to the triumph of peace but to the corruption and ultimate decline of Roman civilisation. In this republican tradition, deriving especially from Plutarch (Shakespeare's main source) and from the increasingly influential Tacitus,[12] Brutus and Cassius (whom Antony in the play boasts of having destroyed at Philippi) were at least partly heroes, even if they were bound to fail; while Octavius, Antony and Lepidus, despite the conflicts between them, could all be seen as the self-seeking heirs of Julius Caesar, whose insatiable ambition for power had led (according to Plutarch) to wars, tyranny and the destruction of the republic, after which single rule became inevitable. The wars of the triumvirs, on this view, marked primarily the decline of the old Roman virtues or order, discipline, valour, selfless concern for the State, and firm anti-absolutist principles, all embodied for the Renaissance in admired republican figures like Cato and Scipio.

This second version of history was much used by European writers seeking analogies with the advance of imperial despotism and the fall of republics in their own day. Montaigne, who regarded Plutarch as 'the most judicious author of the world,' wrote of Tacitus: 'His service is more proper [than Livy's] to a crazed and troubled state, as is ours at this present.' The famous radical tract *Vindiciae Contra Tyrannos*, justifying tyrannicide against monarchs repressing true religion, written by Philip Sidney's Huguenot friend Du Plessis Mornay and signed with the pseudonym Junius Brutus, denounced Julius Caesar as a typical tyrant.[13] Earlier dramatisations in English of the Antony and Cleopatra story drew on this reading. Thus *Antonie*, translated by Sidney's sister, the Countess of Pembroke, from the *Marc Antoine* of Garnier,[14] shows the flawed doctrine of 'all for love' in confrontation with Caesar's equally false doctrine of military supremacy tied to self-aggrandisement;[15] and her Caesar speaks after victory as a hubristic tyrant prepared to safeguard his own safety by general massacre:

> We must with blood mark this our victory
> For just example to all memory.
> Murder we must, until not one we leave
> Which may hereafter us of rest bereave.

The chaotic world of Antony and Cleopatra could, then, be seen as moving towards the reign of corrupt emperors described by Tacitus, who had first been translated into English in the 1590s and promoted as the favoured historian of Essex, Greville and the aristocratic critics of absolute monarchy. Shakespeare is thought to have read him at that time while writing *Henry V*, and would certainly have done so by 1607. As an anti-providentialist, sceptical, scientific, 'politique' historian, widely looked to for tactical lessons in state-craft, Tacitus saw the expansion, corruption and decline of republics as inevitable and cyclical. His sombre analysis of disorder points not to any ordered resolution of chaos but to the need for hard-headed pragmatism in order to survive under a despotic state, and his account of the later career of Augustus, prefaced to his *Annals* of imperial history, is a searing contrast to the triumphalist view.

Tacitus' growing influence was deeply distrusted by King James, who thought him favourable to tyrannicide, and who also attacked Plutarch as biased against Caesar and monarchy. The King had a point. Although classical republican ideas were an inspiration or a warning, rather than a programme, for dissident aristocrats and intellectuals in early Stuart England, they were not purely nostalgic and backward-looking, but survived underground among the classi-cally educated (notably in the Sidney and Neville families) and were to surface again as one strand of revolutionary thought in the 1640s. More generally, Thomas Hobbes in *Behemoth* notes among the causes of the civil war the influence of their classical education on the Parliamentarian leaders:

> There were an exceeding great number of men of the better sort, that had been so educated as that in their youth having read the books written by famous men of the ancient Grecian and Roman common-wealths concerning their polity and great actions, in which books the *popular* government was extolled by the glorious name of liberty and monarchy disgraced by the name of tyranny, they became thereby in love with their forms of government. And out of these men were chosen the greatest part of the House of Commons; or, if they were not the greatest part, yet, by advantage of their eloquence, they were always able to sway the rest.[16]

A generation earlier, *both* the Virgilian *and* the Tacitean perspec-tive are inescapably part of the imaginative context of *Antony and Cleopatra*. When Caesar in victory declares, 'The time of universal peace is near', does this signal that order and reason are about to be restored, or merely that his own single supremacy has been estab-lished for the time being? Like so much else in the play the question remains open-ended, uncertain: it is for the audience to decide. And some of them would certainly recall Tacitus' bleak verdict on the Augustan years:

The violent deaths of Brutus and Cassius left no Republican forces in the field. Defeat came to Sextus Pompeius in Sicily, Lepidus was dropped, Antony killed. So even the Caesarian party had no leader left except the 'Caesar' himself, Octavian . . . Indeed, he attracted everybody's goodwill by the enjoyable gift of peace. Then he gradually pushed ahead and absorbed the functions of the senate, the officials, and even the law. Opposition did not exist. War or judicial murder had disposed of all men of spirit. Upper-class survivors found that slavish obedience was the way to succeed, both politically and financially . . .

By the end of his time, says Tacitus,

Even most of the older generation had come into a world of civil wars. Practically no one had ever seen truly Republican government. The country had been transformed, and there was nothing left of the fine old Roman character. Political equality was a thing of the past; all eyes watched for imperial commands.[17]

It is even possible to feel that the older values asserted in the 'high Roman' deaths of the 'famous pair' are at least preferable to those implied in Caesar's victory.

IV

Negative Capability

The variety of viewpoints and judgements presented, the refusal of a single historical or ethical centre, is an especially marked feature of *Antony and Cleopatra*. However, the ability *not* to draw what Dryden called an 'excellent moral' from the flux of events has been noted (in various terms) as a central point of Shakespearean dramaturgy over many generations from Dr Johnson to Keats and Brecht, whether the critics approved of it or not. Thus for Johnson, Shakespeare 'is so much more careful to please than to instruct that he seems to write without any moral purpose. He makes no just distribution of good or evil. He carries his persons indifferently through right and wrong, and at the end dismisses them without further care, and leaves their examples to operate by chance' (*Preface to Shakespeare*, 1765). Keats observes but admires the same process when he notes 'that quality which Shakespeare possessed so enormously – I mean *negative capability*, that is, when a man is capable of being in uncertainties, mysteries, doubts, without any irritable reaching after fact and reason' (*Letters*, December 1817). And the young Brecht similarly praises the refusal to impose a constructed order on disorder:

> With Shakespeare the spectator does the constructing . . . In the lack of connection between his acts we see the lack of connection in a human destiny, when it's recounted by someone with no interest in tidying it up to provide an idea (which can only be a prejudice) with an argument not taken from life.
>
> (*Macbeth* radio prologue, 1927)

This is the same effect referred to by Barrault when he speaks of Shakespeare as a committed writer in a time of chaos, committed to observe and bear witness, not to take sides as a propagandist. For the generation of Montaigne, living through the French religious wars, scepticism had a strong appeal; Shakespeare read him in Florio's translation about this time.[18]

'Negative capability' is not absolute, of course (though it may seem so relatively to what we find in Jonson or Marlowe). The very selection Shakespeare makes from the mass of rich material in Plutarch inevitably implies preferences and analyses, brings out some contradictions and omits others, highlights some conflicts of values and softens others.[19] Censorship, and the need to avoid irritating King and court, also encouraged a degree of reticence. All the same, the technique does leave the spectators (as well as later students) some room to choose their sympathies and judgements for themselves, and perhaps change their minds later, rather as we do in life, where despite the insolubility of contradictions action is necessarily arbitrary and involves taking sides (since to do nothing is also, as *Hamlet* demonstrates, inescapably to do something). The audience are thereby stimulated, even compelled, to think about what they see.

V

Indeterminacy and the Plays in Performance

It is now generally conceded that 'negative capability' and ambivalence allows of new, widely differing theatrical productions, none of which will be definitely 'right'. Even 'what Shakespeare intended' is no longer accepted as a privileged criterion (though there is still something to be said for it). Where Romantic critics like Goethe or Charles Lamb stressed mainly the imaginative *losses* in performance, we feel enormous gains in vividness, coherence, the element of intermittent illusion which enables spectators to identify with an experience not their own, and thereby see their own in a new perspective. But today's powerful Shakespearean directors often overdo the coherence.

In principle, alternatives, conflicting feelings and judgements, surprises and shocks ought to be there within a single performance. Whichever aspect of the conflict is made dominant, differences and swings of sympathy must still be possible. Otherwise the sense of dismaying complexity and chaos is defeated by 'tidying up' in the interests of unity and clarity what Shakespeare left open-ended and uncertain. Insoluble contradictions and unpredictable risks are too easily smoothed out by the all-knowing director, and 'complex seeing' of unresolved human situations is avoided. And with this disappears the whole terrifying resemblance to our own chaotic time with its seemingly unpredictable and uncontrollable events. This removes the pressure on the audience to observe, think and imagine for themselves, and not to take predigested conclusions for granted.

No performance, of course, can or should be as open and indeterminate as the text, read and reread in the reader's imagination. *Choices* have to be made, about casting, movement, cutting, clothing, the meaning of particular speeches. The actor cannot walk down the stage ambivalently or speak every line ambiguously. Nevertheless spectators need not be passive consumers of pre-packaged emotions. In the Shakespearean theatre, it is through the clash of successive contrasting episodes which distance one another, as much as through subtle portrayal of individual roles, that divided values are made apparent and human potentiality, through all inconsistencies, becomes convincingly alive.[20]

NOTES

[This was one of the last essays that Margot Heinemann wrote before her death in May 1992. The essay was originally prepared for a colloquium on Shakespeare which was held at Weimar in 1991, but was subsequently revised. The colloquium was on the subject of 'Shakespeare and Chaos Theory', and was held in Weimar after the Berlin Wall had been dismantled. The context of this essay is important in that Margot Heinemann, herself a Marxist of some considerable conviction, thinks through in this essay a particular literary analogue of the theme of 'chaos' consequent upon the loss of values previously held dear. For her, one of the functions of literature was to illuminate the problems of the present, and her reading of *Antony and Cleopatra* finds in Shakespeare's play an analogue of a modern situation whose own contours are only now beginning to become clear. It was significant that at the colloquium session where she was invited to read a shorter version of this paper, she was prevented from doing so by the intervention of a senior West German academic. Ed.]

1. J.-L. Barrault, 'Shakespeare and the French', in O. Le Winter (ed.), *Shakespeare in Europe* (Harmondsworth, 1970), pp. 347–58.

2. Barrault has in mind here 'the protracted anguish which followed the production of *Coriolanus* at the Comédie Française in 1937 at the time of the Popular Front. Shakespeare was very nearly transformed into an apologist of Fascism . . . He never preaches morality or politics: he is only concerned with justice' ('Shakespeare and the French', p. 353).

3. Charmian and Iras, Eros and Scarus, and pre-eminently Enobarbus are cases in point.

4. For example *Antonie*, translated from Robert Garnier's *Marc Antoine* by the Countess of Pembroke; Samuel Daniel's *Tragedy of Cleopatra*; Samuel Brandon's *Virtuous Octavia*; Dryden's *All for Love*.

5. See David Bevington's analysis of these cuts in his admirable New Cambridge edition of the play (Cambridge, 1990), pp. 44–70, which provides a detailed stage history.

6. This 'depoliticising' of the drama begins with Dryden's *All for Love* in Restoration times. Evidently the play was felt to have some dangerous connotations, for in his preface to Lord Danby Dryden explicitly disclaims any sympathy with republicanism. His adaptation itself focuses on a 'well-meaning' Antony who 'weeps much, fights little, but is wondrous kind', torn between two loving women who fight over him – a hero much more pleasing, he claims in the Prologue, to an audience which includes women and the 'keeping Tonies of the pit'.

7. M. R. Ridley (ed.), *Antony and Cleopatra* (London, 1954), p. xliii.

8. Ibid., p. xlvii.

9. Fulke Greville, *Life of Sir Philip Sidney*, ed. Nowell Smith (Oxford, 1907), p. 156.

10. Geoffrey Bullough, *Narrative and Dramatic Sources of Shakespeare* (London, 1964), vol. 5, p. 216.

11. Emrys Jones (ed.), *Antony and Cleopatra* (Harmondsworth, 1977), p. 46. There is in fact no evidence that the play was ever performed at court. Nothing definite is known beyond the entry of the title in the Stationers' Register for May 1608, and the note in the Lord Chamberlain's records for 1669 that it was 'formerly acted at the Blackfriars'. If

there had been a court performance it would probably have been mentioned. On internal evidence, the view of this as 'the most courtly of Shakespeare's tragedies' seems easy to resist.

12. For Tacitus and his influence at this period, see Alan T. Bradford, 'Stuart Absolutism and the Utility of Tacitus', *Huntington Library Quarterly*, 46 (1983), 128–38; Blair Worden, 'Classical Republicanism in the English Revolution', in *History and Imagination*, ed. H. Lloyd-Jones et al. (London, 1984). P. Burke, 'Tacitism', in T. A. Dorey (ed.), *Tacitus* (London, 1969).

13. *The Tragedy of Cleopatra*, commissioned by the Countess of Pembroke from her protégé Samuel Daniel, took a similar line, and was apparently known to Shakespeare.

14. The Countess and her brother also translated works by Mornay.

15. See G. Jondorf, *French Renaissance Tragedy* (Cambridge, 1990), pp. 61–3.

16. Thomas Hobbes, *Behemoth* (1679), p. 3.

17. Tacitus, *The Annals of Imperial Rome*, trans. M. Grant (Harmondsworth, 1964), pp. 29–31.

18. Shakespeare apparently read and used Montaigne, probably in Florio's translation, around the time of writing *King Lear* and *Timon*, as well as later in *The Tempest*.

19. Thus Antony's capacity for savage cruelty, underlined in *Julius Caesar* for contrast with Brutus, is rather understated in the later play. Cleopatra's concern to save her children from Caesar's vengeance, which in *Antonie* delays her suicide, disappears here after a single threat: and so on.

20. See my essay on 'Drama for Cannibals? Notes on Brecht and Shakespearean Characterisation', *Shakespeare Jahrbuch* (1990), 135–9.

7

Egyptian Queens and Male Reviewers: Sexist Attitudes in 'Antony and Cleopatra' Criticism

LINDA T. FITZ

> And of Cleopatra what shall be said? Is she a creature of the same breed as Cato's daughter, Portia? Does the one word woman include natures so diverse? Or is Cleopatra . . . no mortal woman, but Lilith who ensnared Adam before the making of Eve?
>
> (Dowden)

Most critics are united in proclaiming that *Antony and Cleopatra* is a magnificent achievement; unfortunately, they are not united on the question of exactly what the play achieves. It is difficult to think of another Shakespearean play which has divided critics into such furiously warring camps. A. P. Riemer describes, fairly accurately, the positions defended by the two main critical factions: '*Antony and Cleopatra* can be read as the fall of a great general, betrayed in his dotage by a treacherous strumpet, or else it can be viewed as a celebration of transcendental love.'[1] Derek Traversi also speaks of this interpretive impasse: 'The student of *Antony and Cleopatra* has, in offering an account of this great tragedy, to resolve a problem of approach, of the author's intention. Sooner or later, he finds himself faced by two possible readings of the play, whose only difficulty is that they seem to be mutually exclusive.'[2] A significant difficulty indeed; however, I would suggest, not the 'only difficulty'.

Both the reduction of the play's action to 'the fall of a great general' and the definition of the play's major interest as 'transcendental love' make impossible a reasonable assessment of the character of Cleopatra. There is a word for the kind of critical bias informing both approaches: it is *'sexism'*. Almost all critical approaches to this play have been coloured by the sexist assumptions the critics have brought with them to their reading. These approaches, I believe, have distorted the meaning of what Shakespeare wrote. Before I take up the sexist criticism in its particulars, I have one general observation. I have noticed, in male critical commentary on the character of Cleopatra, an intemperance of language, an intensity of revulsion uncommon even among Shakespeare critics, who are well enough known as a group for their lack of critical moderation. I do not think it would be going too far to suggest that many male critics feel personally threatened by Cleopatra and what she represents to them. In Cleopatra's case, critical attitudes go beyond the usual condescension toward female characters or the usual willingness to give critical approval only to female characters who are chaste, fair, loyal, and modest: critical attitudes toward Cleopatra seem to reveal deep personal fears of aggressive or manipulative women. Alfred Harbage, in his *Conceptions of Shakespeare*, looked at the personal lives of some anti-Stratfordians and found evidence of persistent neurotic delusions of the sort Freud had labelled 'family romance fantasies';[3] perhaps it would be revealing to examine the lives of anti-Cleopatra critics for evidence of difficulties in relationships with women.

I

But to the particulars. Obviously, most of the sexist distortion has centred on Cleopatra, and it is most revealing to observe with whom Cleopatra has been compared. A favourite game among Shakespeare critics has always been to compare characters from one play with characters from another; so Hamlet is said to have more 'inner life' than Othello, King Lear is said to die less self-centredly than Hamlet, and so forth. With whom is Cleopatra compared? Lear? Macbeth? Othello? No, Cleopatra is compared only with female characters – Viola, Beatrice, Rosalind, Juliet.[4] Juliet is most frequent, and it must be confessed that there are certain similarities. Both appear in tragedies (the rest of the women used for comparison are comic heroines); both are allegedly in love; and they share the distinction of being two of the three women to have made it into the titles of Shakespeare plays. Otherwise, the two are as apt for comparison as Mae West and St Cecilia. Critics do not compare King Lear with Osric, Bottom the Weaver, or Sir Toby Belch because they are all men, but they persist in comparing Cleopatra (usually unfavourably) with female characters because they are all women. Clearly, Cleopatra is cut off at the outset from serious consideration as a tragic hero by being relegated to consideration alongside various heroines, most of whom inhabit the comedies.

Related to this habit of discussing female characters as a group is the critical tactic of describing Cleopatra as 'Woman'. Cleopatra is seen as the archetypal woman: practiser of feminine wiles, mysterious, childlike, long on passion and short on intelligence – except for a sort of animal cunning. Harold C. Goddard, referring to the end of the play, states, 'Now for the first time she is a woman – and not Woman'.[5] S. L. Bethell informs us, 'In Cleopatra [Shakespeare] presents the mystery of woman'.[6] Swinburne sees Cleopatra as Blake's 'Eternal Female'.[7] Georg Brandes calls her 'woman of women, quintessentiated Eve'.[8] E. E. Stoll says, 'Caprice, conscious and unconscious is her nature. . . . She is quintessential woman'.[9] Harley Granville-Barker enlightens us: 'The passionate woman has a child's desires and a child's fears, an animal's wary distrust; balance of judgement none, one would say. But often . . . she shows the shrewd scepticism of a child'.[10] And Daniel Stempel brings us up to date on the alleged Elizabethan attitude:

> Here our knowledge of Elizabethan mores can come to our aid . . . . Woman was a creature of weak reason and strong passion, carnal in nature and governed by lust. She could be trusted only when guided by the wisdom of her natural superior, man. . . . The misogyny of Octavius Caesar is founded on right reason.[11]

It is surely questionable whether there is such a thing as a 'typical woman' or even a 'typical Elizabethan woman'. And if there is such a thing as a 'typical Shakespearean woman', Cleopatra is not the woman. In particular, she is almost unique among Shakespeare's female characters in her use of feminine wiles – by which I mean her deliberate unpredictability and her manipulative use of mood changes for the purpose of remaining fascinating to Antony.

> If you find him sad,
> Say I am dancing; if in mirth, report
> That I am sudden sick
>
> (I. iii. 3–5)

It is ironic that her use of feminine wiles has been one of the only Cleopatran features to have proven appealing to critics. Dowden writes:

> At every moment we are necessarily aware of the gross, the mean, the disorderly womanhood in Cleopatra, no less than of the witchery and wonder which excite, and charm, and subdue. We see her a dissembler, a termagant, a coward; and yet 'vilest things become her'. The presence of a spirit of *life* quick, shifting, multitudinous, incalculable, fascinates the eye, and would, if it could, lull the moral sense to sleep.[12]

Schlegel writes: 'Cleopatra is as remarkable for her seductive charms as Antony for the splendour of his deeds'.[13] Philip J. Traci defends the feminine wiles on the grounds that such behaviour is prescribed for courtly lovers by Andreas Capellanus and Ovid.[14]

It is ironic, I say, because it seems probable that Shakespeare disapproves of such behaviour. With the exception of Cressida,[15] no other woman in Shakespeare's plays practises it. Indeed, Shakespeare's women for the most part actively resist it, preferring instead to woo their men, straightforwardly, themselves. It is Miranda's father, in *The Tempest*, who tries to put obstacles in love's way 'lest too light winning / Make the prize light' (I. ii. 454–5), while Miranda forthrightly approaches the man she has known for about an hour with 'Hence, bashful cunning . . . I am your wife, if you will marry me' (III. i. 81–3).

Of course, if I am to claim that Shakespeare treated his women as individuals, I can hardly postulate that he criticises Cleopatra for behaving differently in this respect from other Shakespearean women. But there is evidence in the play that Shakespeare sees such behaviour as humanly undesirable: he has Cleopatra herself try, in the latter part of the play, to overcome her deliberately inconstant behaviour[16] – behaviour which she (not Shakespeare) sees as being quintessentially female:

> My resolution's placed, and I have nothing
> Of woman in me: now from head to foot
> I am marble-constant: now the fleeting moon
> No planet is of mine.
>
> (V. ii. 238–41)

But while Shakespeare may disapprove of feminine wiles, he understands why Cleopatra feels (perhaps rightly) that she must practise them: she is getting old, and Shakespeare understood that women, unlike men, are valued only when they are young and beautiful. Cleopatra's famous self-portrait –

> Think on me,
> That am with Phoebus' amorous pinches black
> And wrinkled deep in time
> (I. v. 27–9)

– comes at the point where she has just characterised her fantasy of Antony ('He's speaking now, / Or murmuring, "Where's my serpent of old Nile?"' [I. v. 24–5]) as 'delicious poison' – delicious in its confirmation of Antony's loyalty, poisonous in its contrast with the fact of Antony's absence and the fact of her decaying beauty. This passage is immediately followed by a reverie on sexual successes of her youth. The scene is, I think, too often read with attention only to Cleopatra's rejoicing in her own sexuality, to the neglect of its clear undercurrent of fear and insecurity.

The feminine fear of ageing had been introduced early in the play, with Charmian's 'Wrinkles forbid' (I. ii. 21). That Shakespeare well understood the danger of a woman's losing the affection of her lover as she loses her looks to age is clear from the discussion between Duke Orsino and Viola (masquerading as a boy) in *Twelfth Night*:

> **Duke**   Let still the woman take
> An elder than herself: so wears she to him,
> So sways she level in her husband's heart;
> For, boy, however we do praise ourselves,
> Our fancies are more giddy and unfirm,
> More longing, wavering, sooner lost and worn,
> Than women's are . . .
> Then let thy love be younger than thyself,
> Or thy affection cannot hold the bent;
> For women are as roses, whose fair flow'r,
> Being once displayed, doth fall that very hour.
> **Viola**   And so they are; alas, that they are so.
> (II. iv. 29–40)

There is no evidence in Shakespeare (or in Plutarch, his source) that Cleopatra employed feminine wiles when she was younger. It seems more reasonable to conjecture that in Shakespeare's interpretation, she has adopted desperate measures to compensate, by being fascinating, for the ravages of age.

II

Although many critics see Cleopatra as the archetypal woman, others more magnanimously recognise that there are, in fact, two types of woman in the world, both of which appear in *Antony and Cleopatra*: the wicked and manipulative (Cleopatra), and the chaste and submissive (Octavia). This dipolar view usually results in an overemphasis on Octavia, who after all speaks only thirty-five lines in the play,[17] as a viable alternative to Cleopatra. These critics seem to be united in their belief that the love of a good woman could have saved Antony and prevented the whole tragedy. A. C. Bradley complains bitterly of Antony's mistreatment of Octavia.[18] Charles Bathurst feels that 'The character of Antony [Shakespeare] meant to elevate as much as possible; notwithstanding his great weakness in all that concerns Cleopatra, and unmistakable misconduct with regard to his wife.'[19] Laurens J. Mills regrets that 'after the seeming cure during his marriage to Octavia, he falls more and more inextricably into the coils of the Egyptian'.[20] Harley Granville-Barker, who places Octavia third, after Antony and Cleopatra, in his group of character studies for the play,[21] says 'How should we not, with the good Maecenas, trust to her beauty, wisdom, and modesty to settle his chastened heart?'[22]

Leaving aside these touching encomia and turning to the play, one notes that Antony calls his marriage to Octavia 'the business' (a term favoured by the Macbeths in reference to the murder of Duncan). It is very likely that had Antony lived in connubial bliss with Octavia from the time he first remarked 'Yet, ere we put ourselves in arms, dispatch we / The business we have talked of' (II. ii. 167–8), the remaining three-and-a-half acts would have been very different, less concerned with disaster and death, although perhaps somewhat lacking in those qualities we have come to associate with drama. Nevertheless, it is a fact that in Shakespeare Antony treats Octavia better than he does in Plutarch, where he turns her out of his house.[23] And Shakespeare much reduced Octavia's importance: Plutarch's account ends with a vision of Octavia bringing up all of Antony's children, including one named Cleopatra.[24]

Another sexist response to the play has resulted from a distaste for the play's overt sexuality. Traci claims that Shakespearean critics, even bawdry expert Eric Partridge, have been loath to acknowledge the extent of sexual double entendre in the play, and that when they have acknowledged it, they have been disgusted by it.[25] Traci gallantly takes up the challenge by declaring that the whole play is structured in imitation of the sex-act, starting with foreplay in the first several scenes, proceeding to pre-sex drinking and feasting, and finally culminating, after the significant entrance of the character Eros, in intercourse itself – represented, according to Traci, by twenty-one uses of the word 'Eros', twenty-three uses of the word 'come', and sixteen puns on 'dying'. Traci's theory may be a little far-fetched, but it brings a whole new world of meaning to passages like 'What poor an instrument may do a noble deed'. 'The soldier's pole is fallen', and 'Husband, I come'.[26]

Traci feels that critical neglect of the naughty bits in the play has been prompted by prudery, from which he, fortunately, does not suffer. 'Drink . . . like lechery', he declares, 'is a universal manly, social sin. . . . Indeed, they are surely heroic sins, when compared to gluttony and sloth, for example'.[27] What Traci fails to account for is the oddity of encountering critical prudery in *this* day and age. After all, the days of Bowdlerising are over; nobody blenches any more at 'an old black ram is tupping your white ewe'. I submit that what bothers critics about the bawdy remarks in *Antony and Cleopatra* is that so many of them are made by Cleopatra – like 'O happy horse, to bear the weight of Antony!' (I. v. 21), or 'Ram thou thy fruitful tidings in mine ears, / That long time have been barren' (II. v. 23–4). The prudery is of a sexist variety: what appals the male critic is that a *woman* would say such things. It is, to a certain extent, Cleopatra's frank sexuality that damns her. Robert E. Fitch, writing from his post at the Pacific School of Religion, observes, 'It is altogether incredible that the Shakespeare who . . . early and late in his career rejoiced in innocence, loyalty, and love, before lust with all its cruel splendours, could have presented Cleopatra as a model of the mature woman in mature emotion'.[28] J. W. Lever tells us that 'Her wooing of Antony is comic and sensual, immoral and thoroughly reprehensible'.[29]

One might expect Cleopatra to appeal at least to the closet prurience of a few readers. And indeed there are a number of grudging and embarrassed tributes to the power of Cleopatra's sexuality. Schlegel writes: 'Although the mutual passion of herself and Antony is without moral dignity, it still excites our sympathy as an insurmountable fascination.'[30] Coleridge writes, 'But the art displayed in the character of Cleopatra is profound in this, especially, that the sense of criminality in her passion is lessened by our insight into its depth and energy, at the very moment that we cannot help but perceive that the passion itself springs out of the habitual craving of a licentious nature.'[31] Traci sums up the attitude of several modern Cleopatra apologists: 'From beneath the exuberance of the adjectives . . . there emerges the critic's apology for having himself become a slave of Passion'.[32]

Antony and Cleopatra has never been admitted to the holy circle of the 'big four' Shakespearean tragedies – Hamlet, Othello, King Lear, and Macbeth. Many reasons for this have been adduced. Perhaps the most popular reason, as stated by A. P. Riemer, is that Antony and Cleopatra 'deals with issues intrinsically much less important than those of the great tragedies'.[33] Nevertheless, Cleopatra's first line, 'If it be love indeed, tell me how much' (I. i. 14), is strikingly similar to Lear's opening question to his daughters. Both Antony and Cleopatra and King Lear are, as far as I can see, concerned with love and its relationship to public issues like proper ruling, as well as love's place in the individual's hierarchy of values. If Antony and Cleopatra deals with 'much less important issues', it would seem to follow that love between the sexes, as in Antony and Cleopatra, is 'much less important' than familial love, as in King Lear. This is an argument one might expect of Victorian critics, perhaps, but why should we find it today? And if love between the sexes is an unworthy topic for tragedy, why is Othello permitted to stand as one of the 'big four', while Antony and Cleopatra is not? The unavoidable answer, I believe, is that Othello focuses uncompromisingly on a male hero.

III

Another way in which sexism rears its head in Antony and Cleopatra criticism is that in assessing the respective actions of Antony and Cleopatra, critics apply a clear double standard: what is praiseworthy in Antony is damnable in Cleopatra. The sexist assumption here is that for a woman, love should be everything; her showing an interest in anything but her man is reprehensible. For a man, on the other hand, love should be secondary to public duty or even self-interest. Almost every scene in which either character appears has been subjected to this double-standard interpretation. I will focus on three examples.

First, in the Thidias scene, where Cleopatra apparently makes some political overtures to Caesar after Caesar has defeated Antony in the battle of Actium, Cleopatra has repeatedly been damned by critics for trying to save her political skin, and perhaps her actual skin, at the expense of her love for Antony. At the beginning of the play, when Antony follows his fervent protestations of love for Cleopatra by leaving Egypt to patch up his political situation in Rome through marriage to the sister of Octavius Caesar, he receives nothing but critical praise – for putting first things first and attempting to break off a destructive relationship with Cleopatra. According to the critics, men may put political considerations ahead of love; women may not.

Second, while Antony is roundly criticised when he neglects public affairs, critics never take seriously Cleopatra's desire to play an active part in great public enterprises. Cleopatra's participation in the battle of Actium, it must be confessed, is less than an unqualified success, but there is no warrant in the play for doubting her motives for being there in person:

> A charge we bear i' th' war,
> And as the president of my kingdom, will
> Appear there for a man. Speak not against it;
> I will not stay behind.
>   (III. vii. 16–19)

Nevertheless, Julian Markels infers, on no evidence, that 'the entire function of the president of her kingdom is to become the object of universal gaze and wonder. . . . Her business at Actium was to cavort upon that stage where Antony made war'.[34]

Third, a double standard is almost always applied in discussions of Antony's and Cleopatra's respective motives for suicide. Cleopatra is repeatedly criticised for thinking of anything but Antony: this would seem to follow from the sexist precept that nothing but love is appropriate to a woman's thoughts. 'Does she kill herself to be with Antony or to escape Caesar? It is the final question', Mills tells us, after explaining to us the difference between Cleopatra's unworthy death-bed thoughts and Antony's noble ones:

> In her final moments, as she carries out her resolution, Cleopatra has 'immortal longings', hears Antony call, gloats over outwitting

Caesar, addresses Antony as 'husband', shows jealousy in her fear that Iras may gain the first otherworld kiss from Antony, sneers at Caesar again, speaks lovingly to the asp at her breast, and dies, with 'Antony' on her lips and a final fling of contempt for the world. But, it should be noted, she does not 'do it after the high Roman fashion', nor with the singleness of motive that actuated Antony.[35]

Stempel, coming upon the lines, 'He words me, girls, he words me, that I should not / Be noble to myself' [V. ii. 191–2], is indescribably shocked that Cleopatra speaks two whole lines without reference to Antony: 'No word of Antony here. Her deepest allegiance is to her own nature.'[36]

If, however, we look at the play, we see that Cleopatra adduces the following reasons for taking leave of the world: (1) she thinks life is not worth living without Antony;[37] (2) she sees suicide as brave, great, noble, and Roman;[38] (3) she wants to escape the humiliation Caesar has planned for her, and desires to have the fun of making an ass of Caesar;[39] (4) she sees suicide as an act of constancy which will put an end to her previous inconstant behaviour and to the world's inconstancy which has affected her;[40] and (5) she wants to be with Antony in a life beyond the grave.[41] Antony adduces the following reasons for his suicide: (1) he has lost his final battle, and he thinks Cleopatra has betrayed him;[42] (2) he (later) thinks Cleopatra is dead, and feels that life is not worth living without her;[43] (3) he wants to be with Cleopatra in a life beyond the grave;[44] (4) he thinks Cleopatra has killed herself, and he cannot bear to be outdone in nobility by a mere woman;[45] (5) he wants to escape the humiliation Caesar has planned for him;[46] and (6) he sees suicide as valiant and Roman.[47] It is thus apparent that the 'singleness of motive' which Mills thinks 'actuates Antony' is a myth: Antony has six motives to Cleopatra's five, and four of Cleopatra's five motives are identical with Antony's. Yet although Cleopatra is constantly taken to task for the multiplicity of her suicide motives (we all know that women cannot make up their minds), I have yet to see the critic who complained of the multiplicity of Antony's motives.

This double standard, arising from the critics' own sexist world view – that is, that love, lust, and personal relationships in general belong to a 'feminine' world that must always be secondary to the 'masculine' world of war, politics, and great public issues – can seriously distort the play. Some critics see the tragedy as growing out of the finally irreconcilable conflict between public values and private values, but many critics come down unequivocally on the side of public values – assuming, of course, that these public values belong to a world of men. Symptomatic of this tendency is the fact that Enobarbus, a boringly conventional anti-feminist who voices just such a view in the play, is almost always taken to be a mouthpiece for Shakespeare. E. C. Wilson, for example, writes:

> Antony, sobered by news of Fulvia's death, declares that he must from 'this enchanting queen break off'. Enobarbus banteringly cries, 'Why, then we kill all our women. We see how mortal an unkindness is to them. If they suffer departure, death's the word.' But in his next speech, a reply to Antony's 'I must be gone', his clear sense of Antony's folly pierces through his banter. 'Under a compelling occasion, let women die. It were pity to cast them away for nothing, though, between them and a great cause they should be esteemed nothing.' Nowhere in the play is there a more incisive judgement on Antony's conduct.[48]

Because these interpretations of the play are slanted in favour of the 'rightness' of public, Roman values (in spite of the unsavoury character of almost all the Roman activities which appear in the play, from the bride-bartering of Octavius and Antony, to the cut-throat scramble for political ascendancy, to the unctuous hypocrisy of Octavius in the closing scenes),[49] Cleopatra, who after all shares top billing with Antony in the play's title, is demoted from the position of co-protagonist to the position of antagonist at best, nonentity at worst.

IV

The most flagrant manifestation of sexism in criticism of the play is the almost universal assumption that Antony alone is its protagonist. The following are only a few critical pronouncements on the subject, which I have culled from a mass of interpretive writings that make the same point. Oliver Emerson: 'the dramatic movement of the play is the ruin of Antony under the stress of sensual passion'.[50] Georg Brandes: 'Just as Antony's ruin results from his connection with Cleopatra, so does the fall of the Roman Republic result from the contact of the simple hardihood of the West with the luxury of the East. Antony is Rome. Cleopatra is the Orient. When he perishes, a prey to the voluptuousness of the East, it seems as though Roman greatness and the Roman Republic expires with him.'[51] Harley Granville-Barker: 'Antony, the once-triumphant man of action, is

hero. . . . [The play's theme] is not merely Antony's love for Cleopatra, but his ruin as general and statesman, the final ascension of
Octavius, and the true end of "that work the ides of March begun".
. . . If but in his folly, [Antony] has been great. He has held nothing
back, has flung away for her sake honour and power, never weighing
their worth against her worthlessness.'[52] Lord David Cecil: 'the play
would have been better entitled *The Decline and Fall of Antony*.'[53]
S. L. Bethell: 'Antony's position is central, for the choice between
Egypt and Rome is for him to make.'[54] Willard Farnham: 'Shakespeare does not organise his tragedy as a drama of the love of Antony
and Cleopatra, but as a drama of the rise and fall of Antony in the
struggle for world rulership that takes place after he has met Cleopatra.'[55] John F. Danby: 'The tragedy of *Antony and Cleopatra* is,
above all, the tragedy of Antony.'[56] Austin Wright: 'The main theme'
of *Antony and Cleopatra* is 'the clash between Antony and Octavius'.[57]
Julian Markels: '*Antony and Cleopatra* focuses upon the conflict
within Antony between public and private claims.'[58] A. P. Riemer:
'On a strictly formal level, *Antony and Cleopatra* fulfils the requirements of orthodox tragedy in its depiction of Antony's fall (and,
incidentally, Cleopatra's) in reasonably decorous terms.'[59] Janet
Adelman: 'Antony is the presumptive hero of the play.'[60]

When, in 1964, Laurens J. Mills set out to find critics who agreed
with him that Antony and Cleopatra were co-protagonists, he could
find only two other critics who 'agreed'. One of these was Virgil
Whitaker, who I find once remarked that 'the tragic action of the
play is centred upon Antony, who has so yielded himself to the
passion of love that it has possessed his will and dethroned his
reason'.[61] And Mills's own study does little to advance the cause. His
summary of the two tragic falls is that the tragedy of Antony consists
of the 'pathetic picture' of a man who 'by love for a thoroughly
unworthy object comes to a miserable end', whereas the tragedy of
Cleopatra 'cannot be a "tragic fall", for there is nothing for her to
fall from'.[62] The critical camp that sees Antony and Cleopatra as co-
protagonists does not muster impressive forces.[63]

The critical consensus, then, is that Antony is the protagonist.
There is a small catch, however. Antony dies in Act IV, and Cleopatra has the whole of Act V to herself, during the course of which
she speaks some of Shakespeare's greatest poetry. How have the pro-
Antony forces dealt with this embarrassment? A substantial number
of them have chosen the stalwart expedient of ignoring it altogether.
For the rest, the critical contortions to which they have been forced
to resort are instructive and amusing.

V

Some feel that Shakespeare knew what he was doing when he gave Cleopatra the last act to herself. For example, Daniel Stempel says, 'If . . . the major theme is the safety of the state, then the death of Antony does not remove the chief danger to political stability – Cleopatra: she has ensnared Julius Caesar, Pompey, and Antony – how will Octavius fare? This last act shows us that Octavius is proof against the temptress, and the play ends, as it should, with the defeat and death of the rebel against order. The theme is worked out to its logical completion, and the play is an integrated whole, not merely a tragedy with a postscript.'[64] Robert E. Fitch says, 'Naturally Antony, the middle-man in the generic tension of values, must be disposed of by the end of Act IV, so that the last act may be given to the stark confrontation of pleasure and of power in the persons of Cleopatra and Octavius.'[65] Julian Markels says, 'the grand climax of the whole action is reserved for Cleopatra, who now learns the lesson of Antony's life . . . and by her loyalty to him confirms Antony's achieved balance of public and private values.'[66] John Middleton Murry says, 'Up to the death of Antony it is from him that the life of the play has been derived. . . . He is magnificent: therefore she must be. But when he dies, her poetic function is to maintain and prolong, to reflect and reverberate, that achieved royalty of Antony's. . . . We [watch] the mysterious transfusion of his royal spirit into the mind and heart of his fickle queen.'[67] Harley Granville-Barker says, 'The love-tragedy . . . is not made the main question till no other question is left. . . . Antony dead, the domination of the play passes at once to Cleopatra. . . . But Antony's death leaves Shakespeare to face one obvious problem: how to prevent Cleopatra's coming as an anticlimax.'[68] Peter Alexander says, 'Antony dies while the play still has an act to run, but without this act his story would be incomplete. For Cleopatra has to vindicate her right to his devotion.'[69] Other critics feel that in giving Cleopatra Act V to herself, Shakespeare simply made a dreadful mistake, one which destroyed the whole structure of the play. As Michael Lloyd quite rightly points out, 'If we see Antony's tragedy as the centrepiece of the play, its structure is faulty'.[70]

Cleopatra is present throughout the whole of the play,[71] she has Act V to herself, and she dies at the end. Thus, she would seem to fulfil at least the formal requirements of the tragic hero. One might think that in the verbose history of Shakespearean criticism, at least one critic would have suggested that she is the protagonist – the sole protagonist – of the play. As a matter of fact, one did. A critic named Simpson – Lucie Simpson – wrote in a forgotten article in 1928 that 'the play, in fact, might have been called *Cleopatra* as appropriately as *Hamlet* is called *Hamlet* or *Othello Othello*'.[72] Although *Antony and Cleopatra* critics as a rule refer to each other's works more often than to the play, I have seen Lucie Simpson's work referred to only once, and then with a summary dismissal.[73] (Such heretical works are hard to get hold of; for example, an intriguing book by a critic named Grindon – Rosa Grindon – which advances the delightful and provocative thesis that 'the men critics in their sympathy for Antony, have treated Cleopatra just as Antony's men friends did, and for the same cause'[74] has been out of print for over fifty years.) In fact, it is for the most part only the occasional female critic who dares to suggest that a women might be the protagonist of any Shakespearean tragedy.[75]

VI

But changes Shakespeare made in using his source, Plutarch's *Life of Marcus Antonius*, indicate that he had a much greater interest than had Plutarch in Cleopatra as a human being. He elevated her position in the play by paying more attention to her motivation, allowing her to speak in her own defence, and making numerous small alterations in Plutarch's story, the effect of which is almost always to mitigate Cleopatra's culpability. That exonerating and elevating Cleopatra was a conscious intention is suggested by the fact that the changes are consistently in that direction. It is also notable that except for these changes, Shakespeare adheres quite closely to his source.

In Plutarch, Antony embarks on his Parthian campaign with 100,000 men. He loses 45,000 of them, we are told, mainly because 'the great haste he made to return unto Cleopatra'[76] caused him to abandon heavy artillery and put his men to forced marches: 'the most part of them died of sickness'.[77] In Plutarch, then, 45,000 men lost their lives because Antony was in haste to meet Cleopatra by the seaside – and then *she* was late! This distasteful episode, which provides Plutarch with ample occasion to revile Cleopatra, is omitted altogether by Shakespeare.

In Plutarch, Cleopatra is given a reason for wanting to appear in person at the battle of Actium: she fears 'lest Antonius should again be made friends with Octavius Caesar by means of his wife Octavia',[78] and the reasons she gives Antony for wanting to appear are spurious. In Shakespeare, there is no hint of this personal reason; Cleopatra simply declares 'A charge we bear i' th' war, / And, as the president of my kingdom, will / Appear there for a man' (III. vii. 17).

Antony's reason for fighting the battle of Actium by sea is reported twice by Plutarch. 'Now Antonius was made so subject to a woman's will that, though he was a great deal the stronger by land, yet for Cleopatra's sake he would needs have this battle tried by sea.'[79] 'But . . . notwithstanding all these good persuasions, Cleopatra forced him to put all to the hazard of battle by sea.'[80] One very frequently finds critics adducing this as one of the charges against Shakespeare's Cleopatra.[81] But in fact the sea battle is not Cleopatra's idea in Shakespeare's play. Shakespeare instead introduces a different motive, not mentioned in Plutarch: Caesar's dare.[82]

> **Antony**   Canidius, we
>   Will fight with him by sea.
> **Cleopatra**   By sea; what else?
> **Canidius** Why will my lord do so?
> **Antony** For that he dares us to't.
> **Enobarbus** So hath my lord dared him to single fight.
> **Canidius** Ay, and to wage this battle at Pharsalia,
>   Where Caesar fought with Pompey: but these offers,
>   Which serve not for his vantage, he shakes off;
>   And so should you.
> **Enobarbus**   Your ships are not well manned;
>   Your mariners are muleters, reapers, people
>   Ingrossed by swift impress. In Caesar's fleet
>   Are those that often have 'gainst Pompey fought;
>   Their ships are yare, yours, heavy: no disgrace
>   Shall fall you for refusing him at sea,
>   Being prepared for land.
> **Antony**   By sea, by sea.
>
>   (III. vii. 27–40)

In Shakespeare, the emphasis is entirely on Caesar's dare. Cleopatra finds the choice of sea-battle a natural one, since Egypt's military strength is in its navy,[83] but she does not initiate the disastrous plan.[84]

Cleopatra's departure from the battle of Actium, which prompts Antony to follow her and results in the loss of the battle, Shakespeare could hardly have omitted from the play, as it eventuates in the tragic deaths of Antony and Cleopatra. Nor would one wish this changed, since, despite Enobarbus' disclaimer (III. xiii. 3–4), it leaves Cleopatra with a large share of the blame for the ensuing tragedy – an important consideration, in view of the fact that in Shakespeare's mature plays the chain of events culminating in tragedy is initiated by the protagonist. In Plutarch, the focus in this scene is entirely on Antony – Cleopatra's leaving the battle is seen only in relation to its effect on Antony. In Shakespeare, Cleopatra considers whether she is to blame ('Is Antony, or we, in fault for this?' [III. xiii. 2]), indicates fear as her motivation ('Forgive my fearful sails' [III. xi. 55]), offers as her excuse that she acted in ignorance of the consequences ('I little thought / You would have followed' [III. xi. 55–6]), and apologises profusely ('Pardon, pardon' [III. xi. 68]). Plutarch does not present Cleopatra's reactions to this crucial turn of events at all.

After the Thidias scene, Plutarch gives no hint of Cleopatra's impassioned declarations of innocence and love for Antony, declarations that do appear in Shakespeare's text. And although Shakespeare includes in the Thidias scene (as Plutarch does not) the imputation that Cleopatra has stayed with Antony out of fear, not love (III. xii. 56–7), this piece of dialogue is a transmutation of a much more damning passage in Plutarch – where *after* Antony's death, 'Cleopatra began to clear and excuse herself for that she had done, laying all to the fear she had of Antony'.[85] Shakespeare has removed this imputation of disloyalty from the latter part of the action, putting it in the mouth of Caesar's messenger, not Cleopatra. And while Cleopatra acquiesces in the interpretation, she prefaces her acquiescence with the very-likely ironic 'He is a god, and knows / What is most right' (III. xiii. 60–1).

As to Antony's suspicion, after the final aborted battle, that Cleopatra 'has / Packed cards with Caesar' (IV. xiv. 18–19), neither Plutarch nor Shakespeare includes any evidence that she has. But Shakespeare has her messenger issue a denial (IV. xiv. 120–3), whereas Plutarch leaves the question entirely open.

In Plutarch, Cleopatra betakes herself to the monument 'being afraid of [Antony's] fury'.[86] Shakespeare gives her much stronger reasons for her fear, since Antony declares four times, very convincingly, that he is going to kill her (IV. xii. 16; IV. xii. 39–42; IV. xii. 47, 49; IV. xiv. 26). This is not in Plutarch.

In both authors, Antony's suicide is a result of Cleopatra's sending word that she is dead. But again, Shakespeare takes pains to mitigate this action. First, he makes the death-message Charmian's idea (IV. xiii. 4), not Cleopatra's. Second, he has Cleopatra foresee the possible effect of her message and send an emissary to revoke it; unfortunately, the emissary arrives too late (IV. xiv. 119–26). This is a significant departure from Plutarch.

In Plutarch, Cleopatra will not open the gates of the monument to Antony, and no reason for this refusal is given. In Shakespeare, Cleopatra gives a reason and apologises: 'I dare not, dear; / Dear my lord, pardon: I dare not, / Lest I be taken' (IV. xv. 21–3).

Plutarch gives three reasons for Antony's suicide, but none at all for Cleopatra's apart from the implication that her wits were distracted 'with sorrow and passion of mind'. She is reduced to a babbling, self-mutilating neurotic: 'She had knocked her breast so pitifully, that she had . . . raised ulcers and inflammations, so that she fell into a fever. . . . her eyes sunk into her head with continual blubbering, and moreover they might see the most part of her stomach torn in sunder.'[87] Shakespeare gives Cleopatra's suicide full motivation, and allows her to die with dignity and even triumph.

Finally, Plutarch reports simply, 'Her death was very sudden'.[88] The great dying speeches of Cleopatra are Shakespeare's addition.

Shakespeare's greater interest in Cleopatra first manifests itself in his changing Plutarch's title from *The Life of Marcus Antonius* to *The Tragedy of Antony and Cleopatra*,[89] and continues to manifest itself throughout the play.

VII

Although Shakespeare's departures from Plutarch are consistently in the direction of mitigating the harshness of Plutarch's view of Cleopatra, they do not by any means amount to a whitewash. By granting Cleopatra motivation and the chance to speak in her own defence, Shakespeare lifts her from the level of caricature, which would be appropriate for satiric treatment, to the level of fully developed individuality, which qualifies her for treatment as a tragic figure. To be treated as a tragic protagonist, Cleopatra need not – indeed should not – be absolved of every failing; after all, no one tries to prove that Macbeth did not really commit murder before granting him the stature of tragic hero.

The most significant difference between Shakespeare's mature tragic practice and Aristotle's tragic theory is that while Aristotle at one point says that 'pity is aroused by unmerited misfortune', Shakespeare insists on eliciting audience sympathy for characters who, to a greater or lesser degree, have brought their misfortunes on themselves. Shakespeare seems to ask his audience to understand, to empathise – even to forgive. In the later tragedies, Shakespeare seeks audience sympathy for inherently unsympathetic figures – a stubborn and mentally infirm octogenarian, a murderer, a misanthrope, a mama's boy, and (most difficult of all) a disreputable woman. As Willard Farnham points out in *Shakespeare's Tragic Frontier*, such an attempt involves great risks – what is gained in granting characters some say in their own destiny might easily be lost in diminution of audience sympathy. It seems to have been a risk that Shakespeare deliberately elected to take. In his last few tragedies, he made increasing demands on the humane tolerance (or perhaps on the Christian charity, in the most radical sense) of his audience. We are not expected to agree, in every case, that the protagonist is more sinned against than sinning; we are expected, on the basis of our common humanity with the offending protagonist, to offer sympathy unqualified by the necessity for exoneration. It is a demand too radical for Aristotle, for Farnham, for most audiences. Most are too ready to rue the absence of less deeply-flawed heroes, too ready to accuse Shakespeare of having sat down to eat with publicans and sinners. But although this is a tendency in the criticism of all the late tragedies, the fact remains that critics have been readier to sympathise with the murderer than with the wanton woman.

VIII

Any attempt to reach a canonical decision on the identity of a single hero in a play of such generic unorthodoxy as *Antony and Cleopatra*[90] is probably foolhardy and possibly distorting in itself. Nevertheless, since so many critics before me have unblushingly insisted on establishing Antony as the play's sole protagonist, for the sake of argument I will suggest that there are good reasons for considering Cleopatra to be the play's protagonist – or, shall we say (ignoring the usual deprecatory sex-designation 'heroine'), the hero. Not only does the play culminate in Cleopatra's death scene, but she has (according to the statistical evidence of the Spevack Concordance) more speeches than Antony; indeed, the most in the play (although, giving the lie to the received opinion that women talk too much, her speeches contain fewer total lines than Antony's). But most important, she learns and grows as Antony does not.

A. C. Bradley declares that the play is not a true tragedy because he cannot find the tragic hero's inner struggle in Antony.[91] But Cleopatra has that inner struggle. She struggles against her own artificial theatricality (as Richard II never does): she who so often threatens to die that Enobarbus credits her with a 'celerity in dying' (I. ii. 145) finally does truly kill herself. She who in a self-dramatising gesture had sent word to Antony that she was dead and asked the messenger to 'Say that the last I spoke was "Antony" / And word it, prithee, piteously' (IV. xiii. 8–9), finally really dies with the words 'O Antony' on her lips. She struggles against her own inconstancy – the inconstancy that had previously led her to change moods and to change lovers – and approaches death with the words

> My resolution's placed, and I have nothing
> Of woman in me: now from head to foot
> I am marble-constant: now the fleeting moon
> No planet is of mine.
> (V. ii. 238–41)

As Lear learns that he is a man before he is a king, so Cleopatra learns that she is a woman before she is a queen:

> No more but e'en a woman, and commanded
> By such poor passion as the maid that milks
> And does the meanest chares.[92]
> (IV. xv. 76–8)

The composition of *Antony and Cleopatra* followed close upon that of *King Lear*, that great play of self-knowledge.[93] Surely, then, it is no coincidence that while Antony simply fears his own loss of self-knowledge, Cleopatra actually admits to her less-than-admirable actions ('I . . . do confess I have / Been laden with like frailties which before / Have often shamed our sex' [V, ii. 121–4]) and tries, however late, to change – to 'be noble to myself'. Surely after watching what Lear was and what Lear became, we should not be too ready to damn what Cleopatra has been while ignoring what she becomes.

Of the critics I have discussed, A. P. Riemer comes the closest to declaring that Cleopatra is the hero of *Antony and Cleopatra*. Rehearsing all the reasons for not considering Antony the hero, he trembles on the verge – and then withdraws, unwilling to take the final step. He tells us that 'Her death (and this assumption must be faced squarely) is not offered in any sense as the play's structural culmination. . . . The play does not share [her] feelings and ideas, and the audience does not participate in [her] emotional state to the extent that it partakes of Hamlet's, Othello's or Lear's emotions at the climactic points of the tragedies in which these characters appear. . . . It is not possible for us to share her emotions.'[94]

I find this statement very odd. Is Cleopatra such an aberrant being that her emotions lie outside the pale of human comprehension? Is her practice of the tawdry old game known as feminine wiles really sufficient to render her forever as mysteriously and darkly inscrutable as male critics suggest? Is it really true that in contrast to the great universal audience which participates with no difficulty in the emotional state of a man who is troubled by incest, court drinking, the feasibility of revenge, and the authenticity of ghosts, there are no readers and no audiences who can participate in the emotions of a woman who dies thinking of politics, wine, her lover, and her baby?

IX

The persistent idea that Cleopatra cannot be understood, underlying as it does so many of the sexist responses I have discussed, owes much to the notion that women in general are impossible for men to understand. But, *pace* Dowden and others, one might ask exactly what she does that is so dazzlingly mysterious. True, she engages in unqueenly activities such as hopping forty paces through the public street or wandering about incognito to observe the qualities of people. But then, Hal drinks in taverns and takes part in robberies as prince, and later wanders incognito among troops as king; there is disagreement over his motives, of course, but at least critics assume that he *has* understandable motives. I cannot recall anyone describing Hal as 'quick, shifting, multitudinous, incalculable'. And as for feminine wiles, Cleopatra's behaviour here, far from being incomprehensible, is so obvious as to be almost crude: having bound herself to performing, not what is unexpected, but what is exactly the opposite of the expected, she has allowed herself no scope for creativity whatsoever. Milton's Satan, by vowing to oppose whatever God initiates, renders himself dependent on God's will; similarly, Shakespeare's Cleopatra, by obliging herself to determine what Antony expects and then to do the opposite, will very soon forfeit the element of surprise in all her actions. 'If you find him sad, / Say I am dancing; if in mirth, report / That I am sudden sick' – this is not the statement of a Woman of Mystery: it is a blueprint for action which, for the reader if not for Antony, renders the unpredictable predictable.

Shakespeare has taken pains to let Cleopatra explain her contrary behaviour and give the reasons for it (I. iii). He has created a complex but far from inscrutable being. Cleopatra's variety is, at last, finite. In short, Cleopatra needs to be demythologised. What she stands to lose in fascination she stands to gain in humanity.

Cleopatra may or may not be the protagonist of *Antony and Cleopatra*. At the very least, however, it should now be clear that her part in the play needs to be reassessed with more fairness – without the sexist bias that has so far attended most efforts to come to terms with her, without the assumption that readers and theatregoers will never be able to treat her as anything more than an exotic and decadent puzzle, inaccessible to rational thought, remote from human feeling.

I find it hard to believe that there are no readers and audiences who find it possible to share Cleopatra's emotions, or even simply to concede to Cleopatra the attributes of a human being. It seems, after all, that Shakespeare did.

From *Shakespeare Quarterly*, 28 (Summer 1977), 297–316.

NOTES

[Linda Fitz's essay is one of the earliest explicitly feminist attempts to redirect the discussion of *Antony and Cleopatra* away from traditional, male-centred literary criticism, towards a more sympathetic view of Cleopatra herself as a positive tragic figure in the play. Fitz challenges the assumption that from the point of view of 'genre' Tragedy is masculine, and that the figure of Antony is the sole embodiment of its values. What is pioneering in Fitz's account is her confrontation of the question of how criticism itself constructs the object of its enquiry, and how in the case of *Antony and Cleopatra*, this has led to an overlooking of what alterations Shakespeare himself made to his source material. Not only does Fitz excavate the sexual politics of the play itself, but she also exposes the sexual politics of traditional criticism which the play has attracted. Ed.]

1. *A Reading of Shakespeare's 'Antony and Cleopatra'* (Sydney, 1968), p. 82. Throughout this essay, I shall discuss critics as their views are pertinent to each topic I take up, rather than attempting any chronological overview of critical development. The reason for this will be-

come apparent as I proceed: there has been no real critical development on this issue, and modern critics are just as sexist in their views as nineteenth-century critics. All quotations from Shakespeare are from Sylvan Barnet (gen. edn), *The Complete Signet Classic Shakespeare* (New York, 1972).

2. *Shakespeare: The Roman Plays* (London and Stanford, 1963), p. 79.

3. 'Shakespeare as Culture Hero', in *Conceptions of Shakespeare* (Cambridge, Mass., 1966), pp. 101–19.

4. E.g., 'If she were a Juliet she would kill herself immediately for love of Antony, not merely talk about suicide' (Laurens J. Mills, *The Tragedies of Shakespeare's Antony and Cleopatra* [Bloomington, 1964], p. 48).

5. *The Meaning of Shakespeare* (Chicago, 1951), vol. 2, p. 199.

6. *Shakespeare and the Popular Dramatic Tradition* (London, 1944), p. 128.

7. *A Study of Shakespeare* (London, 1902 [first published 1880]), p. 189.

8. *William Shakespeare. A Critical Study*, trans. William Archer and Diana White (New York, 1963 [first published 1898]), p. 144.

9. 'Cleopatra', in *Poets and Playwrights* (Minneapolis, 1930), p. 13.

10. *Prefaces to Shakespeare* (London, 1930), III, 91.

11. 'The Transmigration of the Crocodile', *SQ*, 7 (1956), 63, 65. Stempel bases his whole argument on Renaissance misogynistic writings, which represented only one attitude (among many) toward women in the Renaissance. It is gratifying to note that one male critic takes Stempel to task for so glibly characterising Elizabethan attitudes, which he remarks is 'surely as difficult as characterising The Twentieth Century American's Attitude toward the Poles' (Philip J. Traci, *The Love Play of Antony and Cleopatra* [The Hague, 1970], p. 19). Stempel's argument runs this way: romantic and many post-Romantic critics idealise Cleopatra because they have been in the habit of placing Woman on a pedestal, failing to understand that many misogynistic Renaissance writers denigrated Woman. Stempel fails to realise, however, that neither generalised view of Woman does justice to the individuality of Shakespeare's Cleopatra, who is represented not as Woman, but as a person, partly good and partly bad, like most persons. That Stempel has little feeling for the individuality of female characters might be guessed from his description of Chaucer's Wife of Bath as 'a scholar's wife blessed with a retentive memory' (p. 63).

12. Edward Dowden, *Shakespeare: A Critical Study of His Mind and Art* (London, 1957 [first published 1875]), pp. 313–14.

13. Augustus William Schlegel, *Lectures on Dramatic Literature*, trans. John Black (London, 1840), p. 220.

14. Traci, *The Love Play*, pp. 113–14.

15. Cleopatra's only real fellow in the use of feminine wiles, Cressida, is at best an inconsistent practitioner: her defence of feminine wiles is suspect, even though it occurs in soliloquy, in so far as the same soliloquy insists on her love's firmness (I. iii. 320); and she abandons coquetry in the second scene in which she appears (III. ii). Just as her downright faithlessness contrasts with Cleopatra's final faithfulness, so *Trolius and Cressida* is much more clearly a play of conventional anti-feminism than is *Antony and Cleopatra*, which I believe introduces misogynistic convention, through Enobarbus and others, only to repudiate it.

16. It might be argued that giving up inconstancy (changing moods for effect) is no great effort for Cleopatra once Antony, on whom she has practised this brand of feminine wiles, is gone; but her inconstancy, in a larger sense, has involved changing lovers as well (although it should not be forgotten that her lovers have had a way of getting themselves murdered through no fault of her own). She might, had her 'resolution' not been 'placed', have made a play for Caesar, and some critics (Stempel, Mills) have argued that she does, on such slender evidence as her calling Caesar 'my master and my lord'. An actress who interpreted the 'Seleucus' scene this way, however, would undercut the validity of everything Cleopatra says in Act V, scene ii, and change the entire play from tragedy to satire. The several critics who have suggested this interpretation have changed the play drastically, with little or no warrant in the text of the play. Indeed, Mills's characterising of Cleopatra's tone in the 'Seleucus' scene as 'quaveringly piteous' and Octavius' tone in the same scene as 'blunt' (Mills, p. 54) seems to me perverse, and clearly evidence of a theatrical tin ear.

17. Cordelia, too, speaks very few lines and yet is considered a major character; but Shakespeare manages to convey a sense of strength with Cordelia's few lines, in contrast to the sense of insipidity he conveys with Octavia's. Although both women, when given the floor, decline to speak, there is a world of difference between Cordelia's 'I cannot heave my heart into my mouth' and Octavia's 'I'll tell you in your ear'. Octavia is often praised by critics for her becoming silence (women are to be seen and not heard?), but surely one would regret the loss to English poetry had Cleopatra said 'I'll tell you in your ear' when *she* had the chance to speak. Shakespeare does draw subtle contrasts (as well as the obvious contrasts) between Cleopatra and Octavia – for example, through mythological allusion: Octavia prays for aid from a powerful male god ('The Jove of power make me, most weak, most weak / Your reconciler!' [III. iv. 29–30]), while Cleopatra is always associated with female gods – Isis, Venus, Thetis. But if Shakespeare designed the play along the lines of a love-triangle, it was hardly meant to be equilateral.

18. *Oxford Lectures on Poetry* (London, 1909), p. 294.

19. *Remarks on the Differences in Shakespeare's Versification in Different Periods of His Life* (London, 1857), p. 131.

20. Mills, p. 29.

21. Granville-Barker, p. 97.

22. Granville-Barker, p. 73.

23. Plutarch, 'The Life of Marcus Antonius', trans. Sir Thomas North, in T. J. B. Spencer (ed.), *Shakespeare's Plutarch* (London, 1964), p. 246.

24. Plutarch, p. 294.

25. Traci, p. 81.

26. Traci, pp. 136–60.

27. Traci, pp. 41–2.

28. 'No Greater Crack?' *Shakespeare Quarterly*, 19 (1968), 12.

29. 'Venus and the Second Chance', *Shakespeare Survey*, 15 (1962), 87.

30. Schlegel, p. 220.

31. W. G. T. Shedd (ed.), *The Complete Works of Samuel Taylor Coleridge* (New York, 1884), IV, 105–6.

32. Traci, pp. 4–12.

33. Riemer, p. 105.

34. 'The Pillar of the World: *Antony and Cleopatra*', in *Shakespeare's Development* (Columbus, 1968), p. 47.

35. Mills, p. 55.

36. Stempel, p. 70.

37. 'Shall I abide / In this dull world, which in thy absence is / No better than a sty?' (IV. xv. 60–2); 'It were for me / To throw my sceptre at the injurious gods, / To tell them that this world did equal theirs / Till they had stol'n our jewel. All's but naught. . . . then is it sin / To rush into the secret house of death / Ere death dare come to us?' (IV. xv. 78–85).

38. 'We'll bury him; and then, what's brave, what's noble, / Let's do't after the high Roman fashion, / And make death proud to take us' (IV. xv. 89–91); 'It is great / To do that thing that ends all other deeds' (V. ii. 4–5); 'Methinks I hear / Antony call; I see him rouse himself / To praise my noble act' (V. ii. 283–5).

39. 'This mortal house I'll ruin, / Do Caesar what he can. Know, sir, that I / Will not wait pinioned at your master's court / Nor once be chastised with the sober eye / Of dull Octavia. Shall they hoist me up / And show me to the shouting varletry / Of censuring Rome? Rather a ditch in

Egypt / Be gentle grave unto me!' (V. ii. 51–7); 'Mechanic slaves / With greasy aprons, rules, and hammers shall / Uplift us to the view. In their thick breaths, / Rank of gross diet, shall we be enclouded, / And forced to drink their vapor' (V. ii. 209–13); 'O, couldst thou speak, / That I might hear thee call great Caesar ass / Unpolicied' (V. ii. 306–8).

40. 'It is great / To do that thing that ends all other deeds, / Which shackles accidents and bolts up change' (V. ii. 4–6); 'What poor an instrument / May do a noble deed! He brings me liberty. / My resolution's placed, and I have nothing / Of woman in me: now from head to foot / I am marble-constant: now the fleeting moon / No planet is of mine' (V. ii. 236–41).

41. 'Methinks I hear / Antony call. . . . Husband, I come' (V. ii. 283–7); 'If she first meet the curled Antony, / He'll make demand of her, and spend that kiss / Which is my heaven to have' (V. ii. 300–3).

42. 'She, Eros, has / Packed cards with Caesar, and false-played my glory / Unto an enemy's triumph. / Nay, weep not, gentle Eros, there is left us / Ourselves to end ourselves' (IV. xiv. 18–22).

43. 'I will o'ertake thee, Cleopatra. . . . So it must be, for now / All length is torture, since the torch is out' (IV. xiv. 44–6).

44. 'I come, my queen . . . / Where souls do couch on flowers, we'll hand in hand, / And with our sprightly port make the ghosts gaze: / Dido and her Aeneas shall want troops, / And all the haunt be ours' (IV. xiv. 50–4).

45. 'Since Cleopatra died, / I have lived in such dishonour that the gods / Detest my baseness. I, that with my sword / Quartered the world and o'er green Neptune's back / With ships made cities, condemn myself to lack / The courage of a woman' (IV. xiv. 55–60).

46. 'Eros, / Wouldst thou be windowed in great Rome and see / Thy master thus: with pleached arms, bending down / His corrigible neck, his face subdued / To penetrative shame, whilst the wheeled seat / Of fortunate Caesar, drawn before him, branded / His baseness that ensued?' (IV. xiv. 71–7).

47. 'A Roman, by a Roman / Valiantly vanquished' (IV. xv. 57–8).

48. 'Shakespeare's Enobarbus', in James G. McManaway et al. (eds), *Joseph Quincy Adams: Memorial Studies* (Washington, 1948), pp. 392–3.

49. 'If Shakespeare believed the Romans were noble, he surely did not inherit this notion from his source, which only too realistically draws a picture of the pervasive military mentality of the Romans with their might-makes-right ethic of political expediency. Plutarch, of course, was a Greek whose own grandfather had been incommoded by the battle of Actium – it is only to be expected that his attitude toward the Egyptians and Romans would be 'a plague o' both your houses'.

50. *'Antony and Cleopatra'*, *Poet Lore*, 2 (1890), p. 126.

51. Brandes, p. 158.

52. Granville-Barker, pp. 1, 23, 79.

53. 'Antony and Cleopatra', W. P. Ker Memorial Lecture (Glasgow, 1944), p. 21.

54. Bethell, p. 124.

55. *Shakespeare's Tragic Frontier: The World of His Final Tragedies* (Berkeley, 1950), p. 175.

56. *Poets on Fortune's Hill: Studies in Sidney, Shakespeare, Beaumont and Fletcher* (London, 1952), p. 146.

57. 'Antony and Cleopatra', *Shakespeare: Lectures on Five Plays* by Members of the Department of English, Carnegie Institute of Technology (Pittsburgh, 1958), p. 39.

58. Markels, p. 52.

59. Riemer, p. 88.

60. *The Common Liar: An Essay on 'Antony and Cleopatra'* (New Haven, 1973), p. 30. Adelman is the only female critic in this list. However, it should not be overlooked that hers is the only study of the play which attempts to establish, on a scholarly basis, that Shakespeare's audience might have viewed positively the sex-role reversal exemplified by Cleopatra and Antony's exchange of clothing, as well as Cleopatra's association with serpents – almost all other critics see these two aspects of the play as particularly damning to Cleopatra. On the whole, I have found Adelman's study the most useful and responsible that I have read.

61. *Shakespeare's Use of Learning: An Inquiry into the Growth of His Mind and Art* (San Marino, Huntington Library, 1953), p. 315.

62. Mills, pp. 35, 39.

63. A bevy of critics give Cleopatra a measure of favourable treatment as representative of Egyptian values, which according to these critics are set by Shakespeare in opposition to Roman values – Egyptian values are sometimes seen as triumphing, and sometimes as co-existing with the Roman values in a perpetual state of tension. These opposed values have been described as Reason and Intuition by Bethell (p. 122), Power and Pleasure by Fitch (p. 6), the World and the Flesh by Danby (p. 145), Power and Love by Goddard (p. 185), Reason and Impulse by Paul L. Rose ('The Politics of *Antony and Cleopatra*', *SQ*, 20 [1969], 377–89), and 'workaday world' values and 'holiday' values by J. L. Simmons ('The Comic Pattern and Vision in *Antony and Cleopatra*', *ELH*, 36 [1969], 495). The effect of this kind of interpretation is to reduce Cleopatra to an allegorical figure, representing one set of

values. Octavius Caesar is usually seen as representing the other set, and the Everyman left to choose between these alternatives is always Antony, who then becomes the hero of a kind of morality play, but remains the hero, nonetheless.

The Romantic admiration of Cleopatra as rebel – analogous to the Romantic view of Satan as hero of *Paradise Lost* – depended on the trick of extracting her from the play altogether. Even Romantic admirers were loath to give Cleopatra primacy in the context of the play.

64. Stempel, p. 63.

65. Fitch, p. 6.

66. Markels, p. 140.

67. *Shakespeare* (London, 1936), pp. 372, 377. Murry's essay has been much admired and is often quoted, notwithstanding the fact that his application of the adjective 'royal' to the republican Antony and only by extension to the technically royal Cleopatra ('She has yet, crowned queen though she is, to achieve her "royalty"; and she will achieve it by her resolution to follow her "man of men" to death') is a little bizarre. Cleopatra is often called 'royal' in the play; Antony never is.

That Cleopatra is the queen of Egypt, considering how much it is harped upon in the play, is a fact that critics seem remarkably willing to forget. Several critics, for example, interpret Antony's calling her 'Egypt' as evidence of his subliminal association of all things Egyptian (serpents, slime, fecundity, decadence) with her. Such an interpretation overlooks the conventional use of names of nations as titles for monarchs: Cleopatra is called 'Egypt' in *Antony and Cleopatra* much as the King of France is called 'France' in *King Lear*; both titles bring to mind the political position of the character.

Finally, as regards the royalty of Cleopatra, much critical scorn has been heaped upon Cleopatra for the queenly decking-out of her death scene, which is often seen as one last instance of her manipulative histrionics. Critics seem to have been lulled, by phrases like 'Show me, my women, *like* a queen', into forgetting the fact that she is the queen. Few complain of 'I am Duchess of Malfi still' (perhaps because the Duchess is, at least arguably, respectably married), but Cleopatra's last act is often denied this dignity. To my way of thinking, the 'infinite variety' of Cleopatra's last scene is not the deliberate changefulness of feminine wiles (Antony, after all, is dead), but rather a variety arising out of a real complexity of character. In her last moments Cleopatra thinks of herself as lover, sybarite, mother, politician, and queen. Being queen of Egypt gives Cleopatra a great opportunity for splendour, to which she is not averse; but it is also (let it not be forgotten) her career. The irreconcilability of political life and private life has always been emphasised in Antony's case, but the conflict is there in Cleopatra as well. There have been few enough Cleopatras in history, but with passing time the conflict between a career and private life has become more and more a woman's conflict. Nor were contemporary examples completely lacking for Shakespeare: Henry VIII did not, as it turned out, have to forego marriage (to the women of his choice) in favour of his political career; but his illustrious daughter did. I cannot help feeling that had Elizabeth lived to see Shakespeare's play, virgin queen that she was, she might have amended her famous statement to 'I am Cleopatra, know ye not that?'

68. Granville-Barker, pp. 4, 38–9. What Philip Traci might do with that last line of Granville-Barker's boggles the imagination.

69. *Shakespeare's Life and Art* (London, 1939), p. 178.

70. 'Cleopatra as Isis' *Shakespeare Survey*, 12 (1959), 94.

71. When she is absent from the stage, dialogue and action continually remind the audience of her. Shakespeare departs from Plutarch several times by introducing references to Cleopatra in the midst of Roman scenes: for example, he changes the position of the barge description so that it enters the Roman context, and he has the soothsayer advise, 'Hie thee to Egypt', where in Plutarch the soothsayer had contented himself with remarks on the respective luck of Caesar and Antony.

72. 'Shakespeare's "Cleopatra"', *Fortnightly Review*, NS 123 (March 1928), 332.

73. Traci, p. 36.

74. *A Woman's Study of 'Antony and Cleopatra'* (Manchester, 1909), p. 68.

75. I would not like to leave the reader with the notion that Cleopatra is entirely devoid of male defenders. Credit must be given, for example, to Ralph Behrens, who in an essay promisingly entitled 'Cleopatra Exonerated' (*Shakespeare Newsletter*, 9 [November 1959], 37) declares that 'all apparent lapses in her love for Antony can be accounted for by . . . "feminine frailties". It is true that she teases Antony . . . and feigns illness, but these are simply feminine wiles. . . . It is true that she flees too early with her ships . . . but [this] is a case of feminine fear.' Such a defence would warm the cockles of the sternest feminist heart, were it not for the fact that it is prompted less by a desire to demonstrate that Cleopatra is a significant character in her own right than by a more urgent desire to redeem Antony. As Behrens puts it, 'If the object of Antony's overpowering love were a totally unworthy one, it is likely that his character would be greatly weakened in its command of the reader's sympathy'. The usual forms that 'defences' of Cleopatra take are these: critics admire her for the wrong reasons (appreciating her use of feminine wiles); offer in defence of her questionable actions the fact that she is only a woman and therefore does not really know any better; seek to exonerate her only for the purpose of exonerating Antony; or (often under the guise of countering Bradley's pernicious character-

based approach) argue that she is not a real character at all but an embodiment of certain values. Such defences almost never take the form of arguing that Cleopatra is the protagonist of the play, and therefore to be blamed *and* empathised with, like other tragic protagonists.

76. Plutarch, p. 239.

77. Plutarch, p. 238.

78. Plutarch, pp. 244–5.

79. Plutarch, p. 250.

80. Plutarch, p. 254.

81. E.g., Bradley: 'He fights by sea simply and solely because she wishes it' (p. 297).

82. In Plutarch, Caesar challenges Antony to fight him on land, and offers to withdraw his army 'from the sea as far as one horse could run, until [Antonius] had put his army ashore and had lodged his men' (p. 251).

83. Cf. 'Let the Egyptians and the Phoenicians go a 'ducking' (III. vii. 63–4).

84. Canidius, of course, attributes Antony's decision to the fact that 'our leader's led / And we are women's men' (III. vii. 69–70), but this is interpretation, not fact. Canidius, like Bradley and most critics, is hypothesising an offstage conversation between Cleopatra and Antony in which Cleopatra suggests (or demands) a sea-battle. Critics have often questioned the Bradleyan tactic of speculating on offstage or even pre-play events, but I do not recall that they have questioned it in this particular case. Interpreting the scene on the basis of Canidius' conclusions is a chancy business as well, in a a play which (as Adelman and others have observed) consistently offers various perspectives on the same action. The point is arguable. My objection, however, is that critics have not bothered to argue it, but have instead imported Plutarch's conclusions into the play – in spite of the fact that Shakespeare has so clearly departed from Plutarch in his dramatisation of the incident.

85. Plutarch, p. 287.

86. Plutarch, p. 276.

87. Plutarch, pp. 286–7.

88. Plutarch, p. 291.

89. Although I find the addition of Cleopatra's name to Plutarch's title somewhat significant, I do not think that the fact that Antony's name remains in the title is clear evidence that the two were meant to be co-protagonists. Shakespeare's titles are not always clear indications of who the plays' major figures are to be: witness *Julius Caesar, Henry IV, Henry VI,* or *Cymbeline.*

90. I have, for lack of space, sidestepped the knotty genre question. If the play is seen, for example, as a history play, the search for *one* protagonist becomes irrelevant. Even earlier tragedies had co-protagonists (*Romeo and Juliet*) or lacked a clearly-defined single hero (*Julius Caesar*). It is a fact, however, that all the tragedies from *Hamlet* on have clearly-defined single heroes. I am arguing for Cleopatra as sole hero to show that it can be done, and with as much basis in the play as the argument for Antony as hero. If counterarguments can be produced, well and good. I only ask that their basis be textual, not sexual.

91. Bradley, pp. 286–7.

92. Of this passage, Stempel remarks, 'The death of a queen is levelled to the death of a woman, an exceptional woman, but still only a woman' (p. 71). Goddard, more graciously, makes the comparison with Lear, and also with Othello. In so doing he is one of the few critics to have granted Cleopatra the dignity of comparison with Shakespeare's male heroes. Unfortunately Goddard concludes that although the final transformation of Cleopatra's 'a miracle', Antony's 'devotion to her, even unto death, is what does it' (p. 198).

93. Cf. Paul A. Jorgensen, *Lear's Self-Discovery* (Berkeley and Los Angeles, 1967).

94. Riemer, p. 100.

8

Shakespeare's 'Antony and Cleopatra' and the Rise of Comedy

BARBARA C. VINCENT

> . . . yet the Alexandrians were commonly glad of this
> jolity, and liked it well saying verie gallantly,
> and wisely: that Antonius shewed them a comicall
> face, to wit, a merie countenaunce: and the Romanes
> a tragicall face, to say, a grimme looke.
> *(The Life of Marcus Antonius)*

I

That *The Tragedy of Antony and Cleopatra* contains many elements
of comedy is increasingly noticed in criticism.[1] Cleopatra has been
called 'the queen of comedy',[2] and the play has been regarded as a
transition between the tragedies and the romances.[3] Yet the study of
the opposing dramatic genres and their interrelations can be pursued
more specifically than one might at first imagine. Borrowing the
play's geographical imagery, we can say that Shakespeare provides a
map of his literary universe, with its worlds of tragedy and comedy,
in the play's opposing realms of Rome and Egypt. Only the map is
not static; like an evolving political map, it chronicles the relations
between the two generic worlds. These relations undergo a total
revolution in the course of the play: from the dominance of tragedy
and the separate, subordinate existence of comedy of the Roman
literary world (as Shakespeare portrays it), to the inclusion of trag-

edy in comedy and consequent elevation of the latter in Renaissance and Shakespearean literature.

But before tracing the vision of literary history in the play, it must be shown why we can properly identify Rome as the world of tragedy, and Egypt, comedy. Ironically, the concept of the 'Roman play', which is traditionally used to define the genre of *Antony and Cleopatra*, has sometimes been used to set the play off from Shakespeare's preceding tragedies, as if it were some new form Shakespeare slid into as he grew tired of writing tragedies. Instead, I think, the Roman play, and particularly the Roman world of *Antony and Cleopatra*, should be regarded as Shakespeare's attempt to portray the archetype of tragedy. As Reuben Brower has shown, the world of Shakespearean tragedy is influenced by the Graeco-Roman heroic tradition.[4] Hence, what more fit setting for tragedy than the source of this tradition, the world in which it was not mere literature, but the dominant ethos, as yet unchallenged by the later comic ethos of romantic literature or Christianity? The figure of the great warrior, who embodies a potent ideal of manhood in three of the four 'great' tragedies, is naturally a central figure in the imaginative life of Rome. As Hamlet's father's ghost and the manly ideal he embodied haunts Hamlet, so the Homeric ideal warrior haunts the more modern, limited, civilised society of Rome on the verge of the Augustan era.

That Rome is a pre-Christian world is also convenient for tragedy. Roman culture sanctions the pursuit of power and individual greatness more uninhibitedly than the post-Roman, Christian world, and tragedy, like Rome, is the world of the supreme individual. The ironic religious vision which counterpoises the heroic individualism in tragedy is also best associated with the classical world. The classical gods are jealous of human greatness, and seek to destroy great men lest they rival the gods, as Cleopatra says she and Antony threatened to: 'It were for me / To throw my sceptre at the injurious gods, / To tell them that this world did equal theirs, / Till they had stol'n our jewel' (IV. xv. 75–8). The feeling in tragedy that human greatness is likely to provoke a fatally jealous reaction from the gods is, on the other hand, not well suited to the personality of the Christian God, who, far from seeking to prevent man from becoming god, himself became man.

Rome fulfils the special blend of the heroic and the ironic which is tragedy in many other ways. It is an elevated world by virtue of its antiquity and its enduring literary models. Roman civilisation can be imagined as a great creator of forms, not the least reason being that it developed the rules of decorum, both ethical and dramatic, which are central in Shakespeare's characterisation of it. Cleopatra's ideal of 'the high Roman fashion' acknowledges Rome as the standard-maker for what is noble and lofty in conduct. The elevated verbal style which tragic decorum demands sounds unusually appropriate on the lips of Romans, who can employ Latinate diction more naturally than most characters. Rome is also an ironic world, because it is dead. Not only has its empire vanished, but its values and vision have been supplanted.

According to the principles of dramatic decorum, tragedy is generally based on an historical subject, while the subject of comedy, in contrast, is the poet's invention.[5] Shakespeare both sharpens and expands this point of distinction between the kinds. Rome on the verge of fulfilling her imperial destiny is not just any tale out of a chronicle. The establishment of Augustan Rome could be seen from Shakespeare's viewpoint as *the* historical subject: the vision of the world of the past, the old order of our civilisation. The historicity of Rome also contributes to our sense of it as an ironic world: it is a realistic, unpredictable, nightmarish world from which we would like to awake. It has been called 'the sublunar world',[6] or simply 'the World'.[7] Perhaps because Caesar's Rome does not have its energies deflected by the contemplation of unearthly kingdoms, it seems a concentratedly temporal world, hyperactive in the world of time: 'With news the time's in labour, and throws forth, / Each minute, some' (III. vii. 80–1).

The comic world of Egypt, in contrast, is serenely unburdened by any historical mission, and love, playing, and eating are the central activities. More than just an invented world, Egypt is an archetypally poetic realm. Cleopatra is a particularly compelling embodiment of the conventions of romance. Like the maiden in the Song of Songs, Cleopatra is a woman who is also a nation, calling herself Egypt. She is a cynosure of magnetic attractive powers at her appearance on Cydnus. She is a serpent-woman. She is a dying and reviving heroine, usually with the aid of the conventional amatory trope identifying death with sexual consummation. As Antony is identified with the sun, 'the fire / That quickens Nilus' slime', so is Cleopatra with the Nile Valley. Like Spenser's Garden of Adonis, the Nile Valley is a kind of golden world or earthly paradise, a place of seed where things grow to their fullest effortlessly and without cultivation: 'The higher Nilus swells, / The more it promises: as it ebbs, the seedsman / Upon the slime and ooze scatters his grain, / And shortly comes to harvest' (II. vii. 20–3). As well as imaging a beneficent and intriguingly polymorphous sexuality in Egypt, overflowing Nilus also offers an analogue for the vitalising effect of experiencing the swollen torrents of magnified human passions projected by the histrionically gifted queen. In contrast to the busily temporal world of Rome, Egypt is an eternal realm, which transfixes Romans in the endlessly recurrent and fertilising experience of love.[8]

Rome is also a fitting setting for tragedy because it is an unabashedly masculine world, in contrast to female-dominated Egypt. The anti-romantic attitudes which seem such a sinister aspect of Iago's tragic villainy in *Othello* are practised freely in the open daylight in Rome, not simply by Caesar, who is as quick as Iago to equate love with lust, but also by such a genial spirit as Enobarbus. While Egypt has as its symbol of female ascendancy Mardian, the eunuch, Rome has a female eunuch – Octavia. In Egypt Antony is a lover and a lady's man, in danger of losing his manly self-sufficiency; in Rome Antony is a man's man, a soldier-general, and a competitor with Caesar, and he is subject to some embarrassment for having been a lady's man. This simple and profound distinction is not generally cited in discussions of the principles of decorum, yet it accurately dramatises more explicit points of decorum, such as that comedy conventionally treats of love, while tragedy of violence and war, or that tragedy deals with illustrious actions of great public significance, while comedy treats of private and domestic actions. The sexual dimension of generic distinction also generally accords with previous Shakespearean practice in the genres. The male hero does tend to be the imaginative centre in Shakespearean tragedy, while the heroine tends to overshadow the hero in comedy, much as Cleopatra generally upstages Antony in Act I.[9]

Women are not heroic individuals in comedy, as men are in tragedy; rather, they act as conduits of natural feeling which seeks to form marriages and knits societies together. Another generic commonplace is that while tragedy is concerned with man as an individual, comedy sees man as a member of a social group. Shakespeare signals this distinction even in his titles: in all his tragedies and in the generically akin histories, the name of the play is the name of an individual, while none of his comedies (except two of the romances) have an individual's name in their titles. And Rome is like tragedy in being most interested in man as an individual. The stoic ideals of constancy and imperturbability, of remaining 'like oneself', fortify the individual man and help him resist the pull of common, natural appetites and passions – comic impulses, which appear vulgar, promiscuous, or somehow perverse in the value system of tragedy.

While Rome exalts aloof individuality, Egypt brings about the loss of individual identity, the dissolving of discrete forms, or the overflowing, like Nilus, of the boundaries of form. In Egypt, Antony loses himself and becomes like Cleopatra. This confusion of identities which is typical of romantic lovers is grossly indecorous in the Roman world; Caesar complains that Antony 'is not more manlike / Than Cleopatra; nor the queen of Ptolemy / More womanly than he' (I. iv. 5–7). Cleopatra generally disregards advice to 'keep yourself within yourself' (II. v. 75), she threatens to burst 'the sides of nature' (I. iii. 16), and Antony 'o'erflows the measure' especially under her influence. Always the actress, she nonetheless has an emotional integrity behind her 'becomings' which gives her acting great power. When Antony senses an histrionic storm approaching as he prepares to leave Egypt and accuses her of cunning, Enobarbus, astute detector of frauds, ascribes the sensational power of her passions to their authenticity: 'Alack, sir, no, her passions are made of nothing but the finest parts of pure love. We cannot call her winds and waters sighs and tears; they are greater storms and tempests than almanacs can report' (I. ii. 144–8).

Cleopatra fittingly has immense and vital passions, for she is Eros, that comic deity. She takes Eros' place at the arming scene (IV. iv. 14–15), she enters to his name (IV. 12. 19–20), and Antony mingles her with Eros when apostrophising the presumably dead Cleopatra: 'Eros! – I come, my queen: – Eros! – Stay for me' (IV. xiv. 50). Cleopatra is less troubled than ordinary mortals by the loss of self, since Eros thrives as discrete individual identities are dissolving. Thus, in contrast to the form-making and individuating energies of the tragic Roman world, the comic Egyptian world is governed by form-dissolving Eros.

Rome and Egypt are also like tragedy and comedy in their relationship of opposition, which structures more detail than can ever be mentioned in a list of the elements of tragic or comic decorum. Although one point of the idea of decorum is that each world has its appropriate place, neither world is content with a discrete half of the universe. Rome and Egypt go beyond the sets of values, attitudes or styles appropriate to central areas of human experience like war or love. They are also mental worlds, which become modes of interpreting all experience – the tragic and the comic vision. Each world o'erflows the measure of decorum and seeks to appropriate the entire universe of human experience, ratifying its own vision by showing the values and pursuits of its rival world to be illusory, ephemeral, or childish. The claims of Rome, which seem to Antony like urgent matters of great public concern, or tragic material, after a Roman thought has struck him in I. ii., are reduced by Cleopatra to the petulant demands of shrewish women and youths:

> Fulvia perchance is angry; or who knows
> If the scarce-bearded Caesar have not sent
> His powerful mandate to you, 'Do this, or this;
> Take in that kingdom, and enfranchise that;
> Perform't, or else we damn thee.'
>
> (I. i. 20–4)

Like all Shakespeare's comic and tragic worlds, Egypt and Rome are neither static nor unmixed models; in fact, each at times resembles its opposite because of its imperialistic ambitions. Octavius wants to extend Rome's dominion to the realm of Antony's love life: he arranges a marriage. At Actium, Cleopatra wants to perform in the Roman theatre of war. Shakespeare characteristically mingles the genres for good dramatic reason: each kind is most lively as it is invading and conquering the provinces of its rival, though this attempt also brings on its dissolution.

One might object to the attribution of personality to the genres implied in seeing them as rivalrous and imperialistic. But the worlds of Rome and Egypt each do have a human personality attached to them: the characters of Caesar and Cleopatra. These characters owe their mighty assurance to their roles as spokesmen for a tragic or a comic vision. The more unstable Antony at times seems weak beside the forceful authority of both Caesar and Cleopatra. Yet Antony, unstable because he participates in both worlds, exercises the imaginations of Cleopatra and Caesar profoundly, because he also belongs in ways neither Caesar nor Cleopatra can to their rival world, which both stimulates and threatens them.

If seen as part of the action of the play, the contest of genres explains the conflict of interpretations which the play has generated. Does Cleopatra unman and destroy Antony, ironically weakening and dividing him until he suffers the torment of defeat by a lesser man? Or does she help him achieve his quest for identity, completing the Roman warrior in a greater, more magnanimous hero, and raising him out of the dying world of history – the fortunate Caesar's dominion – into the sublime comic realm of legends, demi-gods, and ever-reviving theatrical heroes? Since each genre is all-encompassing, each can supply a credible interpretation of almost any aspect of Antony's story. One man's 'dotage' is another man's (or woman's) 'nobleness of life'. Each vision elicits the beholder's profound imaginative participation and inspires him with a strong conviction of its truth. Yet so does its opposite. There is no ultimate value structure outside the genres to judge them by; the genres, in their largest conceptions, are the source of all value judgements, as they are of all interpretation. This is why their contest matters, as well as why it is not easily resolved. Yet, although the tragic and ironic vision is never invalidated, the play does move, I think, from a world in which the tragic vision predominates to one in which the comic vision does.

Seeing Rome and Egypt as generic worlds also helps us account for their curiously changing relationships better than other dichotomies – such as power and love, reason and intuition, public life and private life, or the World and the Flesh[10] – into which Rome and Egypt have been allegorised. (The content of these dichotomies is encompassed by the generic one.) The opposition between the worlds is insisted upon for the first three acts, reflecting the fact that in the first half of the play we are in the Roman literary universe, where the classical ideal of decorum, or the separation of the kinds, reigns. Rome and Egypt here have a relationship which is typical of tragic dichotomies: they are mutually exclusive. At the end of this tragic Roman phase of the action, Antony, who belongs to both worlds and to 'be himself' must bestride the ocean which separates them, sinks symbolically beneath the ocean in his failure at Actium. Yet in the latter half of the play, the opposition disappears. All the Romans come to Egypt, and Egypt and Rome become less important as geographical places than as qualities; hence they can enter into a comic, mutually enhancing integration, and take on individual human form in Antony.

II

The contest of genres begins in the opening scene, as spokesmen of each claim their values encompass those of their rival world. The Roman commentary of Philo and Demetrius surrounds the appearance of the lovers, and it also morally claims to comprehend entirely the value of the world which Antony is deluding himself about. This Roman bid for dominance is quite self-assured, because tragedy is unquestionably the dominant kind in the contemporary literary world. When Antony in Egypt steps aside from the epic, public, heroic, martial world of Philo's Roman ideal (the world of tragedy), he enters that society of buffoons and courtesans which populates Roman comedy: 'The triple pillar of the world transform'd / Into a strumpet's fool' (I i. 12–13). Romantically attuned audiences, of Shakespeare's age and later, may be surprised to hear love and the stuff of comedy treated with such contempt, and many feel that the Romans' commentary does not comprehend the experience of seeing the famous pair.

This feeling is created in part by the prophetic glimpse we are given of the coming comic dispensation, when the world of comedy will no longer be a low one. The lover's appearance, ushered in with the biblical echo 'behold and see', has the quality of a revelation, and Antony's reference to 'new heaven, new earth' also hints of a great mythic change to come. Antony's bold conceit, 'Let Rome in Tiber melt', may remind us that Rome's worldly power has indeed melted by the time of this enactment. He declares that love is 'the nobleness of life', which love indeed becomes in future literary worlds, such as the world of heroic romance. Antony uses a word which points us toward this literary world in his challenge to 'the world to weet / We stand up peerless' (I. i. 39–40). 'Weet' is a literary archaism in the seventeenth century; this is its only use in Shakespeare, and it is associated with Spenserian romance.

Yet Antony's commitment to an exalted romantic conception of the comic world is as yet only 'mouth-made', as Cleopatra says. We see two conceptions of the comic world subtly conflicting in the lovers' interchange. Cleopatra wants Antony to hear the news from Rome; she argues from a romantic conception of the comic world, in which it can contain seriousness and the matter of tragedy. In contrast, Antony resists her by arguing for the observance of decorum, from a classical conception of the comic world, in which serious business is out of place: 'Let's not confound the time with conference harsh: / There's not a minute of our lives should stretch / Without some pleasure now. What sport to-night?' (I. i 45–7). Although he appears to be flattering Cleopatra and her world by sweeping Rome aside entirely, Antony's Roman conception of decorum leads to the eventual triumph of Rome and tragedy, because it trivialises the comic world. Cleopatra's attempt to make Antony 'be himself', including his Roman self, is an effort to involve the whole Antony in her comic world, and hence make his valuing of it more permanent

220 BARBARA C. VINCENT

– an attempt which is thwarted by the argument for keeping decorum. The classical ideal of decorum as Shakespeare dramatises it elevates tragedy at the expense of comedy not just by trivialising the comic world, but by disallowing its basic impulses. Like Caesar in his disapproval of mingling business and pleasure ('our graver business / Frowns at this levity', II. vii. 119–20), classical decorum frowns not only on the mingling of dramatic genres, but on all the minglings and marriages of opposites which comedy delights in. Comedy must break decorum and o'erflow its restraining, separating measures if it is not to remain subordinate.

After the prophetic glimpses of scene i, things begin falling apart, and the Roman literary schema of separation reasserts itself in scene ii. The scene is in two halves, visiting each of the separate camps into which the women and men have drifted. In the first half of the scene, we are given a *tranche de vie* portrayal of the female-dominated comic realm in one of its typical serene, unthreatened, and thoughtless moods. Charmian and Iras aggressively tease Alexas and try to cajole the soothsayer into 'giving' them good fortunes. A banquet is being brought out; the conventional feasting of comedy goes on constantly in Egypt. The soothsayer tells Charmian and Iras of their inevitable tragic fortunes and they make fun of him. Fortune is one of the many things taken seriously in Roman moods and mocked in Egyptian ones.

In the second part of the scene, 'a Roman thought' has invaded the thoughtless, playful, passionate feminine world and reversed its value for Antony: 'He was dispos'd to mirth; but on the sudden / A Roman thought hath struck him' (I. ii. 79–80). From the Roman, masculine perspective, Egypt now appears an irrational world of monstrous fertility, an ever-breeding female which has none of masculine regard for the active cultivation of individual worth, and hence produces a nightmarish growth of cripples, weeds, and serpents: 'O then we bring forth weeds, / When our quick minds lie still, and our ills told us / Is as our earing' (I. ii. 106–8). Antony himself has become female in his inactivity, helping to breed this loathesome excess of dangerous vitality: 'Ten thousand harms, more than the ills I know, / My idleness doth hatch' (I. ii. 126–7). Roman thoughts bring a dark vision of Antony's identification with Cleopatra – of that exchange of identities which is so natural and typical of lovers in the comic world of romance. At the same time, Roman thoughts elevate, rather flatteringly, the importance of Antony's manly, individual Roman self. The ever-breeding female who brings forth life without male assistance (as weeds grow up without an 'earing' cultivator, or as serpents grow asexually from horsehairs) is not confined to Egypt, but has spread to the world of Roman politics in Antony's absence. Antony says of Pompey's rising, 'Much is breeding, / Which like the courser's hair, hath yet but life, / And not a serpent's poison' (I. ii 190–2). Antony himself represents that masculine discipline and control that the world lacks – an implication flattering to the Roman Antony, though Pompey and Caesar soon confirm Antony's impression of his own consequence. Since no one fears Caesar's soldiership, Antony's absence from Rome leaves a power vacuum and is responsible for the dangerous political fecundity there.

'A Roman thought' is thought conditioned by the awareness of intractable external realities, such as Roman public opinion: 'Name Cleopatra as she is called in Rome' (I. ii 103). Like the tragic vision, Antony's Roman thoughts originate in messages from the outside world – outside, that is, the world of one's desires, that personal comic realm which often seems subjective and illusory, but which is given a wonderful substantiality by the experience of love. Messages from the outside have been actively trying to reach Antony, in the persons of the messengers, since early in scene i. Though Antony's Roman thoughts, like the tragic vision, begin in an awareness of external realities, they go beyond them, accumulating the power to effect a complete reinterpretation of all Antony's Egyptian experience, and extending, with the wholeness of a generic structure, to the interpretation of things that cannot be known from experience: 'Ten thousand harms, more than the ills I know, / My idleness doth hatch.'

The messengers import more of the matter of tragedy. There is a grim reminder of the fact of death – a messenger brings word of Fulvia's – and some guilt-generating news of the great deeds of younger men such as Pompey. This news of martial adventure injects the presence of heroic epic, recalling the glorious and spacious realm of Homer, or the theatrical recreation of the heroic universe in *Tamburlaine*:

> Mess.   Labienus –
> This is stiff news – hath with his Parthian force
> Extended Asia: from Euphrates
> His conquering banner shook, from Syria,
> To Lydia, and to Ionia;
> Whilst –
> Ant.   Antony, thou wouldst say.
>
> (I. ii. 96–101)

The geographical world, the wide-arched empire which Antony cheerfully dismissed in scene i ('Here is my space'), now seems wider and more impressive. The ideal of martial heroism, and the sovereign sway and masterdom over the earth to which it entitled one, is a compelling one in most of Shakespeare's tragedies, and is fittingly one of the strongest attractions of the tragic world of Rome.

Roman thoughts gain further ascendancy over Antony when, in his discussion with Enobarbus at the end of scene ii, a Roman, masculine kind of comedy supplants the feminine, romantic kind. Enobarbus presents a vision of love found in the Ovid of the *Amores* or the *Arts Amatoria*. English readers are most familiar with the features of this classical comic kind in the amatory verse of Donne – the frankly sexual interest in women, the playful and ironic enacting of romantic extravagances, the celebration of masculine wit. In spite of the amatory subject, the dramatic situation closest to the experience of Ovidian lyric would not consist of a man talking to a woman, but instead, one man talking to another *about* a woman. This is the situation we have in Antony's discussion of Cleopatra with Enobarbus, a man-to-man talk which helps Antony, in the throes of romantic involvement, acquire some comic detachment on the lover in himself.

In his Ovidian mode, Enobarbus demonstrates an ability to appreciate the comic Egyptian world which can yet be encompassed within a Roman, masculine hierarchy of values. After Antony's comic viewpoint is put to rout by Roman thought, he wants to excise the stuff of comedy from his life completely: 'Would I had never seen her!' (I. ii. 150). But for Enobarbus, masculine ascendancy need not be maintained by a rigid exclusion of women:

> Under a compelling occasion let women die: it
> were a pity to cast them away for nothing, though
> between them and a great cause, they should be
> esteemed nothing. Cleopatra catching but the least
> noise of this, dies instantly. I have seen her die
> twenty times upon far poorer moment: I do think there
> is mettle in death, which commits some loving act upon
> her, she hath such a celerity in dying.
>
> (I. ii. 134–42)

As in the Ovidian amatory tradition, Enobarbus allows the experience of love to be included, with some ironic detachment, in a world which believes in the supremacy of masculine pursuits.

The Ovidian mode is not simply ironic; it also genuinely celebrates love, as in *Hero and Leander*, or Enobarbus' account of Cleopatra's appearance on Cydnus. Because Enobarbus can appreciate Cleopatra and her world (unlike Octavius, who, as J. L. Simmons says, can make every moment of life a 'compelling occasion', leaving no room for comedy)[11] and yet maintain his masculine, Roman priorities (which Antony tends to forget in Egypt), his Roman self seems admirably comprehensive. He is the only major character besides Antony whom we see in both Egypt and Rome in the first half of the play, and he is notably better than Antony at recalling the claims of the absent world and balancing them against those of the present world. He does not 'go to, and back, lackeying the varying tide'; he has sufficient individuality to stand against the tide in each world, speaking in favour of Egypt in Rome, and vice versa. Because of his ironic detachment, in the unintegrated Roman system with its separated genre worlds, Enobarbus appears to have more integrity than Antony, whose heroic desire for a total engagement of himself leads him to over-commit himself in each world.

Since he is a Roman comic character, Enobarbus naturally exemplifies classical comic decorum better than Cleopatra. He speaks in the plain, humble, colloquial diction of comedy (his plainness is pointed out by Pompey in II. vi. 78), while she of course lays claim to the styles of greatness and invades the verbal provinces of tragedy. As we move toward the tragic world of Rome, we hear at the end of II. ii. a distinct transition from the playful, bawdy, low diction of comedy to the elevated, Latinate, authoritative, impersonal voice of tragedy, which is also punctuated by a shift from prose to blank verse:

> **Ant.**   The business she [Fulvia] hath broached in the state
>   Cannot endure my absence.
> **Eno.**   And the business you have broach'd here cannot be
>   without you, especially that of Cleopatra's, which
>   wholly depends on your abode.
> **Ant.**   No more light answers. Let our officers
>   Have notice what we purpose. I shall break
>   The cause of our expedience to the queen,
>   And get her leave to part. For not alone
>   The death of Fulvia, with more urgent touches,
>   Do strongly speak to us; but the letters too
>   Of many our contriving friends in Rome
>   Petition us at home.
>
>   (I. ii. 169–81)

Enobarbus, the comic Roman, is a helpful intermediary for Antony between Egypt and Rome. Encountering the comic in this more detached, masculine form makes it easier to control than in the person of Cleopatra.

The Roman counterpart to I. ii. in its juxtaposition of the opposing genres is II. ii., the reconciliation scene between Antony and Caesar. The first part of this scene is conducted in tragic decorum; in fact, there is a heavy emphasis on decorum. Self-consciousness about the need for rhetorical dignity is betrayed by repeated congratulations of the speakers on their fine styles: ''Tis spoken well', ''Tis noble spoken', 'Worthily spoken, Maecenas'. Caesar and Antony jealously insist upon the dignity and decorousness of their treatment of one another, concealing their personal rancour by defensively observing the punctilios of an increasingly evanescent honour:

> Caesar   I must be laugh'd at,
>   If for nothing, or a little, I
>   Should say myself offended, and with you
>   Chiefly i' the world: more laugh'd at, that I should
>   Once name you derogately, when to sound
>   Your name it not concern'd me.
>   (II. ii. 30–5)

> Ant.   . . . as nearly as I may,
>   I'll play the penitent to you. But mine honesty
>   Shall not make poor my greatness, nor my power
>   Work without it. Truth is, that Fulvia,
>   To have me out of Egypt, made wars here,
>   For which myself, the ignorant motive, do
>   So far ask pardon, as befits mine honour
>   To stoop in such a case.
>   (II. ii. 91–8)

To gain acceptance in the exclusivist tragic world, Antony must disavow allegiance to the comic one. A recurrent theme of the reconciliation scene is Antony's lack of control over his women, a source of grievance between Antony and Caesar, and of increasing embarrassment to Antony. Antony coolly betrays Cleopatra, calling his hours with her 'poisoned', to excuse his betrayal of an oath to aid Caesar. Octavia is brought forward to fill the need for a submissive woman, who will make love serve the designs of masculine policy rather than disrupting them.

The hierarchies of tragedy suppress the concerns of comedy by making them appear insignificant: 'Small to greater matters must

give way' (II. ii. 11). Personal and private feeling, of central importance in comedy, is here out of place. ''Tis not a time / For private
stomaching' (II. ii. 8–9), Lepidus, the fatuous keeper of decorum,
tells the aggressively personal and passionate comic Roman,
Enobarbus. Caesar and Antony come to realise that their differences
are based not so much on material injuries, but on differences of
personality and style:

> Caesar I do not much mislike the matter, but
> The manner of his speech; for't cannot be
> We shall remain in friendship, our conditions
> So differing in their acts.
> (II. ii. 111–14)

Yet both men are willing to suppress this vital truth, because of the
decorum of their situation. Mere personal differences are trivial and
embarrassing, and ought to be suppressed in the grave public arena
of world politics. The hierarchies of tragedy smother the viewpoints
of comedy most dramatically when Antony silences Enobarbus, who
keeps violating tragic decorum. As a spokesman for comic values, for
personal and private feelings, Enobarbus refuses to behave as if he
were Antony's subordinate. Unlike Caesar's officer Agrippa, he doesn't
politely ask leave before he speaks. He resists the decorous tragic
fiction that the leaders' expedient alliance out of fear of Pompey is
'noble', and should be grounds for a permanent accord. And he
registers his dissent by divagating into the comic low style: 'Or if you
borrow one another's love for the instant, you may, when you hear
no more words of Pompey, return it again: you shall have time to
wrangle in, when you have nothing else to do' (II. ii. 103–6).
    At the end of the reconciliation, the scene becomes comic without
having to return to Egypt. The recently suppressed Enobarbus now
asserts himself; he speaks with intimacy and licence about the great,
enacting the saturnalian side of comedy. His description of Cleopatra
on Cydnus is of course a powerful celebration for its own sake of
those comic and romantic elements which the Roman leaders seek to
subordinate to their political ends. We also hear of a genuinely
courteous Antony, unlike the pretender to courtesy we see in Rome.
And we hear of a Cleopatra who is all the more majestic while
flouting the decorum which weighs so heavily upon the would-be
magisterial Romans. So II. ii. dramatises the human consequences of
classical decorum. The comic world is a distinctly subordinated one
in Rome; Enobarbus is not allowed a jest in the presence of the great,

let alone his account of Cleopatra's marvellousness as she appeared on Cydnus. However, the potency of his description is part of that groundswell of forces we sense building toward the release of the suppressed energies of comedy.

III

As we have seen, the classical principle of the separation of the genres tends to favour the dominion of tragedy. Antony generally obeys this Roman schema in the first half of the play: he resists Cleopatra's desire to include Roman business in Egypt, leaves Egypt for Rome, and tries to get along in the Roman world by subordinating Egyptian values. Yet each genre is undermined by decorous separation from its opposite. When Antony attempts to make Egypt into a realm which contains only pleasure, Egypt instead becomes the reverse of pleasurable: 'The present pleasure, / By revolution lowering, does become / The opposite of itself' (I. ii. 121–3). When Antony returns to Rome and works at eliminating all things Egyptian from his life, we see the genre world he is trying to build again dissolve in the feast on Pompey's galley. The plan for fighting with Pompey, for an heroic, tragic action, degenerates instead into a comic feasting and drinking bout with him, and the Roman world becomes, rather queasily, the opposite of itself:

> Pom.   This is not yet an Alexandrian feast.
> Ant.   It ripens toward it.
> (II. vii. 95–6)

Shakespeare's critique of classical decorum emerges in the paradox that one cannot fulfil the distinctive natures of either genre without mingling them.

The Roman world ends as a parody of the Egyptian one. Language used about Octavia presents her as a simulacrum of Cleopatra, a love goddess who can make opposites mingle and become one: 'her love to both / Would each to other and all loves to both / Draw after her' (II. ii. 135–7). But Octavia can't encompass and harmonise opposition; instead she becomes a part of it, a further source of hostility between Antony and Caesar. Rome is like Egypt, but it is also Egypt's opposite – the world of ironic comedy. It co-opts and preys upon the matter of comedy, while depriving comic actions of their meaning and value, like the ironic action of Caesar and Antony's imperial rivalry, which, as Enobarbus remarks, devours and makes empty the world: 'Then, world, thou hast a pair of chaps, no more, / And throw between them all the food thou hast, / They'll grind the one the other' (III. v. 13–15). These haunting lines are a comment upon the liquidation of Lepidus, who is another would-be comic mediator, like Octavia, between Antony and Caesar. At the feast on Pompey's galley, Lepidus tries to contain the hostilities between the leaders in himself and convert them to comedy. He tries to divert the other men 'as they pinch one another by the disposition' by making himself more and more drunk. But he 'raises the greater war between him and his discretion'; the attempt to internalise the conflict seems to explode the mediator's ability to maintain a discrete identity, and Lepidus is blown up into a titanic nonentity: 'To be called into a huge sphere, and not to be seen to move in 't, are the hole where eyes should be, which pitifully disaster the cheeks' (II. vii. 14–16). This eyeless Lepidus is a parody of the titanic being which Antony eventually does become in Cleopatra's dream, after he has brought together opposing worlds in himself and 'bestrid the ocean':

> His face was as the heaven, and therein stuck
> A sun and moon, which kept their course, and lighted
> The little O, the earth.
> (V. ii. 79–81)

Caesar, the personality of Rome, expands and fleshes out the ironic vision. In responding to a rumour that Pompey 'is belov'd of those / That only have fear'd Caesar', he dissociates himself from the Roman people, popular leaders, and the processes of history since 'the primal state':

> I should have known no less;
> It hath been taught us from the primal state
> That he which is was wish'd, until he were;
> And the ebb'd man, ne'er lov'd till ne'er worth love,
> Comes dear'd, by being lack'd. This common body,
> Like to a vagabond flag upon the stream,
> Goes to, and back, lackeying the varying tide,
> To rot itself with motion.
> (I. iv. 40–7)

The great classical metaphor of the body politic, which typically endows collective humanity with the virtues of an individual man, is subverted here by Caesar to deny the individuality and humanity of the populace. He emphasises inert, bodily qualities in the body politic: it is mindless, whorish, passive, determined by processes outside itself, and rotten. Like the Parthian darters, those ironic warriors who shoot backwards while retiring from the zone of combat, Caesar withdraws from the world of temporal processes as he attacks it. Past participles – 'wish'd', 'lov'd', 'dear'd', 'lack'd' – turn processes into fixed states, making them more purely ironic. Pompey is loved because he is lacked; he is lacked because his fortunes have ebbed; his fortunes have ebbed because he is worthless. Caesar's is an objective vision: he refuses to identify with the world outside his mind and animate it with any humanising qualities. Instead his vision transforms people into inert objects, in a kind of inversion of the poetic act of personification.

Caesar's objective vision of Pompey's rise to power may be contrasted with Antony's view of it. Antony also remarks upon the ironic tardiness of the people's love:

> Our slippery people,
> Whose love is never link'd to the deserver
> Till his deserts are past, begin to throw
> Pompey the Great, and all his dignities
> Upon his son, who high in name and power,
> Higher than both in blood and life, stands up
> For the main soldier: whose quality, going on,
> The sides o' the world may danger.
>   (I. ii. 183–90)

Antony increasingly respects Pompey; the son begins to grow into the borrowed robes of his father's fame, perhaps because the memory of the heroes of the past has for Antony, a genuine power to raise the men of the present. Pompey's ambition to be 'the main soldier' is identifiable with Antony's own conception of himself. Pompey becomes, to Antony, a considerable and threatening figure, while Caesar sees Pompey's power as a mindless, effeminate creation. A masculine principle – the principle represented in Antony's reflections by Pompey's father, who, together with the 'slippery people' helps generate Pompey's greatness – does not seem to exist for Caesar in the world outside his mind. A dramatic irony lies behind Caesar's emasculating criticisms of both Pompey and Antony (whom he chides 'as we rate boys') in I. iv. Caesar feels himself inadequate to deal with the masculine aggressions, the 'hot inroads' (I. iv. 50) that Pompey and his pirates are making in Italy, without the assistance of Antony's soldiership.

Caesar both speaks from an ironic vision and dwells in an ironic world, the polar opposite of Cleopatra's vision and world. Northrop Frye elucidates some aspects of this polarity: 'All myths have two poles, one personal, whether divine or human, and one natural: Neptune and the sea, Apollo and the sun. When the world of sea and sun is thought of as an order of nature, this polarisation becomes a god or magician who controls the natural machine at one end, and the natural machine itself at the other. Tragedy, irony, and realism see the human condition from inside the machine of nature; comedy and romance tend to look for a person concealed in the mechanical chess player.'[12] Caesar gives us an inhuman, mechanical, threatening vision of what we see in human form in Cleopatra. In Cleopatra, who identifies with the moon goddess Isis, we glimpse a personality in the tides and the ebb and flow of human desire, those fluctuating processes which Caesar sees as devoid of and destructive to human personality. Combining the human and natural worlds, she makes the winds lovesick and the waters amorous at her manifestation on Cydnus. Her passions are like the elements – 'greater storms and tempests than almanacs can report'. Caesar doesn't see the same Cleopatra that the other characters and the audience do. His famously imperceptive entering line, 'Which is the Queen of Egypt?' (V. ii. 112) indicates more than a social maladroitness. The majesty which is Cleopatra's identifying attribute is understandably invisible to Caesar, since it is made up of qualities which erode or threaten his notion of human greatness. Caesar of course only sees others, not himself, as 'inside the machine of nature'. His aloof perspective seems an appropriate way to dramatise a purely ironic vision – a vision of the world entirely devoid of human sympathy, with which its creator refuses to identify himself.

Antony returns to Rome hoping to find a freer, more spacious and heroic realm than Egypt. He finds instead an anti-Egypt, which is engaged in co-opting and destroying the stuff of comedy. The central actions of Antony's Roman sojourn are his empty political marriage and the treacherous feast on Pompey's galley. That the world of Rome devolves from an high heroic world into a world of ironic comedy is significant in the characterisation of Shakespeare's literary universe. Shakespearean tragedy has many affinities with what was a comic world in Rome, and what we would call the world of ironic comedy. Many critics have noticed that *Othello* makes tragic use of characters and situations associated with the Roman comic tradition.[13] Frye remarks that "*Hamlet* and *King Lear* contain subplots which are ironic versions of stock comic themes, Gloucester's story being the regular comedy theme of the gullible *senex* swindled by a clever and unprincipled son.'[14] The affinity of Shakespeare's tragic worlds with the world of Roman or ironic comedy is understandable when we realise the extent to which the world of tragedy is the world of comedy reversed, frustrated, turned inside out – in short, the world of ironic comedy. The realisation of the opposition of the genres is also prelude to their union: the conception of tragedy as an anti-comic world allows it to be subsumed into a comic structure, as the anti-comic movement typical of comedy.

A central difference between Shakespearean tragedy and Roman comedy is the heartlessness of the latter. Situations that were evidently mirth-provoking in a Roman comedy can be heart-breaking in a Shakespearean tragedy, where we become more engaged with the inner lives of the characters. 'Heart' is an important word in *Antony and Cleopatra*. The heart often stands out as the central subject of the action, and the word (or its relatives, like *hearts, hearty*, or *hearted*) occurs forty-nine times, making its most memorable appearances especially resonant:

> Phil.   . . . his captain's heart,
> Which in the scuffles of great fights hath burst
> The buckles on his breast. . . .
> (I. i. 6–8)

> Cleo.   I would I had thy inches, thou shouldst know
> There were a heart in Egypt.
> (I. iii. 40–1)

> Cleo.   'Tis sweating labour,
> To bear such idleness so near the heart
> As Cleopatra this.
> (I. iii. 93–5)

> Ant.   Egypt, thou knew'st too well,
> My heart was to thy rudder tied by the strings,
> And thou shouldst tow me after.
> (III. xi. 56–8)

> Ant.   Cold-hearted toward me?
> Cleo.   Ah, dear, if I be so,
> From my cold heart let heaven engender hail. . . .
> (III. xiii. 158–9)

> Eno.   A diminution in our captain's brain
> Restores his heart.
> (III. xiii. 198–9)

Ant.   Ah, let be, let be! thou art
The armourer of my heart.
          (IV. iv. 6–7)

Eno.   This blows my heart:
If swift thought break it not, a swifter mean
Shall outstrike thought, but thought will do't, I feel.
          (IV. vi. 34–6)

Ant.   O thou day o' the world,
Chain mine arm'd neck, leap thou, attire and all,
Through proof of harness to my heart, and there
Ride on the pants triumphing!
          (IV. viii. 13–16)

Eno.   Throw my heart
Against the flint and hardness of my fault,
Which being dried with grief will break to powder,
And finish all foul thoughts.
          (IV. ix. 15–18)

Ant. O this false soul of Egypt! this grave charm, . . .
Like a right gipsy, hath at fast and loose
Beguil'd me to the very heart of loss.
          (IV xii. 25–9)

Ant. I made these wars for Egypt, and the queen,
Whose heart I thought I had, for she had mine:
Which whilst it was mine, had annex'd unto't
A million moe, now lost.
          (IV. xiv. 15–18)

Ant.   Off, pluck off,
The seven-fold shield of Ajax cannot keep
The battery from my heart. O, cleave, my sides!
Heart, once be stronger than thy continent,
Crack thy frail case!
          (IV. xiv. 37–41)

'Heart' is a frequently-used word in many Shakespearean plays, and it is fittingly prominent in a work which characterises Shakespeare's own literary world in relation to that of his predecessors. The importance of hearts is linked to the elevation and expansion of the domain of comedy in Shakespearean and Renaissance literature. The world of human desire, the life of the heart, becomes noble and heroic, rather than clownish and low, in the course of literary history from Rome to the Renaissance. As Frye has said, 'Shakespearean comedy illustrates, as clearly as any mythos we have, the archetypal function of literature in visualising the world of desire'.[15] The importance of hearts also provides a link between the genres. It also manifests a deepening tragic world, a greater vulnerability to emotional hurt – to what Antony feels about Cleopatra's presumed betrayal, or what Enobarbus feels upon discovering that his desertion was a mistake. In the Shakespearean universe we grow into in the course of the play, characters can be both more high-hearted and joyous, and also more broken-hearted, than in the Roman world of the first half of the play, in which the genres and the emotional life they embody are kept separate.

The play achieves a unity of the kinds which also preserves and indeed heightens their opposition. Such a unity is difficult for the logical mind to accept, which is another reason the play has provoked such controversy about whether it is finally comic and romantic, *or* tragic and ironic. The kind of unity most congenial to the rational mind is a golden mean which balances extremes and cancels out the excesses of each. But the unity of the play is more like that 'heavenly mingle' which Cleopatra admires in Antony as he leaves Egypt:

> O heavenly mingle! Be'st thou sad, or merry,
> The violence of either thee becomes;
> So does it no man else.
>
> (I. v. 59–61)[16]

The achievement of unity in opposition depends upon the power of language to be at once single and double; the simplest form of this power is seen in the pun, which is at once one word and two discrete words. Antony's lament at hearing that Cleopatra is dead, 'now / All length is torture: since the torch is out' (IV. xiv. 45–6), links with wordplay the opposites (in terms of desire) of his torch and his torture. The sound suggests that Cleopatra is both, even while the sense seems to make an ultimate distinction between them. The crucial pun of the play is of course the one on 'dying', which identifies the culminating act of a tragic action with that of a comic, romantic one.[17]

The dramatic image of Antony falling on his own sword is also a kind of gestural pun: it gives profound and powerful expression to opposite meanings. It is the ultimate ironic action, since Antony is turned against Antony. This is what Caesar, the complete ironist, has been trying more and more explicitly to accomplish: 'Plant those that have revolted in the van, / That Antony may seem to spend his fury

/ Upon himself' (IV. vi. 9–11). Yet this ultimate ironic act also puts an end to irony; it prevents Caesar from taking Antony alive and continuing to humiliate him. This image shows the ironic merging into the heroic, as befits tragedy. Falling on the sword is also a romantic and erotic gesture. In heroic romance, one of the signs of love is the stab wound, usually self-inflicted. Swords are inevitably phallic symbols, and Antony talks himself into suicide by imagining it as an erotic act. To achieve heroic stature, Antony must manage to effect a noble death (at least on some level), so falling on his sword, like an erotic act, is also a regenerative one: it entitles Antony to his rebirth in poetry and the theatre.

IV

The play, then, moves beyond the Roman world of Antony and Cleopatra's historical origin. The hero and heroine earn their transcendence of time, for they take the stuff of comedy more seriously than men do in the Roman world, a world in which Antony is accused of 'lightness' and 'traduc'd for levity' (III. vii. 13). Charles Hallett has argued recently that *Antony and Cleopatra* would have been recognised by a Jacobean audience as a portrayal of the 'sublunar' world, an ironic world in which permanent value cannot exist, for everything is subject to change, time, and fortune.[18] Hence we must beware of exalting the characters of such a world, who are distanced from their intended audience by an inevitable, historically-determined inferiority of metaphysical knowledge. But we do not stay in the dead Roman past, nor in the sublunar world, which becomes the fortunate Caesar's dominion. And while Hallett accurately compiles all the evidence presenting the play world as the ironic, lost, sublunar realm, he has neglected to notice the presence of the moon's personification in Cleopatra, who practises changeableness deliberately, as a stimulus to passion. Cleopatra becomes identified with the moon in her manifestations as Isis, the moon goddess, and in Antony's beautiful epithet for her, 'our terrene moon' (III. xiii. 153). Her hoisting of Antony aloft in his death scene symbolises his rising out of the mutable sublunar realm, where Caesar and fortune are all-powerful. 'Our terrene moon' laments that, upon the death of Antony, 'there is nothing left remarkable / Beneath the visiting moon' (IV. xv. 67–8). The visiting moon prepares to depart for a sphere of greater fixity. Striving to be 'marble-constant' in her resolution to die, Cleopatra bids farewell to the moon: 'now the fleeting moon / No planet is of mine' (V. ii. 239–40). As Cleopatra claims to become 'fire and air' and consigns her lower elements to baser life, Charmian's choric comment, 'O eastern star!' (V. ii. 307), suggests a transformation beyond the lunar sphere. Though higher than the moon, the eastern star, Venus, enskies another goddess with whom Cleopatra has been associated, and who, rising from the foam, contains the remembrance of Cleopatra's lower elements and fluid, changeable nature. To see the world of temporal flux and passionate change as a self-destructive, ironic one is true enough to the play, but it is only one of the play's visions – the Roman view, where things rot themselves with motion. We can also glimpse in the mutable world the emergent personality of a majestic queen, whose powers to destroy stability and masculine self-sufficiency are consummating, providential. Antony escapes the world of time and tide by passing through its vortex. For any coherent perception about life one finds in the play, the opposite genre always has an eloquent contrary vision.

After Antony departs from Rome, we have suggestions that we are moving beyond the Roman literary world. In the middle of Act III, allegorical characters, Eros and Scarus, appear on the scene and indicate that we are nearing the precincts of romance. In IV. iv, Antony crosses the threshold into the serious comic realm of Christianity. This scene is repeatedly concerned with meaning: 'What means this?'; 'What does he mean?'; 'What mean you, sir, . . .?' Antony is holding a last supper, at which one of the men present, 'perchance tomorrow', will betray him. He talks of a resurrection of his honour, redeemed with his blood, of the identification of one man with many men, of masters and servants changing places, and of being married to his loyal followers.[19] His meaning is lost on his immediate, pre-Christian audience; only his off-stage audience can find meaning in these biblical *topoi*. Enobarbus is somewhat sympathetic at first, but he becomes too moved himself, and accuses Antony of an unmanly indulgence in feeling. But Antony's critic here has a particular reason to desire the concealment of feeling. He has recently disclosed that 'I will seek / Some way to leave him' (III. xiii. 200–1). So Antony's meditative reflection, 'Perchance to-morrow / You'll serve another master', applies only too accurately to the naturally anguished Enobarbus. Antony's response to his followers' tears, 'Grace grow where those drops fall, my hearty friends', calls for a larger-hearted kind of comic response, for hearts that are capable both of sympathy and joyousness. Antony heartily invites them 'to burn this night with torches', and to 'drown consideration' in a communal feast. He is o'erflowing the measure of his Roman context.

The following scene (IV. iii), of Hercules' departure, also deals with the subject of the changing of the gods. After the brilliance of the preceding scene, we are back out in the uncertain dark, and in the classical religious world of darkness and mystery, omens and portents. The form of this scene is that of mystery play. The stage space is used emblematically to represent the world, with soldiers placed in every corner of it. The characters are simple watchmen, and they witness a miracle, represented by hautboys under the stage. Instead of shepherds watching the appearance of a new star in the sky which portends the birth of a divinity, we have soldier-watchmen hearing music under the earth which signifies the disappearance of a god. The scene is a classical version of a mystery play, a kind of inverse nativity play. It reveals a mythic dimension to Antony's story: the change in Antony from the warrior-general to the lover is involved with the great transformation of our civilisation from Roman antiquity (and the Greek antiquity which informs Rome) to the Renaissance. The change in the hero's identity is one that seems to impinge on an encyclopaedic variety of literary styles, while his quest for identity is a human form of the literary quest to find an order behind and coherent relationships among divergent ancient and modern styles.

The scenes of Antony's successful land battle (IV. iv–viii) move us into the heroic comic world of romantic epic. Antony is at last, for the first time in the play, an inspiring warrior-general as he fights for his love. He calls Cleopatra his 'squire'. In his triumphal return to Alexandria, he speaks of his 'gests', and addresses Cleopatra as 'this great fairy', recalling the greatest literary fairy, the faerie queene. Out of the ashes of the Homeric warrior hero, who is withering away, made obsolete by policy in the ironic world of Rome, is born the hero of romance, who reanimates the warrior ideal – 'O Antony, O thou Arabian bird!' (III. ii. 12). Antony recalls an Homeric hero in praising his men: 'you have shown all Hectors'. In defending Egypt, he has achieved the heroic soldierly ideal of Rome; he has bestrid the ocean. His comic integration of the opposing worlds seems threatened not so much from without, by Caesar, but from within, by its own expansive dynamic; Antony's forces threaten to grow too large and o'erflow the measure of all worldly containers: 'Had our great palace the capacity / To camp this host, we all would sup together, / And drink carouses to the next day's fate, / Which promises royal peril' (IV. viii. 32–5). The comic union of former opposites is inauspicious for wars. Battle is not joined between Antony's navy and Caesar's; instead, the navies themselves join, and Antony is festively defeated: 'My fleet hath yielded to the foe, and yonder / They cast their caps up, and carouse together / Like friends long lost' (IV. xii. 11–13).

As in Antony's naval defeat, comic and tragic actions are also deeply intermingled in Enobarbus' death scene. The *coup de grace* for Enobarbus is not a tragic gesture of exclusion or rejection, but a comic one of love. Enobarbus too at last o'erflows the measure of the Roman world at his death; the Roman watchmen who witness his last scene without his knowledge, and without themselves comprehending that what he utters does not concern Caesar, dramatically give the measure of the distance Enobarbus has come from the Roman world. Formerly a detached mocker of other men's displays of passion, now he pours out his heart to the 'blessed moon'. He has previously spoken in the light, witty, detached mode of Ovidian lyric, in which love has the same effects on men as it has on horses. As Antony enters a new Renaissance heroic mode, Enobarbus at his death scene broaches the new mode of Petrarchan lyric:

> O sovereign mistress of true melancholy,
> The poisonous damp of night disponge upon me,
> That life, a very rebel to my will,
> May hang no longer on me. Throw my heart
> Against the flint and hardness of my fault,
> Which being dried with grief will break to powder,
> And finish all foul thoughts.
>
> (IV. ix. 12–18)

Enobarbus uses familiar Petrarchan tropes: sovereign mistresses, inward rebellions, naked thinking hearts. As the possibilities for jubilation go beyond anything in Roman comedy in the scenes of Antony's triumph, so new possibilities for serious feelings are opened up in these signs of a lyric style which aims at absolute sincerity, sanctions introspection, elevates women and the life of the feelings, and makes love an entirely serious, even tragic poetic theme. As in Shakespeare's own sonnets, the theme is a universal one, not confined to sexual love. Another echo of the sonnets can be felt in IV. v. Antony perfectly embodies that high constancy of love in Sonnet 116; his response to Enobarbus' desertion is a firm refusal 'to bend with the remover to remove'. The high seriousness about love and the life of the feelings embodied in the Renaissance lyric has of course been suppressed in the worldly, classical, masculine vision which Enobarbus has embodied so admirably.

The bursting of Enobarbus' heart, as he gasps out Antony's too great, too noble name with his dying breaths, seems a physical enactment of the expansion of the world of comedy. In his Ovidian mode, Enobarbus has represented a comic vision which is *contained within* a Roman set of values. Hence, as comedy o'erflows the measure of its place in the Roman world, Enobarbus fittingly bursts. Enobarbus also seems to cross quietly into the Christian world in the manner of his death; he repents, and prays for forgiveness.

V

John Danby, who has given one of the most interesting accounts of the play as a tragedy, sees *Antony and Cleopatra* as a vision of the world in terms of two great contraries, with no 'third term' which reconciles them.[20] But for those who see in the play a comic pattern which includes and completes tragedy, Antony is clearly cast in the role of a reconciling third term, who bestrides the ocean and unites the realms of Egypt and Rome. Qualities which can enter into a destructive conflict in Antony, such as youth and age, brown hairs and grey ones, at the Battle of Actium (III. xi. 13–15), can also form a mutually enhancing mixture in him, as when the brain power of the older man seems to nourish the 'nerves' – the toughness, strength, and valour characteristic of a youth (VI. viii. 19–22). Each failure and disintegration of Antony's identity is prelude to his grander and more powerful integration of himself, a pattern that is reinforced by his association with the sun. Antony's sinking and rising again prepares for his glorious re-creation after death in Cleopatra's dream, as well as his many revivals as a theatrical hero.

The image of an Antony who gives human personality and form to the cosmos in Cleopatra's dream is more than an idle fantasy or airy nothing. This god-like, triumphant Antony is a metaphor for the paradoxically comic, integrating and renewing powers of tragic art. The paradox of tragedy is closely analogous to that at work in religious communion, which, as Frye describes it, involves 'the dividing of a divine or heroic body among a group which brings them into unity with, and as, that body'. One way of interpreting the Antony of Cleopatra's dream is as an image of the new larger identity created in the society of play-goers and readers out of the division and fall of Antony.

The possibility of an integrative, comic outcome arising out of a tragic action depends for its credibility not, primarily, on Christian analogies, but on an awareness of the literary and theatrical realm which enables such paradoxes to occur – which is one reason why this play is self-conscious about its identity as a work of art. In literature and the theatre, of course, one does not participate in the hero's identity by eating a piece of his body, but rather through the imaginative process of identification with him. The identity of the hero, and the role in it of other people's identification with him, is a recurrent subject of the play's internal action; attending to it enables us to see the most powerful connection between the genres, as well as some mature Shakespearean reflections on the theory of art.

It is a convention of Shakespearean tragedy that the identity of the hero is a central concern and a unifying principle, and concern with the hero's identity is especially emphatic in *Antony and Cleopatra*. Most of the major characters – Caesar, Cleopatra, Enobarbus – as well as a number of minor choric figures, and of course Antony himself, participate with passionate intensity in the motive of wanting Antony to be a good Antony, as well as in the dramatic debate about what that is. Their concern is related to the degree to which the audience identifies with him, or, conversely, feels detachment and criticism. Though the preoccupation of so many characters with Antony augments our interest in him, the audience is at first inhibited in its identification with him by the presence of critical audience-surrogate commentators on stage. The ironic remarks of Philo and Demetrius, or Enobarbus with Maecenas and Agrippa or with Menas, can foster critical detachment in the off-stage audience. However, the on-stage critical attitudes toward Antony are disarmed in the course of the play. At the last supper scene, for example, the on-stage critic, Enobarbus, is himself inadequate to understand the meditations of this Antony who is fast outgrowing Roman horizons. Antony's off-stage audience here is in a better position to sympathise with his desire for a last communion with his loyal followers. This outer audience seems alluded to in the identification of one man and many men Antony desires, because of his use of an odd term – 'clapp'd' – for uniting people: 'I wish I could be made so many men, / And all of you clapp'd up together in / An Antony.' The failure of Antony's attempt at a communion with his Roman audience is painful to his modern one, and tends to deepen his communion with them.

Detachment and dissociation from Antony is made to seem a most untenable position in the desertion of Enobarbus, an action which ironically recoils on Enobarbus. After Enobarbus leaves, there are no more detached observers in Antony's camp; Antony's attendant is the devoted Eros. At Antony's death scene, all the on-stage observers participate profoundly in, echo, and amplify his agony. In a discussion of the generic associations of engagement and detachment, Maynard Mack observes that 'the total moral weight of comedy inclines generally toward the detached man as that of tragedy inclines toward the man engaged'.[21] Detachment is of course fundamental to an ironic vision, so it naturally is characteristic of ironic Roman comedy. Yet the engaging powers of tragedy can serve comic ends: because it can move the audience to identify with the hero, tragedy can work to create a new comic society which is unusually unified – which is one man and many men. In the desertion of the witty and ironic comic Roman, Enobarbus, the detachment of comedy is being repudiated in the service of a greater comic end.

Even Caesar, in spite of being Antony's enemy and embodying the desire for detachment from the rest of humanity in its purest form, cannot help identifying with Antony at the last. After the Battle of Actium, the conflict between Antony and Caesar becomes a contest between the actions of engagement and detachment on many levels, from the inner psychic lives of the two men, to the quality of their forces which are embarking upon a world war. Caesar's camp, the camp of detachment, is associated with the deserters who detach themselves from Antony; they take the vanguard of Caesar's army. Caesar remains aloof even from his own soldiers, and his cause is associated with the triumph of impersonal bureaucratic methods – 'coin, ships, legions', and 'lieutenant' – over heroic personal power. Caesar employs indirect, personally evasive tactics, such as trying to madden Antony by detaching Cleopatra's affections through the detached 'eloquence' of a hireling, Thidias. Antony, in contrast, seeks a direct personal confrontation, 'sword to sword', and a last passionate engagement of his previously divided self for its own sake. He engages the hearts of his men and makes them identify passionately with his cause, and he refuses to dissociate himself from Enobarbus in spite of the latter's desertion. At the land battle where these forces of engagement and detachment finally encounter, the dramatic engagement culminates as Caesar's lieutenant gives the order 'Retire, we have engag'd ourselves too far' (IV. vii. 1).

Antony and the powers of engagement ultimately win the dramatic contest, if they lose the military one. Though he has seemed to operate with cool detachment to defeat and destroy Antony as efficiently as possible, Caesar rather surprisingly weeps upon hearing that Antony is dead. Maecenas and Agrippa, who know Caesar best, are genuinely struck by the degree to which 'Caesar is touched'. They offer some conventional eulogies of Antony, and then, among themselves, a more sincere explanation for their leader's unusual emotion: 'When such a spacious mirror's set before him, / He needs must see himself' (V. i. 34–5). Though containing the ironic hint that Caesar is capable of tears only for himself, these lines also point out Antony's remarkable capacities as a tragic hero, who can all but compel men to identify with him. Even Caesar, with his stringently objective vision, his utter lack of sympathy for the universe outside his mind, can't help but see himself in Antony.

This notion of a 'spacious mirror' signals a shift in the theory of art from that embodied in conventional mirrors for magistrates, such as Hamlet's mirror held up to nature. The spacious mirror metaphor for drama implies less interest in moral realism than Hamlet's theory of drama evinces; it gives a more flattering reflection to its beholders, magnifying them and giving greater scope to their desires for images of human greatness. Though the concept of a spacious mirror perhaps strains the analogy of art with actual mirrors, it emphasises the emotional mirroring process of identification. Since it is flattering, the spacious mirror works better to make us see ourselves than mirrors which give less scope to our desires.

VI

The theory of art embodied in *Antony and Cleopatra* could be characterised as comic because desire plays a greater role in creating the reality of the play than allegiance to an objectively realistic vision. The attempt to achieve an objective vision is of course discredited in the characterisation of Caesar; it is presented as a negative enterprise, a vision of the world unendowed with any of the imaginative life of the perceiver, and hence a reductive, ironic vision. If as Frye says, Shakespearean comedy is engaged in 'visualising the world of desire', it is not surprising that desirers play an active and creative role in shaping the reality of the play's final comic triumph.

Cleopatra is the prime desirer in the play, and she also plays a prominent role in creating Antony's ultimate identity. In contrast to Caesar, who can always easily believe the worst, Cleopatra's desires so govern her perception of reality that she has great difficulty crediting news, such as Antony's marriage to Octavia, which contradicts them. The opposite ontological positions of Caesar and Cleopatra are dramatised in the two characters' treatment of messengers, who bring news from and symbolise the presence of an unmanipulable external reality. While Caesar listens with diligent attention and respect to messengers, Cleopatra tries to bribe, seduce, or threaten them into telling her what she wants to hear.[22] Cleopatra's relationship to external realities may not always be admirable, but it is consistent with her role in helping to create a more elevated and heroic Antony. Both the hero and the heroine are ennobled by their attempts to live up to the spacious images of themselves in the desiring imaginations of their lover. Antony's belief in Cleopatra's noble death (which the audience knows to be a lie) helps inspire him to attempt the same, which in turn elevates Cleopatra, moving her to realise the spacious image of herself which Antony's suicide has reflected. The soothsayer in I. ii. jokingly suggests that wishes might have wombs, and Caesar also (contemptuously, of course) attests to the creative role of desirers: 'It hath been taught us from the primal state / 'That he which is was wish'd, until he were' (I. iv. 41–2). Cleopatra's desiring imagination is the womb of the heroic Antony. Not only does she inspire him, but she speaks, in her dream of Antony, for the most glorious and transcendent image of him; she is the guardian, through her loyalty, of his image as a hero, rather than a dupe; and she is the agent of his final triumph over Caesar.

Critics with a preference for realism might disapprove of the degree to which Antony is a creation of the desires of those who identify with him. Yet it is the case with many fictive heroes that their identities are dependent on the process of identification: their final consequence to the world depends on how successfully they engage the desires of beholders. *Antony and Cleopatra* is simply more explicit than preceding tragedies about the role played by audience responses in creating its reality, and it contains built-in versions of them. Its realism includes the realities of art. Cleopatra's vision of Antony parallels and eloquently articulates the response of auditors who identify with him. As Antony meditates on the evanescence of earthly pageants and even of his own visible shape, and movingly laments his loss of a million hearts, he is annexing millions more in the theatre and is on his way to acquiring the visionary shape of Cleopatra's dream.

In Cleopatra's final scene we are perhaps in the most sublime

comic world in our language, a world which encompasses tragedy
and is only made the loftier for it, which grows the more by reaping.
We are witness to a comic victory over death, as Cleopatra the
actress prepares for suicide as her last 'noble act'. The queen is at her
most becoming – both beautiful, and full of transformation. She uses
all the resources of the tiring house to dramatise her discovery of her
immortal theatrical identity. In dressing up to die, she plays against
the conventional association in Renaissance drama of death with
undressing. The end of an actor's role, the dissolution of his identity,
is often symbolised by the removal of costume. Antony removes his
armour and is 'no more a soldier' as he prepares to die. The most
perfect dramatic contrary to Cleopatra's regal dressing for death is
perhaps Lear's simple 'Pray you, undo this button'. Cleopatra's
deliberate dressing 'like a queen' for her death tells us visually that
death is not here, as it usually is, the end of role-playing; it is the
beginning of theatrical life.

Cleopatra reminds us of the theatrical world she is entering by
repudiating a version of it:

> Cleo.   The quick comedians
>   Extemporally will stage us, and present
>   Our Alexandrian revels: Antony
>   Shall be brought drunken forth, and I shall see
>   Some squeaking Cleopatra boy my greatness
>   I' the posture of a whore.
> Iras   O the good gods!
>   (V. ii. 215–20)

This theatre is not, of course, the same as the one Cleopatra enters in
Shakespeare's play; it is a return to the Roman comic world of
strumpets and fools in which Philo sees Antony and Cleopatra
performing in scene i. Caesar's triumph over Antony and Cleopatra
would result in their enforced relocation back into the debased,
captive comic world of Roman comedy. But the boy actor strikes
closer home. This allusion to the theatre serves primarily as a reminder of the theatrical being that Cleopatra is becoming.

The references to the theatre and to Cleopatra's immortality as an
actress have a paradoxical effect on our sense of closure, especially in
a live performance, where we have a stronger sense of the temporal
sequence of the drama, since we must surrender to it – we cannot
stop and go back as in reading. In a performance, as Cleopatra
prepares to die, we feel the unmistakable approach of the ending of

this long and powerfully engaging drama. Yet the reminders we are given that Cleopatra is an actress, and this is a play, a recurrent event, make this ending filled with an unusually lively sense of beginning anew: 'I am again for Cydnus, / To meet Mark Antony' (V. ii. 227–8). As we feel the time frame of her death closing in on her, she o'erflows the measure yet once more.

VII

Though Shakespearean comedy typically contains and completes a tragic movement, the union of the genres in *Antony and Cleopatra* is on an epic scale, and informs a coherent vision of literary history. Tragedy here includes its literary matrix in the Graeco-Roman tradition, and comedy, the Renaissance, romantic tradition. One achievement of this coherent vision of literary history is the resolution of one of the central artistic problems of Renaissance heroic tragedy, the problem of reconciling the ancient warrior ideal of heroic manliness with modern, Christianised conceptions of greatness, which is at the heart of *Hamlet* and *Macbeth*. Antony successfully bestrides the ancient and modern heroic traditions. He is a gentle, Renaissance hero, capable of reflection and selfless feeling at his last supper scene, in his forgiveness of Enobarbus and Cleopatra, or in his meditations on evanescent pageants with Eros; he is also capable of the glorious and exuberant martial prowess and the passionate egotism of ancient heroes. He can out-rage Hercules, or be 'more mad / Than Telamon for his shield'. No other hero, I think, acts out these opposing versions of greatness so fully and eloquently.

The central action in the play's vision of literary history is a movement from a world in which the *mythos* of tragedy dominates to one in which that of comedy does. The perspectives of tragedy are not, however, disallowed, as many readings of the play attest. It is the nature of the comic vision to include, not to reject, and Shakespeare revitalises the values and vision of his literary forebears at the same time that he encompasses them in his own more capacious structure.

From *English Literary Renaissance*, 12 (1982), 53–86.

NOTES

[Barbara C. Vincent's essay deals specifically with the question of genre in relation to *Antony and Cleopatra*. The issue of genre generally is a complex one, and more attention has been paid to it since feminists have attempted to distinguish between the masculine world of tragedy and the feminine world of comedy. Basically, Vincent sees the play structured around the opposition between the demands of tragedy and those of comedy, from which the action itself derives a considerable amount of its dramatic impact. Ed.]

1. Quotations from *Antony and Cleopatra* are taken from the New Arden edition, ed. M. R. Ridley (Cambridge, Mass., 1954).
   Among the best discussions of comic elements in the play are J. L. Simmons, 'The Comic Pattern and Vision in *Antony and Cleopatra*', *English Literary History*, 36 (1969), 493–510, and Janet Adelman, *The Common Liar* (New Haven and London, 1973). Adelman has an excellent discussion of how 'the entire tragic vision of the play is subjected to the comic perspective' in her first chapters (pp. 1–52), but she seems uninterested in the converse – the critique of the comic vision by the tragic perspective – or in the part generic worlds play in governing our interpretations. She eschews pursuing literary and critical issues in the play in favour of its 'human fact' (pp. 12–13), while I will argue that the human situations of the play dramatise its literary concerns and are not separable from them.

2. Matthew N. Proser, *The Heroic Image in Five Shakespearean Tragedies* (Princeton, 1965), p. 234.

3. Robert Ornstein, 'The Ethic of the Imagination: Love and Art in *Antony and Cleopatra*', in *Later Shakespeare, Stratford-upon-Avon Studies*, 8, ed. John Russell Brown and Bernard Harris (London, 1966), pp. 31–46, and Julian Markels, *The Pillar of the World: Antony and Cleopatra in Shakespeare's Development* (Columbus, Ohio, 1968).

4. *Hero and Saint: Shakespeare and the Graeco-Roman Heroic Tradition* (New York and Oxford, 1971).

5. Something should be said about the conceptions of tragedy and comedy used here. I think the most significant elements of generic identification – that comedy deals with love and festivity and is generally characterised by mirth, and that tragedy deals with wars and great political events, contains deaths, and is characterised by a generally grimmer view of things – is still a part of the common understanding of the genres and needs no explanation. Other conventional points of classical decorum – that the characters of tragedy are great persons, that its actions are often historical, and that it employs an elevated verbal style, while comedy deals with private and domestic actions of ordinary

citizens or even slaves in a plain, humble style – are familiar enough to students of the period. (Though Cleopatra is in fact a queen, this doesn't prevent her from being classed by various Romans as a strumpet, trull, or whore, a low and conventionally comic character.)

The main sources for the conceptions of tragedy and comedy informing the characterisations of Rome and Egypt are previous Shakespearean practice in the genres and classical theory, which is used to sharpen and amplify points of generic distinction. The chief difference between these components – that Shakespearean practice in comedy typically manifests a more elevated, romantic conception of the comic world than that found in classical theory – is at the centre of my argument about the rise of comedy embodied in the play. A good contemporary discussion of classical decorum can be found in Sidney's *Defense of Poetry*. Discussion of the elements of classical decorum, its relationship to Aristotle's theory of tragedy and to Roman and Elizabethan dramatic practice can be found in Madeleine Doran, *Endeavours of Art* (Madison, 1964), pp. 101–11 and passim, and also J. E. Spingarn, *A History of Literary Criticism in the Renaissance* (New York, 1920), pp. 60–106 and 282–90.

Reuben Brower has enlarged my conception of Shakespearean tragedy in his demonstration of its affinity with the Graeco-Roman heroic tradition in *Hero and Saint*. Northrop Frye has revealed a similar generic affinity between Shakespearean comedy and romance in its characters, situations, and ethos. My generic analysis is indebted also to Frye's perceptions of how the genres can mingle (in opposition to classical decorum) and comedy can contain and complete tragedy, in 'The Argument of Comedy', *English Institute Essays, 1948* (New York, 1949). Frye's defence throughout *Anatomy of Criticism* (Princeton, 1957) of comedy and romance from criticism which judges them by the standards of tragedy, irony, and realism is a most interesting exposition of the intellectual and philosophical content of the contest of genres. (Frye's conceptions of tragedy and comedy are based on or else consistent with classical formulations.)

Warning should be given that Shakespeare's generic thinking in this play, although it has elements of a grand, overarching simplicity, is also highly complex, and would require much longer exposition to be handled with adequate subtlety. For example, the generic worlds are not static entities, although the geo-political metaphor might at first lead one to expect them to be. The generic worlds are mental realms as well as external realities, and they shift with the rhythms of Antony's psychic life. The festive spirit disappears and Egypt becomes a mere colony of Rome when Roman thoughts strike Antony and make him re-evaluate Egypt in I. ii. Rome becomes Alexandrian in II. vii. The forms of tragedy and comedy, which we usually think of as so distinct, tend here to dissolve and flow back and forth into one another. Of course, external geographical entities are themselves surprisingly fluid as conceived in this play, which asks us to entertain thoughts of Rome in Tiber and Egypt into Nile melting, and lets us travel in the theatre from one world to another with the speed of thought.

Another complexity arises from the fact that, as I will discuss, both Rome and Egypt seek to expropriate elements of their adversary worlds. Like any Shakespearean tragic or comic world, neither Rome nor Egypt is unmixedly tragic or comic.

6. Charles Hallett, 'Change, Fortune, and Time: Aspects of the Sublunar World in *Antony and Cleopatra*', *Journal of English and Germanic Philology*, 75:1 & 2 (1976), 75–89.

7. John Danby, '*Antony and Cleopatra*: A Shakespearean Adjustment', *Poets on Fortune's Hill* (London, 1952), pp. 128–51. [Reprinted in this volume. Ed.]

8. Many excellent discussions of the play turn upon this point of decorum, e.g. Herbert Rothschild Jr, 'The Oblique Encounter: Shakespeare's Confrontation of Plutarch with Special Reference to *Antony and Cleopatra*', *English Literary Renaissance*, 6 (1976), 404–29.

9. This aspect of generic decorum, mentioned cursorily by many, is concentrated upon by Linda Bamber, 'Comic Women, Tragic Men: Genre and Sexuality in Shakespeare's Plays', Diss. Tufts 1975. Bamber uses *Antony and Cleopatra*, among other plays, to demonstrate the thesis that 'the central comic woman is whole, whereas the central comic man becomes whole'. This applies well to Antony's quest for identity, I think; as he integrates the conflicting aspects of himself, Antony becomes in the course of the play more like Cleopatra, who has embodied from the first a more seamless union of paradoxical contraries.

10. These interpretations are set forth in the following studies: Harold Goddard, *The Meaning of Shakespeare* (Chicago, 1951), S. L. Bethell, *Shakespeare and the Popular Dramatic Tradition* (Durham, NC, 1944), Markels, *The Pillar of the World*, and Danby, *Poets on Fortune's Hill*.

11. 'The Comic Pattern and Vision', p. 502. It should also be noted how beautifully the historical Octavius' banishment of Ovid fits in with Shakespeare's characterisation of him.

12. Northrop Frye, *A Natural Perspective* (New York, 1965), p. 70.

13. Rosalie Colie, *Shakespeare's Living Art* (Princeton, 1974), pp. 135 and 147. See Colie's notes, p. 147, for other treatments of this subject.

14. *Anatomy of Criticism*, p. 175. Frye's word 'ironic' here seems to me redundant, since these comic themes are from a tradition which is itself already ironic to begin with.

15. *Anatomy*, p. 184.

16. The play is clearly distinguishable from the genre of tragi-comedy in that rather than seeking a middle ground between the genres, it mingles extremes without modifying them. It proceeds straight into a full-blown tragedy, and its final comic elements arise out of the development of the tragic action rather than being any kind of check on it. The play's treatment of the genres can be contrasted with the spirit of compromise in conventional tragi-comedy, which can be seen in Guarini's definition of the genre. He says that the writer of tragi-comedy takes from tragedy 'great persons but not great action; a plot which is verisimilar but not true; passions, moved but tempered; the delight, not the sadness; the danger, not the death; from the other [comedy], laughter which is not dissolute, modest amusement, feigned complication, a happy reversal, and above all, the comic order.' Taken from Eugene Waith's translation in *The Pattern of Tragi-comedy in Beaumont and Fletcher* (New Haven, 1952), p. 48.

17. The luxuriance of puns in the play is more than a means of forging links between opposing genres and interpretations. See Sigurd Burckhardt's richly suggestive discussion of the role of punning in creating an artistic medium out of language, which builds on Empson's demonstrations that one word in great poetry can have many meanings, but changes the emphasis to the ability of many meanings to have one word. In 'The Poet as Fool and Priest', *Shakespearean Meanings* (Princeton, 1968), pp. 22 ff.

18. Hallett, pp. 77 ff.

19. John Middleton Murry, *Shakespeare* (London, 1936, rpt. 1954), also calls this scene 'Antony's Last Supper' (p. 362). And he says that the story of Enobarbus is Shakespeare's version of the story of Judas (p. 367).

20. Danby, p. 149.

21. Engagement and Detachment in Shakespeare's Plays', *Essays on Shakespeare and Elizabethan Drama in Honor of Hardin Craig*, ed. Richard Hosley (Columbia, Mo., 1962), p. 287.

22. Antony, when 'stirr'd by Cleopatra' in scene i, refuses to listen to messengers too.

9

'Antony and Cleopatra': *Virtus* under Erasure

JONATHAN DOLLIMORE

In Jonson's *Sejanus*, Silius, about to take his own life in order to escape the persecution of Tiberius, tells the latter: 'The means that makes your greatness, must not come/In mention of it' (III. 311–12). He is of course exposing a strategy of power familiar to the period: first there occurs an effacement of the material conditions of its possibility, second, a claim for its transcendent origin, one ostensibly legitimating it and putting it beyond question – hence Tiberius' invocation only moments before of 'the Capitol,/. . . all our Gods . . . the dear Republic,/Our sacred Laws, and just authority' (III. 216–18). In *Sejanus* this is transparent enough. In other plays – I choose for analysis here *Antony and Cleopatra* and *Coriolanus* – the representation of power is more complex in that we are shown how the ideology in question constitutes not only the authority of those in power but their very identity

Staged in a period in which there occurred the unprecedented decline of the power, military and political, of the titular aristocracy, *Antony* and *Coriolanus*, like *Sejanus* before them, substantiate the contention that "'tis place,/Not blood, discerns the noble, and the base' (*Sejanus*, V. i. 11–12). Historical shifts in power together with the recognition, or at least a more public acknowledgement of, its actual operations, lead to the erasure of older notions of honour and *virtus*. Both plays effect a sceptical interrogation of martial ideology and in doing so foreground the complex social and political relations which hitherto it tended to occlude.

In his study of English drama in the seventeenth century C. L. Barber detects a significant decline in the presence of honour as a martial ideal and he is surely right to interpret this as due to changes in the nature and occupations of the aristocracy during that period. These included the professionalising of warfare and the increasing efficiency of state armies. The effect of such changes was that by the end of the seventeenth century there was considerably less scope for personal military initiative and military glory; honour becomes an informal personal code with an extremely attenuated social dimension.[1]

More recently, and even more significantly for the present study, Mervyn James has explored in depth the changing conceptions of honour between 1485 and 1642; most striking is his conclusion that there occurred 'a change of emphasis, apparent by the early seventeenth century . . . [involving] . . . the emergence of a "civil" society in which the monopoly both of honour and violence by the state was asserted'.[2]

Such are the changes which activate a contradiction latent in martial ideology and embodied in two of Shakespeare's protagonists, Antony and Coriolanus. From one perspective – becoming but not yet residual – they appear innately superior and essentially autonomous, their power independent of the political context in which it finds expression. In short they possess that *virtus* which enables each, in Coriolanus's words, to 'stand/As if a man were author of himself' (V. iii. 35–6). 'As if': even as these plays reveal the ideological scope of that belief they disclose the alternative emergent perspective, one according to which Antony and Coriolanus are nothing more than their reputation, an ideological effect of powers antecedent to and independent of them. Even as each experiences himself as the origin and embodiment of power, he is revealed in the words of Foucault to be its instrument and effect[3] – its instrument because, first and foremost, its effect. Bacon brilliantly focuses this contradiction in his essay on martial glory: 'It was prettily devised of Æsop: *The fly sate upon the axle-tree of the chariot wheel, and said, What a dust do I raise!*'. Throughout Bacon's essay there is a dryly severe insistence on that fact which martial ideology cannot internally accommodate: 'opinion brings on substance'.[4] Such is the condition of Antony and Coriolanus, and increasingly so: as they transgress the power structure which constitutes them both their political and personal identities – inextricably bound together if not identical – disintegrate.

VIRTUS AND HISTORY

Antony and Cleopatra anticipates the dawn of a new age of imperialist consolidation:

> The time of universal peace is near.
> Prove this a prosp'rous day, the three nook'd world
> Shall bear the olive freely
>
> (IV. vi. 5–7)

Prior to such moments heroic *virtus* may appear to be identical with the dominant material forces and relations of power. But this is never actually so: they were only ever conterminous and there is always the risk that a new historical conjuncture will throw them into misalignment. This is what happens in *Antony and Cleopatra*; Antony, originally identified in terms of both *virtus* and these dominant forces and relations, is destroyed by their emerging disjunction.

In an important book Eugene Waith has argued that 'Antony's reassertion of his heroic self in the latter part of the play is entirely personal. What he reasserts is individual integrity . . . Heroism rather than heroic achievement becomes the important thing'.[5] On this view Antony privately reconstitutes his 'heroic self' despite or maybe even because of being defeated by circumstances beyond his control. I want to argue that the reverse is true: heroism of Antony's kind can never be 'entirely personal' (as indeed Bacon insisted) nor separated from either 'heroic achievement' or the forces and relations of power which confer its meaning.

The reader persuaded by the Romantic reading of this play is likely to insist that I'm missing the point – that what I've proposed is at best only true of the world in which Antony and Cleopatra live, a world transcended by their love, a love which 'translineates man (sic) to divine likeness'.[6] It is not anti-Romantic moralism which leads me to see this view as wholly untenable. In fact I want to argue for an interpretation of the play which refuses the usual critical divide whereby it is either 'a tragedy of lyrical inspiration, justifying love by presenting it as triumphant over death, or . . . a remorseless exposure of human frailties, a presentation of spiritual possibilities dissipated through a senseless surrender to passion'.[7] Nor do I discount the Romantic reading by wilfully disregarding the play's captivating poetry: it is, indeed, on occasions rapturously expressive of desire. But the language of desire, far from transcending the power relations which structure this society, is wholly in-formed by them.

As a preliminary instance of this, consider the nature of Antony's belated 'desire' for Fulvia, expressed at news of her death and not so dissimilar to his ambivalent desire for Cleopatra (as the sudden shift of attention from the one to the other suggests):

> Thus did I desire it:
> What our contempt doth often hurl from us
> We wish it ours again; the present pleasure,
> By revolution low'ring, does become
> The opposite of itself. She's good, being gone;
> The hand could pluck her back that shov'd her on.
> I must from this enchanting queen break off.
> (I. ii. 119–25)

True, the language of the final scenes is very different from this, but there too we are never allowed to forget that the moments of sublimity are conditional upon absence, nostalgic contemplation upon the fact that the other is irrevocably gone. As for present love, it is never any the less conditioned by the imperatives of power than the arranged marriage between Antony and Octavia.

VIRTUS AND *REALPOLITIK* (1)

In *Antony and Cleopatra* those with power make history yet only in accord with the contingencies of the existing historical moment – in Antony's words: 'the strong necessity of time' (I. iii. 42). If this sounds fatalistic, in context it is quite clear that Antony is not capitulating to 'Time' as such but engaging in *realpolitik*, real power relations. His capacity for policy is in fact considerable; not only, and most obviously, is there the arranged marriage with Octavia, but also those remarks of his which conclude the alliance with Lepidus and Caesar against Pompey:

> [Pompey] hath laid strange courtesies and great
> Of late upon me. I must thank him only,
> Lest my remembrance suffer ill report;
> At heel of that, defy him.
> (II. ii. 159–62)

In fact, the suggestion of fatalism in Antony's reference to time is itself strategic, an evasive displacing of responsibility for his impending departure from Cleopatra. As such it is paralleled later by Caesar when he tells the distraught Octavia,

> Be you not troubled with the time, which drives
> O'er your content these strong necessities,
> But let determin'd things to destiny
> Hold unbewail'd their way.
>
> (III. vi. 82–5)

The cause of her distress is divided allegiance between brother and husband (Caesar and Antony) who are now warring with each other. Caesar's response comes especially ill from one scarcely less responsible for her conflict than Antony; her marriage to the latter was after all dictated by his political will: 'The *power* of Caesar, and/His *power* unto Octavia' (II. ii. 147–8; my italics). 'Time' and 'destiny' mystify power by eclipsing its operation and effect, and Caesar knows this; compare the exchange on Pompey's galley – **Antony:** 'Be a child o' th' time./**Caesar:** Possess it, I'll make answer' (II. vii. 98–9). Caesar, in this respect, is reminiscent of Machiavelli's Prince; he is inscrutable and possessed of an identity which becomes less fixed, less identifiable as his power increases. Antony by contrast is defined in terms of omnipotence (the more so, paradoxically, as his power diminishes): the 'man of men' (I. iv. 72), the 'lord of lords' (IV. viii. 16).

In both *Antony and Cleopatra* and *Coriolanus* the sense of *virtus* (virtue) is close to 'valour', as in 'valour is the chiefest virtue' (*Coriolanus*, II. ii. 82), but with the additional and crucial connotations of self-sufficiency and autonomous power, as in 'Trust to thy *single virtue*; for thy soldiers/. . . have . . ./Took their discharge' (*King Lear*, V. iii. 104–6). The essentialist connotations of 'virtue' are also clearly brought out in a passage from *Troilus and Cressida* already discussed [not included here]: 'what hath mass or matter by itself/ Lies rich in virtue and unmingled'. In *Antony and Cleopatra* this idea of self-sufficiency is intensified to such an extent that it suggests a transcendent autonomy; thus Cleopatra calls Antony 'lord of lords!/ O *infinite virtue*, com'st thou smiling from/The world's great snare uncaught?' (IV. viii. 16–18). Coriolanus is similarly described as proud, 'even to the altitude of his virtue' (II. i. 38). Against this is a counter-discourse, one denying that virtue is the source and ethical legitimation of power and suggesting instead that the reverse is true – in the words of Macro in *Sejanus*, 'A prince's power makes all his actions virtue' (III. 717). At the beginning of Act III for example Silius urges Ventidius further to consolidate his recent successes in war, so winning even greater gratitude from Antony. Ventidius replies that, although 'Caesar and Antony have ever won/More in their officer than person' (III. i. 16–17), an officer of theirs who makes that fact too apparent will lose, not gain favour. It is an exchange which nicely illustrates the way power is a function not of the 'person' (l.17) but of 'place' (l. 12), and that the criterion for reward is not intrinsic to the 'performance' (l. 27) but, again, relative to one's placing in the power structure (cf. *Sejanus*, III. 302–5: 'all best turns/With doubtful princes, turn deep injuries/In estimation, when they greater rise,/Than can be answered').[8]

Later in the same act Antony challenges Caesar to single combat (III. xiii. 20–8). It is an attempt to dissociate Caesar's power from his individual virtue. Enobarbus, amazed at the stupidity of this, testifies to the reality Antony is trying, increasingly, to deny:

> men's judgements are
> A parcel of their fortunes, and things outward
> Do draw the inward quality after them,
> To suffer all alike.
>
> (III. xiii. 31–4)

In Enobarbus' eyes, Antony's attempt to affirm a self-sufficient identity confirms *exactly the opposite*. Correspondingly, Caesar scorns Antony's challenge with a simple but devastating repudiation of its essentialist premise: because 'twenty times of better fortune' than Antony, he is, correspondingly, 'twenty men to one' (IV. ii. 3–4).

As effective power slips from Antony he becomes obsessed with reasserting his sense of himself as (in his dying words): 'the greatest prince o' th' world,/The noblest' (IV. xx. 54–5). The contradiction inherent in this is clear; it is indeed as Canidius remarks: 'his whole action grows/Not in the power on't' (III. vii. 68–9). Antony's conception of his omnipotence narrows in proportion to the obsessiveness of his wish to reassert it; eventually it centres on the sexual anxiety – an assertion of sexual prowess – which has characterised his relationship with both Cleopatra and Caesar from the outset. He several times dwells on the youthfulness of Caesar in comparison with his own age (e.g. at III. xiii. 20; IV. xii. 48) and is generally preoccupied with lost youthfulness (e.g. at III, xiii. 192; IV. iv. 26; IV. viii. 22). During the battle scenes of Acts III and IV he keeps reminding Cleopatra of his prowess – militaristic and sexual: 'I will appear in blood' (II. xiii. 174); 'There's sap in't yet! The next time I do fight,/I'll make death love me' (III. xiii. 192–3); and:

> leap thou, attire and all,
> Through proof of harness to my heart, and there
> Ride on the pants triumphing.
> (IV. viii. 14–16)

All this, including the challenge to single combat with Caesar, becomes an obsessive attempt on the part of an ageing warrior (the 'old ruffian' – IV. i. 4) to reassert his virility, not only to Cleopatra but also to Caesar, his principal male competitor. Correspondingly, his willingness to risk everything by fighting on Caesar's terms (III. vii) has much more to do with reckless overcompensation for his own experienced powerlessness, his fear of impotence, than the largesse of a noble soul. His increasing ambivalence towards Cleopatra further bespeaks that insecurity (e.g. at III. xii and IV. xii). When servants refuse to obey him he remarks 'Authority melts from me' – but insists nevertheless 'I am/Antony yet' (III. xiii. 92–3): even as he is attempting to deny it Antony is acknowledging that identity is crucially dependent upon power. Moments later even he cannot help remarking the difference between 'what I am' and 'what . . . I was' (III. xiii. 142–3).

It is only when the last vestiges of his power are gone that the myth of heroic omnipotence exhausts itself, even for him. In place of his essentialist fixedness, 'the firm Roman', the 'man of steel' he once felt himself to be (I. iv. 43; IV. iv. 35), Antony now experiences himself in extreme dissolution:

> That which is now a horse, even with a thought
> The rack dislimns, and makes it indistinct
> As water is in water . . .
>   Eros, now thy captain is
> Even such a body: here I am Antony,
> Yet cannot hold this visible shape
> (IV. iv. 9–14)

Virtus, divorced from the power structure, has left to it only the assertion of a negative, inverted autonomy: 'there is left us/Ourselves to end ourselves' (IV. xiv. 21–2). And in an image which effectively expresses the contradiction Antony has been living out, energy is felt to feed back on itself: 'Now all labour/Mars what it does; yea, very force entangles/Itself with strength' (IV. xix. 47–9). Appropriately to this, he resolves on suicide only to bungle the attempt. The bathos of this stresses, uncynically, the extent of his demise. In the next scene it is compounded by Cleopatra's refusal to leave the monument to

kiss the dying Antony lest she be taken by Caesar. Antony, even as
he is trying to transcend defeat by avowing a tragic dignity in death,
suffers the indignity of being dragged up the monument.

There is bathos too of course in Caesar's abruptly concluded
encomium:

> Hear me, good friends –
> *Enter an Egyptian*
> But I will tell you at some meeter season.
> The business of this man looks out of him
> (V. i. 48–50)

The question of Caesar's sincerity here is beside the point; this is,
after all, an encomium, and to mistake it for a spontaneous expression of grief will lead us to miss seeing that even in the few moments
he speaks Caesar has laid the foundation for an 'official' history of
Antony. First we are reminded that Caesar *is* – albeit regrettably –
the victor. He then vindicates himself and so consolidates that victory by confessing to a humanising grief at the death of his 'brother'
(though note the carefully placed suggestion of Antony's inferiority:
'the *arm* of mine own body'). Caesar further vindicates himself by
fatalising events with the by now familiar appeal to necessity, in this
case 'our stars,/Unreconcilable'. Earlier Caesar had told Octavia that
'The ostentation of our love . . . left unshown,/Is often left unlov'd'
(III. vi. 52–3). Such is the rationale of his encomium, a strategic
expression of 'love' in the service of power. The bathos of these
episodes makes for an insistent cancelling of the potentially sublime
in favour of the political realities which the sublime struggles to
eclipse or transcend. Actually, bathos has accompanied Antony
throughout, from the very first speech of the play, the last three lines
of which are especially revealing (Philo is speaking of Antony):

> Take but good note, and you shall see in him
> The triple pillar of all the world transform'd
> Into a strumpet's fool. Behold and see.
> (I. i. 11–13)

The cadence of 'triple pillar of all the world' arches outward and
upward, exactly evoking transcendent aspiration; 'transformed' at
the line end promises apotheosis; we get instead the jarringly discrep-
ant 'strumpet's fool'. Cynical, perhaps, but Philo's final terse injunction – 'Behold and see' – has prologue-like authority and foresight.

After Antony's death the myth of autonomous *virtus* is shown as finally obsolescent; disentangled now from the prevailing power structure, it survives as legend. Unwittingly Cleopatra's dream about Antony helps relegate him to this realm of the legendary, especially in its use of imagery which is both Herculean and statuesque: 'His legs bestrid the ocean; his reared arm/Crested the world'[9] (V. ii. 82–3). Cleopatra asks Dolabella if such a man ever existed or might exist; he answers: 'Gentle Madam, no'. Cleopatra vehemently reproaches him only to qualify instantly her own certainty – 'But if there be nor ever were one such' – thereby, in the hesitant syntax, perhaps confirming the doubts which prompted the original question.

His legs bestrid the ocean: in dream, in death, Antony becomes at last larger than life; but in valediction is there not also invoked an image of the commemorative statue, that material embodiment of a discourse which, like Caesar's encomium, skilfully overlays (without ever quite obscuring) obsolescence with respect?

HONOUR AND POLICY

If the contradiction which constitutes Antony's identity can be seen as a consequence of a wider conflict between the residual/dominant and the emergent power relations, so too can the strange relationship set up in the play between honour and policy. Pompey's reply to Menas' offer to murder the triumvirs while they are celebrating on board his (Pompey's) galley is a case in point:

> Ah, this thou shouldst have done,
> And not have spoke on't. In me 'tis villainy:
> In thee't had been good service. Thou must know
> 'Tis not my profit that does lead mine honour:
> Mine honour, it. Repent that e'er thy tongue
> Hath so betray'd thine act. Being done unknown,
> I should have found it afterwards well done,
> But must condemn it now.
> (II. vii. 73–80)

Here honour is insisted upon yet divorced from ethics and consequences; the same act is 'villainy' or 'service' depending on who performs it; ignorance of intent to murder is sufficient condition for approving the murder after the event.

Elsewhere in the play we see these inconsistencies resolved in favour of policy; now honour pretends to integrity – to be thought to possess it is enough. Once again it is a kind of political strategy which takes us back to Machiavelli's *The Prince*. Antony tells Octavia: 'If I lose mine honour/I lose myself' (III. iv. 23–3). Octavia has of course been coerced into marriage with Antony to heal the rift (now reopened) between him and Caesar, her brother. So, for Antony to speak to her of honour seems hypocritical at least; when, however, Antony goes further and presents himself as the injured party ready nevertheless to forego his revenge in order to indulge Octavia's request that she be *allowed* to act as mediator – 'But, as you re-quested/Yourself shall go between's' (III. iv. 24–5) – the honour in question is shown to be just another strategy in his continuing exploitation of this woman.

When Thidias is persuading Cleopatra to betray Antony and capitulate to Caesar, honour is now a face-saving strategy for *both* sides; because she 'embraced' Antony through fear, says Caesar, he construes the scar upon her honour as 'constrained blemishes,/Not as deserv'd'. Cleopatra quickly concurs: 'He [Caesar] is a god, and knows/What is most right. Mine honour was not yielded,/But conquer'd merely' (III. xiii. 59–62).

In Enobarbus we see how policy aligns positively with realism and judgement. He, like Philo at the outset of the play, Ventidius in III. i and the soldier in III. vii who urges Antony not to fight at sea, occupies a role in relation to power very familiar in Jacobean trag-edy: he possesses an astuteness characteristic of those removed from, yet involved with and dependent upon – often for their very lives – the centre of power; his is the voice of policy not in the service of aggrandisement so much as a desire for survival. So, for example, we see in III. vi Enobarbus attempting to dissuade Cleopatra from participating in the war and Antony from fighting on Caesar's terms. Failing in the attempt, Enobarbus leaves Antony's command but is struck with remorse almost immediately. Since he left without his 'chests and treasure' (IV. v. 8) we are, perhaps, to presume that material gain of this kind was not his motive. Enobarbus, like Antony, comes to embody a contradiction; the speech of his begin-ning 'Mine honesty and I begin to square' (III. xiii. 41) suggests as much, and it becomes clear that he has left his master in the name of the 'judgement' which the latter has abdicated but which is integral still to his, Enobarbus', identity as a soldier. Yet equally integral to that identity is the loyalty which he has betrayed.

The extent of people's dependence upon the powerful is some-thing the play never allows us to forget. Cleopatra's beating of the messenger in II. v is only the most obvious reminder; a subtler and perhaps more effective one comes at the end of the play when Cleopatra attempts to conceal half her wealth from Caesar. In the presence of Caesar she commands Seleucus, her 'treasurer', to confirm that she has surrendered all; 'speak the truth, Seleucus' she demands and, unfortunately for her he does, revealing that she has kept back as much as she has declared. Cleopatra has ordered him 'Upon his *peril*' (V. ii. 142) to speak the truth (i.e. lie) while he, with an eye to Caesar, replies that he would rather seal his lips 'than to my *peril*/Speak that which is not'. Here, truth itself is in the service of survival. Cleopatra, outraged, finds this unforgivable; for servants to shift allegiance is, in her eyes (those of a ruler) 'base' treachery (V. ii. 156). The play however, in that ironic repetition of 'peril' (my italics) invites an alternative perspective: such a shift is merely a strategy of survival necessitated precisely by rulers like her.[10] Yet doubly ironic is the fact that while Seleucus is described as a 'slave, of no more trust/Than love that's hir'd' (V. ii. 153–4) her own deceit is approved by Caesar as the 'wisdom' (V. ii. 149) appropriate to one in her position. Elsewhere Caesar speaks in passing of the 'much tall youth' (II. vi. 7) that will perish in the event of war; Octavia speaks of the consequence of war between Caesar and Antony being as if 'the world should cleave, and that slain men/Should solder up the cleave' (III. iv. 31–2; cf. III. xiii. 180–1; IV. xii. 41–2; IV. xiv. 17–18). It is a simple yet important truth, one which the essentialist rhetoric is never quite allowed to efface: to kiss away kingdoms is to kiss away also the lives of thousands.

SEXUALITY AND POWER

Those around Antony and Cleopatra see their love in terms of power; languages of possession, subjugation and conspicuous wealth abound in descriptions of the people. More importantly, Antony and Cleopatra actually experience themselves in the same terms. Antony sends Alexas to Cleopatra with the promise that he will 'piece/Her opulent throne with kingdoms. All the East/(Say thou) shall call her mistress' (I. v. 45–7). Later Caesar describes the ceremony whereby that promise was honoured, a ceremony aiming for an unprecedented *public* display both of wealth and power: 'Cleopatra and himself in chairs of gold/Were publicly enthron'd'; Antony gives to Cleopatra the stablishment of Egypt and makes her 'Absolute Queen' of Syria, Cyprus and Lydia. 'This in the public eye?' inquires Maecenas; 'I' th' common showplace' confirms Caesar (III. vi. 4–12). Cleopatra for her part sends twenty separate messengers to Antony. On his return from Egypt Enobarbus confirms the rumour that eight wild boars were served at a breakfast of only twelve people, adding: 'This was but as a fly by an eagle: we had much more monstrous matter of feast, which *worthily deserved noting*' (II. ii. 185, my italics).

Right from the outset we· are told that power is internal to the relationship itself: Philo tells us that Antony has been subjugated by Cleopatra (I. i. 1–9) while Enobarbus tells Agrippa that Cleopatra has 'pursed up' (i.e. pocketed, taken possession of) Antony's heart (II. ii. 190). As if in a discussion of political strategy, Cleopatra asks Charmian which tactics she should adopt in order to manipulate Antony most effectively. Charmian advocates a policy of complete capitulation; Cleopatra replies: 'Thou teachest like a fool – the way to lose him!' (I. iii. 10). Antony enters and Cleopatra tells him: 'I have no power upon you', only then to cast him in the role of treacherous subject: 'O, never was there queen/So mightily betrayed. Yet at the first/I saw the treasons planted' (I. iii. 23–6). Whatever the precise sense of Cleopatra's famous lines at the end of this scene – 'O my oblivion is a very Antony,/And I am all forgotten' – there is no doubt that they continue the idea of a power struggle: her extinction is conterminous with his triumph.

Attempting to atone for his departure, Antony pledges himself as Cleopatra's 'soldier-servant, making peace or war/As thou affects' (I. iii. 70). This is just one of many exchanges which shows how their sexuality is rooted in a fantasy transfer of power from the public to the private sphere, from the battlefield to the bed. In II. v Cleopatra recalls with merriment a night of revelry when she subjugated Antony and then engaged in cross-dressing with him, putting 'my tires and mantles on him, whilst/I wore his sword Phillipan' (II. v. 22–3). Inseparable from the playful reversal of sexual roles is her appropriation of his power, military and sexual, symbolised phallically of course in the sword. Later Antony takes up the sword-power motif in a bitter reproach of Cleopatra for her power over him; here he sees her as his 'conqueror' (III. xi. 66, and compare IV. xiv. 22–3). Another aspect of the power-sexuality conjunction is suggested in the shamelessly phallic imagery which the lovers use: 'Ram thou thy fruitful tidings in mine ears,/That long time have been barren' (II. v. 24–5), although again Cleopatra delights in reversing the roles (as at II. v. 10–15).

Here then is another aspect of the contradiction which defines Antony: his sexuality is informed by the very power relations which he, ambivalently, is prepared to sacrifice for sexual freedom; correspondingly, the heroic *virtus* which he wants to reaffirm in and through Cleopatra is in fact almost entirely a function of the power structure which he, again ambivalently, is prepared to sacrifice for her.

Ecstasy there is in this play but not the kind that constitutes a self-sufficient moment above history; if *Antony and Cleopatra* celebrates anything it is not the love which transcends power but the sexual infatuation which foregrounds it. That infatuation is complex: ecstatic, obsessive, dangerous. Of all the possible kinds of sexual encounter, infatuation is perhaps the most susceptible to power – not just because typically it stems from and intensifies an insecurity which often generates possessiveness and its corollary, betrayal, but because it legitimates a free play of self-destructive desire. In Antony's case it is a desire which attends and compensates for the loss of power, a desire at once ecstatic and masochistic and playing itself out in the wake of history, the dust of the chariot wheel.

From Jonathan Dollimore, *Radical Tragedy: Religion, Ideology and Power in the Drama of Shakespeare and his Contemporaries* (New York and London, 1984), pp. 204–17.

NOTES

[Jonathan Dollimore's *Radical Tragedy*, first published in 1984, and revised in 1989, is one of the most influential books to have been published during the 1980s. Dollimore argues that the tragic drama of Shakespeare and his contemporaries appeared at a time when society itself was undergoing radical change, and these plays consciously and unconsciously mediate, rather than simply reflect that change. Dollimore draws on a range of French poststructuralist theory in order to substantiate his arguments, in particular the work of the late Michel Foucault. Subsequent commentators have frequently made connections between the methodology deployed by Dollimore, which has come to be known as Cultural Materialism, and the movement known as New Historicism, whose leading exponent is the American critic Stephen J. Greenblatt. The tradition within which Dollimore writes, however, unlike Greenblatt, is that of a poststructural Marxism, although Dollimore frequently uses a recognisably Brechtian kind of analysis, and his discussions of cultural formations owe much to the work of the late Raymond Williams. Crucial to Dollimore's argument throughout *Radical Tragedy* is the Renaissance 'decentring' of Man, and the crises of identity to which that process leads. It is Dollimore's contention that a number of Renaissance writers were conscious of this process, and discussed it in their writings. His own reading of the symptoms of this crisis in their work, and the work of contemporary Renaissance dramatists, is what makes this book so important as a ground-breaking study. Ed.]

1. C. L. Barber, *The Idea of Honour in the English Drama 1591–1700* (Gothenburg, 1957), pp. 269–79.

2. Mervyn James, *English Politics and the Concept of Honour 1485–1642* (Oxford, 1978), p. 2. See also Lawrence Stone, *The Crisis of the Aristocracy 1558–1641* (Oxford, 1965), pp. 239–40, 265–7; Ruth Kelso, *The Doctrine of the English Gentleman in the Sixteenth Century* (Urbana, Illinois, 1929), pp. 11 ff.

3. Michel Foucault, *Power/Knowledge*, ed. Colin Gordon (Brighton, 1980), p. 98.

4. Francis Bacon, *Essays* (London, 1972), p. 158.

5. Eugene Waith, *The Herculean Hero* (London, 1962), p. 118.

6. G. Wilson Knight, *The Imperial Theme* (London, 1965), p. 217.

7. Derek Traversi, *An Approach to Shakespeare* (London, 1969), vol. 2, p. 208.

8. Machiavelli concurs: 'it is impossible that the suspicion aroused in a prince after the victory of one of his generals should not be increased by any arrogance in manner or speech displayed by the man himself' (*The Discourses*, ed. Bernard Crick [Harmondsworth, 1970], p. 181).

9. Compare the dying Bussy: 'Here like a Roman statue; I will stand/Till death hath made me a marble' (*The Revenge of Bussy D'Ambois*, V. iii. 144–5).

10. In North's Plutarch, Shakespeare's source, we are told that Cleopatra engineered this 'scene' in order to deceive Caesar into thinking she intends to live (*Antony and Cleopatra*, ed. M. R. Ridley [London, 1965], p. 276). It is difficult to infer this from the play, but, even if we are inclined to see her anger as feigned, it still presupposes the point being made here, namely that a double standard works for master and servant.

10

'Antony and Cleopatra'

MARILYN FRENCH

It is interesting that Shakespeare would choose two figures who are
remembered not only for their grand passion, but also their sexual
freedom and inconstancy, on whom to build his broadest and most
realistic study of constancy. *Antony and Cleopatra* is *about* constancy in a way that comedies containing a chaste constant figure
are not.[1] In terms of values, the closest analogue to the tragedy is
A Midsummer Night's Dream, a comedy about constancy that is
filled with inconstant figures. And, significantly, both plays separate
constancy from chastity.

Chastity, the form of constancy that seals female subordination to
the male and guarantees male legitimacy, is an element in the tragedy, in Octavia. But she is unimportant to the action; like
Andromache in *Troilus and Cressida*, she provides a 'cause' for the
males – first, to seal their compact, and second, to serve as justification for Octavius' war on his former partner. Her chaste constancy
is not exalted as a quality necessary and adequate for 'redemption' of
the world from its own viciousness. As a result, *Antony and Cleopatra* is more realistic than many other Shakespeare plays – not that
realism is necessarily more desirable than other modes.

The removal of a high value placed on chastity is concomitant
with the removal of sexual guilt from one area of the play. That guilt
is present, but in a very muted way: it underlies Roman values, and
directs many elements of Roman behaviour, many Roman attitudes.
But it is missing in Egypt. As a result, a quality – sexual freedom –
Shakespeare played with in an earlier play (*Love's Labour's Lost*)
and worked with seriously but unsympathetically in *All's Well*,
placing sexual freedom in Bertram and then proceeding to damn

him – is given the only sympathetic treatment Shakespeare was ever to award it. This is not to say that Egyptian values are depicted with complete sympathy by the playwright, but that they are shown with *some* sympathy.

As a result of Shakespeare's separation of chastity from constancy in this play, constancy itself is redefined. As I have discussed earlier, constancy is a 'masculine' quality, a permanence; when affixed to sexual love, it effects a synthesis of the two gender principles. But in this play, constancy is totally integrated with the united feminine principle and provides what is, to my mind, the most profound vision possible of human constancy.

In most of Shakespeare's work, indeed, in most Western thinking, there is an unconscious identification between the genuine and the enduring: only that which lasts is *true*. So true love is love that does not swerve for the lifetime of the lovers. A fashion, that which passes, is automatically seen as less serious, less profound than things that endure. So institutions of various sorts are viewed with awe as incarnations of 'true' values. This association is no doubt rooted in humans' needs to fix – make permanent – something or someone so as to keep their bearings in this wild world.

But the identification seems to me fallacious, unless the word *true* is defined as *enduring* (which it sometimes implicitly is). One can have a genuine and intense experience of love, hate, charity, or guilt that cannot be called anything but true, yet which does not last. Life is made up of millions of such moments, many of which contradict or overlay each other. The only human experience which lasts unalterably is death, as Cleopatra realises, death 'which shackles accidents, and bolts up change;/ Which sleeps, and never palates more the dung' (V. ii. 6–7). Not only people, but empires, institutions, and even art die. This knowledge underlies *Antony and Cleopatra*.

The tragedy occurs in a vacillating world. The near chaos of the structure has frequently been noted, and in recent decades accepted as organic to the play, and not a sign of Shakespeare's diminished powers. The alternation of scenes set in Rome, Egypt, and other places that are under the influence of one or the other is paralleled by alternations in domination by Roman or Egyptian values. In addition, within this large dichotomy, there are shifts in alignments, alliances, and attitudes, accompanied by images of shift and transiency.[2] The huge scope of Shakespeare's canvas and the grandeur of the allusions – for example, repeated references to Roman rulers and possessors and upholders of the entire world, Cleopatra's identifica-

tion of herself with Egypt, pervasive references to the Roman pantheon with identification of the principals with the gods – suggest
that Shakespeare felt himself to be making a large, perhaps even a
definitive statement, and a statement about more than the handful of
characters who dominate the play.[3] More than Antony, Cleopatra,
and Octavius, more than Rome versus Egypt, the play is concerned
with portraying the opposition of the gender principles in the world
at large.

The play is unique in the canon because it alone presents in a
positive way the outlaw feminine principle embodied in a powerful
female. The mature and sexual woman is rare in Shakespeare; mature women are not common, and most of those who exist seem to
spend all their fruitful years in convents of some sort. There is the
Nurse in *Romeo and Juliet*, but one has the sense that she is *very*
mature, and that her sexual life is lived mostly in memory. At any
rate, she is a comic figure. And there is Gertrude, who, in the context
of the play, is guilty. Presumably Lady Macbeth has a sexual life, but
she seems to renounce that when she renounces pity and compassion.
So far is Cleopatra from the idealised Shakespearean heroine, young,
nubile, chaste and constant, so far also from the heavy panting Venus
of the early poem, that it seems that when he wrote this play, he got
up and went into a different room, one he had never worked in
before, and shut the door on everything else he had done. If this were
his last play, we would see it as a resolution to his conflicts. Unfortunately for those of us who like neat lives, it isn't.

For a time, then, Shakespeare put aside his ordinary demands of
the female, as well as his ordinary demands of the male: no character
in the tragedy is either idealised or demonised. If there is no Cordelia,
no Desdemona, no Henry V, there is also no Lady Macbeth, Goneril,
or Richard III. What this means is that there are no absolute values
in the play.

Yet it seems to yield not an absolute, but a high good, although
this is a matter of contention. On the one hand, the grandeur and
beauty of the language of the lovers is a statement of value, whatever
flaws we may see in their behaviour.[4] On the other hand, we have
seen how the beauty and power of the language of Hamlet, Othello,
Lear, and Macbeth sweep us up into their values, whether or not
those values are affirmed by the play. On the whole, however, I think
that what the great poetry in the plays affirms is not strictly speaking
a moral stance, but an approach to life. For great poetry is the
language of feeling, and that is the characteristic each of these heroes

most fully incarnates. Whether Hamlet is responding in shock to the world around him, or Othello is fighting off his feelings for Desdemona in order to bring himself to kill her, or Lear is satirically and savagely anatomising the arrangements of society, or Macbeth is preparing to put his feelings aside in order to kill Duncan, each of these characters feels his experience deeply. So too do Antony and Cleopatra. Thus, on a level quite above the immediate values of the play, feeling is the quality most affirmed by it, by all the tragedies. (For this reason, Aristotelian categories seem to me quite irrelevant to Shakespearean – and even to Greek – tragedy. A fall, a flaw, a recognition: the pattern must be stretched into one-size-fits-all dimensions to fit the plays, and is not illuminating even then.) And to the degree that the poetry of this play celebrates feeling, it affirms the lovers as well.

There are two opposing motions in the surface structure: submission to Circe, a 'strumpet', leading to loss of worldly power; and the triumph of love over a world well lost. The world is lost *to* Octavius, the unemotional, powerful, possessive, rational, structure-building masculine figure. The world is lost *for* Cleopatra, the shifting, variable, capricious, passionate, sexual, playful, and beautiful feminine figure. The losing, of course, is done by Antony who, because of his participation in both worlds, is a synthetic figure, blending both but in unequal and shifting, seesawing balance. In the world at large, whether in Shakespeare's time or our own, the prejudice of most people leans towards power, possession, and structure, whatever their daydreams. But the play subverts that prejudice in its presentation: there is no question of which, Rome or Egypt, is a diminished world, which richer.

Although the number of scenes set in Egypt is only slightly less than the number set in Rome or Roman territories, Roman values dominate the play. The voice of Rome opens and closes the drama. In addition, as the Roman forces slowly invade Egypt, Roman material increasingly intrudes on Egyptian material. Yet the Egyptian values never change. To see the significance of this requires comparison: consider how Iago's terms invade and poison Othello's idealised world, or how even the quiet domestic scene in Lady Macduff's castle is permeated by the fear and bitterness that have come to characterise Scotland. Increasingly, in *Antony and Cleopatra*, war becomes central to the 'Egyptian' characters. Yet they are never 'masculinised'. There is no completely 'Egyptian' scene, that is, no scene that is totally free from allusion to Rome or Roman actions or Roman values. Egyptian material finds its way to Rome as well, but it is nowhere near as pervasive, and is usually brought in in a sniggering, fascinated 'locker-room' style – which is to say, Rome does not really comprehend Egypt (just as Venice cannot comprehend Belmont). And there are several Roman scenes that contain no mention whatever of Egypt, Cleopatra, or 'Egyptian' values.

Roman values are strongly 'masculine', concerned with power, hierarchy, ownership, and above all contest, war, rivalry. Beneath all Roman statements is the assumption that aggressive war and the establishment of a centrally ruled, constantly expanding sovereignty are good. The Romans make claims on the basis of treaties and agreements (codifications of alliances), but in fact they have no hesitation in breaking those agreements when it suits their purposes. Power does not derive from traditional and hereditary 'right', but from *de facto* power and possession. Thus, although the notion of legitimacy functions in the tragedy as a justification for actions, it is not seriously questioned by any character because no character seriously believes in it.

Despite its concern with permanencies and structure, the defining characteristic of Rome is competition, rivalry, squabbling of all sorts. In these arguments or battles, the notion of right, of justice, sometimes appears, but it is used like food colouring, to make the claims appear more attractive. At issue in all the conflicts is power-in-the-world, dominance, and as rivals are swept aide, it becomes the single and highest good.

The Egyptian world is rooted in the feminine principle, but in this play, uniquely, it is unified. Since it is unified, wholly itself, it is powerful and not on the moral defensive. It does not have to maintain chaste constancy as a guarantee to the 'masculine' world of its division of itself, its castration, and consequent subordination to 'masculine' values. It is fully the pole of nature and procreation and beauty (magnetic power, as opposed to the power of force, imposition). Thus, it is nourishing and sometimes compassionate and merciful; it is also tempestuous, cruel, and variable. It is above all generative and highly erotic. It is also sensuous, anarchic (or democratic), rooted in pleasure, play, and sex. Its great threat lies in its great appeal and its lack of respect for 'masculine' qualities like authority, hierarchy, order, and possession. It is thus anti-civilisation; yet it is the principle of life. The feminine principle rests on the ability to give birth; and many of Cleopatra's images, or allusions to her or Egypt, concern fertility, whether of the 'natural' or of the 'monstrous'.

Like all humans, all the characters participate in the masculine principle. Cleopatra holds Egypt by power and 'rights' made secure by Antony. When she is threatened, she attempts to secure some possessions. She believes in her own royal privilege; her government is hierarchical and she is an absolute ruler. But we almost never see her in such a context. We see her, or hear about her, being playful, passionate, tempestuous, variable, beautiful. She and Antony *play* – they go fishing, walk the streets incognito, stitch clothes, tease, feast lavishly in a court full of luxury and games like fortune-telling. Cleopatra hops in public, or sails down the Cydnus looking like a goddess.

Although all of Shakespeare's characters contain 'masculine' qualities, many demonstrate a weak or missing 'feminine' side. Iago seems to have no 'feminine' qualities at all; Goneril and Regan are 'feminine' only in that they are sexual; Macbeth eradicates his 'feminine' side and dies inwardly as a result. Coriolanus has only tenuous connections to 'feminine' qualities which exist outside, not inside him, but which nevertheless destroy him. Of all Shakespeare's extremely 'masculine' figures, Octavius is the only successful one. He achieves his goals; he does not destroy his world or himself. He destroys only what he sets out to destroy – Antony and Cleopatra.

Thus *Antony* has some similarity to *Macbeth*, as well as *Coriolanus*. All three tragedies contain a powerful figure who ignores or scorns 'feminine' values and who is successful in the world because of this. But whereas *Macbeth* and *Coriolanus* focus on the consequences of this victory from the point of view of the victor, *Antony and Cleopatra* concentrates on portraying that which is lost.

There is a suggestion that Caesar seriously intends the establishment of 'universal peace' (IV. vi. 5), the *pax romana* that was in actuality achieved during the rein of Augustus. But this is mentioned only once, and in passing. Idealistic authoritarian totalitarianism is not a strong element in Shakespeare's Octavius. Rather, the force that drives him is rivalry. He is a mechanic, a hollow man who uses trumped-up self-justifications to mask his competitiveness, his real envy of Antony. Because of the way Rome and its values gradually move in on Egypt, the overall motion of the play feels like a crusade led by a puritanical Octavius against the intractable and 'sinful' feminine principle. What Macbeth kills in himself, Octavius kills in the world. With Octavia, the inlaw feminine, supporting him, he saves the world from sin.

The portrait of Octavia is as astonishing, coming from Shakespeare, as the portrait of Cleopatra. Chaste, constant, meek and mild, she is made in the image of many heroines. She is a sister to Isabel, although she lacks that figure's force; and to Imogen, although she lacks her spirit; and to Hero, although she has a bit more toughness. And as described by Enobarbus, she is 'holy, cold, and still' (II. vi. 119–20): quite correctly in a wife, as Menas points out, but not very interesting. Thus Shakespeare judges – in this play – the ideal he himself has erected in a series of plays.

Within the large and definitive movement of Rome into Egypt that occurs in the tragedy are a series of seesaw motions on every level – scene structure, character alignments, behaviour from moment to moment, and images as well. Variability, betrayal, and flux are the only absolutes in the play.[5] In addition, every character of any importance whatever is either betrayed or betrays others, or both. Inconstancy is this world's defining characteristic: let us examine some examples of it.

The play opens with the phrase 'Nay, but', which Janet Adelman points out indicates the argumentative, dialectical mode of the play.[6] Philo's Roman judgements – Cleopatra is a gypsy and a strumpet, Antony has dwindled from his stature as a great soldier and 'triple pillar of the world' (I. i. 12) into a bellows and fan – give way immediately to a teasing dialogue between the lovers. Inherent here is the motion of the whole play: Roman values dominate the world; the feeling between Antony and Cleopatra extends beyond it, into 'new heaven, new earth' (I. i. 17).

Instantly appears a messenger from Rome; instantly Cleopatra is angry and challenges. Some readers interpret this passage as meaning that Cleopatra does not want him to listen to the messenger, and by challenging Antony to listen, taunts him into ignoring the message instead. Others, including myself, think she is angry about his ambivalent feelings about Rome – and about her – and taunts him about that. In any case, he ignores the messenger for a time, in her presence, and enunciates the outlaw feminine values that dominate their love:

> Let Rome in Tiber melt, and the wide arch
> Of the rang'd kingdom fall! Here is my space,
> Kingdoms are clay; our dungy earth alike
> Feeds beast as man; the nobleness of life
> Is to do thus. . . .
>
> (I. i. 33–7)

The final words of the scene are left to Rome. In sixty-two verses, the terms of the struggle have been defined.

Alternations pervade more than the scenic shifts from Rome to Egypt (and places associated with them). The entire surface of the play is a wavering series of betrayals, reversals, and realignments. Antony ignores the messenger and goes off with Cleopatra, protesting the absoluteness of their love. But suddenly he is struck by a 'Roman thought' and confers with the messenger privately. The news is Fulvia's death.

He is saddened: 'She's good, being gone' (I. ii. 126). He wishes he could bring back the wife he abandoned. He muses: 'Thus did I desire it. / What our contempt doth often hurl from us, / We wish it ours again' (I. ii. 122–4). Cleopatra's earlier taunting of Antony: 'Why did he marry Fulvia, and not love her?' (I. i. 41), or her charge that his love for her is as insincere as his love for Fulvia shows that she understands Antony's nature and his attitudes. Although she is not without some ambivalences herself, and although she is using the attack to manipulate him and keep him with her, her charges are not inaccurate. Shortly after receiving the news about Fulvia's death, Antony exclaims about Cleopatra: 'Would I had never seen her!' (I. ii. 152).[7] Enobarbus ironically consoles him by reminding him that there are other women in the world. And indeed, as soon as Antony returns to Rome, he repudiates Cleopatra, describing his stay in Egypt as 'poisoned hours' that 'bound me up / From mine own knowledge' (II. ii. 90–1). In brief span, he marries Octavia and moves to Athens.

In time, of course, he betrays Octavia and returns to Cleopatra, but his return does not end his vacillations. He blames Cleopatra for the defeat at Actium; in this case, her tears instantly melt his anger. He moves from defeated despair to a hollow-sounding heartiness as he attempts to retrieve their fortunes; then he turns bitterly and dangerously against her again (without a clear cause) after the defeat in IV. xi. He threatens wildly to kill her. Nevertheless, news of her suicide throws him into total despair and precipitates his own suicide.

Yet when he discovers she is alive, he reproaches her for nothing. He is hauled up to her monument and the two are as loving as we have ever seen them. Antony tells Cleopatra to seek her honour and safety with Caesar, and warns her to trust none of Caesar's men except Proculeius. This is a small point, and it is seemingly irrelevant to the action. There is no question that Antony thinks he is giving Cleopatra good advice. But Proculeius does as Caesar orders, and if the Queen trusted him, she would be betrayed. Shakespeare's inclusion of this minute detail is of a piece with everything else that happens in the play: shift and betrayal – betrayal in fact, or betrayal of expectations – are the only absolutes in the play.

In contrast to Antony, Cleopatra languishes while he is away, and nearly kills the messenger who brings word of his remarriage. Oddly, the 'strumpet' is faithful; it is the hero who is not. But Cleopatra is only *sexually* faithful to Antony. Politically, she is ambivalent. When their forces have been defeated, she toys with Caesar's envoy, sending Antony into an insane rage. To calm his fury after the defeat, she sends false word that she is dead. By the time she rescinds that word, Antony has stabbed himself. And even as he dies, she refuses to risk leaving the monument. After Antony's death, she hedges with Caesar, trying to feel or sense his intentions. There is little question that if she could protect herself, her children, and keep her kingdom, she would make terms with Caesar. Her suicide is a response not simply to Antony's death, but also to Caesar's intentions for her future.

Antony's suicide is of the same sort. He performs it – clumsily – after hearing of her death, but if he had won the battle, if there was a chance of mustering his forces and re-engaging Caesar and winning a real victory, the chances are most unlikely he would have done any such thing. Thus, they kill themselves not entirely for love. What both assert by their deaths is that they will not live in worlds too severely diminished. Without each other, and without power over their own lives, they choose death. Unless one has a rather idiotic view of romantic love, it is perfectly understandable that they would choose to survive if the terms of survival were not too degrading.

The behaviour of the lovers towards each other, however, is hardly ideal. The play of Shakespeare's that most exalts mature sexual love is also the play that least idealises love. The lovers quarrel with real animus, they betray each other, they move between love and renunciation, as ordinary lovers do.[8] They play together, they exchange roles, and they remain erotically bound to each other. And they are, at the last, faithful: if the causes of their fidelity are contingent, so are the causes of their infidelity. They live in an unfaithful world.

Consider:

Antony speaks of the 'slippery people' (I. ii. 183), the fickle populace that follows the current leader, and how the 'hated, grown to strength / Are newly grown to love' (I. iii. 48–9). Caesar speaks of the 'common body', which 'like to a vagabond flag upon the stream, / Goes to, and back, lackeying the varying tide, / To rot itself with motion' (I. iv. 44–7). For Caesar, of course, anything not fixed is intolerable, anything not permanent is rotten.

Pompey plans in II, i to continue his war: in II. vi he is flattered or frightened out of that plan. He has no objection to Menas' plan to destroy the triumvirate except that Menas consults him and he does not want to take the responsibility for such an act. Consequently, Menas abandons Pompey, and Caesar destroys him: two more betrayals.

Lepidus, who tries, to the amusement of the underlings, to steer an even course between Antony and Caesar, and to conciliate the continual wrangling and contention between them, is betrayed and destroyed by Caesar. Yet Enobarbus' suggestion that Antony and Caesar should 'borrow one another's love for the instant' (until Pompey is disposed of), and then 'return it again' (II. ii. 103–5) – which is precisely what they do – is reprimanded.

Ventidius, in a short scene that is irrelevant to the plot, shows how competition functions in hierarchy. He 'betrays' Antony in order not to be betrayed by him: 'I could do more to do Antonius good, / But 'twould offend him' (III. i. 25–6). In one passage reminiscent of Antony's feelings about the dead Fulvia, Agrippa and Enobarbus recall Antony crying at the sight of the dead Brutus: 'What willingly he did confound, he wail'd' (III. ii. 58). After the defeat at Actium, many of Antony's allies and soldiers abandon him. After watching even Cleopatra dally with the notion of making terms with Caesar through his envoy, Enobarbus too decides to leave Antony.

The war vacillates: Antony is defeated, then Caesar, then Antony, again and finally. Eros 'betrays' Antony by reneging on his promise to kill him. Caesar betrays Cleopatra as to his intentions. Like Antony for Fulvia and Brutus, Caesar is 'touch'd' by the news of Antony's death: 'I have follow'd thee to this . . . But yet let me lament' (V. i. 33, 36, 40), Cleopatra deceives Caesar about her withheld treasures and her intentions: Seleucus betrays Cleopatra, hoping to ingratiate himself with Caesar. Proculeius is not honest with Cleopatra, betraying our expectations. Dolabella, however, is, and so betrays Caesar out of pity and affection for the Queen.

Even those who attempt like Lepidus to avoid or transcend the shifting winds and seas are betrayed or destroyed. Octavia is torn between her love for her brother and her duty to her husband. 'Her tongue will not obey her heart, nor can / Her heart inform her tongue – the swan's down-feather, / That stands upon the swell at full of tide, / And neither way inclines' (III. ii. 47–50).

'You must think, look you, that the worm will do his kind', says the Clown, whose speeches offer in little the contradictions and paradoxes of the play. Utter constancy is impossible: 'were man but constant, he were perfect'.

> Sometime we see a cloud that's dragonish;
> A vapour sometime like a bear or lion,
> A tower'd citadel, a pendant rock,
> A forked mountain, or blue promontory
> With trees upon't, that nod unto the world,
> And mock our eyes with air . . .
> That which is now a horse, even with a thought
> The rack dislimns, and makes it indistinct
> As water is in water.
>
>   (IV. xiv. 2–7, 9–11)

The only absolute besides inconstancy is constancy in death:

> 'Tis paltry to be Caesar:
> Not being Fortune, he's but Fortune's knave,
> A minister of her will: and it is great
> To do that thing that ends all other deeds,
> Which shackles accident and bolts up change,
> Which sleeps, and never palates more the dung,
> The beggar's nurse, and Caesar's.
>
>   (V. ii. 2–8)

In such a world, and this is how the actual world is, any constancy is a miracle, a gift. Love that endures in spirit, even if not in the letter, is the greatest gift one can grant or get. Thus Enobarbus remains in the imagination as a type of loyalty despite his defection, and Eros *because* of his broken promise. In ironical fulfilment of the Sooth-sayer's prophecy, Iras and Charmian die shortly after their mistress; their words suggest they accompany her in love and admiration more than out of fear of Caesar. And so too Antony and Cleopatra, despite their alternations and removals, remain constant to each other, and take on mythic size.

Part of what makes them so large-sized is their understanding and forgiveness of alteration.[9] Despite Cleopatra's rage at hearing of Antony's marriage, she accepts him back with no diminution of love. Although she is terrified by his threats against her in IV. xii she forgives him enough to risk the consequences of his rage to send word that she is really alive – once she is safely in her monument.

Antony, after his first defeat, expects and even encourages his allies to abandon him. He understands the world and does not hold up idealistic (and self-serving) demands. After his tantrum, he forgives Cleopatra for dallying with Caesar's envoy. He fully forgives Enobarbus and sends his treasure after him. Part of his love of Cleopatra is founded on what Enobarbus calls her 'infinite variety'; she expresses everything, and everything becomes her. Inconstancy may be the cause of much human sorrow, but under its other name, variety, it is the spice of life.

Thus, as in *A Midsummer Night's Dream*, constancy is wrested directly out of the fact of inconstancy. Like the moon images in the comedy, which offer a concrete example of constancy within inconstancy, all elements of *Antony* – scenic structure, plot, characterisation, and language and allusion – repeat in multiple ways the same notion. The Romans disapprove of Egypt; Cleopatra has contempt for Rome: but the two realms are in some way contained in each other.

Roman values and manners dominate the play in terms of time and attention devoted to them; Egyptian values dominate the emotional dimension of the tragedy. The activities of Rome are war and contention. The only pleasure shown or described as Roman is a male drinking bout conducted not in the sensuous abandon and pleasure of Egypt, but as a contest, which Lepidus loses. Presumably, turning the drinking session into a competition cleanses it of any associations with the feminine principle, and so purifies it. The drinking contest is a metaphor for what will happen to Lepidus: we do not need to see his destruction – it is implicit in the drinking contest.[10]

But if Roman values dominate in the plot, they do not triumph in most readers' sense of things: it is the emotional dimension of the play that matters. There is no question that the lovers are magnified. This is accomplished through the allusive level, which is idealising; and through the poetry, which is magnificent. The use of Enobarbus as the vehicle of much praise of Cleopatra (the tough old soldier who sees her tricks still praises her inordinately) and Cleopatra's words about Antony when he is dead and she can no longer try to manipulate him – these elements function as a kind of reinforcement or validation for the large notions of the lovers themselves. In addition, the lovers are continually associated with nature, fertility, and wealth in its best sense – the heaped-up richnesses of the world. Antony is repeatedly described or shown as generous in word or deed. He is even lavish: his magnanimity is dramatically presented in his under-standing and forgiveness of betrayal in 'this wild world'. Cleopatra is majestic and tempestuous, without shame and without guilt. Her speeches after Antony's death have a dignity, a largeness of reference, and an authority that amounts to wisdom. In drawing her idealised portrait of Antony, she makes a statement about spirit, not flesh, about largeness of being and doing and feeling.[11]

Still, the lovers are not idealised. Generous Antony takes Pompey's house in a spirit of petty greed. Both are at times unreasonable, capricious, cruel, weak, and treacherous to each other and other people. It is clear that Shakespeare's intention in magnifying them is not to create exemplary moral models, not even to idealise these particular characters. Rather, the magnification serves to exalt their feeling for each other, and to link it with eternity, the realm beyond the changes of the moon. In the process, the play exalts feeling itself, guiltless eroticism, play, free-flowing emotion of all sorts, the rich high vividness of living when experience is its own end.[12]

The pole of nature does not mask or enrobe the dung and slime of earth and flesh; it accepts the worm who does its kind, the transiency of every human experience, and accepts its participation in time, in contrast to Caesar, who wants to 'possess' the time (II. vii. 99). The images associated with Egypt are alternately luxurious, fertile, and baleful; 'the serpent theme culminates in a brilliant union of the fruitful and the lethal powers of the Nile.'[13] They are, however, all peaceful, and they frequently link the great Queen Cleopatra with beggars, just as she herself describes herself as a milkmaid: although this kingdom is ruled hierarchically, legitimacy is not a major issue in it.

One critic has claimed that love is always ambiguous in Shake-speare, and that in this tragedy, the love is a dream, the slime is the reality.[14] But Shakespeare's great triumph in this play, it seems to me, is to portray love in all the ambivalence and ambiguity it has in actuality, and to persuade us nevertheless of its authenticity and intensity. Slime is never far from love, as Yeats's Crazy Jane might say, but this does not make one real and the other an illusion.

The play is about the human conflict between seemingly contra-dictory impulses. Robert Ornstein writes that Shakespeare's 'arche-typal imagery suggests that the worlds of Rome and Egypt are eternal aspects of human experience and form a dichotomy as elemental as that of male and female'.[15] I am not at all sure that these impulses are necessarily contradictory, or that the dichotomy of male and female is anything like as elemental as we have come to believe, but I will reserve such comments for the conclusion. It certainly appears that Shakespeare thought this way, however. And since he did, and since in this play he aggrandised the very pole that was seen as immoral, not just sexually, but in terms of overall response to life, he was offering a radical criticism of his culture.

Although some critics believe that Antony suffers from 'a deep-seated defect of will', and that the play is 'a conflict between passion and human weakness, and duty and self-denial'; or that passionate love is 'sinful and dangerous', and Antony a type of Hercules in thrall to Omphale, one can only respond that the richer experience, in a life in which one may not have everything, is the more desirable.[16]

Just as the tragedy brings together the two principles at war with each other (as they were in the problem plays), but focuses equally on them, so the structure focuses on linear scenes that advance the plot, and scenes irrelevant to plot that create texture or are significatory. That it violates conventional tragic form made it seem a failure to generations of readers. A. P. Riemer claims that it violates tragic tradition in that it contains flashes of comedy, vulgarity, and swift changes of tone.[17] To challenge convention is to challenge attitude, even if that convention is a literary one. V. K. Whitaker says that only *Lear* and *Antony and Cleopatra* seriously question 'the validity of the concept of universal harmony or order', and that the latter denies 'that the achievement of fixity is possible'.[18]

Perhaps the most daring thing Shakespeare did in the play was to present illegitimate sexuality as glorious. Many critics still find romantic or erotic love a trivial subject, not worthy of tragedy.[19] But it is impossible to deny the seriousness and grandeur of this tragedy, and impossible – largely because of Shakespeare's language – to deny that he glorified something that is seen as sinful, trivial, and contemptible by many of the characters. Once sex and sin are not seen as identical – as they are not in Egypt – then Egypt is as hot as Rome is cold, and 'as inevitably self-renewing as the other is inescapably deadly.'[20] Reason, what we call reason, which is linear and goal-directed, is far less encompassing than emotion.[21] It is true that the unified feminine principle is anti-civilisation; but the masculine principle is anti-life. In the plays that follow this tragedy, Shakespeare will pursue the second perception to its ugly and barren conclusion.

And in fact, how civilised is the civilising principle? Roman values – order and degree, power-in-the-world, structure and possession – do not create harmonious order and a protective pale for procreation. They create contention and rivalry, one order superseding another, and a thin, pleasureless, stiff existence. The feminine principle may be doomed; it may always be defeated. But in the meantime it offers the richness of emotional and erotic dimensions of life – pleasure, play, and sex. At the end of *Antony and Cleopatra*, Caesar has the world; Antony and Cleopatra had the living.

From Marilyn French, *Shakespeare's Division of Experience* (London, 1982), pp. 251–65.

NOTES

[Marilyn French's book was one of the first full-length studies of the Shakespeare oeuvre from the perspective of feminism to have emerged during the early 1980s. In terms of the history of feminist criticism of Shakespeare it should be compared with Juliet Dusinberre's earlier *Shakespeare and the Nature of Women* (London, 1975), and the influential collection edited by Carolyn Lenz, Gayle Greene and Carol Thomas Neeley, entitled *The Woman's Part* (Urbana and Chicago, 1980); French's commitment to what is now regarded as an 'essentialist' feminism, that is that gender difference is rooted in essential differences between the sexes, is now unfashionable, and has been superseded by the view that gender difference is socially produced, and hence amenable to change. Ed.]

1. John Arthos sees the tragedy as being concerned with 'the manner in which love, given its range in at once the greatest and most ordinary natures, arrives at apotheosis. The drama is the preservation of constancy, in this world, and afterwards' (*The Art of Shakespeare* [London, 1964], p. 62).

2. 'Mutability rules *Antony and Cleopatra*' (M. C. Bradbrook, *Shakespeare the Craftsman* [London, 1969] p. 117).

3. Caroline Spurgeon (*Shakespeare's Imagery and What it Tells Us* [Cambridge, 1935], p. 352) points out that the word *world* occurs forty-two times, more than double its occurrence in any other play. Theodore Spencer adds that the word *fortune* also appears more frequently than in any other play (*Shakespeare and the Nature of Man* [New York, 1942] p. 167). Maurice Charney claims that the magnitude of the issues in the play is emphasised by the many words of cosmic reference and by the *world* theme (*Shakespeare's Roman Plays* [Cambridge, Mass., 1961], p. 80).

4. Critics who believe that Shakespeare (like Virgil) upheld the claims of Rome against the charm of Egypt must juggle or ignore the language. Brents Stirling, *Unity in Shakespearean Tragedy* (New York, 1956), p. 169, manages to find Cleopatra's ending 'comic'; Daniel Stempel,

'The Transmigration of the Crocodile', *SQ*, 7 (1956), 59–72, explains away all the poetry. T. J. B. Spencer attempts to deal directly with the problem. He writes, 'The splendour of language given to Antony and Cleopatra captures our imaginative sympathy for the . . . "wrong" side' (*Shakespeare: The Roman Plays* [London, 1963], p. 31). His statement, however, makes one wonder about his respect for the playwright, who surely used language to indicate his meaning.

5. The pervasiveness in the play of what Maynard Mack calls 'mobility and mutability' has been noted by nearly all its modern readers (*'Antony and Cleopatra*: The Stillness and the Dance', *Shakespeare's Art: Seven Essays*, ed. Milton Crane [Chicago, 1973]).

6. Janet Adelman, *The Common Liar* (New Haven, 1973), p. 26.

7. Antony's reversals are discussed by John Danby, 'The Shakespearean Dialectic: An Aspect of *Antony and Cleopatra*', *Scrutiny*, 16 (1949), 196–213.

8. John Holloway, *The Story of the Night* (London, 1961), p. 117, describes the behaviour of Antony and Cleopatra as 'sometimes exalted and sometimes abject'. In this play, he asserts, 'the highest and the lowest, the most exalted and the base . . . [are] one' (p. 106).

9. Antony and Cleopatra 'transcend their environment through their capacity for change and mutation' (A. P. Riemer, *A Reading of Shakespeare's 'Antony and Cleopatra'* [Sydney, 1968], p. 35). He adds that the lovers 'thrive on impermanence' (p. 113).

10. Riemer, *A Reading*, p. 45, sees the drinking scene as a premonition of a 'dissolving world'.

11. Barbara Everett find the language of Antony and Cleopatra 'expressive of a whole radically different way of living and feeling: a language of immediate individual experience . . . Love or desolation, exhilaration or rage become their own argument' (Intro., Signet *Antony and Cleopatra* [New York, 1963]).

12. The play offers 'transcendent justification of passion in terms of emotional value and vitality', wrote Derek Traversi, *An Approach to Shakespeare* (Garden City, NY, 1969), p. 117. In this early work, Traversi claims that in *Antony and Cleopatra*, Shakespeare 'came nearest to unifying his experience into a harmonious and related whole' (p. 127). John Arthos, *The Art of Shakespeare*, p. 62, suggests that the drama is about the transformation of love into apotheosis: 'the drama is the preservation of constancy.'

13. Maurice Charney, *Shakespeare's Roman Plays* (Cambridge Mass., 1961), p. 101.

14. Charles R. Lyons, *Shakespeare and the Ambiguity of Love's Triumph* (The Hague, 1971), p. 186.

15. Robert Ornstein, 'The Ethic of Imagination: Love and Art in *Antony and Cleopatra*', in *Stratford-upon-Avon Studies*, 8 (London, 1966), 31–46. Philip Edwards, *Shakespeare and the Confines of Art* (London, 1968) p. 121, insists on the 'impossibility of single vision and simple judgement' of the play.

16. Maurice Charney, *Shakespeare's Roman Plays*, p. 126; Irving Ribner, Intro. *Antony and Cleopatra* (New York, 1976); Franklin Dickey, *Not Wisely But Too Well* (San Marino, Calif., 1967), p. 1. Daniel Stempel sees the 'domination' of Antony by Cleopatra as 'an unnatural reversal of the roles of man and woman', and approves the end – the 'defeat and death of the rebel against order' ('The Transmigration of the Crocodile', *SQ*, 7 (1956), 63). Derek Traversi hardens his attitude against the lovers in *Shakespeare: The Roman Plays* (London, 1963). Although he continues to find the lovers an image of integration and constancy, he also continually equates Cleopatra with 'mortal weakness' and 'corruption' (p. 94).

17. Riemer, *A Reading of Shakespeare's Antony and Cleopatra* (Sydney, 1968), p. 15.

18. Virgil K. Whitaker, *A Mirror Up to Nature* (San Marino, Calif., 1965), p. 111.

19. Whitaker, *A Mirror up to Nature*, p. 104, and Dickey, *Not Wisely But Too Well*, chap 1, among others.

20. John Danby, 'The Shakespearean Dialectic: An Aspect of Antony and Cleopatra'.

21. Doubting his emotions, Enobarbus follows reason and dies, suggests Janet Adelman, *The Common Liar*, p. 123. She adds that to be convinced to love is to have 'faith in what we cannot know'.

11

'Travelling thoughts': Theatre and the Space of the Other

ANIA LOOMBA

NEGATIVE CAPABILITY RECONSIDERED

The assumption of dominant Anglo-American criticism, that tragedy must arrive at 'some comprehensive vision of the relation of human suffering to human joy'[1] and must lead via catharsis to moral certainty, was central in both bringing the privileged text to a closure and in institutionalising this by framing a hierarchical canon of 'great' art. The exalted stature of Shakespearean drama, its affirmation of a moral (i.e. conservative) order and its movement towards a final and unquestionable truth are interdependent claims which are invoked to confirm one another.[2] On the other hand, Middletonian drama (for example) was dismissed as 'not the highest kind of tragedy' because its protagonists do not arrive at any 'recognition of truth'.[3] Truth-telling was an attribute of the Godlike and 'detached' artist, and yet this criterion was selectively applied on a slanted principle: precisely what was celebrated as 'negative capability' in the case of Shakespeare was dismissed as an 'ironically detached unheroic view of life not attuned to the heroic passions of early tragedy' in the case of Middleton.[4]

Bertolt Brecht has increasingly been used to re-read the plays of the period because he found a 'complex, shifting, largely impersonal, never soluble' conflict, a 'disconnectedness' of both structure and perspective that approximated to his own[5] in what had been regarded as an omniscient authorial detachment. This has radical implications, not only for the reading of the plays, but for 'democratising' the Renaissance canon, with its Shakespearean apex, for Brecht observed similar characteristics in at least twenty of Shakespeare's contemporaries.

Brecht's analysis was important also for focusing in a new and self-conscious way on structure and form as an aspect of textual meaning and perspective. The blurring of distinctions between comedy and tragedy had often been disparagingly noted by critics in relation to the plays of Middleton; *Women Beware Women*, for example, has been called an 'unsuccessful attempt to create tragedy out of the materials and conventions of satiric comedy', its central theme 'more appropriate to a broadside balladeer than the tragic poet'.[6] Brecht read such 'impurities' in the context of the various ways in which Renaissance drama resisted artistic isolation into the world of make-believe. He noted that its language incorporated the speech of the beer-hall audiences; that daylight performances and open stages prevented hypnotic illusion, that the dramatisation of material familiar to the audience encouraged a critical approach; that the collective nature of the theatre companies and their life-style encouraged montage and epic construction which opposes the idea of drama as a self-sufficient microcosm. All this, says Brecht, led to a 'naive surrealism', practised not only by Shakespeare but also by other dramatists of the period.[7]

Robert Weimann has demonstrated that 'the basis of Shakespeare's "negative capability" is itself socio-historical', located partly in the 'freedom, the detachment, and the imagination made available to him by the popular tradition in the theatre' and partly in the fact that while older feudal values could already be questioned, those of capitalism 'were not yet their *necessary alternative*'; the 'myriad-mindedness' of Shakespeare's art is contextualised by Weimann in terms of the positioning of both artist and the playhouse,[8] and is interwoven with the structural looseness of the plays. More recently, Jonathan Dollimore has elaborated the implications of the Brechtian connection by drawing upon Brecht's critical and dramatic approach to identify the materialist 'realism' of Renaissance drama, its emphasis on discontinuity of form and character and its radical questioning of the philosophical and political status quo.[9]

My own purpose here is to insert the dimension of gender more fully into such proto-Brechtian multiplicity and montage, and to suggest that the epic structure is at least partly derived from and closely related to the drama's interrogation of gender roles and patriarchal authority. Conversely, the non-teleological form itself becomes an important vehicle for resisting closure: it suggests, as Brecht claimed, the open-endedness of a situation – that if things could happen one way, they could also have happened in a totally different manner. Open-endedness in this sense does not connote a free-wheeling vacuum: 'the realism has to do more than just make reality visible on the stage . . . One has to be able to see the laws that decide how the processes of life develop'.[10]

An invocation of the sanctity of a linear and teleological structure was crucial for the colonial deployment of the Western canon. On the one hand, it ensured that questions of form and structure flooded (and still do) the examination papers, inviting the reader yet again to squeeze the text into a straitjacket and to erase the possible fractures of experience in reading it. On the other, it imposed Western aesthetics (for example, the Aristotelian demarcation of tragedy from comedy) upon traditions, such as that of Indian drama (both classical and folk), which had acknowledged the intermingling of moods and genres. Westernised theatre groups, and imported British troupes (often playing melodramatic versions of Shakespeare) ensured the hegemony of such ideas in actual performance, and generations of actors were taught to forget the proto-Brechtian epic traditions of the Indian theatre.

Today there have been some efforts to revive such a heritage, and to enrich it by infusing it with contemporary relevance. This has included adaptations of Western drama; and when Habib Tanvir, for example, has performed Brecht's plays in the style of folk theatre from Chattisgarh, using the latter's actors and music, it has illustrated, among other things, the extent to which much Indian drama had worked on assumptions and techniques analogous to Brecht's. There is not the space here to consider the ways in which third world literatures, both traditional and modern, both writers unknown to the West and those who have become current objects of its gaze, like Rushdie, Márquez, and recently, Ghosh, step out from the model of linear time and space and transgress the dominant Western literary model. It may be said, however, that such a movement cannot be explained simply by analogies to Western rejections of linearity (such as those of Miller or Beckett) for it refers specifically to the disjunctures and complexities of a non-Western experience.[11]

However, it will not do simply to demarcate the two either; for the refusal of a Western text to comply with the structural or ideological unity demanded of it by dominant criticisms is equally useful for questioning the preferred textual model. Hence to seize upon what Brecht saw as the 'disconnectedness' of Renaissance drama is one way to contest its institutionalised usage as the barricade around a series of privileged positions. Finally, since the patriarchal gaze on women and the colonial one on its others is one-dimensional, because it aims both to obscure their depth and to deny their potential for mobility, we may usefully consider how montage, as a structural and thematic perspective, can challenge the dominant portrayals of women and other colonised peoples. At the same time, by identifying these perspectives and techniques as not exclusive to the hitherto privileged author or text and by bringing excluded ones into related focus, we may question the sanctity of the Western syllabus as it has been inherited and preserved by Indian departments of English.

MONTAGE

Middleton's frequent collaborations with other writers possibly contributed to the loose and episodic structure of his plays. For example, the comic scenes in *The Changeling*, supposedly the work of Rowley, are interspersed with Middleton's tragic scenes. Many readings have been at pains to establish the harmony between the two. But the two plots also serve to puncture and comment upon each other. In that sense, they do not merely 'blend' into one another, but create a collage which serves to demystify certain issues.

Both the main plot and the sub-plot reinforce the different ways in which people change. In both the heroine is tempted to be unfaithful: whereas Beatrice actually succumbs and changes, Isabella remains faithful. But this does not serve to condemn Beatrice; rather the almost surrealistic treatment of madness in the sub-plot serves to alienate us in the Brechtian sense from the 'madness' of Beatrice's story. Bradbrook notes that the masque of madmen reinforces the idea of love as madness, as something that confounds discretion and darkens reason. On the contrary, the madhouse splices the main story to create a montage which prevents us from reacting hypnotically to a romantic and mystical conception of love, which even within the main plot is not a fixed category, but expands, erodes and changes as people do: it is both socially created and affects events, but is never absolute.

The point here is that montage expresses what I have previously considered as the *unresolved* tensions of Beatrice's 'giddy turning'.

Measured against the contingency of character and social construction of subjectivity which the plays emphasise, the 'spectacular catastrophe(s)' of Jacobean tragedy noted by critics[12] do not constitute the 'revelation' which is considered the proper end of drama, for they only confirm what the almost cool depiction of violence in the earlier acts has relentlessly underlined. Hence to Muir's complaint that Beatrice does not attain knowledge we may reply that this is precisely the point: neither the protagonists nor the plays arrive at that famous final moment of closure. Examining this in relation to *The White Devil*, Dollimore cites a passage from Brecht which is worth re-quoting at this point:

> The tragedy of Mother Courage and of her life ... consisted in the fact that here a terrible contradiction existed which destroyed a human being, a contradiction which could be resolved, but only by society itself and in long, terrible struggles . . . It is not the business of the playwright to endow Mother Courage with final insight . . . his concern is, to make the spectator see.[13]

I have earlier commented on the rape scene in *Women Beware Women* where Bianca internalises the violence committed upon her and, at the same time, is alienated from the beliefs by which guilt is measured. The rape is inserted into a long scene, framed by the chess game and broken up by clusters of smaller scenes of courtly life. The chess game has been used elsewhere in the drama as a political metaphor, as for example in Middleton's own *A Game at Chess*; what is especially important in the case of *Women Beware Women* is that he employs it to de-sensationalise the rape. Violence on the female body has become a sort of courtly game in which those outside the royal circle are pawns. What lifts the scene from being just a cynical comment on power is the violence and unexpectedness of Bianca's reaction: even as she adapts to her status as victim, she retains a sense of her own agency. Bianca is one of the three women involved in the rape scene - Livia's machinations and the Mother's helplessness place women in a series of different relationships with patriarchal power. As the three interact with each other we glimpse the relativity and contingency of each relationship – the Mother seeks to confine her daughter-in-law but is herself ensnared in the chess game, Livia will shortly be out-manoeuvred. Again, none of the three attain any final insights; Bianca's dying belief – 'Like our own sex, we have no enemy' (V. ii. 215) – is pitifully inadequate in explaining her fate.

The non-linear, non-climatic, episodic structure, and montage, usually disclose the *construction* of identity and social relations. For example, as we saw in *Othello*, Iago's downstage position serves to hoist popular notions of racism or misogyny onto the stage itself, where they become particular and contested perspectives instead of confirmed truths. In Webster's *The White Devil* characters repeatedly overhear, watch and secretly observe each other, so that at most points we watch the action through a series of eyes, not just our own. Such successive framings have been often regarded as 'stock-devices', stereotypical versions of a play within a play. But their effect is far from stereotypical. Consider, for example, Vittoria's first 'private' interchange with Brachiano, which is watched by Zanche, Flamineo and Cornelia. Whereas Romeo and Juliet's balcony scene fills the entire arena, this affair is interrupted and interpreted for the audience by different comments:

> **Brachiano**   Excellent creature.
>   We call the cruel fair, what name for you
>   That are so merciful? (*Embraces her*)
> **Zanche**   See now they close.
> **Flamineo**   Most happy union.
> **Cornelia**   (*aside*) My fears are fall'n upon me, oh my heart!
>   My son the pander: now I find our house
>   Sinking to ruin.
>
> (I. ii. 202–8)

Zanche invests the liaison with her own desire for romance, which is ridiculed by others because she is black (see V. iii). Flamineo's comment is ironic, for he is hardly concerned with the lovers' *happiness*, and yet, his own viciousness can be seen as a consequence of his poverty and marginalisation.[14] Cornelia's remark serves to swerve the gaze away from Vittoria's transgression to her brother's part in it. Montage here insists that the relationship is no privatised ideal of spontaneity and instant attraction, it is something planned and manipulated, and *always public*. The act of watching constantly punctures the illusion of privacy and individual agency; the resultant 'broken' focus ties in with Vittoria's public trial and punishment and thus prepares us for the interplay of private and public, which is the main theme of the play:

> **Lawyer**   My lord Duke and she have been very private.
> **Flamineo**   You are a dull ass; 'tis threat'ned they have been very public.
>
> (III. i. 17–19).

SPATIAL POLITICS

Let us examine the effects of montage more closely by focusing on a text that is supposed to achieve the kind of tragic harmony that is seen to elude *The Changeling*. Three centuries of critical opinion, from Samuel Johnson onwards, has been preoccupied with 'overcoming' the heterogeneous nature of both the form and the content of Shakespeare's *Antony and Cleopatra*: the focus has variously been on its disjointed structure, mingling of tragic and comic, flux in character; its divisions between private and public, male and female, high and low life; on what Danby has called the 'dialectic' of the text.[15] However, a correlation of these various binaries – the thematic oppositions, the broken structure, its treatment of fluid gender and racial identity – has yet to be attempted. An 'epic effect' has been noted, but in the classical sense of the word;[16] we might more usefully employ the term in its Brechtian sense to analyse these various schisms. 'The continual hurry of the action, the variety of incidents, and the quick succession of one personage to another . . . the frequent changes of scene'[17] then emerge as contradicting the classical elevation of character or teleological progression towards catharsis, as achieving a Brechtian alienation from character to posit a radical interrogation of the imperial and sexual drama.

The geographical turbulence of the first three acts involves a redefinition of femininity and of female space: patriarchal Rome contests Egyptian Cleopatra for her geographical and sexual territory. Into the contest is woven the theme of imperial domination. Dominant notions about female identity, gender relations and imperial power are unsettled through the disorderly non-European woman. These ideas appear to be reinstated as the quick shifts of scene are abandoned in favour of a more orthodox climax at the end of the play, an apparent resolution of the dilemma. Whereas in the first three acts of the play there are twenty-three changes of scene, and shifts of location within each as well, as the play proceeds there is a change in the quality and quantity of movement: in Act IV alone there are fifteen changes of locale, but all within Egypt. Act V contains only two scenes, and both are confined to the area of Cleopatra's monument. Alongside this, different characters strive to rise 'above' their earlier turbulence and assert an inner unity of being. However, this harmony is precarious; the manner of its achievement conveys the very opposite of a resolution and the various sets of oppositions noted by critics are not subscribed to but eroded by the play.

The issues of imperial expansion, political power and sexual domination are dramatically compressed into spatial and geographical shifts and metaphors. The almost cinematic movements – 'panning, tracking, and playing with the camera'[18] – are designed to reveal the complexity of the terrain on which men and women move as well as of their inner spaces. They penetrate into different aspects of power, which is at once something concrete – land, kingdoms, wealth – and something relatively abstract – emotions, ideology, and sexuality. Theatrical space is not just an inert arena but interacts with the text's treatment of social and psychological space.

Not only does the locale constantly shift, but in each setting we are reminded of another. In Egypt, Rome is evoked, and vice versa. While leaving for Rome, Antony tells Cleopatra: 'thou, residing here, goes yet with me, / And I, hence fleeting, here remain with thee' (I. iii. 103–4). This is a common enough lovers' platitude but it serves to remind us that in addition to the purely geographical shifts of terrain, there are also those of conceptual settings; the lovers' private world is constantly contrasted to the political space. Antony identifies the former with Egypt, and in preferring it to Rome is trying to privatise love, to locate his relationship with Cleopatra in a domestic arena. But he also attempts to expand this space so that it excludes the other, threatening world of masculine politics, and crowds out other concerns:

> Cleopatra   I'll set a bourn how far to be belov'd.
> Antony   Then must thou needs find out new heaven, new earth.
> (I. i. 16–17)

This is what Donne's lovers are also trying to do as they seek ever more expansive metaphors for their relationship and for each other: 'She's all States, and all Princes I'; their room becomes an 'everywhere' (p. 73).

Roman patriarchy demonises Cleopatra by defining her world as private (Antony is no longer a serious general by entering it); as female (Egypt robs Antony and his soldiers of their manhood); and as barbaric (Antony is now a slave of gypsies). But both Antony and Caesar are aware that Egypt is not merely a private space and that its female, non-European nature only intensifies its challenge to imperial Rome:

> **Antony**   My being in Egypt, Caesar
> What was't to you?
> **Caesar** No more than my residing here at Rome
> Might be to you in Egypt. Yet, if you there
> Did practise on my state, your being in Egypt
> Might be my question.
>
> (II. ii. 39–44)

Objective space is always invested with political or emotional connotations; as Caesar indicates, Egypt is a place from which subversion can be practised, and as such it can never be merely a lovers' retreat. Antony too courts Cleopatra with territorial and political gifts: he will 'piece / Her opulent throne with kingdoms; all the East / ... shall call her mistress' (I. v. 45–7). Caesar complains precisely of this:

> Unto her
> He gave the establishment of Egypt; made her
> Of Lower Syria, Cyprus, Lydia,
> Absolute queen.
>
> (II. vi. 8–11)

Passionate as the relationship between Antony and Cleopatra is, 'the language of desire, far from transcending the power relations which structure this society, is wholly informed by them'.[19] These relations are both sexual and racial. In the beginning Antony thinks he is in control of what he regards as the opposition between politics and pleasure; therefore he assumes that he can simultaneously possess the Roman matron Octavia through the legal bonding permitted by imperial patriarchy, and the oriental seductress Cleopatra, through a sexually passionate and 'illicit' relationship:

> I will to Egypt;
> And though I make this marriage for my peace,
> I'th' East my pleasure lies.
>
> (II. iii. 39–41)

He alternately views Egypt as his retreat from Roman politics and a place to consolidate his bid for power. In short, he oscillates between Cleopatra's territory and Caesar's, both literally and otherwise. As the play proceeds he is no longer in command of such a divide: his position in both Rome and Egypt becomes unstable and manifests itself as a dislocation of personality: 'I / Have lost my way for ever', 'I have fled myself', 'I have lost command' (III. x. 3–4, 7, 23).

'Authority melts from me', he cries, but like Faustus, the Duchess of Malfi, and Parolles, he invokes his lost 'essential' self: 'Have you no ears? I am / Antony yet' (III. xiii. 90–3). Even as Antony complains that Caesar keeps 'harping on what I *am*, / Not what he knew I *was*' (III, xiii, 142–3; emphasis added), he is aware of the change in himself. Without power, without space, without Rome and without Cleopatra, Antony disintegrates.

It is important that Cleopatra's transformation into the 'whore' and 'witch' occurs precisely at this point: the language of what Antony perceives as a betrayal reduces Cleopatra's 'infinite variety' to both patriarchal and racist stereotypes. Helen Carr has pointed out that 'although the substitution of "witch" for "whore" as the primary image of the deviant woman signifies a greater degree of horror at the possibility of female sexuality, at the same time it represses the idea of a consciously sexual woman (the witch's fantasies are alien and evil intruders in her mind)'.[20] Cleopatra, I have argued, is both: her sexuality is an aspect of her blackness and as such can only be erased later, when she herself adopts token Roman-ness. Whereas, in falling from Othello's favour, Desdemona became 'begrim'd' and morally black and false to her true self, Cleopatra as the 'foul Egyptian' only realises her 'true' position as the complete outsider. As Antony perceives that he is only nominally the site of the conflict which is actually between Cleopatra and Caesar, the latent struggle for power between him and Cleopatra escalates. The meta-phors for this three-way struggle become those of the land and the sea. Whether the fight should take place on the Roman element, the land, or Cleopatra's medium, the water, is at once a matter of military strategy and a measure of Antony's emotional and political affiliations. The erosion of the absolute space of love stems from his increasing perception of his own marginality, and Cleopatra's refusal to share her space. With all worlds being lost, Antony's vacillations cease, and so do the structural shifts.

Such a movement is also dependent on the play's treatment of Cleopatra. If Cleopatra's political being threatens patriarchy it also catalyses the contradictions within her, which are inherent in the position she occupies as a sexually active non-European female ruler. Although she is unique among the independent women in Renais-sance drama, for she appears to command her own spaces, these are precariously constructed: as the ruler of Egypt her space is threatened by the expansionist designs of the Roman empire, and as a woman, by the contradictions of heterosexual love. Her insecurity, her fear of invasion – not just as a ruler, but also as a woman who is threatened even (or especially) by her lover – is evident in her physical stasis, her reluctance to move from her territory. However slippery, inconstant and variable Cleopatra may be, however she may threaten the boundaries between male and female, political and private worlds, she remains geographically stationary. She resents the intrusions of Roman messengers who remind her not only of Antony's wives, first Fulvia and then Octavia, but also of the imperial threat.

Cleopatra fluctuates between establishing her emotional and her political spaces: a vacillation without end for she cannot simultaneously occupy both. She finds it much harder to locate her own territory in relation to Antony than *vis-à-vis* Caesar. She can either function within the private life of a man, or enter politics as a honorary man and chaste woman, like Elizabeth. In any case it is a double bind. As 'foul Egyptian' she will always stand outside Roman society: Antony can never fully trust her and will marry safe and obedient Roman women like Octavia to ensure his stability within that society. Her gender renders her politically unacceptable, her political status problematises her femininity, and her racial otherness troubles, doubly, both power and sexuality. To the extent that she acts as a ruler, she is perfectly comprehensible to Caesar: he even praises her for concealing her treasure from him; 'nay, blush not, Cleopatra; I approve / Your wisdom in the deed' (V. ii. 148–9). But whereas he will not haggle over 'things that merchants sold' (V. ii. 83), he refuses to grant her autonomy even in respect of her death.

The last act appears to 'resolve' the various tensions of the play; the style now changes from montage and a mingling of comic and tragic to that of classical tragedy. It appears that Cleopatra is tamed; the wanton gypsy becomes Antony's wife, the queen is stripped to an essential femininity that attaches to all women irrespective of class: 'no more but e'en a woman, and commanded / By such poor passion as the maid that milks / And does the meanest chares' (IV. xv. 73–5). The variable woman is now 'marble constant'; the witch gives way to the penitent goddess as Egypt tries to do 'what's brave, / what's noble ... after the high Roman fashion' (IV. xv. 86–7).

Several aspects of this resolution serve to contradict its apparent implications. Firstly, Cleopatra is able to capitulate to Roman matrimony only after Antony has died, and when one aspect of her conflict has dissolved rather than being resolved. The prospect of sharing power with Antony no longer exists, and she begins to approximate the lovers in Donne's poems, or Antony's own earlier expressions of absolute emotion. After his death Antony can fill her world in a way that Antony alive could never be allowed to do:

> His face was as the heav'ns, and therein stuck
> A sun and moon, which kept their course and lighted
> The little O, the earth ...
> His legs bestrid the ocean; his rear'd arm
> Crested the world.
>
> (V. ii. 79–83)

The poetry has been seen as sublime. Cleopatra's words display an effort to cloak personal and political loss in the language of a transcendental, eternal romance. Given the conditions of its utterance, the poetry reveals the politics of sublimation, rather than a transcendence of politics. Antony can now comfortably be called 'husband' (V. ii. 285) without the risk to freedom that actual matrimony implies.

Cleopatra also lets her own fierce identification with Egypt slip for the first time. Literally, of course she still does not accept Caesar's Rome, which remains a threat:

> Shall they hoist me up,
> And show me to the shouting varletry
> Of censuring Rome? Rather a ditch in Egypt
> Be gentle grave unto me!
>
> (V. ii. 55–8)

But Rome was also Antony's space and as his wife she can adopt the 'Roman fashion'.

Secondly, if these moves reflect Cleopatra's contradictions, they are also strategic and constitute the unruly woman's last performances. Having lost power, it now becomes 'paltry to be Caesar' (V. ii. 2); it is now time to speak of things other than power. Her suicide clouds her political defeat with mystic glamour and a show of autonomy. Her own body is the last 'space' to be wrested from Roman control. The asp will bring her 'liberty' in the absence of real territory. The maternal image of the snake at her breast tames her own earlier identification with the serpent, replacing the deadly Eastern inscrutibility with a comprehensible version of the Madonna. Of course, *both* are patriarchal constructions of women. The first demonises the alien woman while the second seeks to domesticise her.

THEATRE AND THE SPACE OF THE OTHER 291

Till the end, Cleopatra attempts to maintain some vestiges of power even as she acknowledges Caesar as 'the sole sir o'th' world' (V. ii. 119). It is only when every effort has failed that she has 'immortal longings' (V. ii. 279). Without power 'What should I stay – / In this vile world?' (V. ii. 311–12).

As Cleopatra achieves these false resolutions, the play also abandons the cinematic montage that so adequately expressed the discontinuity of character, the dialectic between inner and outer, political and personal, male and female spaces. The shifts of scene which conveyed both the vacillations of Antony and the unruly theatricality of Cleopatra give way to the elevation of the 'Roman' suicides; to the conventional 'climax' and the stock devices of formal drama, as patriarchal roles and divisions are apparently reinstated. If Cleopatra's fluid identity and play-acting demanded one kind of theatrical form, her new role as Antony's marble-constant wife employs the more classical technique. The Roman theatre takes over from the volatile Egyptian one. The closed space of the monument, the measured actions and tones, the slow, drawn-out scenes and the elevated language all tone down the fiery and unpredictable performances of the earlier Cleopatra. The narrative of masculinity and imperialism regains control but Cleopatra's final performance, which certainly exposes her own vulnerability, not only cheats Caesar but denies any final and authoritative textual closure.

ANOTHER PURPOSE OF PLAYING

Robert Weimann has suggested several reasons for perceiving an approximation of the Brechtian epic in Renaissance drama;[21] an increasing focus on discontinuous identity and on female changeability may be another. In the play just discussed, elements of the disorderly woman are identified with those of the popular stage, and therefore the foregrounding of such women also interrogates the controls and limitations of theatrical space. If there are two styles and forms in the play, they also explore the popular drama's own position within an authoritarian state.

Louis A. Montrose's important essay, 'The purpose of playing' suggests a relationship between authority and Renaissance theatre which we can trace as analogous to that between authority and women.[22] The public theatre and the professional player resisted the drive towards fixity in several ways: their profession was based on a kind of duplicity, or temporary donning of identity; players were upwardly mobile in real life; their costumes were often the discarded clothes of the nobility and defied the dress code;[23] and the plays themselves reveal a pervasive concern with 'fictional situations in which human characters are confronted by change within the self, the family, the body politic, the cosmos'.[24] The protean nature and concerns of the theatre are placed by Montrose against the background of the desperate attempt of the authorities to contain – ideologically, economically and spatially – the enormous and varied mobility of various sections of society; I have suggested that this scenario is also the ideological and political backdrop for the foregrounding of female changeability, duplicity, mobility in the drama.

The drive to limit and contain theatre space was concurrent with and similar to the effort to limit and contain women. In both cases transcience, mobility, alteration, disguise and changeability are seen as subverting a dominant need for stability. Contemporary tracts explicitly connect actors with other unruly social groups; conversely, theatre becomes acknowledged as a disruptive force. As Jean Howard has shown, women figure 'prominently in the anti-theatrical narrative of social disruption . . . (they) are constructed in these texts as the duplicitous, inherently theatrical sex'.[25] Both Howard and Peter Stallybrass[26] quote from Philip Stubbes, in whose writings this comparison becomes very clear: his suspicion of the 'painted sepulchres' of the stage employs the language common in the theme of the white devil. Conversely, he accuses women of proteanism ('Proteus, that Monster, could never chaunge him self into so many fourmes and shapes as these women do') and goes on to level the same charge against actors. Attacks on changeable fashion and clothing draw together the threats of female cross-dressing as well as theatrical disguise – interestingly, transgressive women are accused of being masculine, whereas popular theatre is accused of being effeminate. In both cases the fears are that social and sexual boundaries will be erased. The woman who puts on male clothing is warned '. . . if you will walke without difference, you shall live without reverence: if you will contene order, you must endure the shame of disorder; and if you will have no rulers but your wills, you must have no reward but disdaine and disgrace' (*Haec-Vir*).[27]

Both women and theatre are seen to stray from their allotted spaces in various ways. The physical confines of the home and the playhouse are challenged: for example, Elizabeth fears the subversive potential of Shakespeare's *Richard II* not merely because of its timing before the Essex rebellion, not merely because 'I am Richard II. Know ye not that?' but also because the play, she complains, was performed in 'open streets and houses'.[28] Social and political boundaries are defied by the drama and women as they dress in the garments of their superiors, and if women are seen as attempting to usurp authority, the players are accused of inciting political trouble or rebellion. Ideologically, women threaten the demarcation of the 'private' sphere and popular theatre resists the confinement of dramatic performance.

We may pursue the connections further. The theatre of the period involves not just the general disguise that all drama calls for, but specifically an interchange of gender roles, both literally by boy-actors and thematically by the further exchange of male–female roles. At the same time, female cross-dressing functions as a version of theatricality that extends disguise from the playhouse to social space. Again, parallel to the theatre's growing concern with women, the public controversy on gender-roles becomes increasingly theatricalised: the authors of the pamphlets speak from within adopted roles such as that of the masculine woman, Haec-Vir, or the effeminate man, Hic Mulier. The pamphlets are also a self-consciously dramatic public dialogue between the authors whose pseudonyms confer a particular identity upon them: thus Esther Sowernam replies in 1617 to Joseph Swetnam's *Arraignment of Lewde, Idle, Unconstant and Froward Women* published two years earlier also by letting her name (sour-name) play on the ironies of his (sweet-name). The controversy finally culminates in a straightforward play *Swetnam the Woman-Hater Arraigned by Women* (1620), in which Swetnam is brought on trial before an all-female jury. Shepherd points out that this 'is probably the nearest women of the time got to writing a publicly performed play . . . (which is also) the first case of a female mob sympathetically treated on the Jacobean stage'.[29]

During James's reign there was a drive towards formalising theatre, which can be seen as an attempt precisely to contain and define the audience–theatre relationship. James himself had likened the king to 'one set on stage, whose smallest actions and gestures, all the people gazingly do behold'.[30] The effort to make theatre as well as architecture a part of James's statecraft implicitly acknowledged not only the power of theatre but the theatricality of power.[31] Wotton testified that the Banqueting House at Whitehall, planned by Inigo Jones, James's chief architect, as a place where masques were performed and where ambassadors and royal guests were received, was a place where 'Art became a piece of State'.[32]

Jones created elaborate masques and imported European Palladianism and the Italian proscenium stage with its perspective scenes. The latter relied heavily on arches, which were designed to separate audience from performer, and to reinforce the impression of power and grandeur through formality and distance.

No spatial structure is free of social implications, including those of gender: architecture (and theatre design) is not ideologically inert.[33] The arch was increasingly being used as an emblem of state power; Inigo Jones was exploiting its potential as a symbol of order and grandeur both in the theatre and in public construction. There were arches for James's entrances into London which were carefully designed to be 'triumph(s) in the high Roman style'.[34] Stephen Harrison's *Archs of Triumph* (1603–4), which Ben Jonson described as 'the expression of state and magnificence' were typical of such usage. They can be contrasted to the *ad hoc* stages that were constructed for Elizabeth I's earlier entrances.[35] If the arch effected a separation between the royal actor and his audiences, it also served the purpose of distancing the events of the stage. Formal theatre enacted on the picture frame stage sought to exalt the power of the state as much as the public theatre was seen to threaten it. Later the arch was repeatedly used in colonial architecture as emblematic of imperial might. Hence it is significant that as Antony repudiates Rome in favour of Cleopatra, he uses the arch as a symbol of the Roman empire:

> Let Rome in Tiber melt, and the wide arch
> Of the rang'd empire fall! Here is my space.
>   (I. i. 33–4)

In this context, the opposition of Caesar and Cleopatra in the play can be seen as partially deriving from the contrasting styles of James and Elizabeth. The arch here becomes one of the various spatial signifiers of the conflict between the Egyptian theatre and the Roman, one more way of establishing the dimensions of Cleopatra's theatricality, of suggesting that Egypt and Rome are invested with implications deriving from theatrical practice.

James's anti-woman bias was also picked up by the new architecture and theatre. Inigo Jones conceived of his own architecture and theatre design as 'solid, proportional, *masculine* and unaffected'.[36] If masculinity connotes order and power, then the variety and disorder of the popular theatre is connected yet again to the disturbance offered by unruly femininity.

THE VOLATILE STAGE

Webster's preface to *The White Devil* confesses that 'this is no true dramatic poem'; that it was written for an 'open and black' stage which lacked 'a full and understanding auditory' and on whose audience, resembling 'ignorant asses', 'the most sententious tragedy . . . observing all the critical laws' would be wasted.[37] Jonson's note to the readers of *Sejanus His Fall* makes a similar excuse for writing 'no true poem': '*Nor is it needful, or almost possible*, in these our times, and to such auditors . . . to observe the old state, and splendour of dramatic poems, with preservation of any popular delight'.[38] While formally deferring to the superior status of classical art and deprecating the very audiences they invoke to justify their own departures from it, both these notes indicate the liberating influence of the same open stage that had terrified Elizabeth, and of an interactive audience. Montrose has suggested that

> the actual process of theatrical performance, marked off from the normal flow of social activity, offers its audience (and of course, its performers) an imaginative experience which temporarily removes them from their normal places. In this sense, to go to the playhouse to take part in a play is voluntarily to undergo a marginal experience; it is to cross the interstices of the Elizabethan social and cognitive order.[39]

If the subversive potential of any theatre depends to some degree on such a removal, it also requires, conversely, an *intersection* with social reality. The dynamics of audience participation, as Brecht's dramaturgy demonstrated, generates a certain power in itself. For example, the involvement of the entire population of a town may be elicited by traditional theatre performances in India. Anuradha Kapur describes the annual *Ramlila*, or dramatisation of the epic *Ramayana*, as staged in the town of Ramnagar. Here the city becomes the stage, and all the audience who await the return of the hero-god Rama from exile become actors. Rama's return is endowed with enormous emotional power by the mass participation which renders the stage 'volatile' and 'there is then the hope of great happenings'. The opposite, suggests Kapur, is the effect of a stage where the spectator is isolated:

... the auditorium, and especially the picture-frame stage, creates a series of *calculable* relationships: the enclosed space, the static set and the imprisoned spectator. Short of jumping on to the stage there is scarcely any possibility of transgression ... naturalistic theatre, under the tyranny of certain architectural features is unable to make its space anything other than verisimilar.[40]

The power of theatre therefore derives from its ability to employ strategically both its privileged *removal from* and *extension into* social space. Such a duality is also responsible for the dialectic of its own position – playwrights and players may transgress the social order but are also constituted by it. Thus drama may simultaneously question and confirm normative behaviour; it may both challenge and reinforce the prescriptions for order.[41] The three-way intersections of theatrical, social and female spaces during the Renaissance allow a simultaneous examination of all three.

'TRAVELLING THOUGHTS'

The rigidity of the Western canon, especially as it operates in the colonial situation, was discussed in the first chapter. Reverence for the bard has led to a devaluation of other dramatists of the period. Marlowe leads *up to* Shakespeare and Webster and Jonson *down from* him, but almost no one else is admitted to the charmed circle. In relation to the Romantic poets, Marilyn Butler proposes that 'poets we have installed as canonical look far more interesting individually, and far more understandable as groups, when we restore some of their lost peers'.[42]

I will therefore turn to a somewhat later and almost totally neglected writer, Richard Brome, in order to suggest that some of the issues just discussed are brilliantly focused by his play *The Antipodes*; it could well be a key-text in an alternative curriculum.[43] But Brome's play is useful beyond providing a gloss on Shakespeare. As Walter Cohen points out, one serious limitation of current 'political approaches to Shakespeare' is their almost exclusive emphasis on that dramatist.[44] Pragmatic concerns, even those which have to do with re-reading what we are made to read in the classroom, inevitably lead to such a bias; one of my purposes in interlacing key issues raised by Shakespeare's plays with those of others has been precisely to disallow such a prioritisation. Of course, from the perspective of post-colonial education, the validity of replacing one master-text with another can be questioned, a problem which requires full discussion but is outside the scope of my argument at this point.

More self-consciously than the texts previously considered here, *The Antipodes* looks forward to Brechtian theatre politics – not only preferring fragmentation and multiplicity to the definitive statement, employing various alienation devices, combining the didactic and the comic but also explicitly positing the formation of identity and the function of theatre as related issues. It is truly 'in advance of its time as a contribution to criticism and aesthetics, albeit in a somewhat disguised form'.[45] Even more significantly, the play considers the interrelation of social and psychic space by locating the production of male and female fantasies in the different spaces occupied by men and women. Although focusing neither on the disorderly woman, nor any actual black person, it brings together the issues of race and gender by showing geographical expansion and the attendant production of travel mythology as profoundly gendered.

Criticism of the play (at least prior to Martin Butler's *Theatre and Crisis*) has been, like the label generally attached to Brome, conservative, and has largely ignored the radical thrust of the method as well as the subject of the play. The plot is fairly simple, and revolves around the cure of Peregrine Joyless, a young man so obsessed with 'travelling thoughts' (I. ii. 27), with the wonderful lands, strange peoples, and other 'strangest doings' (I. iii. 10) portrayed in travel books, that he has lost all contact with his actual existence, and most critically with his wife Martha, who is still a virgin after three years of marriage.

Peregrine's name, also used by Jonson in *Volpone*, is derived from the Latin *peregrinus* meaning 'foreign' and means also 'outlandish; . . . an alien resident: a pilgrim or traveller in a foreign country' (*Chambers 20th Century Dictionary*). His sickness in this play dramatises the hold of the enormous range of travel literature during the early years of colonial expansion upon the public imagination. Such literature, as I have remarked in relation to *Othello*, combined myth and facts, entertainment and enquiry, and was filtered through cultural, political and religious prejudice. The ideological effects of the images of strange lands and peoples were not necessarily expansive, but often strengthened existing chauvinism. The racist implications of this have been considered; *The Antipodes* demonstrates the psychological effects of such literature.

In 1555 there appeared Richard Eden's accounts of the first two English voyages to Africa, which combine actual description with fantastic stories. In 1577 Richard Willes's *The History of Travayle* and in 1589 Hakluyt's *Principal Navigations* contributed to the growing fund of travel account-fantasies. Peregrine's visions of 'monsters / Pigmies, and giants, apes and elephants, / Griffins, and crocodiles, men upon women, / And women upon men, the strangest doings' are, however, more specifically drawn from *The Travels of John Mandeville* and especially from the notion therein of an antipodal land.[46]

For Peregrine fantasy results in alienation from his reality, especially from Martha. If his mind soars beyond the colonial horizons, hers withdraws and shrinks to a preoccupation with her bodily fertility in what amounts to a classic case of womb hysteria. Both husband and wife are neurotic, but the 'disorder' of their minds is derived from typically defined gender roles – his is based on the male colonial fantasy of travel, power and excitement; hers on the female one of domesticity and children. Earlier I have considered how the spatial and ideological ghettoisation of women indicates their subordination and conditions their subjectivity; in *The Antipodes* its psychological effects are related to those of colonial expansionism. Once again imperialism and sexism reinforce the prescribed spaces of the female mind. Also typically, whereas Martha's fantasy is dependent upon Peregrine's co-operation, his has no room for her at all. In Christian allegory, ironically, Martha's name symbolises the active life; in the play, we witness her inability even to fantasise about it.

One may here refer usefully to modern studies on the spatial behaviour of the sexes, which have documented how boys' play is obsessed with movement and exterior landscapes whereas girls tend to concentrate on still objects and interior spaces.[47] There is a tendency to explain this by biological differences alone, by referring to girls' awareness of the inner spaces of their bodies instead of seeing how gender differentials in spatial perception are socially induced.[48] Brome's play allows us to locate female hysteria in relation to the gradual expulsion of woman from outer arenas until only her womb remains for her to act her fantasies upon. Even more importantly, it addresses the usually glamourised male sense of 'adventure' as a form of hysteria. Peregrine's disorders are the predecessors of Gulliver's alienation and Kurtz's madness. Significantly, his relationship with his wife emerges as a measure of his cure; 'real knowledge of a woman' will indicate his readiness to adjust to English society. At the end of Act IV, Peregrine consents to embrace Martha because he has been led to believe that she is transformed into a Princess of the Antipodes; so she is integrated into his fantasy.

The Antipodes has been called 'a dramatisation of psychiatric therapy;'[49] apart from Corax in Ford's *The Lover's Melancholy*, Doctor Hughball, to whom Peregrine's father Joyless brings him, is 'the first practising psychiatrist to appear on the English stage'.[50] Hughball lives with Letoy, a 'Phantastic Lord' whose house 'in substance is an amphitheatre of exercise and pleasure' (I. v. 52–3). The two form a sort of director–producer partnership whereby theatre becomes the medium of psychotherapy. They stage a show in which Peregrine is made to live out his fantasy – made to believe that he is actually in Mandeville's 'world of Antipodes', where the people

> In outward feature, language and religion,
> Resemble those to whom they are supposite:
> They under Spain appear like Spaniards,
> Under French Frenchmen, under England English
> To the exterior show; but in their manners,
> Their carriage, and condition of life
> Extremely contrary.
>
> (I. vi. 107–13)

By Brome's time, the phrase 'to act the antipodes' had become a proverbial expression for a reversal of the expected order of things.[51] Brome is also generally drawing upon a long tradition of the world turned upside down which was recurrent in satiric or Utopian literature.[52] There are Shakespearean echoes too in the theme of finding one's 'true' self after a temporary sojourn into the madness of the inverted world. *The Antipodes* in fact draws together various common Saturnalian strands – madness, dislocation, eventual cure, flouting of hierarchy and social criticism. Reversal can be used for a variety of political ends and can serve either as a safety-valve to maintain the status quo or as a radical critique of society, as in More's *Utopia*. In Brome's text, as Martin Butler argues, inversion operates as a 'brilliant structural and analytical tool' for a specifically political critique of Charles's government[53] and also for a more general indictment of all hierarchical societies.

First Hughball describes the Antipodes and its principle of reversal by which 'the people rule / The Magistrates', 'the women overrule the men' and 'As parents here, and masters, / Command there they obey the child and servant' (I. vi. 119–27). The doctor tells Diana, Joyless's young wife, that it is nature, not art that enables Antipodian women to rule over men. Diana's comment, 'Then art's above nature, as they are under us', not only holds art responsible for male domination in her own world but opens up the play's consideration of another sort of theatre and art which can work as therapy, correctively. The ability of art to intervene in both private fantasy and social existence, to mould identity, is repeatedly emphasised. Joyless fears the possible effects of theatre upon Diana and is adamant that she shall not see a play. The Doctor insists that 'she must, if you can hope for any cure' (I. vi. 201). Art has an effect on nature, ideas can shape reality.

As Butler has pointed out, there are two categories of reversal in the Antipodean world. The first are simply amusing and confirm our social beliefs – such as those where old men go to school or merchants ask gentlemen to cuckold them. But the second are more disturbing, firstly because they offer a deeper and more political critique of existing social and gender relations, and secondly because they reveal that a large part of what goes on in the Antipodes actually exists surreptitiously in London. In other words, reversal here is not pure fantastical inversion but part of actual suppressed subversion, as for example when servants rule masters, or women hunt and 'deale abroad / Beyond seas, while their husbands cuckold them, / At home' (I. vi. 169–71). Peregrine is most shocked by sexual inversion:

> Can men and women be so contrary
> In all that we hold proper to each sex?
> (IV. v. 31–2)

At another point, we see a courtier who is a beggar; Diana's repeated comments that such things are the *opposite* of reality only serve to question whether they really are so far removed from the truth. Is it not that courtiers *are* a variety of beggars and churchmen are usurers? So while some illusions here point to the upside-down quality of Charles's England,[54] others depict what is lacking in that society.

There are several aspects of Brome's handling of reversal which lifts it above the common-play-within-the-play device. One is that unlike usual reversals or escapes from reality, neither the Antipodes nor the real world are simply idealised or maligned. Of course the didactic purpose is obvious: just as Letoy and Hughball cure their patients so Brome the doctor-playwright hopes to cure his audience through what has been called comic catharsis. Brome probably drew upon Burton's *Anatomy of Melancholy*, which explained that 'perturbations of the mind' may be rectified by 'some feigned lie, strange news, witty device, artificial invention' and particularly recommended the utility of mirth.[55] Brome refuses to allow the spectator/reader to regard the Antipodean critique of reality as Utopian fantasy; social criticism is not dependent upon idealisation but is made part of a more complex, wry and pluralist approach – such as we encounter in a more self-conscious and polemical way in Brecht. Swinburne was not far from the truth when he commented that the play reveals that life is always and everywhere 'an incongruous congruity of contradictions'.[56]

An aspect of the reversals that has been ignored by existing criticism is the manner in which the relation between England and the Antipodes, and hence of imperial power and its others, is subjected to examination. The scholarly discourses pursued by Peregrine construct it as a land of 'monsters more', but the Antipodes is in fact far from the fantasy land of the grotesque, of all that is alien to European and Christian civilisation: the theatrical enactment visualises it as uncomfortably like England. Moreover, both its similarities and differences are determined by the actors, or the participants in the imperial drama: it is a constructed and not an actual world, created by the imagination of the white traveller, Peregrine, the Doctor, or anyone else who cares to participate in myth-making. Thus the play comes close to apprehending the process whereby cultural, racial and geographical differences are transposed into that curious blend of fact and fiction, fantasy and fears that one finds not just in the travel literature of the period but in most Orientalist writings.

The free interplay of the actors and spectators in *The Antipodes* is also important. Actually, there is not one but three plays: the first is the staging of the Antipodal world for Peregrine's benefit; in the second Letoy pretends to court Diana, the young wife of Peregrine's intensely jealous father Joyless and by witnessing her refusal, the old man is cured; finally there is the masque of the last scene celebrating the triumph of harmony over discord. None of the plays is presented naturalistically – we are never allowed to forget that they are staged, that spectators and participants mingle and interchange positions. Consider the first show, which is primarily put on to cure Peregrine. Besides being the principal spectator, he is also the most crucial actor, for the effect of the drama depends upon his participation. At the same time, the presence of Letoy, Joyless, Diana, Martha and Barbara is a constant reminder that this is but a play. An alienation effect is achieved, not only through the spectators, but also through the Doctor, who is both director and actor in the Antipodean theatre and also in the stage of Peregrine's mind. Letoy similarly punctures the illusion by stepping in and out of the drama: the actors are his men and he plays director to them. The audience are his guests and he plays host to them. At the same time he initiates the second play while the first is still on by beginning to flirt with Diana. The two plays are interwoven, preventing any total absorption in or totalising effect of either of them. The audience is made aware of the significance of its participation; in the manner of epic theatre they are invited to step in and to comment on the action.

There is no tight story either, so that the total effect is one of fragmentation. *The Antipodes* could be said to return, like Brecht's own plays are seen to do, 'to the theatre's simplest elements instead of trying to foster an illusion of reality'.[57] It is, finally, claiming quite a lot for art – in fact no less than Brecht himself: ideological practices and theatre particularly have a definite and material effect on reality and are agents of its change. One might argue that this is not special to Brome, that the notion of comedy as criticism dates back to ancient Greek drama. But Brome goes further than that, for art is a corrective practice only if the audience accepts its diagnosis – the participation of the patient is essential. Theatre then is lifted from a minority entertainment and, again anticipating Brecht, derives its power from audience involvement.

Finally, the play takes a dig at its own practice, for the world it has brought Peregrine back to is not much better than his illusory one. Fantasy also has the power to distort perception in a retrogressive way, as in Peregrine's case. But most importantly, neither kind of imagination is arbitrary but is based on what is available or denied to human beings.

The Antipodes, then, suggests that the basis for male and female spatial fantasies, expansive and contractive respectively, is the gender roles that are socially defined for them, and the desires and fantasies of an entire culture, as they are organised by its mobility or stasis. In other words Brome is examining the formation of subjectivity, including its most elusive and 'private' aspects – through powerfully imposed ideologies, and more self-conscious alternative fantasies that deliberately engage with and subvert them.

From Ania Loomba, *Gender, Race, Renaissance Drama* (Manchester, 1989), pp. 119–41.

NOTES

[Ania Loomba's book deals with the relationship between Gender and Race in a range of Renaissance plays. Central to her argument is the concept of Gender as a social construction which positions women culturally, and Race as a further determinant of social position. In her trenchant analysis of female 'subjectivity' – involving both the characteristics which are socially ascribed to women, and also the sense in which they are 'subjected', and oppressed by men – Loomba evolves a reading which is very sensitive to the ways in which female dramatic characters occupy particular geographical spaces, and the extent to which they are able to subvert and hence change the conditions of their existence. Loomba's analysis derives a considerable added force from her own experience of teaching in India. Ed.]

1. Irving Ribner, *Jacobean Tragedy: The Quest for Moral Order* (London, 1962), p. 1.

2. See also Margot Heinemann, 'How Brecht read Shakespeare', in Jonathan Dollimore and Alan Sinfield (eds), *Political Shakespeare* (Manchester, 1985), p. 203.

3. Kenneth Muir (ed.), *Thomas Middleton, Three Plays* (London, 1975), pp. xiii–xiv.

4. Robert Ornstein, *The Moral Vision of Jacobean Tragedy* (Madison and Milwaukee, 1965). Some thirty years earlier T. S. Eliot (*Selected Essays*, London [1932]) had found that Middleton 'has no point of view, is neither sentimental nor cynical; he is neither resigned nor disillusioned nor romantic; he has no message' (p. 162); Una Ellis-Fermor (*The Jacobean Drama*, London [1936]) detected in him a 'belittling of those human figures which his contemporaries exalt', 'a pitiless abstemiousness' (p. 152). It had been generally concluded, as Eliot did, that Middleton is merely a 'great recorder', 'merely a name which associates with six or seven great plays' (p. 162). So whereas Shakespeare's detachment was seen to stem from a positive morality, that of others was made to neatly tie in with the 'hectic portraits of vice and depravity' to be found in Jacobean drama (Ornstein, p. 3).

5. Bertolt Brecht, *Brecht on Theatre*, ed. and trans. John Willett (London, 1964), p. 161.

6. Robert Ornstein, *The Moral Vision of Jacobean Tragedy*, p. 140.

7. See Heinemann 'How Brecht read Shakespeare', p. 209.

8. Robert Weimann, *Shakespeare and the Popular Tradition in the Theater* (Baltimore, 1978), pp. 176–7.

9. Jonathan Dollimore, *Radical Tragedy: Religion and Ideology in the Drama of Shakespeare and his Contemporaries* (Brighton, 1983).

10. *Brecht on Theatre*, p. 27.

11. See P. K. Datta, Review of A. Ghosh's *The Circle of Reason, Social Scientist*, October 1986.

12. Brian Gibbons, *Elizabethan ad Jacobean Tragedies* (Kent, 1984), p. xviii.

14. Ibid., pp. 322–5.

15. John F. Danby, 'The Shakespearean dialectic: an aspect of *Antony and Cleopatra*', *Scrutiny*, 16 (1949), 196–213. L. C. Knights comments: 'In *Macbeth* we are never in any doubt of our moral bearings. *Antony and Cleopatra*, on the other hand, embodies different and apparently irreconcilable evaluations of the central experience' (quoted J. R. Brown [ed.], *Antony and Cleopatra* [London, 1958], p. 172). Janet Adelman, *The Common Liar* (New Haven, 1973); Catherine Belsey, *The Subject of Tragedy* (London, 1985); Lisa Jardine, *Still Harping on Daughters* (Brighton, 1983); John Holloway, *The Story of the Night* (London, 1961); Maynard Mack, '*Antony and Cleopatra*: the stillness and the dance', in *Shakespeare's Art: Seven Essays*, ed. Milton Crane (Chicago and London, 1973); Julian Markels, *The Pillar of the World: Antony and Cleopatra in Shakespeare's Development* (Columbus, Ohio, 1968); Mark Rose (ed.), *Twentieth Century Interpretations of Antony and Cleopatra* (New Jersey, 1977); Martha Rozett, 'The comic structures of tragic endings: the suicide scenes in *Romeo and Juliet* and *Antony and Cleopatra*', *Shakespeare Quarterly*, 36 (Summer 1985); J. L. Simmons, 'The Comic Pattern and Vision in *Antony and Cleopatra*', *English Literary History*, 36 (1969), 483–501; and Stella Smith, 'Imagery of union, division and disintegration in *Antony and Cleopatra*', *Clafflin College Review*, 1 (May 1977), 15–28, all emphasise different aspects of the heterogeneity foregrounded by the play.

16. Mark Rose (ed.), *Twentieth Century Interpretations of Antony and Cleopatra*, p. 2.

17. Dr Johnson, in J. E. Brown, *The Critical Opinions of Samuel Johnson* (London, 1926), p. 26.

18. John F. Danby, 'The Shakespearean dialectic', p. 197.

19. Dollimore, *Radical Tragedy*, p. 203.

20. Helen Carr, 'Woman/Indian: "the American" and his others', in Francis Barker et al. (eds), *Europe and its Others*, vol. 2 (Colchester, 1985), p. 51.

21. Robert Weimann, *Shakespeare and the Popular Tradition in the Theater*.

22. Louis A. Montrose, 'The purpose of playing: reflections on a Shakespearian anthropology', *Helios*, 7 (1980), 51–74.

23. Lisa Jardine, *Still Harping*, pp. 141–2.

24. Montrose, 'The purpose of playing', p. 63.

25. Jean E. Howard, 'Renaissance anti-theatricality and the politics of gender in *Much Ado About Nothing*', in Jean E. Howard and Marion F. O'Connor (eds), *Shakespeare Reproduced: the Text in History and Ideology* (New York and London, 1987), p. 168.

26. Howard, ibid., p. 168; Peter Stallybrass, 'The history of sexuality in the English Renaissance' (unpublished manuscript), pp. 1, 12.

27. *Haec Vir, or the Womanish Man* (1620) in Barbara J. Baines (ed.), *Three Pamphlets on the Jacobean Anti-feminist Controversy* (New York, 1978).

28. Stephen Greenblatt (ed.), *The Power of Forms in the English Renaissance* (Norman, Oklahoma, 1982, pp. 3–4); see also Jonathan Dollimore, 'Shakespeare, cultural materialism and the new historicism', in Jonathan Dollimore and Alan Sinfield (eds), *Political Shakespeare* (Manchester, 1985), p. 8.

29. Simon Shepherd (ed.), *The Woman's Sharp Revenge: Five Pamphlets from the Renaissance* (London, 1985), p. 55.

30. Dollimore, 'Shakespeare, cultural materialism', p. 8.

31. Architecture and stage design are only one aspect of the interrelation between power and theatricality during the Renaissance, which has been richly focused, for example, by Stephen Greenblatt, *Renaissance Self-Fashioning* (Chicago, 1980); Jonathan Goldberg, *James I and the Politics of Literature; Shakespeare, Donne, and their Contemporaries* (Baltimore and London, 1983); Louis Montrose, 'The purpose of playing'; Leonard Tennenhouse, 'Strategies of State and political plays: '*A Midsummer Night's Dream, Henry IV, Henry V, Henry VIII*, in *Political Shakespeare*, ed. Jonathan Dollimore and Alan Sinfield, and (Tennenhouse) *Power on Display: The Politics of Shakespeare's Genres* (London, 1986).

32. Goldberg, *James I*, pp. 40–4.

33. The ideological loading of spatial structures has to do with the contexts in which they are created, with associations that gather around them, with their settings and usages. The dome, for example, was a symbol of perfection under the Mughals: the Taj Mahal conferred upon it multiple associations of love (it was built by Shah Jahan for his wife Mumtaz Mahal); of might (it took twenty years, much wealth and a vast army of labour to construct it); and of ruthless power (the master-craftsmen who executed it had their thumbs cut off on completion so that they could never build another such monument and the exclusivity of the Taj could be preserved). Coleridge's dome in 'Kubla Khan' carries Orientalist connotations of the glamour, pleasure as well as despotism of the

east. It may be conjectured that the arch codes for power because its shape, like that of the dome, required careful planning and meticulous execution.

34. Goldberg, *James I*, p. 33.

35. D. M. Bergeron, *English Civic Pageantry 1558–1642* (London, 1971), pp. 75–8.

36. Anne Thorne, 'Women's Creativity: Architectural Space and Literature' (unpublished Dip. Arch thesis, Polytechnic of Central London, 1979), p. 57 (emphasis added).

37. John Webster, *The White Devil*, ed. Elizabeth M. Brennan, in *Elizabethan and Jacobean Tragedies* (Kent, 1984), p. 491.

38. Ben Jonson, *Sejanus His Fall*, ed. W. F. Bolton, in ibid., p. 247 (emphasis added).

39. Louis Montrose, 'The purpose of playing', p. 63.

40. Anuradha Kapur, 'Actors, pilgrims, kings and gods: the Ramlila at Ramnagar', *Contributions to Indian Sociology*, 19 (1985), 57 (emphasis added).

41. See Louis A. Montrose, 'Renaissance literary studies and the subject of History', *English Literary Renaissance*, 16 (Winter 1986), 9–11.

42. Marilyn Butler, 'Revising the canon', *TLS*, 4–10 December 1987, p. 1349.

43. Richard Brome, described in the title page of the 1658 version of his comedy, *The Weeding of the Convent Garden* as 'An Ingenious Servant and Imitator of his master: that famously renowed poet Ben Jonson', wrote mainly comedy. *The Antipodes* was composed in 1637 for a new company, Queen Henrietta's, and was first acted at the Salisbury Court playhouse in 1638. Martin Butler has argued that Caroline drama did not break with the concerns of earlier drama, and 'did persistently engage in debating the political issues of the day' (*Theatre and Crisis, 1632–1642* [Cambridge, 1984], p. 1). Institutionalised criticism tends to rigidly demarcate literature of different periods (and to classify these according to the prevailing monarch) – hence Elizabethan, Jacobean and Caroline dramas are often treated as three completely distinct types of theatre.

44. Walter Cohen, 'Political criticism of Shakespeare', in Jean E. Howard and Marion F. O'Connor, *Shakespeare Reproduced*, p. 20.

45. Joe Lee Davis, 'Richard Brome's neglected contribution to comic theory', *Studies in Philology*, 40 (1943), 527.

46. See Richard Brome, *The Antipodes*, ed. Anne Haaker (London, 1966), pp. 16–17.

47. See E. H. Erikson, 'Inner and outer space: some reflections on woman-hood', in Lee and Sussman (eds), *Sex Differences: Cultural and Developmental Dimensions* (London, 1976).

48. See Shirley Ardener (ed.), *Women and Space: Ground Rules and Social Maps* (London, 1981), *passim.*

49. Catherine M. Shaw, *Richard Brome* (London, 1980), p. 123.

50. R. J. Kaufman, *Richard Brome: Caroline Playwright* (New York, 1961). As John Drakakis has suggested to me, Pinch in Shakespeare's *The Comedy of Errors* might be considered as another predecessor of Hughball.

51. Shaw, *Brome*, p. 127.

52. See A. L. Morton, *The English Utopia* (London, 1969).

53. Martin Butler, *Theatre and Crisis*, pp. 215, 220.

54. Ibid., p. 217.

55. See Joe Lee Davis, 'Richard Brome's neglected contribution', p. 524.

56. Quoted ibid., p. 524.

57. Robin Ridless, *Ideology and Art: Theories of Mass Culture from Walter Benjamin to Umberto Eco* (London, 1984).

12

Renaissance Anti-theatricality, Anti-feminism, and Shakespeare's 'Antony and Cleopatra'

JYOTSYNA SINGH

I

Audiences and readers of Shakespeare's *Antony and Cleopatra* generally remember Cleopatra in terms of her varied histrionic moments. In wooing Antony, she displays contrary and shifting moods: 'If you find him sad, / Say I am dancing; if in mirth, report / That I am sudden sick' (I. iii. 3–5).[1] In ruling her subjects, she commands distant adulation by staging herself in pageants, displays a playful familiarity toward her serving-women, or cruelly strikes a slave; and in responding to Caesar's victory, she declares her obedience, but then undermines his authority by enacting a grand suicide and an imaginary union with Antony: 'I am again for Cydnus, / To meet Mark Antony' (V. ii. 228–9). While the range and virtuosity of Cleopatra's performances is dazzling, one is particularly struck by a pervasive connection between her histrionics and the blurring of gender boundaries. A scene that immediately comes to mind is when Cleopatra finds delight in her memory of cross-dressing with Antony:

> . . . and next morn,
> Ere the ninth hour, I drunk him to his bed;
> Then put my tires and mantles on him, whilst
> I wore his sword Philippan.
>
> (II. v. 20–3)

Here, Cleopatra stirs the worst Roman fears of effeminacy by bringing to life the myth of Hercules in women's clothes serving Omphale,
or of Venus armed in victory over Mars. Why this image of Antony
in female attire makes the Romans anxious is understandable. Very
quickly in the play one can note that their condemnation of Egypt,
where Antony is 'transformed / Into a strumpet's fool' (I. i. 12–13),
is in essence a fear of a mutable, and thereby 'effeminised', identity.
In fact, what they consistently uphold as the 'true' Roman self –
whether individual or collective – reveals itself as an ideal of masculinity premised on an exclusion of the feminine. From their perspective, when Antony is with Cleopatra, he is 'not Antony' (I. i. 57), as
his 'sport' in Egypt makes him 'not more manlike / Than Cleopatra,
nor the queen of Ptolemy / More womanly than he' (I. iv. 5–7). Thus,
if Antony is to remain the Roman hero, Cleopatra must be
marginalised as the temptress, witch, adultress.[2]

This ideology of exclusion through which the Romans perceive
the power relations – and gender relations – of their world is repeatedly dismantled by Cleopatra as she represents, and in the scene of
cross-dressing literally reconstitutes, the Roman divisions between
the masculine and the feminine. Categories such as these, she demonstrates, are flexible and open to improvisation. In her dramatic plots
Antony can play both warrior and lover as she shows him that these
roles are not antithetical to one another, and that combining them
does not imply effeminacy. Moreover, Antony's Roman 'honour
[that] calls [him] hence' to Rome, Cleopatra points out, can be
played as a 'scene / Of excellent dissembling' (I. iii. 78–80) so that
Egypt and Rome can enact the same fiction of 'perfect honour',
which need not be a Roman or masculine prerogative. By thus
drawing attention to the particular ways in which gender differences
are constructed, the theatrical queen puts into question the very
notion of a unified, stable identity.

To suggest that Cleopatra is a performer and playmaker has
become a critical commonplace. While traditionally, critics considered the Egyptian queen's histrionics intrinsic to her nature as a
femme fatale, recent feminist studies view her theatricality as a
source of empowerment and as a positive value in the play.[3] Most,

however, essentialise Cleopatra into a special, charismatic individual given to self-dramatisation. My interest lies in examining Cleopatra's theatrical function in the play, as outlined above, in relationship to specific, historically situated debates about the theatre and women in the sixteenth and seventeenth centuries, especially as they were articulated in the anti-theatrical and anti-feminist writings of the period. I am not seeking to establish a direct influence between the documents and the play – which has its recognised sources in Plutarch's *Lives of the Romans* and Vergil's *Aeneid*; but rather, I wish to explore the ways in which the associations between women and the theatre emerge as a significant concern in both dramatic representation and social commentary.[4]

It has already been suggested that the sixteenth- and seventeenth-century detractors of the theatre and of women represent theatricality in the rhetoric of feminine appeal and vice versa.[5] In their response to Cleopatra, the Romans also perceive the feminine and the theatrical in similar interchangeable terms. For them, as for the tract writers, authentic human identity is clearly the prerogative of a universalised and coherent male subject, who must resist being seduced and 'feminised' by the possibility of changeable, multiple selves. The fact that both the social and dramatic contexts focus on the notion of a histrionic personality suggests the lingering influence of the orthodox doctrine of a hierarchical universe. In the official homily of obedience of 1559, as read in Elizabethan services, all English subjects were exhorted to accept their God-given roles:

> Everye degre of people in theyr vocation and callyng, and office hath appointed to them [by god], theyr duety and ordre. Some are in hyghe degree, some in lowe, some kynges and prynces, some inferiors and subjects, . . . Fathers and chyldren, husbandes and wives, riche and poore. . . . For where there is no ryghte ordre, there reigneth all abuse, carnal libertie, synne and Babilonicall confusyon.[6]

While this picture of the world was undoubtedly appealing to those who benefited from it, it could not contain the sweeping social and economic transformations affecting English society in the sixteenth and seventeenth centuries. Social historians testify to unprecedented displacements in society caused by a complex interplay of factors such as population growth, inflation, changes in agrarian modes of production, and a widening gap between the privileged and growing numbers of poor, masterless, landless, and indigent.[7] The effect of this social flux was a widespread perception of a 'crisis of order', a major feature of which was a perceived threat to the patriarchal structures of the time – or specifically, to 'natural' distinctions between gender roles.[8]

While the polemicists respond to these social changes by discursively constructing a static society in which identities are fixed, Shakespeare's text, which itself is a play, celebrates theatricality – with all its implications of social and ontological instability – even as it dramatises a resistance to it. Thus, read in relationship to the anti-theatrical and anti-feminist tracts, *Antony and Cleopatra* seems both to reproduce and to contest their conception of a social order in which women and actors are seen as duplicitously subverting the 'natural' boundaries of social and sexual difference. Through this formulation, I open the play to the historical moment of its genesis, underscoring its particular response to the tension between 'official' theories of order and the actual disruptions in traditional social hierarchies and gender roles in Renaissance England.

II

The proponents of anti-theatricalism in sixteenth- and seventeenth-century England launched their attacks on the stage from 1577 to the closing of the theatres in 1642. There are variations in the approaches taken by individual polemicists, suggesting in part an increasing unease about the popularity of drama, but there are also remarkable similarities that express consistently shared concerns.[9] I will examine some tracts of writers such as Northbrooke, Gosson, and Rankins among others, covering the years till about 1600, in an attempt to show that while some of their objections are grounded in practical reasons such as the fostering of idleness by the public theatres, in general, the polemicists' overwrought rhetoric is aimed sweepingly at anything associated with pleasure, sexuality, femininity, with succumbing to feeling, and consequently, with the dissolution of all familiar boundaries.[10] In conceiving of theatrical performance in these erotic terms, the anti-theatricalists, it seems, are revealing their fear of both effeminacy and femininity. As an overt expression of their concern, they condemn transvestism on the stage for effeminising the young actors and their male audiences who, supposedly titillated by homoerotic fantasies, lose their manhood or manliness.[11] But in a more insidious sense, their criticism of the stage, I believe, reflects a dread of an unrestrained femininity disrupting the conventional boundaries of sexual difference crucial to the preservation of the patriarchal culture of the time.[12] Thus their attack on the 'immoral' effects of stage plays reveals itself as an anxiety about fixing the meaning of masculinity and femininity.

The condemnation of plays and other pleasurable pastimes, found as early as 1577 in John Northbrooke's *A Treatise wherein Dicing, Dauncing, Vaine playes, or Enterluds . . . are reproved*, carries with it a prescriptive definition of manhood and womanhood.[13] Northbrooke's criticism of all forms of idleness expresses the Protestant work ethic in a developing mercantile economy.[14] Within this context, however, he constructs an ideal of stoic manhood whereby in a dialogue between youth and age, the (male) youth is exhorted to distinguish between a 'beastly and slothfull idlenesse . . . [and] an honest and necessarie idlenesse' (F. iij), and to remember that the Sabbath is not for 'carnall pleasures, as the wicked and ungodlye are wonte, but for godlynesse and virtues sake' (F. iij). 'Vaine playes and Enterludes', like Bathsheba's charms that snared David, are among the pastimes that Northbrooke considers a threat to men's virtue (J. iij). Furthermore, as plays and players represent 'whoredome', 'no wives or maydens, . . . that . . . content and please . . . honest men, [should] be found and seene at common Playes' (J. iij). Being seen at the theatre where she may be 'desired with so many eyes', and where her virtue may be compromised, a woman may lose her socially acceptable identity.

Northbrooke's anxiety about the theatre as a site of idleness and immorality pales in contrast to the intensifying dread of the disruptive effects of theatricality found in later tracts. Stephen Gosson, in his last tract, *Playes Confuted in Five Actions* (1582), launches a broad attack on all plays as the creations of the devil.[15] In Gosson's idealist construction of the world, 'there can bee no truce, no league, no manner of agreemente [between God and the Devil], because the one is holy, the other unpure; the one good, the other evill' (B4).[16] Central to his moral scheme is the notion of a fixed God-given human identity; 'God hath made us in his owne likenesse' (B4), Gosson reminds his readers, and goes on to attack plays as satanic inventions that draw actors and audiences to participate in lying fictions: 'In Stage Playes for a boy to put on the attyre, the gesture, the passions of a woman, to take upon him the title of a Prince with counterfeit porte and traine, is by outward signes to shewe themselves, otherwise than they are, and so within the compasse of a lye' (E4). Like the other polemicists, Gosson is particularly disturbed by the blurring of gender boundaries on stage. Citing a number of biblical and medieval religious sources, the writer asserts, 'The Law of God straightly forbides men to put on women's garments that are set downe for signes distinctive between sexe and sexe, to take unto us those garments that are manifest signs of another sexe is to falsifie, forge, and adulterate contrarie to the express rule of God' (E3).

In Gosson's eyes the stage is a site of contamination – a place where natural distinctions of identity are blurred, confused, and adulterated in a parody of God's act of forming human nature.[17] Audiences are simply seduced by the dramatic effect that 'whets [them] to wantonness . . . and [through which] the mind like a stringe, being let downe, [is] pitcht . . . to his key of carnall delight' (F5). Repeatedly, in Gosson's attack, theatricality is represented in the rhetoric of feminine sexual appeal: theatrical spectacles evoke troubling desires that 'breedeth a hunger, a thirst after pleasure' (F6), and make gazers 'unfit for manly discipline' (C2), as they 'effeminate and soften the hearts of men' (G4). What emerges from this line of argument is an assertion of masculinity predicated on a denial of pleasure, of desire – and of anything associated with female sexuality.

Not only Gosson, but other anti-theatrical writers also emphasise the erotics of dramatic performance. William Rankins, in *A Mirrour of Monsters* (1587),[18] views players as deceiving 'monsters' who are sent by Satan 'to lead the people with intising shewes to the divell, to seduce them to sinne' (B.ii), and envisions the stage as a site on which the marriage of pride and lechery takes place – a site which Rankins terms 'for [its] abhomination, the chappell Adulterinum' (B. iiij). The union of the bride and bridegroom in this simple allegory signals the loss of a heroic manliness: the bridegroom is 'Like as Mars when he hadde beene wearied with warlike exployts, used to entertaine his Lady Venus when . . . they were taken in a nette' (C. ii). Rankins goes on to attack players for a host of undesirable attributes such as idleness, flattery, ingratitude, and blasphemy, but, in general, seems obsessively focused on their threat to virtuous masculine identity: players present before the eyes of 'young wits' such 'inchaunting Charmes, and bewitched wyles, to alienate theyre mindes from vertue, that hard wyll it for a wit well stayde to abyde the same' (E. i). Weakening masculine discipline, plays 'bewitcheth the myndes of menne' away from 'the profitable fruits of virtuous labour' (C. iii). Frequently comparing the deceitful flattery of players to seductive female charms, Rankins exhorts his readers to beware of their dangerous allure: 'Let us arme ourselves against the damnable enticings of these hellish feendes [the players] with the wise regard of prudent Ulises, who for feare lest he should be mooved with the pleasant harmonie of singing Syrens, bound himselfe and his Mates to the mast of his Shippe' (E. i). In another instance, he rallies theatre audiences to resist temptation as the 'young Egyptian did' when placed in a 'sumptuous Chamber' with the 'fayrest Concubine in all his Courte, with her embracings and sweete perswasions' (E. i).

Such cautionary anecdotes are typical of the views held by most polemicists. However, it is interesting to note that while they recognise that theatres may snare 'faire women' into wantonness and adulterous trysts, they generally imagine the spectators as male. And nothing preoccupies them as much as the pernicious effects of plays on the 'manhood' of their viewers. While there is a certain irony in their fear, considering that corporeal representations of female sexuality were excluded from the stage during the period, the source of it lies in the powerful cultural stereotype of women as duplicitous seducers – a stereotype that is easily transferred to actors.[19] In order to understand fully the connection between the theatre and female sexuality forged by the anti-theatricalists, let us now turn to its parallel in the anti-feminist polemic of the period. Katharine Maus makes a strong case for this interrelationship when she suggests that in the Middle Ages and the Renaissance, women and the theatre were subject to attack from the same rhetorical position – and that 'suspicion of female sexuality and suspicion of the theatre can be considered two manifestations of the same anxiety'.[20] Just as the anti-theatricalists perceive all play-acting as a form of satanic deceit, a cover-up for one's real identity, anti-feminists deride women for hiding their sinful interior by their alluring appearance.

Most anti-feminist tracts draw heavily on the stereotype of the duplicitous seductress. Edward Gosynhill, in *The Schoolhouse of women* (1541?), like other misogynist pamphleteers, warns men against women's 'fair, glozing countenance' and 'sugared utterance' and gives instances of how simple men are 'Deceived . . . where they most trust' (p. 154).[21] Mentioning legendary women, like Herodias, Jezebel, Delilah, whose names are synonymous with sexual appeal and deceit, the critic suggests that all women delude men by their physical attraction, 'Trim[ming] themself every day new, / And in their glasses pore and pry, / . . . to allure the masculine' (p. 145). Female fashions are thus a frequent target of attack among anti-feminists. For instance, Gosson, in his lighthearted pamphlet *Pleas-*

ant quippes for upstart newfangled gentlewomen (1596)[22] asks: 'these painted faces which they [women] weare, / can any tell from whence they cam? / Don Satan, Lord of fayned lyes, / All these new fangles did devise' (p. 5). And Joseph Swetnam accuses women of similar hypocrisies at greater length in *The Arraignment of Lewd, froward, idle, and unconstant women* (1615).[23] Women, according to him, 'are in shape Angels but in qualities Devils. . . . They have myriad devices to entice, bewitch, and deceive men' (p. 205); 'some they keep in hand with promises, and some they feed with flattery, and some they delay with dalliances, and some they please with kisses' (p. 201).

What is under attack in both the anti-theatrical and anti-feminist tracts is the notion of a changeable, histrionic personality. Critics such as Katharine Maus and Jean Howard point out that in the eyes of the polemicists women and actors by their very changeability erase boundaries.[24] In general, the tract writers fear that social hierarchies are no longer stable or clearly demarcated when we 'disdaine the callinge he [God] hath placed us in'.[25] Quite understandably, then, their condemnation of plays and of women reveals itself as a desire to hold in place an essentialist ideology that views human identity as immutable and God-given rather than socially constructed. While actors in this ideal, stratified world are to be suppressed, women are exhorted to curb their fickle, changeable natures and conform to static stereotypes of feminine virtue, often taken from the Bible.[26]

From the polemicists' general concern for the breakdown of established categories by tampering with God's handiwork, there emerges, as we have seen, an obsessive concern for the erotic effects of histrionic displays on gazers. Of course, whether stirred by women or plays, lust characterises disorder and corruption.[27] But when the tract writers condemn all forms of enticing play-acting they are, I believe, expressing a *specific* masculine fear of a loss of identity through attraction to the female. Making little distinction between the self-adornment of women and dramatic spectacles that 'ravish the sence', the polemicists warn against all displays that stir sensual desires in men and 'effeminate the mind like pricks unto vice'. Therefore, for a man to allow himself to be engulfed by sensual pleasures signals a loss of masculinity.

It is particularly telling to observe how this spectre of the effeminised male haunts the anti-theatricalists: while they attack theatres for specific social evils such as the breeding 'of plague and vice, traffic congestion and mob violence, inefficient workers and dangerous ideas',[28] their anxieties about this site of social disorder often co-alesce on the image of threatened masculinity. Gosson, in *The Schoole of Abuse* (1579),[29] explains the appeal of plays and other pleasurable activities by lamenting how the 'olde discipline of Englande' has changed since 'wee were schooled with these abuses' (B8). The prevailing interest in 'banqueting, playing, pipying, and dauncing' (B8v), according to him, has blurred sexual differences by effeminising men: 'Our wreastling at armes, is turned to wallowying in Ladies laps, our courage, to cowardice, our running to ryot, our Bowes into Bolles, and our Dartes to Dishes' (C1). Thus it seems that their discussion of theatricality, so dependent on their fear of changing gender roles, inevitably returns to the issue of what it means to be masculine or feminine. Such polarising tendencies clearly place these anti-theatrical and anti-feminist narratives within a larger body of cultural texts – sermons, homilies, proclamations, and preambles to statutes – devoted to naturalising a hierarchical scheme of social, political, and cosmological order. Common to all these texts are distinct standards of exclusion and inclusion by which the Eliza-bethans and Jacobeans imagined their lived relation to the world, but which were often not sustained by reality.[30]

III

By 1608, when *Antony and Cleopatra* first appeared in the Sta-tioners' Register, Shakespeare, among others, had already glorified on stage a number of histrionic figures – self-conscious actors and dramatists like Richard III, Falstaff, and Hamlet as well as the playful heroines of comedy like Rosalind and Viola. An interest in the theatrical nature of human identity is evident in most of Shake-speare's works. In this play, however, associations between the feminine and the theatrical, as embodied in Cleopatra, function specifically both to reveal and to subvert the existing ideology of order by which traditional sexual and social hierarchies were held in place. Conventionally, the play has been read as a clash between abstract categories such as reason versus passion or politics versus love. Inherent to such readings is the tendency to naturalise patriar-chal stereotypes that often equate Rome with reason and public duty and Egypt with sensuality and emotional excess.[31] Recent critics have tried to break free from traditional gender prejudices, but they too, in most instances, tend to view the play as being non-ideological.

However, when one contextualises the play within the controversial public debates on the theatre and on women, one realises that the issues at stake in the Rome/Egypt opposition are far from being abstract or universal, and instead, are closely linked to the preservation of the patriarchal order in Renaissance England.

The terms of the conflict between the Romans and Cleopatra emerge early in the dialectical structure of the play.[32] While Roman actions and speech promote a hierarchical view of political order and an essentialist conception of human identity, Cleopatra's histrionic mode of being disrupts such notions of fixity. In their formal rhetoric, at least, the Romans evoke the image of a stable empire; Caesar, who rules over the 'third o'th'world' (II. ii. 67) imagines that a 'hoop should hold [him and Antony] staunch, from edge to edge / O'th'world' (II. ii. 120–1). Quite arbitrarily, he draws boundaries: their empire is to be divided among all three 'world Sharers' (Lepidus, Octavius, Antony) whom Pompey acknowledges as 'The senators alone of this great world, / Chief factors for the gods' (II. vi. 9–10), and 'Wars 'twixt [them] would be / As if the world should cleave' (III. iv. 30–1). The basis of such assertions of power is the exclusion or control of women. By the Roman creed, Antony must remain the 'triple pillar of the world', and if he faces a choice 'between [women] and a great cause [women] should be esteemed nothing' (I. ii. 140). Octavia, of course, is quite literally 'esteemed nothing' and therefore acceptable as a woman – and as a convenient pawn in Octavius's and Antony's power struggle.

Implicit to the Roman ideology of exclusion is a fear of the loss of male identity through an attraction to the female. The picture of a threatened masculinity the Romans construct seems to give validity to the anti-theatrical and anti-feminist polemic, especially in its negative associations between female charms and duplicitous shows. The Egyptian queen's 'infinite variety', as they portray it, applies interchangeably to her sexual appeal and to her role-playing, and is clearly antithetical to the Roman myth of a stable and unified male subject. From the opening scene, it is apparent that in Roman eyes Antony's image as a warrior, and as a Roman, becomes diffuse in his moments as lover. Seeing him with the Egyptian queen Antony's comrades regret that the 'plated Mars' has become a 'strumpet's fool' (I. i. 13). Now, they believe, 'he is not Antony, [as] / He comes too short of that great property / Which still should go with Antony' (I. i. 57–9), and wish for 'better deeds' which will make him reject his 'dotage' to a woman and reclaim his honour. This scene prefigures the continuing Roman impulse to defend themselves against Cleopatra's repertoire of charms. Even as they devalue her 'playfulness', they often recognise its appeal to their senses and feelings – a recognition expressed by Enobarbus ('We cannot call her winds and waters sighs and tears; [yet] they are greater storms and tempests than almanacs can report' [I. ii. 148–50]) and more fully experienced by Antony as he seeks to break away from the 'enchanting queen' (I. ii. 129) who alienates him from his Roman self.

Octavius Caesar marks the precise boundaries of the desired Roman identity on his first appearance on stage in I. iv. when he mocks at Antony's 'revels' with Cleopatra in Alexandria:

> he fishes, drinks, and wastes
> The lamps of night in revel; is not more manlike
> Than Cleopatra, nor the Queen of Ptolemy
> More womanly than he . . .
> . . . You shall find there
> A man who is the abstract of all faults.
>   (I. iv. 4–9)

As Caesar sees it, Antony's sport in Egypt has collapsed divisions that are crucial to the Romans. He has conflated his masculinity with femininity, being 'not more manlike than Cleopatra'; he has equated the importance of his 'kingdom' with a 'mirth' and forgotten his noble identity in 'tippling with a slave' (18–19).

Soon afterwards, in the same scene, Octavius wistfully recapitulates Antony's past heroism in battle, extolling masculinity as a form of stoicism:

>   . . . When thou once
> Was beaten from Modena, where thou slew'st
> Hirtius and Pansa, consuls, at thy heel
> Did famine follow, whom thou fought'st against,
> Though daintily brought up, with patience more
> Than savages could suffer. Thou didst drink
> The stale of horses and the gilded puddle
> Which beasts would cough at. Thy palate then did deign
> The roughest berry on the rudest hedge.
> ...
>   On the Alps
> It is reported thou didst eat strange flesh,
>   . . . And all this –
> . . .

Was borne so like a soldier that thy cheek
So much as lanked not.

(I. iv. 56–71)

Speaking in the 'official' Roman voice, Octavius clearly promotes a definition of masculinity that preserves the myth of Roman greatness. And while his distinction between Egypt, where Antony fills 'His vacancy with his voluptuousness' (I. iv. 26), and Rome, which beckons him to 'th'field', anticipates Roman fears about contaminating their manhood with female attributes, it also reveals their impossibly idealist view of the 'true' warrior. There is enough evidence in the play to show that the deeds of Rome's heroes do not conform to their inflated reputations. Therefore, they must mark Cleopatra as an external threat in order to sustain their myth. Throughout the play, Antony's men blame Cleopatra for their general's decline: she is the 'Egyptian dish' (II. vi. 124), and Antony has given his 'potent regiment to a trull' (III. vi. 95). They regret that their 'leader's led, / And [they] are women's men' (III. vii. 69–70) and, in the end, believe that the 'god Hercules, whom Antony loved, / Now leaves him' (IV. iii. 17–18). Thus, instead of allowing Antony his moments as a lover, they label him as effeminate and repudiate his authority.

A useful way of viewing this Roman discourse is to note its resemblance to what one critic describes as 'the logocentric, masculine tradition of Renaissance historiography, written by men, devoted to the deeds of men, glorifying the masculine virtues of courage, honour, and patriotism, and dedicated to preserving the names of past heroes'.[33] Plutarch's moralising history, on which the play is based, is also male-centred, and in its simplest form, tells the tale of a 'Great Man and a Temptress'.[34] Detractors of plays and of women seem equally dependent on these cultural and historical paradigms. Freely, and quite eclectically, they draw on masculine traditions in history and literature to bolster their argument. Just as the Romans in *Antony and Cleopatra* evoke images of Aeneas, Mars, and Hercules as prototypes for Antony's struggle in the snare of female charms, tract writers allude to similar figures – 'Ulises' and 'Mars', for instance – as notable examples of men resisting feminine wiles. In both the Roman discourse and the social texts, the particular choice of literary/historical models is important only in so far as it perpetuates the threat of the alluring, duplicitous female. What we learn here is how particular cultural mythologies are circulated and affirmed in the service of specific interests – in this case those of the patriarchy.

To sum up, the Roman discourse in the play embodies the ortho-dox impulse to fix identity – or, specifically, to secure the myth of the male hero against threats of demystification. Thus, quite understand-ably, their vision in the play closely approximates Plutarch's version of history which privileges the male perspective, and in which the Herculean Antony suffers from the 'sweet poison of Cleopatra's love'.[35] Critics who look for a moral centre in the play often privilege the Roman perspective, reinforcing the intentionality of Plutarch's account, but overlooking Shakespeare's own ambivalent response to an 'official' reading of history.[36] A fact that escapes their notice is that the play does not ask to be seen as a univocal construct, shaped by a single, monolithic tradition. Instead, what is more obvious is that Cleopatra's histrionic revisions of the Roman myth repeatedly disrupt the continuity between Plutarch's account and Shakespeare's play – even though Caesar's final victory is assured by history.

Cleopatra's sense of self, as opposed to the Romans, is consist-ently 'playful'. When life is experienced as a performance, she demonstrates, then all assumptions of selfhood become tenuous. Cleopatra's subversion of the Roman claims to a stable identity gains particular significance when we note her identification with the figure of the alluring, changeable seductress who figures prominently in the anti-theatrical and anti-feminist narratives. There is enough evidence to suggest that the Romans perceive her as bewitching and duplicitous. Creating her own theatrical space in Egypt, where, as Pompey puts it, 'witchcraft join[s] with beauty, lust with both!' the Egyptian queen transforms the noble Antony into a 'libertine in a field of feasts' (II. i. 22–3).

Cleopatra's changeableness obviously attracts the Romans, who often resemble fascinated but uneasy spectators of a play. In the opening scene, Philo urges his companion to 'Behold and see' (I. i. 13) as Cleopatra incites and stages their general's transformation:

> . . . his goodly eyes,
> That o'er the files and musters of the war
> Have glowed like plated Mars, now bend, now turn
> . . .
> . . . [and] His captain's heart,
> . . .
> . . . is become the bellows and the fan
> To cool a gypsy's lust.
>
> (I. i. 2–10)

Later, Enobarbus's imaginative response to her grand self-presentation on the barge dramatises her effect over her own people as well as the suppressed Roman attraction for her and for Egypt. On this occasion, when her femininity is synonymous with 'seeming' as her person 'beggared all description' (II. ii. 203), the Romans listening to Enobarbus seem enthralled by the 'infinite variety' of Cleopatra's histrionic and sexual enticements. Like them, the play's audiences are forced to recognise that 'Age cannot wither her, nor custom stale / Her infinite variety' (II. ii. 240–1).

Clearly then, we can make a significant connection between Cleopatra's performances and stage plays in the light of the anti-theatrical conception of theatrical experience as female and of the generic spectator as male. A stage play, the polemicists argue, is like a 'painted woman', beckoning its viewers into a sexualised engagement that few can resist. In *Antony and Cleopatra*, Shakespeare does not refute this argument, but he clearly puts a more positive construction upon the conflation of the feminine and theatrical than was found in the cultural orthodoxies of the time. The very qualities that characterise the Renaissance stereotype of the duplicitous female – beauty, eroticism, changeability, ingenuity – are those that enrich and empower Cleopatra's artistry in shaping her own self-representations and in challenging those of the Romans.

Why does the playwright make the Egyptian queen's specifically 'feminine' qualities the source of her theatrical power? To answer this question, I will first examine some aspects and effects of Cleopatra's distinctive mode of dramatic *improvisation*.[37] Throughout the play one can observe how Cleopatra uses the Roman myth of honour as a manipulable fiction. Philo evokes one version of this myth in the opening scene when he idealises Antony as Mars and implicitly designates Cleopatra as a Venus of sensual temptation, weakening the great general.[38] Cleopatra does not accept this or any other fixed identity. Instead, she constantly revises and reworks their narrative of Venus and Mars to dramatise in positive terms her 'playful' engagement with Antony and her queenly role before her subjects.

In the opening scene, she undermines Philo's judgement by enacting before Antony a vital and positive scenario of their love, leading him to exult in the dissolution of familiar Roman boundaries: 'Let Rome in Tiber melt. . . . The nobleness of life / Is to do thus' (I. i. 33, 37). Later, when Antony departs for Rome, with the firm resolve to break the 'Egyptian fetters', Cleopatra challenges the reductive Roman view of herself and Antony with a transcendent vision of love: 'Eternity was in our lips and eyes, / Bliss in our brows' bent' (I. iii. 35–6). Her model of eternal love, however, immediately reveals its tenuousness when faced with Antony's wavering affections: 'I am quickly ill and well, / So Antony loves' (I. iii. 72–3).

These exchanges establish the pattern for Cleopatra's strategy of improvising on Roman fictions and revealing them as constructed and arbitrary. At one moment, she upholds the Roman view of Antony as the 'greatest soldier of the world', and then calls him the 'greatest liar' (I. iii. 38–9) in denying their love. Or, when she addresses Antony as a 'Herculean Roman' (I. iii. 86), she suppresses the Roman view of him as an enfeebled Hercules held captive by feminine charms. By improvising on Antony's identification with Hercules, Cleopatra questions not only the Roman version of the myth, but also their assumptions about her marginality. After these opening scenes, we do not see Antony in Egypt again until III. vii, but through her many 'becomings', Cleopatra reminds us of his role as a lover – which the Romans trivialise and Antony tries to suppress. She plays out his divided disposition in Rome: 'He was not sad . . . / . . . he was not merry, / . . . his remembrance lay / in Egypt with his joy' (I. v. 55–8). More subversively, she violates the Roman concept of manhood by evoking the famous cross-dressing scene, mentioned earlier in this essay. On this occasion, the exchange of clothes, and to some extent of sexual characteristics, disrupts the sexual hierarchy of the Romans whereby Rome is perceived as a heroic and masculine empire and Egypt a kingdom of women and eunuchs.

While Cleopatra evokes an association with the armed Venus in the cross-dressing scene, she enhances and complicates her role as Venus in the public pageant described by Enobarbus. Here, her feminine charms – her sensuality and eroticism – coalesce with her artifice to hold her audiences in rapture:

> For her own person,
> It beggared all description . . .
> . . .
> O'erpicturing that Venus where we see
> The fancy outwork nature...
> . . .
> . . . From the barge
> A strange invisible perfume hits the sense.
> . . . The city cast
> Her people out upon her.
> (II. ii. 203–19)

In Cleopatra's various roles, then, the legend of Venus emerges as many-sided and contingent: while seeming to threaten Antony's masculinity in the cross-dressing scene, she also transforms the Venus/Mars myth into a context for a playful eroticism in which sexual identities are confused. But when she plays Venus on the 'burnished throne', her erotic appeal merges into a larger picture of queenly grandeur and power. In thus shaping her self-representations, for public or private consumption, Cleopatra seems particularly responsive to assertions of power through improvisational role-playing.

These histrionic revisions of the Venus/Mars myth afford one instance of the diverse, manipulable elements making up Cleopatra's repertoire. They are clearly a part of her sustained strategy of collapsing the distinctions made by the Romans between Antony's role as effeminised lover and masculine warrior. Repeatedly in the play Antony tries to deny his attraction for Cleopatra and thereby, to deny his fickle and changeable nature. Near the end of the play, however, a new character, Eros, appears on stage, and his name signals Antony's fuller acceptance of his own role as lover, and more importantly, of a new playful sense of self. Only now is he able to experience an utter dissolution of personality:

Sometime we see a cloud that's dragonish:
A vapour sometime like a bear or lion,
. . .
That which is now a horse, even with a thought
The rack dislimns, and makes it indistinct
As water is in water . . .
My good knave Eros, now thy captain is
Even such a body. Here I am Antony,
Yet cannot hold this visible shape.
(IV. xiv. 2–14)

In response to Antony's feelings of annihilation, Cleopatra, the consummate actress, improvises a moment of high tragedy: 'To th'monument! / Mardian, go tell him I have slain myself; / Say that the last I spoke was "Antony"' (IV. xiii. 6–8). The purpose of Cleopatra's fiction is to help him recover a sense of selfhood that is heroic in a fuller sense of the word than the Romans allow. As a result, even while committing suicide in the high Roman way, Antony ascribes more meaning to his role as lover: 'I will be / A bridegroom in my death, and run into't / As to a lover's bed' (IV. xiv. 99–101).

At the moment of his death, Antony transcends the rigid boundaries dividing Egypt and Rome – as well as the rigid conception of self. If the Roman value system defines him as a feminised male, a Hercules in bondage to Omphale, a Mars trapped by Venus, Cleopatra invests his effeminacy with a richness not in exclusion from, but within the context of, the Roman heroic model.[39] We still see him in the image of Aeneas, but her vision reformulates the Roman ideal of public duty by emphasising Aeneas's commitment to Dido over his duty to war. Therefore, beyond death, Antony can visualise his reunion with Cleopatra in a transmuted image of Aeneas and Dido in the Elysian Fields, rather than forever separated as in Vergil's version: 'Where souls do couch on flowers, we'll hand in hand. / . . . / Dido and her Aeneas shall want troops, / and all the haunt be ours' (IV. xiv. 51–4).

If Antony dies by imaginatively evoking the values of love – what the Romans decry as the effeminate in him – Cleopatra resolves her suicide by infusing into her feminine being the masculine constancy claimed by the Romans: '. . . I have nothing / Of woman in me. Now from head to foot / I am marble-constant' (V. ii. 238–40). And subsequently, in her imaginative rendering of an afterlife, all human categories of sexual difference seem to dissolve in their union: 'Husband, I come. / . . . / I am fire and air; my other elements / I give to baser life' (V. ii. 286–9). Cleopatra daringly celebrates love's victory in a world of dramatic illusion in these final moments of the play, even while acknowledging that if removed from her milieu – and from the Renaissance stage – 'Some squeaking Cleopatra [will] boy [her] greatness' (V. ii. 220). While the autonomy of her histrionic role is curtailed by the image of the boy actor emerging from his disguise, it also ironically serves as a reminder that no identity is fixed and immutable, and that agents of representation on the Renaissance public stage could freely take on identities that transgressed boundaries of gender and hierarchy. To shape life as a performance and to improvise a part of one's own, rather than accept a God-given role, emerged as an increasingly appealing concept in the sixteenth and seventeenth centuries, even though the choices implied by such rhetoric were limited.[40] While Cleopatra embodies such assertions of power through role-playing, the dialectical structure of the play evokes the conditions of existence of the fiercely contested site of the Renaissance public theatre. More significantly, the work reminds us that a fear of theatrical power – both in the play and in the culture – inevitably reveals itself as an anxiety about female dissembling.

IV

In Shakespeare's *Antony and Cleopatra*, as in the anti-feminist and anti-theatrical narratives, the figures of the alluring, histrionic temptress and the effeminised male repeatedly emerge as the focus of concern about changing gender boundaries in Renaissance England. The tract writers' preoccupation with preserving 'true' masculinity is, in effect, an attempt to naturalise the orthodox doctrine of a static social and sexual order. In Shakespeare's play, however, this ideology of order – with its clear standards of otherness and exclusion – is revealed as a contingent fiction open to revision. Human identity, as Cleopatra dramatises it, is multiple, varied, and protean, and, as we have seen, the playwright affords her many occasions to exult in her playful disruptions of the Roman gender polarities. Thus both dramatic text and public debates, when read in relationship to each other, present a complex picture of Renaissance society caught between the pressures of mobility and a desire for stasis. Or more specifically, they bring to light the cultural dilemma of choosing between God-given identities and new, socially constructed ones.

Another, related concern that gains urgency in such a reading of the literary and social texts deals with the use and control of theatrical power. Considering that all spectacles were popularly conceptualised as female and viewers as male, it is not surprising that the Renaissance culture feared feminine displays even as it acknowledged their overwhelming appeal. Thus when the anti-theatricalists attack actors for effeminising themselves and their audiences, they seem to concede immense theatrical power to unrestrained femininity, and to counter that, exhort women to conform to static models of virtue. Shakespeare radically revises these negative associations between women and actors. By conflating femininity and theatricality in such positive and powerful terms in the figure of Cleopatra, the playwright is identifying femininity as one of power's crucial modes.

Like the Romans in *Antony and Cleopatra*, the orthodoxies of the Renaissance culture would have certainly been critical of Cleopatra's dramatic shows, considering that they are the creation of female dissembling. Yet, in the Elizabethan and Jacobean periods, large audiences flocked to the theatres every night. So the Egyptian queen has always had her audiences. Caesar's victory is inscribed in history, but by writing this play, Shakespeare has given Cleopatra endless performances.

From *Renaissance Drama*, 20 (1989), 99–119.

NOTES

[As a means of supplementing Ania Loomba's account of the construction of Gender, Jyotsyna Singh extends the discussion of *Antony and Cleopatra* into an area which during the past 10 years or so has begun to attract attention: the area of 'anti-theatricalism'. The theatricality of the play challenges directly the strictures of those who opposed theatrical performance, and Jonas A. Barish's book, *The Anti-Theatrical Prejudice* (Berkeley, 1981) has stimulated a number of studies of particular Shakespearean texts. Singh combines this interest with another, that of the anti-feminism which accompanied objections to dramatic performance. In a variety of ways she takes up and extends into areas of current feminist concern a number of themes which Phyllis Rackin touched on in her earlier article on the play. Ed.]

1. All references are to the New Penguin Shakespeare *Antony and Cleopatra*, ed. Emrys Jones (Harmondsworth, 1977).

2. An analogy for this paradigm can be found in Stephen Greenblatt's *Renaissance Self-Fashioning: From More to Shakespeare* (Chicago, 1980), pp. 1–9.

3. Cleopatra has been variously identified as an actress, dramatist, performer, or in broad terms, as a character wholly defined by her histrionic temperament. Phyllis Rackin, 'Shakespeare's Boy Cleopatra, the Decorum of Nature and the Golden World of Poetry', *PMLA*, 87 (1972), 201–12, describes Cleopatra as a 'dedicated showman' and a 'contriver of shows' whose action throughout is 'like that of playwright or actor' (p. 203). Her essay is important to my argument in that she views Cleopatra's showmanship as Shakespeare's calculated response to those who oppose all 'shows' and 'seeming' – i.e. the 'golden world of poetry' (pp. 204–9). Sidney Homan (*When the Theater Turns to Itself: The Aesthetic Metaphor in Shakespeare* [Lewisburg, 1981], pp. 177–91) relates Cleopatra's artifice and theatricality to her sexuality: 'the word "play", in the sense of sexual play is frequently interchangeable with "play" as it refers to the illusion produced by an actor' (p. 179). Linda Bamber (*Comic Women, Tragic Men: A Study of Gender and Genre in Shakespeare* [Stanford, 1982], pp. 45–70) perceives Cleopatra as a self-conscious actress who, unlike Antony, 'does not deny that she performs her love, plays roles, puts on shows' (p. 67). Her drama, with all its energy and struggle, becomes her vehicle for asserting control over her life. While studies such as these see Cleopatra's theatricality in positive terms, earlier criticism often considered her histrionics as a part of her inscrutable, or even duplicitous, female charm. For an account of the latter, see Linda T. Fitz, 'Egyptian Queens and Male Reviewers: Sexist Attitudes in *Antony and Cleopatra* Criticism', *Shakespeare Quarterly*, 28 (1977), 297–316. (Reprinted in this volume. Ed.]

4. Mary Beth Rose's observations ('Women in Men's Clothing: Apparel and Social Stability in *The Roaring Girl*', *Renaissance Historicism:*

Selections from English Literary Renaissance, ed. Arthur F. Kinney and Dan Collins [Amherst, 1977], pp. 223–7, 246–7) on the interaction between social and dramatic texts have contributed to the way in which I have constructed my argument, in both the introduction and the conclusion.

5. Katharine Maus ('"Playhouse Flesh and Blood": Sexual Ideology and the Renaissance Actress', *English Literary History,* 46 [1979], 603–9) points to the similarities between the rhetoric of the anti-theatrical and anti-feminist tracts. Jean E. Howard ('Renaissance Anti-theatricality and the Politics of Gender and Rank in *Much Ado About Nothing*', *Shakespeare Reproduced: The Text in History and Ideology,* ed. Jean E. Howard and Marion F. O'Connor [London, 1987], pp. 163–87) also reveals pointed connections between anti-theatricalism and the misogyny found in other modes of polemical writing of the period.

6. Cited in Louis Montrose, 'The Purpose of Playing: Reflections on a Shakespearean Anthropology', *Helios,* ns 7 (1980), 53–4.

7. For a full discussion of the social changes of the period, as well of the accompanying preoccupation with problems of order and degree, see David Underdown, *Revel, Riot, and Rebellion: Popular Politics and Culture in England, 1603–1660* (Oxford, 1985), pp. 9–43 and Keith Wrightson, *English Society 1580–1680* (London, 1982) pp. 17–38. See also Karen Newman, 'Renaissance Family Politics and Shakespeare's *The Taming of The Shrew*', *English Literary Renaissance,* 16 (1986), 91–3.

8. Underdown, *Revel, Riot, and Rebellion,* pp. 37–40.

9. For a useful account of the anti-theatrical discourse in Renaissance England, see Jonas A. Barish, *The Antitheatrical Prejudice* (Berkeley, 1981), pp. 80–190.

10. See Jonas Barish's observations (*The Antitheatrical Prejudice,* pp. 85–7) on the connection between the anti-theatricalists' attack on the theatre and their unease about female sexuality.

11. Lisa Jardine (*Still Harping on Daughters: Women and Drama in the Age of Shakespeare* [Brighton, 1983] pp. 8–33) discusses at length the homoeroticism associated with the 'effeminate boy[s] . . . of stage cross-dressing' (p. 17).

12. Both social and literary historians observe that the culture's preoccupation with the changing social arrangements in Renaissance England was frequently expressed as an anxiety about the patriarchal order. See Woodbridge's observations (*Women and the English Renaissance: Literature and the Nature of Womankind, 1540–1620* [Urbana, 1984], pp. 152–83) on the controversial debates regarding the 'nature' of women and the transformations taking place in the traditional sex roles in the early seventeenth century. Also see Underdown (*Revel, Riot, and*

Rebellion, pp. 36–43) for an account of the social fears of the breakdown of patriarchal family arrangements.

13. John A. Northbrooke, *A Treatise wherein Dicing, Dauncing, Vaine Playes, or Enterluds . . . are reproved*, 1577 (?), ed. Arthur Freeman (New York, 1974).

14. Russell Fraser, *The War against Poetry* (Princeton, 1970), pp. 52–76.

15. Arthur F. Kinney, *Markets of Bawdrie: The Dramatic Criticism of Stephen Gosson* (Salzburg, 1974), p. 59.

16. Stephen Gosson, *Playes Confuted in Five Actions*, 1582, ed. Arthur Freeman (New York, 1972).

17. Kinney, *Markets of Bawdrie*, p. 61.

18. William Rankins, *A Mirrour of Monsters*, 1587, ed. Arthur Freeman (New York, 1973).

19. Critics such as Maus and Howard clearly show how the image of the duplicitous seductress occurs frequently in anti-theatrical and anti-feminist literature. For further discussion of this stereotype see Katharine Usher Henderson and Barbara F. McManus (eds), *Half Humankind: Contexts and Texts of the Controversy about Women in England 1540–1640* (Urbana, 1985), pp. 47–50.

20. Maus, 'Playhouse Flesh', pp. 602–3.

21. Edward Gosynhill, *The Schoolhouse of women*, 1541, in Katherine Usher Henderson and Barbara F. McManus (eds), *Half Humankind: Contexts and Texts of the Controversy about Women in England, 1540–1640* (Illinois, 1985).

22. Stephen Gosson, *Pleasant quippes for upstart newfangled gentlewomen*, 1596 (London, 1841).

23. Joseph Swetnam, *The Arraignment of Lewd, idle, froward, and unconstant women*, 1615, in Henderson and McManus (eds), *Half Humankind*.

24. Maus ('Playhouse Flesh', p. 607) and Howard ('Renaissance Antitheatricality', p. 169) arrive at the same conclusion.

25. Gosson, *Playes Confuted*, G7v.

26. Edward Gosynhill's references to biblical stereotypes of female virtue typify such an impulse (*Multerum Paean* [1542?] in Henderson and McManus [eds], *Half Humankind*, pp. 165–6, 168).

27. Maus ('Playhouse Flesh', pp. 606–17) develops the implications of this observation.

28. Montrose, 'The Purpose of Playing', p. 57.

29. Stephen Gosson, *The Schoole of Abuse*, in Kinney, *Markets of Bawdrie*.

30. See Richard Marienstras, *New Perspectives on the Shakespearean World* (Cambridge, 1985), pp. 9–25, and Keith Wrightson, *English Society, 1580–1680* (London, 1982), pp. 18–23.

31. Typical of such traditional approaches is that of Julian Markels (*The Pillar of the World: Antony and Cleopatra in Shakespeare's Development* [Columbus, Ohio, 1968], pp. 3–49), who reads the play as a clash between public and private value systems, and of John Danby, who designates Rome and Egypt as 'the World and the Flesh' (*Poets on Fortune's Hill: Studies in Sidney, Shakespeare, Beaumont and Fletcher* [London, 1952], p. 148).

32. For a useful analysis of the play's dialectical structure, see Janet Adelman, *The Common Liar: An Essay on Antony and Cleopatra* (New Haven, 1974), pp. 14–52.

33. Phyllis Rackin, 'Anti-Historians: Women's Roles in Shakespeare's Histories', *Theatre Journal*, 37 (1985), 329–44.

34. Maynard Mack, Introduction to *Antony and Cleopatra* in *The Complete Pelican Shakespeare* (New York, 1969), p. 1169.

35. Geoffrey Bullough, *Narrative and Dramatic Sources of Shakespeare* (London, 1964), vol. 5, p. 272.

36. Edward Dowden (*Shakespeare: A Critical Study of His Mind and His Art* [London, 1918] pp. 245–309) exemplifies a long and influential tradition of such moral readings. He views the play as Antony's tragedy and considers Cleopatra as putting the 'moral sense to sleep' (p. 278).

37. Greenblatt (*Renaissance Self-fashioning: From More to Shakespeare*, pp. 227–32) identifies improvisation as the talent for perceiving given structures as a manipulable fiction to be reinscribed into one's own scenario. This essay identifies Cleopatra as such an improviser.

38. In her detailed analysis of the play's treatment of the Venus/Mars myth (*Literary Transvaluation from Vergilian Epic to Shakespearean Tragicomedy* [Berkeley, 1984], pp. 167–90), Barbara Bono gives a rich account of the various perspectives on this myth by showing how 'Shakespeare reflects the many Renaissance interpretations of Venus in his characters' responses to Cleopatra and to what she does with the martial Antony' (pp. 167–8).

39. Bono's discussion (pp. 151–90) of Antony's identification with changing images of mythic heroes such as Mars and Hercules contributes to my argument.

40. Greenblatt, *Renaissance Self-fashioning*, pp. 255–7.

Further Reading

The essays that comprise this volume begin at that point when critics began to realise that *Antony and Cleopatra* represented an unusual departure from the normal patterns of Shakespearean tragedy. As the volume develops then it becomes clear that larger cultural and historical questions are at issue than a straightforward engagement with the formal characteristics of the text itself. All studies of Shakespearean texts, however, begin from particular editions, and these are to be treated with some care, since all editors interpose their own views into their introductions, textual choices and commentary notes. As the volume moves out from the text of the play to engage with larger questions, such as those of 'history', 'theatricality', 'race', 'gender' and 'genre', so there is a corresponding need for larger, extra-dramatic contexts for the discussion. The following reading list begins with editions of the play, and then moves out from there to a selected number of traditional approaches and thence to a series of general, theoretically informed critical accounts which have some bearing on the issues raised in *Antony and Cleopatra*. The final section seeks to gather together a wide selection of current approaches to the play.

EDITIONS

G. Blakemore Evans (ed.), *The Riverside Shakespeare* (Boston: Houghton Miffin, 1974).

Barbara Everett (ed.), *The Tragedy of Antony and Cleopatra*, Signet Classics (New York and Scarborough, Ontario: Mentor, 1964).

Alfred Harbage (ed.), *The Complete Pelican Shakespeare* (Baltimore: Penguin, 1969).

Emrys Jones (ed.), *Antony and Cleopatra*, New Penguin Shakespeare (Harmondsworth: Penguin, 1977).

M. R. Ridley (ed.), *Antony and Cleopatra*, The Arden Shakespeare (London: Methuen, 1965).

Stanley Wells and Gary Taylor (eds), *William Shakespeare: The Complete Works* (Oxford: Oxford University Press, 1986).

TRADITIONAL CRITICISM

Jonathan Bate (ed.), *The Romantics on Shakespeare* (Harmondsworth: Penguin, 1992).

John Bayley, *Shakespeare and Tragedy* (London: Routledge & Kegan Paul, 1981).

A. C. Bradley, *Oxford Lectures on Poetry* (London: Macmillan, 1909).

John Russell Brown and Bernard Harris (eds), *Later Shakespeare*, Stratford-upon-Avon Series, 8 (London: Edward Arnold, 1966).

John Russell Brown (ed.), *Shakespeare: Antony and Cleopatra*, Casebook Series (London: Macmillan, 1968).

James C. Bulman, *The Heroic Idiom of Shakespearean Tragedy* (London and Toronto: University of Delaware Press, 1985).

Maurice Charney, *Shakespeare's Roman Plays* (Cambridge, Mass.: Harvard University Press, 1961).

John F. Danby, *Poets on Fortune's Hill* (London: Faber & Faber, 1952).

Emrys Jones, *Scenic Form in Shakespeare* (Oxford: Oxford University Press, 1971).

John Holloway, *The Story of the Night* (London: Routledge & Kegan Paul, 1961).

Ernst Honigmann, *Shakespeare: Seven Tragedies* (London: Macmillan, 1976).

G. Wilson Knight, *The Imperial Theme* (London: Methuen, 1951).

L. C. Knights, *Some Shakespearean Themes and an Approach to Hamlet* (Harmondsworth: Penguin, 1966).

Alexander Leggatt, *Shakespeare's Political Drama: The History Plays and the Roman Plays* (London: Routledge, 1988).

Robert S. Miola, *Shakespeare's Rome* (Cambridge: Cambridge University Press, 1983).

Kenneth Muir, *Shakespeare's Tragic Sequence* (London: Hutchinson University Library, 1972).

Irving Ribner, *Patterns in Shakespearean Tragedy* (London: Methuen, 1960).

J. L. Simmons, *Shakespeare's Pagan World: The Roman Tragedies* (Brighton: Harvester Press, 1973).

Vivian Thomas, *Shakespeare's Roman Worlds* (London: Routledge, 1989).

Derek Traversi, *An Approach to Shakespeare* (Stanford, Calif.: Stanford University Press, 1963).

CRITICAL THEORY

The following list contains a number of books and collections of essays which indicate some of the new theoretically informed work which is emerging in the area of Shakespeare and Renaissance studies.

Catherine Belsey, *The Subject of Tragedy: Identity and Difference in Renaissance Drama* (London: Methuen, 1985).

Michael D. Bristol, *Carnival and Theater: Plebeian Culture and the Structure of Authority in Renaissance England* (New York and London: Methuen, 1985).

Jonathan Dollimore and Alan Sinfield (eds), *Political Shakespeare: New*

Essays in Cultural Materialism (Manchester: Manchester University Press, 1985).

John Drakakis (ed.), *Alternative Shakespeares*, New Accents Series (London: Methuen, 1985).

John Drakakis (ed.), *Shakespearean Tragedy*, Longman Critical Reader Series (London: Longman, 1991).

Margaret W. Ferguson, Maureen Quilliagn and Nancy J. Vickers (eds), *Rewriting the Renaissance: The Discourses of Sexual Difference in Early Modern Europe* (Chicago and London: University of Chicago Press, 1986).

Margretta de Grazia, *Shakespeare Verbatim: The Reproduction of Authenticity and the 1790 Apparatus* (Oxford: Oxford University Press, 1991).

Stephen J. Greenblatt, *Renaissance Self-fashioning: From More to Shakespeare* (Chicago and London: University of Chicago Press, 1980).

Stephen J. Greenblatt, *Shakespearean Negotiations: The Circulation of Social Energy in Renaissance England* (Oxford: Clarendon Press, 1988).

Stephen J. Greenblatt, *Learning to Curse: Essays in Early Modern Culture* (New York and London: Routledge, 1990).

Terry Eagleton, *William Shakespeare*, Re-reading Literature Series (Oxford: Blackwell, 1986).

Malcolm Evans, *Signifying Nothing: Truth's True Contents in Shakespeare's Text* (Brighton: Harvester Press, 1986).

Terence Hawkes, *That Shakespeherian Rag: Essays on a Critical Process* (London: Methuen, 1986).

Thomas Healy, *New Latitudes: Theory and English Renaissance Literature* (London: Edward Arnold, 1992).

Jean E. Howard and Marion F. O'Connor (eds), *Shakespeare Reproduced: The Text in History and Ideology* (New York and London: Methuen, 1987).

Lisa Jardine, *Still Harping on Daughters: Women and Drama in the Age of Shakespeare* (Brighton: Harvester Press, 1983).

Carolyn Lenz, Gayle Greene and Carol Thomas Neely (eds), *The Woman's Part: Feminist Criticism of Shakespeare* (Urbana and Chicago: University of Illinois Press, 1983).

Leah Marcus, *Puzzling Shakespeare: Local Reading and its Discontents* (Berkeley: University of California Press, 1988).

Kathleen McLuskie, *Renaissance Dramatists* (New York and London: Harvester Press, 1989).

Steven Mullaney, *The Place of the Stage: License, Play, and Power in Renaissance England* (Chicago and London: University of Chicago Press, 1988).

Patricia Parker and Geoffrey Hartman (eds), *Shakespeare and the Question of Theory* (New York and London: Methuen, 1985).

Annabel Patterson, *Shakespeare and the Popular Voice* (Oxford: Blackwell, 1989).

Murray M. Schwarz and Coppelia Kahn (eds), *Representing Shakespeare: New Psychoanalytic Essays* (Baltimore and London: Johns Hopkins University Press, 1982).

H. Aram Veeser (ed.), *The New Historicism* (New York and London: Routledge, 1989).

ANTONY AND CLEOPATRA

The following books and articles represent a selection of some of the more stimulating work that has appeared in recent years in relation to the play:

Janet Adelman, *The Common Liar: An Essay on Antony and Cleopatra* (New Haven: Yale University Press, 1973).

Linda Bamber, *Comic Women, Tragic Men: A Study of Gender and Genre in Shakespeare* (Stanford: Stanford University Press, 1982).

Peter Berek, 'Doing and Undoing: The Value of Action in *Antony and Cleopatra*', *Shakespeare Quarterly*, 32 (Autumn 1981), 295–304.

Barbara J. Bono, *Literary Transvaluation: From Vergilian Epic to Shakespearean Tragicomedy* (Berkeley: University of California Press, 1984).

Geoffrey Bullough, *Narrative and Dramatic Sources of Shakespeare*, vol. 5, *The Roman Plays* (London: Routledge & Kegan Paul, 1977).

Jonathan Goldberg, *James I and the Politics of Literature* (Baltimore and London: Johns Hopkins University Press, 1983).

Richard Hillman, 'Antony, Hercules, and Cleopatra: "The bidding of the god" and "The subtlest maze of all"', *Shakespeare Quarterly*, 38 (Winter 1987), 442–51.

Sidney Homan, *When The Theatre Turns to Itself: The Aesthetic Metaphor in Shakespeare* (Lewisburg: Bucknell University Press, 1981).

Lucy Hughes-Hallett, *Cleopatra: Histories, Dreams, and Distortions* (London: Vintage Books, 1990).

Arnold Kettle (ed.), *Shakespeare in A Changing World* (London: Lawrence & Wishart, 1964).

Ronald Macdonald, 'Playing Till Doomsday: Interpreting *Antony and Cleopatra*', *English Literary Renaissance*, 15 (Winter 1985), 78–99.

Philip Lawrence Rose, 'The Politics of *Antony and Cleopatra*', *Shakespeare Quarterly*, 20 (Autumn 1969), 379–89.

Susan Snyder, 'Patterns of Motion in *Antony and Cleopatra*', *Shakespeare Survey*, 33 (1980), 113–22.

Leonard Tennenhouse, *Power on Display: The Politics of Shakespeare's Genres* (New York and London: Methuen, 1986).

William D. Wolf, '"New Heaven, New Earth": The Escape from Mutability in *Antony and Cleopatra*', *Shakespeare Quarterly*, 33 (Autumn 1982), 328–35.

Notes on Contributors

Janet Adelman is Professor of English at the University of California at Berkeley. She is the author of *The Common Liar: An Essay on 'Antony and Cleopatra'* (1973), and *Suffocating Mothers: Fantasies of Maternal Origin in Shakespeare's Plays 'Hamlet' to 'The Tempest'* (1992). She is also the editor of *Twentieth-Century Interpretations of 'King Lear'* (1978).

John F. Danby was Professor of English at University College of Bangor, North Wales. He was the author of *Poets on Fortune's Hill* (1952), and *Shakespeare's Doctrine of Nature* (1958).

H. Neville Davies is Fellow of the Shakespeare Institute and lecturer in English at the University of Birmingham.

Jonathan Dollimore is Reader in the School of English and American Studies at the University of Sussex. He is the author of *Radical Tragedy: Religion, Ideology and Power in the Drama of Shakespeare and his Contemporaries* (1984), and *Sexual Dissidence: Augustine to Wilde, Freud to Foucault* (1991), and the co-editor of *Political Shakespeare: New Essays in Cultural Materialism* (1985).

Linda. T. Fitz (who is now Linda Woodbridge) is Professor of English at the University of Alberta. She is the author of *Women and the English Renaissance 1540–1620* (1984).

Terence Hawkes is Professor of English at the University of Wales College of Cardiff. He is the author of *Shakespeare and the Reason* (1964), *Shakespeare's Talking Animals* (1975), *Structuralism and Semiotics* (1977), *That Shakespeherian Rag: Essays on a Cultural Process* (1986), *Meaning by Shakespeare* (1992). He is also the editor of the journal *Textual Practice* and the General Editor of *The New Accents* series.

Margot Heinemann was, until her recent death, a Fellow of New Hall, University of Cambridge. She is the author of *Puritanism and Theatre: Thomas Middleton and Opposition Drama under the Early Stuarts* (1980), and she has contributed an essay on Brecht and Shakespeare to *Political Shakespeare* (1985).

NOTES ON CONTRIBUTORS *335*

Marilyn French is a novelist and critic. She has taught at Yale University. Her novels *The Women's Room* and *The Bleeding Heart* are well known, as, indeed, is her study of James Joyce, *The Book as World: James Joyce's Ulysses*. Her account of the corpus of Shakespearean drama, *Shakespeare's Division of Experience*, was a significant breakthrough in feminist studies of Shakespeare.

Ania Loomba is a Reader at the Jalawarhal Nehru University in New Delhi. She is the author of *Race, Gender, and Renaissance Drama* (1986).

Phyllis Rackin is Professor of English at the University of Pennsylvania. She is the author of *Shakespeare's Tragedies* (1978) and *Stages of History: Shakespeare's English Chronicles* (1990).

Jyotsyna Singh is assistant Professor of English and Cultural Studies at Southern Methodist University. She is the co-author of *The Feminist Shakespeare* (forthcoming).

Index

Adelman, Janet, 9, 10, 13, 17–18, 22, 30, 56, 77, 98, 193, 207, 210, 244, 268, 277–8, 329, 333
Agrippa, 6, 67, 225, 238, 240, 259, 271
Alexander, Peter, 194, 209
Alexas, 40–1, 220, 258
All for Love (John Dryden), 12, 111, 180
American New Criticism, 20
Anderson, Donald K., 156
Antipodes, The (Richard Brome), 296–302, 306–7
Antonie (Robert Garnier), 169, 175, 180–1
Antony: ambivalence, 51, 81, 123–4, 274, 323; and Caesar, 44, 224–5; based on Christian IV, 16, 139, 153; and Cleopatra, 1, 4–5, 8, 36–7, 40, 43, 96, 112, 117, 127; as seen by Cleopatra, 10, 50–1, 57, 255; view of Cleopatra; 39, 197, 232, 269, 288; death, 36, 42, 79, 90–1, 191, 198, 232–3, 270, 324; disgrace, 12, 18, 38, 50, 53, 81–2; disintegration, 168, 193, 195–6, 239, 288, 319; and Fulvia, 44, 251, 269; hyperbole, 68–70, 76, 235; identity; 24, 34, 238, 318; image, 58, 249–50, 252–6; and Octavia, 120, 187, 252, 257, 287; protagonist, 22, 192–3; between Rome and Egypt, 6, 8, 37, 41, 111, 121, 216, 220–

2, 229, 237, 286–7; sexuality, 24, 119, 258–60
Antony and Cleopatra tragedies: Greville, Fulke, 14–15, 31, 153, 173; Stege, Hans Thomissøn, 152–3, 164–5
Arthos, John, 276–7
Augustus, *see* Octavius Caesar

Babylon, Whore of (Thomas Dekker), 132, 156
Bacon, Francis, 63, 73, 74, 128, 135, 155, 157, 249–50, 261
Baker, Donald C., 95
Bamber, Linda, 246, 326, 333
Barber, C. L., 249, 261
Barish, Jonas, 326–7
Barrault, Jean-Louis, 166–7, 178, 180
Bathurst, Charles, 187, 205
Bayley, John, 2–4, 29–30, 331
Behrens, Ralph, 209
Belsey, Catherine, 331
Bethell, S. L., 184, 193, 203, 207, 246
Booth, Stephen, 77
boy actors, 5, 11, 26, 57, 78–80, 89, 92, 95, 97, 117, 121, 242, 324, 326, 327
Bradbrook, M. C., 35, 276, 282
Bradley, Andrew Cecil, 2, 3, 12, 18–20, 30, 71, 187, 200, 204, 210–11, 331
Brandes, Georg, 184, 192, 203, 207

Brandon, Samuel, 180
Brecht, Bertold, 17, 26, 177–8, 181, 260, 279–81, 285, 291, 295, 301–3
Bristol, Michael D., 331
Brome, Richard (*The Antipodes*), 296–302, 306–7
Brower, Rueben, 213, 244–5
Brown, John Russell, 1, 29, 125, 331
Brutus, Marcus Junius, 174–5, 177, 181, 271
Bullough, Geoffrey, 77, 173, 180, 329, 333
Bulman, James C., 331

Caesar, Gaius Julius, 6, 14, 34, 37, 174–5
Canidius, 210, 253
Caputi, Anthony, 98
Carleton, Dudley, 148–9, 151, 159–60, 163–4
Carr, Helen, 288, 304
Cassius, Gaius Cassius Longinus, 174–5, 177
Cecil, Lord David, 193, 207
Cecil, Robert, 1st Earl of Salisbury, 130–1, 141, 143
Charmian, 40, 77, 93, 95, 180, 186, 197, 220, 259, 272
Charney, Maurice, 276, 277–8, 331
Christian IV, King of Denmark, 16, 137–53, 158–64
Chronicles, see Holinshed
Cleopatra: ageing, 22, 186; and Antony, 1, 8, 36, 39, 43, 96, 112, 117, 127, 190–1, 268; idea of Antony, 10, 56, 70, 76, 94, 240–1, 255, 290; character, 5, 92, 183, 201–2, 208, 234, 267; death, 46, 79, 91, 93–8, 191, 198, 200, 211, 242–3, 270, 291; duplicity, 48, 80, 83, 90, 190, 197, 257, 288; as the East, 4, 6, 27; as Flesh, 8, 49, 114–18; and Fulvia, 40; manipulating, 21, 37–8, 41, 187, 241, 259; on monument, 91, 198; and Octavia, 40, 116; and Octavius, 92, 94, 194,

258; paradox, 66–7, 76; past, 6, 34, 186; protagonist, 195, 199–201; prurience over, 1, 2, 18, 37, 40, 188–9; versus Rome, 25, 27, 29, 229, 288–9; seductive wiles, 2, 4–5, 6, 9, 12, 184–5, 204, 320; sexism, 183–5, 188–93; sexuality, 2, 5–6, 26, 118–19, 171, 258–60, 317; theatrical, 11, 23, 28, 58, 83–4, 86–7, 92, 308–10, 321–4, 326; as whore, 62, 78, 121, 288, 324
Cleopatra (Samuel Daniel), 169, 180
Cohen, Walter, 296, 306
Colie, Rosalie, 74–75, 246
Coleridge, Samuel Taylor, 2, 5, 34, 40, 189, 205, 305
colonisation, 5, 6–7, 22, 25, 245, 298
Conrad, Joseph, *Heart of Darkness*, 7, 298
Cordelia, 52, 104–5, 110, 123, 204
Cornwallis, Sir Charles (Ambassador at Madrid), 130–1, 155
Coward, Rosalind, 19, 31
Critical Theory, 13, 20–1
Croce, Benedetto, 172
crocodiles, 143, 152, 203
Cultural Materialism, 23–4, 260

Danby, John, 5, 8, 10, 13, 17–18, 27, 33–55, 70, 72, 172, 93, 207, 237, 246–7, 277–8, 285, 304, 329, 331
Daniel, Samuel, *Cleopatra*, 169, 180–1
Davies, H. Neville, 15–18, 21, 28
deconstruction, 9, 22
Dekker, Thomas (*The Whore of Babylon*), 132, 156
de Man, Paul, 19, 31
Demetrius, 5, 40, 82, 238
Dido, Queen of Carthage (Christopher Marlowe), 71
Dolabella, 10, 35, 94, 97, 100, 256, 271
Dollimore, Jonathan, 23–5, 28, 31, 248–61, 280, 283, 303–5, 331–2

Donne, John, 6, 30, 65–6, 171, 222, 286, 290
Doran, Madeleine, 72–3
Dowden, Edward, 182, 185, 201, 203, 329
Drakakis, John, 1–32, 332
Dryden, John, 12, 76, 111, 123, 177, 180

Egypt: scene of action, 12, 114–17; carnivalesque, 9, 11–12, 22, 26, 89, 90; colonised, 6, 7, 22; as comedy, 214, 216, 220; eroticisation, 4–5, 16, 23, 113–19, 318; fecundity, 5, 171; feminine, 22, 25, 27, 196, 215, 266, 273, 322; as flesh, 8, 52, 218; and Rome, 1, 6, 27, 34, 40, 48, 226; versus Rome, 12–13, 18, 28, 50, 52, 79, 112, 119–21, 169, 172, 212, 263–4, 285, 317; Rome's attraction to, 5, 97, 192
Eliot, T. S., 303
Elizabeth I, Queen of England, 127, 131–2, 141, 153–4, 209, 289, 292–5
Elizabeth Jonas (warship), 146, 163
Ellis, John, 19, 31
Ellis-Fermor, Una, 113, 125, 303
Emerson, Oliver, 192, 207
Enobarbus, 6, 57, 79, 115; and Cleopatra at Cydnus, 66, 76, 84, 86–7, 94, 117, 225, 321; Cleopatra's passions, 43, 200, 216, 222, 273, 317; desertion and death, 232, 234, 236–7, 239, 257, 272–3; and Egypt, 11, 22, 34–5, 57, 259; ironic comment, 69, 84, 167, 192, 197, 223, 225, 227, 253, 269; and Lepidus, 67, 170; and Octavia, 46, 121, 268
Eros, 36, 188, 216, 234, 243, 254, 271–2, 323
Essex, Robert Devereux, 2nd Earl of, 173–4, 175
Everett, Barbara, 277, 330

Fanon, Frantz, 30
Farnham, Willard, 199

feminism, 21–2, 25–6, 276
Fitch, Robert E., 188, 194, 205, 207–8
Fitz, Linda, 21–2, 182–211, 326
Foucault, Michel, 23–4, 31, 249, 260–1
French, Marilyn, 25–6, 31, 262–78
Frye, Northrop, 20, 229, 231, 237, 240, 245–6
Fulvia, 35, 37, 42, 44, 116, 192, 217, 221, 224, 251, 269, 271, 289

Garnier, Robert (*Antonie*), 169, 175, 180
gender, 5, 12, 22, 25–6, 28–9, 262–3, 276, 280, 285, 298, 302–3, 309, 316, 325–6
Gloucester, Earl of, 106–9, 230
Goddard, Harold C., 184, 203, 207, 211, 246
Goethe, Johann Wolfgang von, 178
Gorboduc, 88
Gosson, Stephen, 311–16, 328–9
Gosynhill, Edward, 314, 328
Granville-Barker, Harley, 83, 99, 113, 125, 162, 184, 187, 192–4, 205, 207, 209
Greenblatt, Stephen J., 260, 305, 326, 329, 332
Greville, Fulke, 165, 175, 180; *Antony and Cleopatra*, 14–15, 31, 153, 173
Grindon, Rose, 195, 209

Hallett, Charles, 223, 246
Harbage, Alfred, 125, 183, 330
Harington, Sir John, 143–5
Harrison, G. B., 71
Hawkes, Terence, 12–13, 17, 22, 121–5, 332
Hayward, Sir John, 15
Healy, Tom, 17, 31, 332
heart, 230–2
Heart of Darkness (Joseph Conrad), 7, 298
Heinemann, Margaret, 17–18, 21, 166–81, 303
Herod, 69
Heylyn, Peter, 137, 157

Hobbes, Thomas (*Behemoth*), 176, 181
Holinshed, Raphael (*Chronicles*), 105
Holloway, John, 277, 381
Honigmann, Ernst, 331
Howard, Charles, Lord Howard of Effingham, Earl of Nottingham, 149–52, 155, 163–4
Howard, Jean, 292, 305, 315, 327–8, 332
hyperbole, 67–76

Iras, 40, 180, 220, 272

James I, King of England, 15–16, 28, 126–37, 140–64, 174, 176, 293–4, 305; policy, 128–32; character, 136–7, 141–2; feasting, 145–53
James, Mervyn, 249, 261
Jardine, Lisa, 98, 327, 332
Johnson, Samuel, 2, 13, 17, 30, 81, 177, 285, 304
Jones, Emrys, 126, 153, 174, 180, 330–1
Jones, Inigo, 293–4
Jonson, Ben, 79, 98, 128, 134–5, 144, 154–7, 160–1, 178, 248, 294, 297; *Sejanus*, 174, 248, 252–3, 295–6, 306
Joseph, Sister Miriam, 74, 98
Julius Caesar, 6, 14, 34, 37, 174–5

Knight, G. Wilson, 3, 9, 17, 20, 31, 40, 72, 172, 261, 331
Knights, L. C., 1, 20, 29, 304, 331
Keats, John, 17, 177

Lamb, Charles, 178
Lee, Robin, 135
Leggatt, Alexander, 331
Leishman, James Blair, 73
Lentricchia, Frank, 20, 31
Lepidus, Marcus Aemilius, 35, 46–7, 67–8, 120, 134, 149–50, 152, 175, 177, 225, 227, 251, 271, 273, 317
Lever, J. W., 188, 205
Lévi-Strauss, Claud, 124

Levin, Harry, 71
Lloyd, Michael, 194, 209
Loomba, Ania, 26–8, 279–307
love, 101–9, 115, 122–5
Lyons, Charles R., 277

Machiavelli, Niccolò, 48, 136, 261; *The Prince*, 252, 257
Mack, Maynard, 122, 125, 239, 247, 277, 329
Maecenas, 259
Mallock, A. E., 74
Mardian, 90, 323
Markels, Julian, 190, 193–4, 205, 207–8, 246, 329
Marlowe, Christopher, 178, 296; *Dido*, 71; *Tamburlaine*, 66, 221
Marxism, 20–1, 179, 260
Maus, Katherine, 314–15, 327–8
McLuhan, Marshall, 13, 124
Menas, 68, 148, 238, 256, 268, 271
Mexia, Pedro, 137, 157
Middleton, Thomas, 279–80, 282–3, 303
Mills, Laurens J., 187, 190–1, 193, 205
Miola, Robert S., 331
Montrose, Louis A., 291–2, 295, 304–6, 326, 328
Muir, Kenneth, 331
Munday, Anthony, 133–4
Murry, John Middleton, 194, 208, 247

Neville, Sir Henry, 129–30, 176
New Historicism, 11–13, 16, 23–4, 28, 260
North, Sir Thomas, *see* Plutarch's *Lives*
Northbrooke, John, 311–12, 328

Octavia, 35, 46–7, 66, 115, 120, 127, 153, 187, 196, 224, 226–7, 241, 251–2, 255, 257–8, 262, 269, 271, 287–8, 317
Octavius Caesar (Gaius Julius Caesar Octavianus *later* Augustus), 29, 44, 46–8, 57, 68, 92, 96–7, 120, 126–9, 134–7, 147, 151,

157, 167, 173–6, 184, 194, 196,
215, 217, 221, 223–5, 227–9,
232–3, 238–41, 251–5, 257–8,
262, 265, 267, 269–71, 274, 287,
289–90, 317–19
Ong, Walter J., 13
Ornstein, Robert, 244, 274, 278,
303
Ovid, 222, 236–7, 246

paradox, 63–7, 72–6
Partridge, Eric, 188
Peacham, Henry, 64, 73–5
Philo, 5, 37, 40, 59, 66, 68, 81–2,
86, 113, 219, 238, 242, 255, 257,
259, 268, 320–1
Phoenix and the Turtle, The, 35,
43, 64
Plato, 57, 81, 84, 87, 90, 92, 99
Plutarch's Lives (translated Sir
Thomas North), 66, 75, 85, 87,
91, 93–4, 135–6, 147–8, 152,
168–9, 175–6, 178, 186–7, 195–
8, 209–10, 261, 309, 319, 320
poetic rhetoric, 2, 4, 9–12, 57–9,
71–2
Pompey (Sextus Pompeius), 42, 44–
6, 145, 147–8, 151, 169–70, 177,
221, 223, 225–8, 251, 256, 271,
274, 317, 320
poststructualism, 19, 21
Practical Criticism, 20
Proculeius, 92, 94, 269, 271
Proser, Matthew N., 72, 100, 244
Pryce, Jonathan, 127, 135
Puttenham, George, 64–6, 73–6

Rackin, Phyllis, 11–13, 17, 28,
78–100, 326, 329
Raleigh, Sir Walter, 7, 30, 150
Rankins, William, 311, 313–14,
328
Ribner, Irving, 303, 331
Ridley, M. R., 172, 330
Riemer, A. P., 135–6, 182, 189, 193,
200, 205, 207, 211, 275, 277–8
Robarts, Henry, 145, 158–9, 161–3
Rome: Augustan, 16, 28, 48, 89,
172–3; coloniser, 5, 6, 22; and

Egypt, 1, 6, 27, 34, 40, 48, 226;
versus Egypt, 12–13, 18, 28, 41,
50, 52, 79, 112, 119–21, 169,
212, 263–4, 285, 317; masculine, 22, 27, 215, 322; political,
8, 44, 47, 90, 217, 266; tragedy,
213–14, 219; values, 4, 5, 9–11,
22, 28, 41, 84, 86, 97, 167, 172,
192, 216, 265–6, 273; words,
12, 115
Rothschild, Herbert Jnr, 246

Said, Edward W., 4, 30
Salisbury, John Gordon, Dean of,
129, 135, 154, 156
Schanzer, Ernest, 172
Schlegel, August Wilhelm von, 2,
185, 203, 188, 205
Seleucus, 258, 271
sexism, 21, 182–203, 298
sexuality, 2, 24, 26–7, 66, 118–19,
121, 171, 186, 258–60, 264–5,
270, 275, 288, 305, 311, 314,
321, 323, 326–7
Shakespeare, William: Cleopatra,
185–6, 194, 197, 275; construction of plays, 52–4, 59–64, 80,
199, 215, 238, 283–4; criticism
of, 20, 136, 166–7, 177–8, 187–
8, 245, 280, 316; dialectic, 36,
40, 43–5, 54; dramatic skill, 8,
22, 33–5, 49, 63, 71, 78, 89,
124; and Holinshed, 105;
Octavius, 47–8, 174; and
Plutarch, 75, 85, 136, 147, 169,
186, 195, 197–8, 320; poetic language, 2, 11, 13, 57–8, 77; text,
7, 10, 13, 52; world of, 14, 74,
109, 117, 126, 135, 144, 148,
152, 172–3; *All's Well That Ends
Well*, 262; *As You Like It*, 60;
Coriolanus, 33, 53, 169, 248–9,
252, 267; *Cymbeline*, 33; *Hamlet*, 144, 159–60, 166, 178, 189,
213, 229, 240, 243, 264–5;
Henry IV, Pt 1, 169; *Henry V*,
76, 176; *Henry VI*, 33; *Julius
Caesar*, 14, 173, 181; *King Lear*,
13, 15, 33, 52–3, 102, 104–11,

122–5, 134–5, 154, 169, 181, 189, 200, 229, 252, 264–5, 267, 275; *Love's Labour Lost*, 63, 262; *Macbeth*, 53, 144, 161–2, 178, 187, 189, 198, 243, 264–5, 267, 304; *Measure for Measure*, 160; *Merchant of Venice, The*, 99; *Midsummer Night's Dream, A*, 59–60, 75, 262, 273; *Othello*, 189, 215, 229, 264–5, 288, 297; *Pericles*, 34; *Richard II*, 66, 293; *Richard III*, 47; *Romeo and Juliet*, 171, 264; *Tempest, The*, 181, 185; *Timon*, 33, 53, 181; *Troilus and Cressida*, 61–2, 171, 204, 252, 262; *Twelfth Night*, 60, 186; *Winter's Tale, The*, 33, 156

Shaw, George Bernard, 58, 72, 81–3, 99, 172
Sidney, Sir Philip, 9, 11, 30, 80, 85–9, 98, 165, 176, 180, 245
Simmons, J. L., 223, 244, 246, 331
Simpson, Lucie, 195, 209
Singh, Jyotsyna, 26, 28–9, 308–29
Southampton, Henry Wriothesley, 3rd Earl of, 173
Spencer, Benjamin T., 72–3
Spencer, T. J. B., 80, 277
Spenser, Edmund, 60, 214
Spurgeon, Caroline, 276
Stallybrass, Peter, 292, 305
Stege, Hans Thomissøn (*Antony and Cleopatra*), 152–3, 164–5
Stempel, Daniel, 184, 191, 194, 203, 205, 208, 211, 276–8
Stirling, Brents, 276
Stoll, E. E., 184, 203
Structuralism, 13, 19, 21, 124
Stubbes, Philip (*Haec Vir*), 292–3, 305

Swinburne, Algernon, Charles, 184, 203, 301

Tacitus, Publius, 17, 137, 174–7, 180
Tamburlaine (Christopher Marlowe), 66, 221
Thidias, 190, 197, 239, 257
Thomas, Vivian, 331
Tillyard, E. M. W., 16
Traci, Philip J., 185, 188–9, 204–5, 261
Traversi, Derek, 72, 162, 182, 277–8, 331
Tre Kroner (Danish flagship), 138–9, 148, 158

Ventidius, 34–5, 67, 140, 170, 257, 271
Vincent, Barbara C., 22–3, 212–47
Virtuous Octavia (Samuel Brandon), 180

Waith, Eugene M., 98, 247, 249, 261
Webster, John (*The White Devil*), 283–4, 295–6, 306
Weimann, Robert, 280, 291, 303–4
Whitaker, Virgil K., 99, 193, 207, 275, 278
White, Hayden, 20, 31
White Bear (English warship), 146–7, 162
Widdowson, Peter, 19, 31
Winchester, Bishop of, 129
Wind, Edgar, 63–4, 73
Williams, Raymond, 23–4, 31, 124, 260
Wilson, E. C., 192, 206
Wright, Austin, 193, 207